Civility and Its Discontents

An AMINTAPHIL Volume

Civility and Its Discontents

Essays on Civic Virtue, Toleration, and
Cultural Fragmentation

Edited by
Christine T. Sistare

University Press of Kansas

Published by the University Press of Kansas (Lawrence, Kansas 66049), which was organized by the Kansas Board of Regents and is operated and funded by Emporia State University, Fort Hays State University, Kansas State University, Pittsburg State University, the University of Kansas, and Wichita State University

Library of Congress Cataloging-in-Publication Data

Civility and its discontents : essays on civic virtue, toleration, and cultural fragmentation / edited by Christine T. Sistare.
    p.   cm.
    "AMINTAPHIL volume."
    Includes bibliographical references and index.
    ISBN 0-7006-1313-7 (cloth : alk. paper) — ISBN 0-7006-1314-5 (pbk. : alk. paper)
    1. Social ethics—United States. 2. Civil society—United States. 3. Social values—United States. 4. Social integration—United States. 5. Liberalism—Moral and ethical aspects. 6. Toleration—United States. 7. Civics.
I. Sistare, C. T. (Christine T.), 1951–
HN90.M6C58   2004
   303.3'72—dc22   2004003031

British Library Cataloguing-in-Publication Data is available.

Printed in the United States of America

10 9 8 7 6 5 4 3 2 1

CONTENTS

PREFACE

Civility, civic virtue, tolerance, and sociocultural unity have been the subjects of considerable discussion in recent years, and their purported demise has been the subject of much lament.* In both popular media and academic publications, social commentators of varied political persuasions have argued over the extent to which these social goods have declined in modern liberal societies, the causes of their decline, and the very meaning of the terms. These and associated problems are addressed in this volume.

At this point in history, when the United States has been subjected to astonishing terrorist assaults and undertaken a war in response, the subject matter of the essays collected here may seem quaintly inapt. Many social commentators, including the current U.S. president, have hailed a reawakening of patriotism and civic concern, even a sense of unity among the peoples of many nations. Without discrediting these claims, I would observe that the problems addressed in this volume are of such a depth as to largely elude the ameliorating effects of the patriotic expressions and charitable impulses typically cited.† The discussions taken up by the contributors to

---

*For example, Benjamin Barber, "The Civic Mission of the University," *Higher Education and the Practice of Democratic Politics,* ed. B. Merchand (Kettering Foundation, 1991) and "Universities and the Decline of Civic Responsibility" from www.college values.org; Stephen Carter, *Civility: Manners, Morals, and the Etiquette of Democracy* (New York: Basic Books, 1998); Martin Marty, *The One and the Many: America's Struggle for the Common Good* (Cambridge, Mass.: Harvard University Press, 1997); Robert Putnam, *Bowling Alone: The Collapse and Revival of American Community* (New York: Simon and Schuster, 2000), Adam Seligman, *The Problem of Trust* (Princeton, N.J.: Princeton University Press, 1997).

†Although many U.S. citizens have been displaying flags and other patriotic emblems and many made generous contributions to emergency relief funds immediately following the events of September 11, the hard data of civic involvement remain unencouraging. Thus, although requests for information about military service, the Central

this volume reach to the nature of civil society, the character of democracy, the relationship between the demands of individual liberty and those of the common good, and the role of law and government policy in weaving the fabric of a social whole.*

The contributors pursue these profound issues with particular focus on three sets of concerns: (1) the constituent elements of civility, civic virtue, and good citizenship; (2) problems surrounding civil rights and the promotion of tolerance and openness, particularly through constitutional devices; and (3) social and legal responses to apparently intensifying social fragmentation. This division of subject matter mirrors the volume's separation into Part 1, "Civic Virtue," Part 2, "Toleration," and Part 3, "Cultural Fragmentation." That separation, however, is approximate, and the reader will find that themes, issues, case examples, and conceptual analyses frequently cross these editorial borders. For this reason, a reader interested in, for example, concepts of civility and civic virtue will profit from essays in Parts 2 and 3 as well as from those in Part 1. Similarly, issues of toleration are pertinent to many of the discussions in Parts 1 and 3, and questions about the use of law that occupy contributors to Part 3 underlie many other discussions throughout the volume.

The reader will discover considerable diversity of subject matter and treatment among these essays, but some similarities are worth noting. First, the great majority of the contributions to this volume are grounded in views that fall under the, admittedly broad, rubric of Liberal thought. (See the Introduction to Part 1 for discussion of this extended notion of liberalism.) All share a general advocacy of fundamental liberal values such as individual freedom, political equality, and democratic process. So, too, all the contributing authors express approval of principles of respect for others, openness to rational discussion, and acceptance of diversity. As to the prac-

---

Intelligence Agency, and volunteer opportunities escalated after the terrorist attacks, applications and active volunteerism have not increased. So, too, although many Americans have reported improved opinions of their government, voting and registration continue to decline.

*All but two of the essays were originally written for the 1998 AMINTAPHIL conference having the general theme "[In]Civility, Civic Virtue, and Democracy." The two exceptions, on hate speech, grew out of paper discussions at the 2001 IVR (International Association for Philosophy of Law and Social Philosophy) in Amsterdam conference on "Pluralism and Law."

tical implications for political and legal policy, however, there is genuine disagreement. In these pages, then, the reader will encounter admirers of Rawlsian liberalism, of varieties of communitarianism, and of libertarian and republican perspectives. Although the discussion takes place among members of a shared intellectual heritage, the disputes are quite as significant and intense as family arguments commonly are.

Second, despite concern for matters of private morality and good manners, contributors are primarily concerned with *public* issues. Economic, legal, and political policies within single nations are the predominant concern here. The nature of civic virtue and citizenship occupies many of the authors, and, again, the ruling approach focuses on dispositions and conduct that affect the public lives of individuals and groups. Thus, what the American Civil Liberties Union (ACLU) describes as a cultural debate over "civil morality"* is a tangential issue throughout most of this volume, although the character and devices through which those debates are carried on is very much in the fore.

Finally, with the exceptions of Lester Mazor's piece on Germany in Part 3 and Christopher Gray's piece on the Canadian secession struggle in Part 2, all the papers in this volume are grounded in the cultural, intellectual, and political contexts of the United States. This is in part a matter of accident, as nearly all the contributors are American and most specialize in American political, social, or legal philosophy. But, it seems true, as well, that we in the United States are particularly concerned with the health of our civil order. However universal the problems of civil society are in Freudian terms, a volume concerning "civility and its discontents" seems a peculiarly American project. Hence, indebtedness to—or, at least, interest in—the thought of the Founders and those who influenced them, of Tocqueville as a sympathetic observer of the United States as a young democracy, and of prominent American social and political philosophers is evident in many of the contributions. So, too, attention to the cultural situation,

---

*The ACLU employs this language in reference to debates over the purported spread of moral relativism, the acceptability of homosexuality, the morality of abortion and other forms of human reproductive control, the meaning of "family," and so on. Although these debates clearly have legal and political import, they are, at bottom, concerned with personal morality rather than with the character of civil interaction. The limits of public tolerance, which marks the intersection of the public and the private, are discussed in several of the essays in this volume.

legal controversies, and other particularities of the United States characterizes the majority of the work included, here.

Although these three areas of congruence necessarily limit the scope of the volume, they function, in turn, to provide some boundaries to a vast area of exploration and argument. Among papers evincing shared perspectives, the reader will find marked disagreement as to the requirements of good citizenship, the demarcation of public and private, and the accurate characterization of liberal democratic ideals and realities. This discrepancy indicates the complexity and depth of the issues surrounding the life of a civil society more adequately, I believe, than a collection that attempted to cover the full political, conceptual, and geographic territory available. The possibility of a satisfactory collection of that scope aside, I am confident that the reader of these essays will find more than enough to consider.

Thanks are owed to many people whose efforts and patience brought this volume to fruition. As always, I am indebted to the members and Executive Committee of AMINTAPHIL, to Nancy Scott-Jackson of the University Press of Kansas, and to my family for their continuing support. Many thanks to Anitra Witkowski of Muhlenberg College for putting it all together.

Special thanks are due to Jonathan Schonsheck for the preliminary work he did for this volume—organizing, selecting pieces, and working with authors in the first stages of the volume's creation.

Christine Sistare
Muhlenberg College

Part I

Civic Virtue

Society means association; coming together in joint intercourse
and action for the better realization of any form of experience
which is augmented and confirmed by being shared.
   —John Dewey, *Reconstruction in Philosophy*

Liberalism as Context

Opening this Introduction with a quotation from John Dewey may strike
some readers as philosophically risky, insofar as the essays that follow might
be taken as examples of the kind of abstract conceptual analysis that Dewey's
experimental pragmatism specifically eschewed. Contributors to this section
of the volume are concerned with an array of ideas—concepts, all—falling
within the general category of *civic ideals*. These ideas include the character
of a healthy civil society, the nature of good citizenship, and the demands
of civic virtue and social justice. However, each contributor is engaged in
the process of understanding these ideals as they implicate concrete practice, a form of analysis to which Dewey was, himself, committed.

Moreover, like Dewey, they are engaged in a particular historical and
cultural context, that of liberal democratic societies of the modern age,
rather than with the empty universalism he rejected. No doubt these
authors believe, as much as did Dewey, that the ideals of liberal democracy
represent the present pinnacle of human social achievement, but their
analyses presuppose the basic context of contemporary Western societies,
particularly the United States. The claims of alternative sociopolitical
ideals, therefore, are here regarded as problematic, that is, they must be ac-
counted for in terms of the liberal democratic context.

That this context is, itself, problematic, is a consequence of its own historical development, as Dewey recognized.[1] In fact, what he criticized as the
universalistic theorizing of early liberal thought contributed to the social,

1

political, and legal developments that brought us to our present situation. For this reason, a brief indulgence in the history of liberal democratic thought and some efforts at conceptual clarification will be useful and, one hopes, forgivable on even the most stringent pragmatic terms.

Without failing to appreciate the influence of Roman and Renaissance republicanism and the oppositional forces of philosophical conservatism on Western liberal democratic thought, we can trace the origins of contemporary perspectives most directly to the democratic rights theories that flourished in the work of seventeenth- and eighteenth-century French, English, and Scottish philosophers. Intellectual historians continue to debate the tenor and details of an adequate narrative of Western liberal thought, but none doubt the significance of thinkers such as Charles-Louis de Secondat Montesquieu, Alexis de Tocqueville, John Locke, Adam Smith, and David Hume. The radical individualism of Thomas Hobbes and the romanticism of Jean-Jacques Rousseau, through the medium of the consent theory of legitimate authority that they shared with more moderate liberal thinkers, brought distinctive elements to the mix. At various points, the moral liberalisms of utilitarianism, Moral Sense theory, and, later, Kantianism have also contributed to the history of Western liberal democratic views. A thorough and balanced story of the development of this line of thought would require, further, an account of the diverse interpretations given to the primary narrative by thinkers and activists from the many nations that now enjoy some part in this intellectual inheritance, as well as the interplay of this liberal democratic heritage with genuinely antiliberal views of all stripes.

With this nod to the requirements of an extended analysis, however, we can turn to a review of core notions and principles of Western liberal democratic thought. Giving this body of thought its full scope, let us treat it as encompassing not only the classical individualist liberalism of thinkers such as Hobbes, Locke, and Smith, but also versions of those perspectives frequently distinguished from garden-variety liberalism under the rubrics of republicanism, libertarianism, and communitarianism. Looked at with this generous eye, liberalism is the base context within which the discussions in this volume, and many of our most heated quotidian political debates, take place. Liberalism, thus understood, was the shared perspective of all the American Founders—federalists and antifederalists, proponents of direct democracy and of representative democracy,[2] populist agrarians and prophets of modern market economy, those who trusted in the omnicompetence of the ordinary citizen and those who hoped for the preeminence of an educated elite. For all their very real disagreements, these thinkers, and others like them in Britain and on the Continent, shared certain fundamental ideals, a common bent that qualifies them all as liberals in our extended sense of the term.

What, then, is this *liberalism*? First among its ideals is *democratism*. By this is meant the advocacy of popular sovereignty as contrasted with monarchy, oligarchy, or inherited aristocracy. However attenuated their notions of citizenship and suffrage appear by contemporary standards, the liberal theorists of the seventeenth and eighteenth centuries maintained that only the consent of citizens could legitimize political authority, and in this they stood against the beliefs and practices of Founders—primarily monarchic and aristocratic Founders—that had dominated Western social organizations since the end of the Roman Republic. It is true that some envisioned a return to Roman-style democracy, with its limited citizenship and participatory rights, and some accepted the remainders of class distinctions and the institution of slavery. Nonetheless, by adapting ancient theories of natural law and natural rights, theorists of the seventeenth and eighteenth centuries committed themselves to the logic of government by consent of, and in the service of, all the people.[3]

Wittingly or not, they also committed liberalism to a progressively egalitarian course. Although the full import and meaning of social equality continues to be a fighting point among the myriad liberal factions, political equality based on some conception of natural equality is a central idea of Western liberalism. As claims of the natural inequality of the propertyless, women, the illiterate, racial minorities, and other social outsiders have given way, the elimination of civil inequalities has become another ideal of all forms of liberalism.[4]

By contrast, elimination of significant economic inequality and the use of political means to mitigate the effects of such inequality have always been disputed as aims of liberalism, even in our extended sense. Patricia Smith addresses some of the ways in which material inequity undercuts civic bonds, and she appeals to the principle that the state should provide for the welfare of all its members, to the best of its abilities. This is, of course, a principle that follows from certain ideals: the fundamental equality of all, the rational consent of the governed as legitimizing the state, the function of the state to serve the interests of all. Other liberals can contest Smith's advocacy of political remedies for economic inequality, but they will do so on the same set of principles. Thus, although the relationship between equality and liberty may be congenitally controversial within liberalism, it is worthy of note that both values do belong to Liberal thought, while neither is particularly valued by the nonliberal traditions.[5]

Democratism and egalitarianism, however practiced, rest on a firm valuation of the individual person and her freedom. To this extent, some variety of *individualism* is the ethic of all liberal theories. But only to that extent, for liberal thinkers are notoriously divided on the subject of social theory. Here, and perhaps most clearly, we encounter the issues that separate communitarianism and republicanism, on the one hand, from libertarianism and other strongly individualistic versions of liberalism, on the other.

This area has become so disputed, as the reader will discover in this volume, that to distinguish liberalism from republican and communitarian thought is as common as it long has been to mark a formal separation of libertarianism and liberalism, *simpliciter*. Communitarians and republicans repudiate what they perceive to be the excessively individualist social theory underlying formal liberalisms and libertarianism. Specifically, they call for more robust conceptions of citizenship, particularly of the duties of citizens to one another and to the social whole, than even moderate liberalisms appear sufficient to support; of libertarian intrasocial isolationism, they want no part. And, to the extent that laissez-faire economics is associated with individualist liberalism, both republicans and communitarians fault that part of the liberal tradition with encouraging a selfish acquisitiveness frequently cited as a cause of diminishing civic responsibility.

In the face of this dispute, can we retain the general nomenclature of liberalism rather than abandoning it to bellicose Hobbesian individualism, to the storied social atomism of Locke, or to the abstract formal individualism of contemporary liberals such as Rawls?

First, it should be noted that much of this is a matter of context. Thus, compared with Hobbes, Locke is the champion of natural sociability and gentle republican virtues. To some libertarians, communitarians and moderate liberals, alike, are disguised social collectivists, and those republican appeals to the common good are the apex of a slippery slope to totalitarianism. On the other hand, as Joan McGregor notes, those who style themselves communitarians or republicans often depict both moderate liberal and libertarian views as radically individualistic and equally incapable of explaining the nature of civic obligations.[6] Without reducing all disagreements to a matter of perspective, then, we should not allow what separates the proponents of various types of liberalism to obscure the profound agreements that unite them against antiliberal views.

Second, we can follow Dewey in distinguishing the psychological and metaphysical individualism of one type of liberal thought from cognate ideals of the moral value of individual freedom and development. He argued that, whereas "earlier liberalism led to a conception of individuality as something ready-made, already possessed, and needing only the removal of certain legal restrictions to come into full play,"[7] individuality should be understood as an *end* of liberalism, in the broadest sense. Thus, while conceptions of individuality change fashion, what liberalism always seeks is "a social organization that will make possible the effective liberty and opportunity for personal growth in mind and spirit in all individuals."[8]

On this view, what is central to liberalism is not metaphysical or psychological individualism but commitment to the well-being, the full flourishing, of every individual member of society. This commitment does not presuppose a state of nature populated by full-grown independent hominids, nor a Newtonian cosmos in which individual humans represent discrete wholes. Nor does it require that we imaginatively reduce each person to an anonymous rational calculator of isolated self-interests. Liberalism, thus understood, simply values individuals *as* individuals. In this attitude, as in its call for democracy and political equality, liberalism stands against traditions that privilege social groups, specific classes, or the state, the church, the race, and other abstractions, and that treat the good or interests of these as the objects of primary valuation. Liberalism, by contrast, announces that individual persons do matter. It need not set the individual against society, but it refuses to wholly subsume the individual within society. It is in this way, then, that individualism is the philosophical anthropology of liberalism, rather than in the metaphysical or psycho-epistemological fashion of seventeenth-century philosophy.

The valorization of individual *freedom*—the *libertas* in Liberalism—makes sense in this light: individuals deserve to be respected as free agents in the pursuit of self-development. This freedom, understood as moral autonomy and personal liberty, is both an end in itself and a means to self-realization. But, again, keeping communitarian and republican liberalisms in mind, we need not depict liberalism as reducing human relations to the balancing of individual rights and interests without reference to shared responsibilities and obligations. Libertarianism is but one form of liberalism, on this account, and both the character and boundaries of individual liberty remain subjects of discussion within our broadly liberal camp. In this respect, we do well to recall that Locke, so often listed among the villains of extreme individualism, was, in fact, a natural law theorist quite convinced that humans are both naturally sociable and bound by moral obligations that preexist any civil order.

Dewey's distinction between liberalism as a set of ends and as specific prescribed means is useful here. For, just as individual identity can be seen as something to be achieved rather than something ready made, so, too, individual freedom can be understood as a goal that liberalism pursues. The *liberation* of individual members of society, which is integral to their self-realization, is what liberalism promotes. How this liberation is to be effected and what its terms will be are contested issues within liberal discourse. Libertarians may see liberty as an original condition best left unencumbered; for them there is little *process* to liberation—it is essentially a matter of keeping the state at bay. For communitarians, republicans, and left-leaning liberals, the aim of liberation may appear to require active social efforts to aid individuals in the development of freedom; any of these perspectives is also more likely than libertarianism to restrict individual interests in promoting maximum free development for all. Nonetheless, all liberalism stands apart from those perspectives that regard individual freedom as a danger or a myth. No doubt it is this thematic element in liberal thought that persuades some beginning students of philosophy to regard Aristotle as the liberal antidote to Platonist corporativism, at least until they encounter Locke.

The Essays

Just as they share in the liberal context, the essays in Part 1 attempt to answer a common question: What virtues define good citizenship and what are ideal civil relations in a liberal democracy? Several contributors look to the nature of public interactions and the proper role of reasoning in civic affairs. Others attend to institutional means of eliminating or ameliorating the tensions that erode feelings of civil connection. As we will see, there is much consensus as to the elements of civility—perhaps a surprising degree of consensus given the authors' apparent agreement that civility is currently in decline.

Mortimer Sellers's "Ideals of Public Discourse" focuses on a concern that appears throughout Part 1: the character of *public discourse*. Sellers attempts to lay out the ideals of public discourse in terms of its primary purpose, which he identifies as the res publica, the "common interest of all members of society."[9] He acknowledges that, sometimes, the existence of common ground must simply be asserted in the face of apparently irreconcilable differences.

In part, this seems to be a logical requirement for public discourse: absent the possibility of common ground, no genuine discourse, or at least none that reaches us as public beings, is possible. Domination through usurping of power or through force is not discourse, ideal or otherwise. But, Sellers clearly intends to make an argument of political morality, as well. He holds that the state should "take everyone's well-being into account and develop," partly through democratic practices, "a public good that harmonizes the various interests and capacities of the citizens into a coherent and satisfying whole"[10] and maintains that citizenship imposes duties of cooperation and commitment to the common good. Sellers's affirmation of a genuinely public good, of the real possibility of a coherent civil union, and of the shared obligations of citizenship evinces the republican character of his approach.

What dispositions and attitudes constitute the civic virtue presupposed by effective public discourse? Sellers notes these as of particular importance: (1) readiness to hear the views of others in a fair manner; (2) a sincere desire to achieve the harmonization of interests; and (3) restraint in mode of discourse and tolerance in reaction to others, so as to not cut off or subvert debate. A particularly interesting feature of his analysis is the treatment of subcommunities within the larger social whole. Although subcommunities contribute importantly to human happiness, he argues, exclusionary "tribal" collectivities endanger public discourse; they do so by both privileging members' interests and insulating the group from interaction with nonmembers. Sellers's recommendation seems to be to encourage what I call "porous" subcommunities—ones that give expression to religious, ethnic, and other subcivil interests, while remaining open to the flow of discourse with the rest of society.

In "Civility, Civic Virtue, and Citizenship," Joan McGregor scrutinizes individualistic liberalism as a cause of current failures of civic virtue. Like Sellers, she takes a republican perspective, but she advocates republicanism specifically as an antidote to what ails us. She rejects both the metaphysical and psychological individualism of much liberalism and what she identifies as the reactionary, regressive possibilities implicit in some communitarianism. She contends that "civic republicanism" offers the conceptual apparatus to conjoin liberal valuations of individual freedom and pluralism with communitarian emphasis on commitment to the public good and transcendence of selfish private interests.

In diagnosing our unhappy social condition and explicating republicanism, McGregor analyzes three core concepts: *civility*, distinguished from good manners; *civic virtue*, as a set of dispositions developed in and valuable to social organization; and *citizenship*, as a mode of life distinguished from mere legal status. The good, or true, citizen exhibits a set of civic virtues, including (1) commitment to, and a sense of, the public good; (2) respect for others and tolerance of differences; (3) self-restraint with respect to the pursuit of private advantages; (4) readiness to accept social responsibilities and burdens; and (5) the capacity to employ deliberative reason. Meaningful civility, which draws from deeper sources than mere politeness, is the visible face of civic virtue.

McGregor's discussion is particularly valuable for its inclusion of both classical and contemporary republican theory. Readers familiar with ongoing debates among intellectual historians as to the relative sway of republican and liberal ideals in the thought of the American Founders[11] will find the analysis of contemporary republican theorists enlightening, as it is their explicit purpose to articulate the common grounds of liberalism in our broad sense. McGregor's use of reactionary communitarianism as a foil for individualist liberalism, especially the formal variety popular among academics, illuminates civic republicanism as a genuine third alternative that affirms both the value of individual growth and the importance of social life for that growth.

Emily Gill takes up the persistent liberal interest in public reason, deliberation, and openness in "Civic Education in the Liberal State." As her title suggests, she sees the demand for rational civil discourse as a social challenge as much as a call to individual virtue. How, she asks, can the virtues we seek in citizens of a liberal state be encouraged and sustained? Indeed, how can we promote any set of virtues without violating the very respect for individual autonomy liberalism demands? Is it not disrespectful of personal freedom to insist that citizens become rational deliberators—to insist, in effect, that they be autonomous?

Surveying the current literature on the problem of civic education, Gill identifies three ways to answer these questions. The approach she ascribes to Amy Gutmann and Eammonn Callan affirms the aim of education for active participation in a democratic polity as including training in critical reflection and development of a capacity for "imaginative engagement" with unfamiliar perspectives. Against this, Gill sets William Galston's call for limiting liberal civic education to the minimal requirements of tolerance: citizens must learn to live in peace with those whose choices they reject but should not be expected to understand those views or to critique their own. As a third alternative, she assesses Stephen Macedo's "muscular version" of liberalism, according to which critical reflection and rational deliberation are central educational goals, and illiberal perspectives—notably religious ones—must retreat to their properly nonpublic corners.[12]

Gill's vision of liberal civic virtues includes many of those identified by Sellers and McGregor, notably (1) willingness to subject our own views to examination and to hear out the views of others, (2) respect for others as equals, and (3) tolerance of nonharmful views and behaviors of which we do not approve. Like Gutmann, Callan, and Macedo, she regards the capacity for critical reflection as requisite for citizenship in a liberal democracy, and she believes that this capacity presupposes "sympathetic and imaginative engagement" with diverse, even disliked, worldviews.[13]

Gill also recommends that the lesson of critical reflection be taken to heart by those who deem themselves liberal as much as by those they perceive as illiberal. She argues that liberals can learn something about their own views by practicing genuine openness, even to illiberal groups. They can learn that they, too, are people who advocate a specific perspective, one that values autonomy, and that this is not a universal valuation. That liberalism is not a value-neutral Archimedean position is an important lesson. As Gill demonstrates, ignoring this lesson may lead us to disguise our values, subvert them in practice, or impose them unreflectively on others.

Patricia Smith, in "Intolerance and Exploitation: Civic Vice, Legal Norms, and Cooperative Individualism," seizes the categorical bull by the horns by differentiating between her liberal vision and that based on social atomism. Cooperative, rather than atomistic, individualism is the view she thinks most appropriate to liberal democracy, on the grounds that interpersonal cooperation and shared obligations are crucial to the institutions of limited constitutional government, the family, and private contract. These institutions she associates with fundamental liberal valuation of individuals. But, she recognizes that individuals sometimes require institutional support to maintain cooperative efforts, particularly in the face of social intolerance and economic exploitation. Good citizens of a liberal democracy *should* be tolerant of one another and *should* refrain from exploiting relative advantages in ways that harm others and undercut cooperation. If individuals cannot be counted on to behave perfectly—as we assume they cannot—she concludes that institutions and policies must be adapted to restrain their vices and to offset ill effects of their failures of virtue.

Smith forcefully rebuts the standard arguments against political responses to persistent poverty, insisting throughout on a collective responsibility to combat economic structures that effectively exploit individual citizens. Thus, she contends, providing for the general welfare is a collective responsibility and "we should recognize it in institutions of law and government that address the wrong" of economic exploitation.[14]

Interpersonal intolerance, on the other hand, appears less susceptible to governmental action, as Smith observes. Distinguishing between "group intolerance" as that based on existential features and "moral/religious intolerance," which focuses on disparaged practices or beliefs, she suggests that the former is antithetical to recognition of the equal worth of every individual. It is, thus, without defense in a liberal polity. Yet, it is often beyond the reach of the law. To mitigate group intolerance, therefore, she recommends "experience" and education, echoing Gill's emphasis on the ideals of education for liberal citizenship.

What she calls moral/religious intolerance poses thornier philosophical issues, particularly for a liberal society wherein morally or religiously motivated judgmentalism is as much to be respected as generous acceptance of differences. Smith recognizes this conundrum and, like Gill, seeks a reasonable accommodation. Her problem, however, is a different one, for the morally intolerant who are of concern to her wish to constrain the conduct of others, whereas Gill's illiberal minorities wish only to be left to their own devices. Smith's solution is the classic Millean one of insisting on allowing everyone to live as they will so long as they do not harm others. Thus, she concludes by encouraging tolerance of and by all and calling, somewhat wistfully, for the inclusion of *On Liberty* in school curricula.

Conclusion

As suggested, Sellers, McGregor, Gill, and Smith share a general view of civic virtue, one appropriate to their common liberalism. The characteristics they identify are all virtues in the philosophical sense, in that they are capacities, dispositions, habits, and attitudes, as distinguished from types of conduct. Naturally, to have the civic virtues of reasonableness, tolerance, concern for the public good, and so forth, precludes certain acts. Thus, one cannot exhibit the liberal virtue of respect for others while excluding them from political participation or seeking to suppress their religious views, and one cannot exhibit the virtue of commitment to the common good while advancing incompatible private interests. But, our authors are concerned to portray the character of the good citizen and the nature of civil relations, more than they are to enumerate prescribed and proscribed behaviors.

Further, I think it fair to say that the authors share a vision of the role and purposes of civic virtue, as well. That is, they would give generally the same answers to the question "Why have the civic virtues?" These answers would be functional, for the most part—or consequentialist, for those who prefer that term. Civic virtue is good for us, good for individuals, and good for society. The particular virtues our authors prescribe for liberal democracies are those that serve the good of liberal democracies and their citizens. Their exercise makes political and daily life practicable and more pleasant than they would be if the majority of citizens lacked them. Indeed, this seems to be the message of current worry over the decline of civic virtue: life is becoming less pleasant, less rewarding, and the business of public life is becoming ever more difficult. Benjamin Franklin, Thomas Jefferson, and other American Founders explicitly confessed their concern for the "virtue" of future citizens. Although this concern did extend to what we would now call private morality, their primary interest lay with the civic virtue of the citizenry. Following Tocqueville, they believed that liberal democracy could not survive without a civic-minded citizenry, no matter how refined the constitutional provisions surrounding political affairs.[15] This was, of course, one reason most of the Founders—including those suspicious of the average citizen—advocated public education, which they assumed would inculcate values of cooperation and self-restraint as well as teach fundamental skills. If anyone had suggested that the primary purpose of education was to enable individuals to maximize their own material welfare without regard to the common good, as we now so often do, the Founders would have been astounded and horrified.[16]

Like the Founders, then, contributors to Part 1 take a functional view of civic virtue, not because of shallow moral perspectives but because they recognize that civic virtues are by their very nature aimed at goods: the good lives of all citizens and the health of the polity. Although some academic philosophers might classify these as "external" goods, they belong to the very heart of public life.

C.S.

Notes

1. John Dewey, *Liberalism and Social Action* (New York: Putnam's Sons, 1935); especially chap. 1, "The History of Liberalism," and *Reconstruction in Philosophy,* 2d ed. (Boston: Beacon Press, 1948); especially chap. 8, "Reconstruction as Affecting Social Philosophy."

2. I include advocates of direct democracy here to acknowledge the honored place of Thomas Paine in U.S. history, although he may have been a lone voice among those usually mentioned as the Founding Fathers.

3. Consequently, participation in the governing process, in the limited form of voting or in more active contribution, is a good proclaimed by genuine liberalism. This may be an instrumental good, serving the interests of individuals and the social whole, or an intrinsic one, valuable simply as fitting for free citizens.

4. In this regard, note that much of the debate over affirmative action policies is carried on in the name of civil equality. Thus, opponents of affirmative action often claim that such policies treat individuals inequitably by referencing illegitimate features such as race and gender.

5. One clue to this distinction lies in the purpose of property expressly recognized by republicans and market liberals alike: that self-sufficiency is necessary for individual freedom and, hence, genuinely free political participation.

6. See Chapter 2 for McGregor. It might be said from the communitarian and republican perspectives that libertarianism is simply more honest than moderate liberalism in acknowledging the absence of genuine civic connection.

7. Dewey, *Liberalism and Social Action,* 39.

8. Ibid., 31.

9. Sellers, p. 15, this volume.

10. Ibid., 18.

11. For an entrée into these quarrels, see James Kloppenberg, "The Virtues of Liberalism: Christianity, Republicanism, and Ethics in Early American Discourse," *Journal of American History* 74, no. 1 (1987); and Joyce Appleby, "Republicanism in Old and New Contexts," *William and Mary Quarterly* 43 (1986).

12. Macedo holds that religious beliefs, as personal worldviews not susceptible to public verification, cannot yield *public* reasons—that is, reasons appropriate to public discourse.

13. On imaginative engagement, "understanding" antithetical worldviews and lifestyles as an element of tolerance, see the Introduction to Part 2.

14. Smith, p. 69, this volume.

15. John Adams, who disputed Jefferson's rosy portrayal of the omnicompetent citizen, placed great faith in constitutional devices to ensure the welfare of the country. Still, like Jefferson and others, he maintained that education of the citizenry was necessary for the ultimate stability of the new democracy.

16. Alexander Hamilton might be cited as an exception to this claim, but I believe that would be unfair. It is true that he advocated commerce and the individual pursuit of material well-being as a means to divert less-than-virtuous citizens from factional meddling in political affairs. But, this recommendation itself evidences his awareness of the importance of civic virtue and the perils of civil vice. Wanting to counterbalance the absence of virtue is not the same as declaring virtue irrelevant.

Chapter 1

Ideals of Public Discourse

Mortimer Sellers

Ergo unum debet esse omnibus propositum, ut eadem
sit utilitas unius cuiusque et universorum; quam si ad se
quisque rapiet, dissolvetur omnis humana consortio.
—Marcus Tullius Cicero, *De Officiis*

This essay considers *public discourse*, defined here as speeches, publications, and other statements concerning the public good. Public discourse in this sense regards public policy, as distinguished from *private discourse* among citizens seeking to develop their own private friendships and interests. This line between public and private discourse may be difficult to draw, because it concerns the fundamental division of power within society and the state. Public discourse defines and limits the power of the government, but also the power of individuals. That which is not public is private, and vice versa, and it is public discourse, itself, that must, in the end, decide the boundaries. The purpose of public discourse is to search for right answers to public questions, so that the state *and* individuals can guide their actions as much as possible in conformity with justice and the common good of the people. The ideals of public discourse depend on constructing a system of human interaction that respects the well-being of every member of society. This entails civility, sincerity, and even the toleration of seemingly dangerous behavior when doing so will aid the public good.

The standards of behavior that should govern public discourse constitute *civility*. With some exceptions, these standards also extend to private discourse. Specific forms of *incivility*, such as simple thoughtlessness to others, ideologically supported thoughtlessness to others, and ideologically supported hostility to others violate the basic premise of public discourse: that is, service to the public good, defined as the common interest of all members of society. Public discourse assumes a res publica—the range of purposes

15

and needs that people have in common, and above all their common need to coordinate private interests, so that the well-being of each individual benefits as much as possible from the shared well-being of the community. Incivility disparages the community of citizenship without which public discourse cannot exist. The argument for public discourse is also an argument for civility. But the boundaries of public discourse do not limit the range of civility, despite their close affinity and similar origins.

Ideals and the Common Good

The purpose of public discourse is to search for right answers to public questions, so that the state and individuals can guide their actions as much as possible in conformity with justice and the common good of the people. These ideals of public discourse seek to guide and preserve the common good of every citizen's private interests, on the basis of a shared public community. Private actions against the public good violate justice and may be restrained or forbidden. Private actions congruent with the public good do not violate justice and should not be constrained by the state. There will also be certain violations of justice that do not rise to a level that warrants public interference. Such legally private activities remain, nonetheless, legitimate subjects of public discourse that seeks to influence or educate citizens to behave civilly in their private lives.

Discourse about ideals is foundational, in the sense that it governs the structure of the enterprise itself. This means to some extent that ideals about discourse must be asserted, not proved, because conversation cannot begin without ideals in place to support it. Of course, public discourse does often begin without an explicit discussion of ideals, because the fundamental ideals of public discourse are implicit in the very act of entering into a conversation. Discourse of any kind entails establishing some common ground, and public discourse implies a broader community. Simply by virtue of trying to convince you of something, I admit that your views are worth influencing and that I must take them into account. Arguments based solely on my own interests will fail to convince you without some reference to a common standard that embraces your views as well as mine. We begin with points on which we can agree and move forward from there.

If ordinary discourse consists in two people finding common ground, public discourse should consist in finding common ground for the people as a whole. This seldom happens. Depending on the political structure of the community in question, one may have only to convince a single person, as in a despotism; a few people, as in an oligarchy; or a majority, as in democracies, to shape public policy. Each situation involves injustices, as the one, the few, or the many disregard the rest to pursue their own private interests on the backs of everyone else. The implicit ideals of actual public discourse are limited by the scope of those included in the conversation. So, in the end, one must simply assert the ideal that public discourse should consider the well-being of every member of the community.

To assume that public discourse should respect the well-being of every member of the community does not require that the well-being of every member of the community be always and everywhere reconcilable or that everyone always agree. Ideal public discourse seeks to reconcile private interests as much as possible, while seeking the public good, and continues to value each individual's well-being, even when individuals do not agree or refuse to participate in the conversation at all. Those who deny the basic premise that everyone's well-being should count will be hard pressed to explain why theirs deserves special attention. Bald assertions of extraordinary entitlement seldom convince in the absence of coercion or generations of strong cultural conditioning.

Any individual will have a wide range of inchoate interests and capacities, formed in large part by the society in which he or she lives. These almost always include the tendency, or at least an ability, to enjoy the happiness of others, along with some familiar but less appealing desires, such as sadism or greed. Not all these human tasks and possibilities can be satisfied at once, so human personalities and careers develop by favoring some aspects of human nature and leaving others undeveloped. Public discourse helps to guide such decisions by discovering the constellation of possibilities that does the most to make everyone's lives worthwhile and disapproving those possible human interests that violate the common good.

People develop social lives and enjoy cooperative projects, even in the absence of stable political institutions. Public discourse makes this possible. Most humans value community as a good in itself and enjoy the complicated shared projects, such as theaters, highways, parks, and monuments, that community makes possible. Public discourse identifies these common needs and stigmatizes private interests that hurt communal institutions or involvements. The common good is a pattern of public coordination that develops all citizens' capacities and interests toward harmony and mutual benefit, without exploiting any individuals for the unreciprocated benefit of others in society.

Most states and participants in public discourse do in fact claim to serve the common good of the community as a whole. I shall call states that successfully do so republics, because they protect the res publica or common good of the people. Republican institutions take everyone's well-being into account and develop a public good that harmonizes the various interests and capacities (*res privata*) of the citizens into a coherent and satisfying whole. Republican discourse is discourse in pursuit of the common good, and to realize its own foundational ideals, all public discourse should be republican.

Republics have a long history of institutional and theoretical development, which has identified certain practices as conducive to republican deliberation and public decision making in a free state. Popular sovereignty, representative government, frequent elections, the separation of powers, a mixed and balanced bicameral legislature, an independent judiciary, and the rule of law have all been demonstrated to secure impartial decisions, in pursuit of the common good.[1]

This discussion of public discourse will not review the details of republican constitutional government except to endorse them, generally, and to express the hope that public discourse will take place under the aegis of free republican institutions. Republican constitutional protections guide governments as much as possible toward making public decisions in service of the common good, but they cannot succeed without a culture of constructive public discourse to discover the policies that best serve justice. Public discourse needs more specific, subconstitutional, laws to protect its integrity, and commitment by participants to nonlegislated standards of behavior.

Civility

Standards of behavior that serve the ideals of public discourse are known as civility, because they promote a sense of citizenship and shared community. Rules of civility encourage taking the well-being of every member of the community equally into account in public discourse and treating every participant in the conversation as a fellow citizen whose interests deserve respect and whose views merit careful consideration. This requires listening to the arguments made by others in the public discussion, trying to understand them, and responding as if they were made in good faith by making reasoned responses even to incoherent or transparently self-interested views.

Civility promotes the ideal of community by example, eliciting civil responses and attitudes from others, but it also promotes the aims of pub-

lic discourse in practice, by finding or developing the public good and justice more effectively than other, uncivil, forms of discourse. This is because
the views of every member of the community are *in fact* worth considering
in pursuit of the common good. Each individual has strong insights into his
or her own needs and circumstances but is also misled by them, guided by
the natural human tendency to confuse reality with one's own self-interest. Civil public discourse makes use of every individual's insights, while
moderating self-interested mistakes and confusion.

Civility reflects a necessary humility about one's own perceptions, while
eliciting the valuable perceptions of others as sources of truth about justice.
Civility educates all participants in sincere public discourse, by encouraging
the reflective exchange of insights in pursuit of truth and justice. This does
not mean that all perceptions and insights are equally valid, but that all
equally deserve to undergo the test of sincere public discourse. Views that
do not convince ought to be reexamined in the light of public criticism.

Sincerity

The measure of sincerity in public discourse is actual commitment to the
ideals of public discourse, which is to say, an actual commitment to the common good of the people concerned. Sincere participants in public discourse
evaluate their own views and the statements of others in the light of this
commitment to create a harmony of interests and worthwhile life for all
members of the community. This entails listening to and considering the
observations of others, without necessarily endorsing them. To disregard the
insights of others would frustrate the purposes of public discourse by limiting the knowledge with which decisions are made and, therefore, their conformity with justice. Public decision makers, deriving authority from the
public-regarding procedures of an ideal republic, still require sincerity to
serve the common good effectively, because even the best procedures cannot completely constrain discretion in applying republican values and legislation to specific cases and circumstances. Insincerity poisons the sources of
public authority by divorcing the exercise of public power from the principles that justified it in the first place.

Insincere public discourse by private citizens deprives public decision
makers of important information in their public search for justice. Public
officials and other citizens will respond to insincere discourse as if offered
in good faith, but insincere arguments do not advance the search for truth

about justice and will not convince well-intentioned citizens in pursuit of the common good. When others are sincere, insincerity will be self-defeating.

When most participants in public discourse are sincere, insincerity constitutes its own self-punishment, because it deprives the speaker of his or her opportunity to make good-faith contributions to the public search for truth about justice. Some forms of insincerity are more dangerous, however, as when factions coordinate their participation in communal discourse to manipulate public decision-making procedures in favor of their own interests, against the common good. Such tactics may vary in their shamelessness. Whenever factional insincerity threatens the integrity of public opinion, factions or would-be factions deserve to face the justified outrage of their angry fellow citizens. Arguments presented as if to serve the common good will seldom evoke justified outrage, because civility requires treating other participants in public discourse as sincere, even when they are not. Yet, openly factional arguments that deny or disparage the common good elicit justified outrage, because they violate the ideals that public discourse exists to serve. Coordinated insincerity presents a more difficult case, because it observes the proper standards of public discourse, *even as* it violates them. Most forms of insincerity require patient refutation through a reasoned argument. Nonetheless, large factions of insincere participants may sometimes deserve public outrage when, as public officials, they abuse their power in the state.

Outrage shuts its victims out of public discourse by disapproving their views and behavior. This makes outrage very dangerous, appropriate only in extreme situations that disrespect the fundamental purposes public discourse exists to serve. Public arguments that rest on racial, ethnic, religious, gender, or other inappropriate references to private affiliation or exclusion are outrageous because they privilege private affinities over the public welfare. Invective, public discussion of another's private affairs, and other incivilities are outrageous because they violate the public values of community, which discourse exists to serve. Outrage patrols the boundaries of public discourse, discountenancing forms of expression that violate the common good.

Community

Constructing the common good implies creating a community to support the harmony of public and private interests that public values develop to serve. At some level, the common good of the people should include all people but, in fact, most communities are smaller, comprising the inhabitants of a very restricted society or territory. This raises questions of legitimacy, in distinguishing illegitimate factions from legitimate communities of interest. Ideals of public discourse disallow assertions of community that improperly exclude the views of those they govern or control.

Public discourse should embrace all members of the community, but not all communities should embrace all people. The boundaries between communities control the scope of public discourse by defining the citizens or people whose interests they serve. Local projects require local discourse, while others have a broader scope. The fundamental community of humanity regulates the borders of all group deliberations without necessarily determining specific regional arrangements in each separate community. Smaller communities reflect historical and geographical developments that group people together in pursuit of common projects. Most such affinities are private, in the sense that they fall into the area of private discretion that public institutions exist, in part, to protect. Other communities, by which I mean primarily geographically based communities, fulfill a public function by encouraging everyone who lives within a given territory to build the harmony and sense of common purpose without which worthwhile lives will be difficult to achieve. Communities that elevate some citizens at the expense of others are factional and should not be encouraged.

Some subcommunities find meaning in nongeographical allegiances, such as race, religion, or ethnicity. Such categories threaten to violate the ideals of public discourse by excluding nonbelievers from their public deliberations. They create *tribes*. To the extent that nongeographical tribal affiliations exercise public authority over nonbelievers or nonaffiliates, they violate the ideals of public discourse, which require public consideration for all members of the community. Private expressions of tribal solidarity do not violate this ideal, so long as public processes do not impose tribal identities onto unwilling citizens.

The tribal identity of private affiliations must be distinguished from the shared public identity of a broader community. Wider communities work in the interests of all, which requires that they consider the insights of all, in pursuit of the common good. Tribal groups serve the common enterprise of some self-selected collectivity who have set themselves apart from others by virtue of their own special interests. Racial and ethnic groups do this expressly, based on ancestry or appearance. Religious groups often do the same, using religion as a marker in place of ancestral or ethnic affiliation.

Broader religious claims of universal application cannot stand without the scrutiny of public deliberation in a free community; simple assertions of universal authority by self-selected leaders will not easily survive this test.

Tribes and religions usually develop around hereditary or moral principles that reflect fundamental human interests and capacities, which can be useful to the wider community. Hereditary affiliations can encourage a sense of family and commitment to multigenerational projects. Moral affiliations can encourage altruistic behavior exceeding the basic requirements of justice. Both commitments may enrich and deepen the meaning of individual lives. Yet, they also threaten public discourse when tribes act collectively to circumvent the public welfare. Tribes and religions contribute to the common good by enriching individual lives. They supplement, but should not replace, the wider community, and they must not be allowed to circumvent the republican requirements of public deliberation.

Toleration

Some types of incivility, insincerity, self-seeking, and tribal or religious solidarity violate the ideals of public discourse without seriously harming the community. Often, these reflect the personal confusion or self-deception of those who commit the violations. Such transgressions are not always conscious or intended and may so closely involve other more desirable aspects of individual personality that interfering would be dangerous or hurtful. Participants in public discourse should tolerate as much as possible the petty intolerance of others to foster the sense of community that makes public discourse possible.

Of course, when powerful figures justify their own violations as tolerable, the weak will suffer and society should be careful. But, when weak or disappointed individuals comfort themselves with invective or self-interest, toleration on the part of others may help to redirect their anger and confusion toward more constructive activities. Toleration always presupposes some violation of otherwise binding standards or norms. When the norms and standards so violated protect the common good of society, then toleration will facilitate faction and oppression. Therefore, one measure of toleration should be power: the more powerful the actor, the less his or her transgressions of the norms of public discourse deserve to be tolerated by other participants in the conversation.

Further, any policy of toleration reflects the natural limitations of human wisdom and judgment. Not everything that seems to violate ideals of public discourse really does so, when properly understood. Mistakes will be made even in the best republics after the best-constructed deliberation by well-intentioned participants. Interference or criticism of any kind is itself a harm to those who face it. Toleration prevents unnecessary friction by overlooking those violations that do the least harm to public discourse, when public outrage might be mistaken or would intensify the damage done by the original transgression.

Conclusion

The ideals of public discourse depend on constructing a system of human interaction that respects the well-being of every member of society. I have argued that this entails civility, sincerity, and even the toleration of apparently dangerous behavior when such toleration advances the public good. Republican government guarantees basic political structures that regulate public action in pursuit of the common good, but even the best structures of government will fail without sincere and civil public discourse to support them. Rudeness has no place in public discourse, but the conflict of competing ideologies may be unavoidable when sincere participants in public discourse strongly disagree. In such cases, when public issues are at stake, firmly expressed disagreement should give way to the public consensus. On the other hand, genuine public outrage and complete disregard of other citizens' views are seldom justified, unless to counter open challenges to the high and equal value of every human being.

Public discourse considers, develops, and balances the potentialities of human nature, viewed in the context of existing historical circumstances. The fundamental community of consideration should embrace all humanity, but narrower, geographically distinct communities will develop regional societies with publics of their own. Communities not based on geography also exist but should not exercise the coercion that properly protects territorial communities against the self-interest of some of their own members or power elites. Public discourse educates and elevates the people so long as participants embrace communal deliberation in pursuit of the common good. The ideals of public discourse are the ideals of human community, which make private projects possible by defining the boundaries of public life.

Notes

1. See Philip Pettit, *Republicanism: A Theory of Freedom and Government* (Oxford: Oxford University Press, 1997); Quentin Skinner, *Liberty before Liberalism* (New York: Cambridge University Press, 1998); M. N. S. Sellers, *The Sacred Fire of Liberty: Republicanism, Liberalism and the Law* (New York: New York University Press, 1998); and M. N. S. Sellers, *American Republicanism: Roman Ideology in the United States Constitution* (New York: New York University Press, 1994).

Chapter 2

Civility, Civic Virtue, and Citizenship

Joan McGregor

There is a general sense that individuals' interactions with one another in modern American society have deteriorated.[1] Public discourse tends to be sharp, short, and angry. Ironically, the "in your face" attitude is often applauded in pop culture—think of the shock jock Howard Stern or television personality Jerry Springer—and, thus, encouraged and perpetuated. Participation in democratic processes has also dramatically declined, including people's willingness to vote and serve on juries. When people do participate in democratic processes, that participation is often self-serving and acrimonious. Special-interest politics is flourishing. Special interest groups are often one-issue groups; many of them are intransigent about their positions and disinterested in other issues. The limiting case of special interest politics is individuals' exclusive interest in their own welfare, so that "vote your pocketbook" appears to be the slogan followed on election day. Getting voluntary compliance from individuals to restrain themselves for environmental or public-safety reasons or other matters of the public good is extremely difficult. The principles of individual sovereignty and absolute control over property and resources are advanced to prevent governmental regulation that might serve the interests of the community.

The idea that we, as citizens of a liberal democracy, should sometimes set aside our own narrow interests for the common interests of society is incongruent in this climate. In this essay, I explore the connection between our contemporary society's commitment to political liberalism, with its preoccupation with individual rights and autonomy, and the deterioration of civility, the decline of democratic participation, and the overemphasis on individuals' self-interest. In particular, I consider whether contemporary society's narrow, self-interested attitudes might reflect contemporary political theory's single-minded pursuit of individual rights and the justice of the basic institutions, to the neglect of recognizing the benefits of participation in and commitment to a genuine republic. If there is a connection between the two, does this mean that liberalism is stuck with that result, or are there alternative ways of construing liberalism that don't result in the decline of civility and civic virtue? In answering that question, I will explore the revival in republican political philosophy and how that theory can modify liberalism.

Civility, Civic Virtue, and Citizenship

Before inquiring into liberalism's complicity in the decay of the tone of modern society, we need to define some of the key concepts. Let's start with *civility.* Civility encompasses everything from good manners to the so-called civic virtues. Civility requires that we use the "magic words" with strangers as well as with friends and family: we must say "please" and "thank you" for services given. It requires that we address others formally until given permission to do otherwise.

Civility is essentially about our treatment of strangers; it is an ethic for relating to strangers. Civility requires in some basic sense that we exhibit respect toward them.[2] Some of this respect is in the form of accepted conventions about good manners, and other forms of respect are exemplified in more generalized but less ritualized treatment of strangers. Civility involves treating others as if they matter. The standards are those that go beyond the moral minimum; that is, they include more than merely not violating people's rights.

Stephen Carter claims that civility is the sum of many sacrifices we are called on to make for the sake of living together.[3] One important question is how much of a sacrifice does civility require of us? Being polite and patient with others sets the baseline for civility, but we might want to ask about actions that go beyond that. For example, is providing positive assistance to strangers part of civility? Bad Samaritan laws might be seen as enforcing an aspect of civility. Bad Samaritan laws punish with criminal sanctions acts of incivility; they ask that people make small sacrifices when others are in need. Treating strangers as if they matter means that when they are in distress one ought to help them, at least if one can do so without threatening one's own life or welfare.[4]

Civil treatment also has a lot to do with how we communicate with others. Being civil extends to our treatment of people who disagree with our political views. Listening to the views of our political opponents and even tolerating reasonable differences of opinion are important aspects of civility. Discussing differences of viewpoints without acrimony, violence, shouting, or ad hominem attacks is a dimension of civility. One might object that failure to treat such people cordially or with courtesy does not harm them in the sense of John Stuart Mill's harm principle. Hence, the objection continues, incivility is not an issue of public concern but, rather, a private matter. That is, of course, part of our question, namely, what role ought civility to play in politics and civil society, and should the state be involved in encouraging it?

Second is the concept of *civic virtue* itself. Civic virtue is tied to the role of the citizen: the good citizen practices civic virtue.[5] Virtues are tied to roles and are understood as a part of one's character. Hence, they refer to "the dispositions to act in accordance with the standards and expectations that define the role or roles a person performs."[6] Civic virtue refers to certain dispositions and characteristics one has to have to be a good citizen. But, before civic virtue can be used to set standards of excellence for the role of a citizen, we need to understand the characteristics of a good citizen.

The republican tradition has a lot to say about good citizenship. Republicanism has a long history, tracing its pedigree to Aristotle through Montesquieu, to Rousseau to Harrington and others, including the framers of the American Constitution.[7] For Aristotle, virtues simply are those characteristics that enable individuals to live well in communities. Full human flourishing can be achieved only in the *polis,* and social institutions depend for their existence on the practice of civic virtue. For Aristotle, politics and ethics are necessarily connected. Civic virtue is, then, a necessary ingredient to human well-being or flourishing, but it is valuable because it promotes the good of the community or society, not because it directly promotes the good of the individual. On some theories, including Aristotle's, these goods cannot be readily disentangled, but clearly the motivation for virtue is not narrow self-interest.

Civic virtue may be defined, then, as the "disposition to further public over private good in action and deliberation."[8] Being disposed to public spiritedness and public service are general character traits of civic virtue. A person with civic virtue, according to Richard Dagger, who has argued for the joining of republicanism and liberalism, has the following traits and dispositions: he or she (1) respects individual rights, (2) values autonomy, (3) tolerates different opinions and beliefs, (4) plays fair, (5) cherishes civic memory, and (6) takes an active part in the community.[9] These traits or

characteristics are ones that may make a good citizen in a liberal republican society but may not be so compelling in other political systems. What
characteristics make one a good citizen is, at least to some degree, a function of the type of political system. Nevertheless, republican theory finds a
prominent place for civic virtue, unlike many other political theories.

Third, we have *citizenship,* which is sometimes defined merely as a legal
status guaranteeing its bearer certain rights and privileges. Another
definition of citizenship conceptualizes it in terms of social roles and the
attendant responsibilities. For example, as Rousseau conceptualizes citizenship, it "is intimately related to civic virtue—so intimately that he practically defined 'citizens' as 'one who acts with the good of the community
in mind.'"[10] This conception of citizenship follows the tradition of Aristotle. For Rousseau and other republicans, "citizenship was not simply a matter of legal status that carried with it various privileges and immunities.
Citizenship was a way of life that required commitment to the common
good and active participation in public affairs."[11]

Citizens, under this model, need to have certain attitudes toward their
country and their fellow citizens. They need to share a sense of identity
with other members of their nation and feel allegiance to the group. Citizenship, according to Will Kymlicka, "should be a forum where people transcend their differences, and think about the common good of all citizens."[12]
They should view the nature and the role of the state as not merely to protect their rights but also as a cooperative enterprise to advance common
goods for all citizens. Citizens should be willing to exercise self-restraint
to advance collective goals for the community—for example, environmental, public health and safety, and aesthetic goals. And when the country asks its citizens for sacrifices in the interests of the country, individuals
must have some basis for seeing their interests as integrated with those of
the nation.

Pluralistic democracies pose particularly difficult challenges for citizenship in this latter sense, according to which citizens normally developed
their shared identity through a common history, religion, language, and culture. Practicing civic virtue in modern pluralistic democracies, by contrast,
means tolerating and respecting those with religious and cultural differences.[13] Practicing civility may be more difficult in these circumstances,
without obvious common goals based on common history, religion, language,
or culture. Nevertheless, pluralistic democracies may have a greater need for
encouraging civil virtue, since there are many opportunities for intolerance

and fragmentation based on cultural differences. Nonetheless, for republican notions of citizenship, the individual needs some basis for identification with the group. Where individuals in pluralistic democracies might get their sense of identity will be a crucial part of our later discussion.

Liberalism and Communitarianism

The relationship between *civility, civic virtue,* and *citizenship,* then, is this: Civic virtue is the virtue of the citizen, and civility is basic to having civic virtue. What do these notions, particularly civic virtue, have to do with the environment in modern liberal America?

Several opponents of modern liberalism charge that one important contributor to the decay of civic virtue in American society is the excessive emphasis that we as a nation place on individual rights and autonomy. Theory and its practice in American society are seen as overemphasizing a crass form of individualism, to the detriment of community. Simultaneously, and because of liberalism's focus, little or no attention is paid to our responsibility to our community and fellow citizens. The argument is that we demand that other people and the government pay attention to our interests and respect our rights, while, on the other hand, we believe that we have a right to be left alone and not participate in the community. We define our relationships with other people and the government in terms of our rights against them. Politics, in this environment, is only important to individuals to the extent that they can secure their rights or advance their own self-interest. Thus, citizenship and civic virtue as defined by republican theory have little or no role.

State institutions, according to liberal theorists, are designed to protect individuals' rights within a structurally just society. On this view, the cardinal virtue of the state is *neutrality* toward different conceptions of the good. State neutrality means that the state is to "ensure for all citizens equal opportunity to advance any conception of the good they freely affirm" and that the "state is not to do anything intended to favor or promote any particular comprehensive doctrine rather than another, or to give greater assistance to those who pursue it." Finally, state neutrality means "that the state is not to do anything that makes it more likely that individuals will accept any particular conception rather than another unless steps are taken to cancel, or to compensate for, the effects of policies that do this."[14]

Many theorists, including communitarians, Marxists, and feminists, have commented on this liberal preoccupation with rights and autonomy.[15] They have argued that the exclusive emphasis on the values of individual rights and personal autonomy in contemporary political theory has led us, in practice, to neglect duties and responsibilities toward others and to our community as a whole—to allow civility, civic virtue, and the ideal of citizenship to wither away.[16]

These critics of liberalism have focused their attention on liberalism's support of what is often called *abstract individualism*.[17] This view considers individual human beings as social atoms abstracted from their social contexts. Society, on this view, is "in some sense constituted by individuals for the fulfillment of ends which were primarily individual."[18] This view of society and individuals "disregards the role of social relationships and human community in constituting the very identity and nature of individual human beings."[19] Individuals are conceived as rationally self-interested maximizers (*homo economicus*), each out to maximize his or her own self-interest.[20] Other liberal theories postulate that individuals are inevitably caught in a battle of all against all in competition for scarce resources.[21] The social context in which individuals find themselves is seen as important for nothing more than its instrumental value for maximizing one's own self-interest. We get the picture of individuals who are atomistic, individualistic, selfish or egoistic, and self-sufficient. That picture of liberalism seems either hostile to civic virtue or one in which civic virtue is irrelevant.

Under this conception of liberalism, the social conditions in which individuals find themselves are undervalued as contributors to the individual's sense of self or prospects for autonomous self-development. Since liberalism places little importance on social relationships, liberal theory has difficulty grounding the importance of civic virtue and the responsibility to the community that goes with civic virtue. Liberalism doesn't, so the argument goes, see communal relationships as a requirement for the effective fulfillment of individuals' autonomous plans. Unlike the view of Aristotle and other republican theorists, for example, liberalism does not value social and political life for its contribution to a full human life. Human beings are not conceptualized as irreducibly social in nature. There is merely a contingent connection for any particular individual between her life plan and the community of which she is a part.

Charles Taylor, among others, has objected to the atomist view of liberalism.[22] To fully understand the criticism, consider what Taylor sees as the alternative to atomism, namely, what he calls the *social thesis*.[23] The social thesis claims that the capacities for self-determination and autonomy can only be cultivated and exercised in particular kinds of societies, namely, societies with a rich array of cultural and social opportunities. In other words, individuals will not develop the capacity for self-determination and autonomy without a society that has made an effort to ensure a social environment where options and opportunities for those capacities can flourish. Liberalism mischaracterizes individuals as self-sufficient, as not needing the state's encouragement and protection of this enriched cultural environment.

Liberalism cannot, according to Taylor, endorse the social thesis because of liberalism's commitment to state neutrality. If the state were to encourage and protect a rich cultural environment—by funding the arts, for example—it would not be neutral among conceptions of the good. Taylor's social thesis rejects liberal neutrality, arguing that a neutral state is unable to sufficiently encourage and protect the rich social and cultural environment required for individuals to exercise self-determination.[24] Liberalism's rejection of the social thesis and its commitment to neutrality, therefore, undermine the possibility that people can develop fully.

Liberalism's rejection of the social thesis, both the view that individuals are to some extent constituted by their social environment and that individuals require certain kinds of social environments for full development of autonomy, raises an important question of how we are going to achieve that group identity required for a robust, republican, view of citizenship. If individuals don't see their connection to their community and, thereby, their nation as necessary for their self-identification and development, then they lose an important source of group identity necessary for citizenship. Another reason to worry about lack of identification with the group is that it may lead to a reluctance and unwillingness to share the burdens that come with liberal justice.[25] Individuals may question why they should sacrifice for others with whom they have little or no identity.

Michael Sandel raises a version of this objection to Rawls's difference principle, which requires that individuals share their assets with others in society. He argues that,

> [the difference principle's] claim on me is not the claim of a constitutive community whose attachments I acknowledge, but rather the claim of a concatenated collectivity whose entanglements I confront. What the difference principle requires, but cannot provide, is some way of identifying those *among* whom the assets I bear are properly regarded as common, some way of seeing ourselves as mutually indebted and morally engaged to begin with.[26]

Citizens in the narrow legal sense of citizenship in liberal democracies, according to Sandel, will not be motivated to share their assets as required by the difference principle or to subordinate their interests for others with whom they share little in terms of common forms of life or common conceptions of the good.

The result, according to Taylor, is that liberal democracies have a legitimacy problem. The citizens of liberal states are required to contribute to the welfare state, thereby setting aside their own interests for others with whom they share very little. Since individuals have no common shared sense of the good, even in a limited fashion, the individuals asked to make the sacrifices will not see the state or its demands as legitimate. Citizens asked to make sacrifices for others will view them as legitimate only when they identify with the state, and that will happen only when there is, says Taylor, "a common form of life [which] is seen as a supremely important good so that its continuance and flourishing matters to the citizens for its own sake."[27] If individuals see themselves as self-sufficient and the government function solely as protecting their own rights so that they might act autonomously, then individuals will have no reason to get involved in politics or make sacrifices for the nation unless their personal interests are compromised. If Taylor is correct that citizens will identify with the state and accept its demands as legitimate only when there is a common form of life, then liberalism is in trouble.

Liberalism seems to be committed to individuals freely choosing their own forms of the good, not requiring the state's support in developing that capacity, and to state neutrality toward those independently chosen goals.[28] Nonetheless, some liberal theorists think that a Rawlsian view avoids the problem of legitimacy by supposing that individuals, even though they might have very different conceptions of the good, will recognize that each person has an equal claim to consideration. It is, then, a shared sense of justice, not a shared conception of the good or even some part of a shared sense of a common form of life, that sustains state legitimacy.[29] Citizens will agree to the burdens of justice even when it means sacrificing for individuals with very different conceptions of the good life.

Is this solution going to be enough to get people to make sacrifices for the nation, to be good citizens, to practice civic virtue? Or does the recognition that people have an equal claim to consideration provide the motivation not to harm others but not much more than that? In contrast to a liberal state, a communitarian state would presumably foster an identification with a common form of life. Engaging in civic virtue, by participating in the political life of the community, sometimes subordinating one's own interests for the community's interest, and being public spirited, would follow naturally for citizens of a communitarian state with its politics of the common good. It seems unlikely that, alone, the insight that we owe everyone equal consideration will give us enough reason to fulfill all the responsibilities of such a robust version of citizenship.

But, are liberal democratic societies having a legitimation crisis simply or primarily because there is no common form of life or shared conception of the good life? Do most individuals see sharing burdens or assets with others with whom they have no connection as illegitimate? Does the rejection of the social thesis and the principle of neutrality truly leave individuals without the requisite identification with group necessary for civic virtue? In sum, is the only way to get people to identify with the state and be willing to make sacrifices for the common good to adopt some version of communitarianism, which seems to require a unified conception of the good life?

Societies in which individuals share goals and ends may not have the same problems as liberal ones in sustaining legitimacy. Nevertheless, communitarian theories have other problems, particularly for modern pluralistic democracies. Since there is plenty of criticism of communitarianism in the literature, I will not reiterate the objections here.[30] Suffice it to recall that the history of early America had plenty of communities with shared forms of life and common conceptions of the good but that those same communities excluded women, blacks, Native Americans, and others from dialogue and participation in the community. Many communitarians seem to hark back to a vision of community with traditional roles for men and women, the church, and so on. Certainly, some of those institutions were rejected, correctly, on liberal grounds because they were oppressive and unjust.

Furthermore, the characterization that communitarians provide of community and our membership in community does not fit with modern experience. Communitarians often imply that we are members of only one, clearly defined community. This mischaracterizes the situation. A more accurate characterization is that we are members of multiple communities that overlap one another in a variety of ways. Someone might be a Chinese American, a Catholic, a Democrat, a feminist, and a physician. Some communities we join voluntarily, for example, a political party, and others are ones in which we find ourselves at birth, whether an ethnic group, a religious community, a town, or a nation. In modern pluralistic democracies, people have multiple memberships in various kinds of communities.

Communitarians talk about our being situated or embedded in our community and how the community gives us roles and responsibilities that are constitutive of who we are as persons. Michael Sandel argues that those allegiances encumber us and define who we are.[31] He supposes that liberals argue for the opposite, that we choose all of our responsibilities and duties. Both these views are extremes. One view claims that none of our allegiances are chosen—that we find ourselves wholly embedded in a web of obligations and roles. The other view claims that all our duties and responsibilities are self-imposed and that we can never merely find ourselves with duties that we have not consented to. Both accounts miss the mark.

Not all our duties to these communities are the same.[32] The strength and nature of the duties and responsibilities differ in different communities. Our membership in communities is neither all involuntary nor all voluntary. Since we voluntarily join some communities, we can voluntarily exit if the conditions of membership seem to us to be, for example, immoral. Other communities are not so easily entered or exited. We may find ourselves situated in a community and feel allegiance, a strong sense of belonging, and owe a duty to that community even though we do not agree with all its norms and practices. But that does not preclude our getting critical distance at some point from that community, objecting to its practices and traditions, and possibly dissociating ourselves from it.

Republicanism

Is there a way to get commitment and responsibility, indeed civic virtue, to the political structure that is not based, as the communitarians would have it, on a single, shared conception of the good? Indeed, is there a way to retain the liberal values of individual rights and autonomy and yet avoid the legitimation problem? Is the only alternative the Rawlsian view that we get commitment to the state based on a shared sense of justice? Are the ideals of autonomy and individual rights, on the one hand, and civic virtue on the other, incompatible?

To the last question, several contemporary theorists advocating versions of civic republicanism—for example, Richard Dagger, Cass Sunstein,[33] and Charles Taylor—say no. Taylor argues for a union of autonomy and civic virtue, which he calls *holistic individualism*. This, he says, is "a trend of thought that is fully aware of the (ontological) social embedding of human agents, but at the same time prizes liberty and individual differences very highly."[34] Taylor argues for a duty to belong to and sustain a certain kind of society as a requirement for a society committed to the values of liberty and autonomy.

Dagger argues that, even though on the face of it there is discord between them, civic virtue and liberal values are consistent. Reaching back to the classical republican tradition, he notes that it focused on the notions of civic virtue and public responsibility, while liberalism focused primarily on individual rights and personal autonomy.[35] Dagger argues that a key concept in classical republican thought is that civic virtue is the "disposition to further public over private good in action and deliberation."[36] Civic republicanism provides the necessary connection between civility, citizenship, and civic virtue. Civic virtue means individuals transcending their own differences, treating others with concern and respect, and working for the common good of all citizens. Republicanism is not antithetical to liberalism and its values, according to Dagger, but complementary and contributory to them. Dagger argues for the following relationship between the quintessential liberal value of autonomy and civic virtue:

> They sometimes pull in different directions, with autonomy leaning toward individual rights and civic virtue toward public responsibility. . . . When autonomy pulls too hard in an individualistic direction, the appeal to civic virtue reminds us that both the development and the exercise of autonomy require the assistance and cooperation of others; when appeals to civic virtue threaten to jeopardize individual rights, the claims of autonomy remind us that the body politic ought to be a cooperative enterprise, composed of individuals who have a right to lead a self-governed life.[37]

Taylor's and Dagger's republican vision doesn't run into the problems of either atomistic individualism or a reactionary version of communitarianism. Civic republicanism, in addition, seems to provide the necessary ingredients for civic virtue. Other essentials to republican politics are, first, that it is deliberative. Citizens come together to solve common problems and deliberate about the best solutions. Citizens must be willing to discuss and debate views, and be willing to revise them in light of the best reasons. Political action is not, then, purely self-interested; it is based on public good. Political equality, particularly in modern republican theories, is another essential element of the theory. Political equality was so important for the political process that some prominent republicans, for example, Thomas Jefferson, argued for the advantage of equal distribution of property to facilitate political equality since gross differences in wealth eventually lead to differences in political power.[38] Citizens, for republicans, are people who are capable of ruling and being ruled. This conception has a long history traced back to Aristotle. Republicans fear dependence of citizens, and that fear indicates, finally, the importance of independence or liberty in the republican conception of civic virtue.[39] The virtuous citizen must be free, but not simply free to go his or her own way. Instead, the citizen is free when he or she participates in the government of his or her community. As part of the community, citizens will recognize that self-government requires an occasional sacrifice of one's own interests.[40]

It is at the point of self-government that the connection between individual rights, autonomy, and civic virtue most clearly emerges. Also, it is self-government working toward common solutions for the common good that gives individuals a sense of belonging and identification with others. Democratic government is the place where the liberal commitment to individual rights and autonomy requires the republican ideal of civic virtue. Liberalism is not merely a theory about the state protections of individual rights and autonomy, but a theory of self-government, of democracy. So, the question whether liberal theories make room for, accommodate, or even embrace civic virtue needs to focus on the nature of democracy. Many versions of democratic theory depend on cultivating civic virtue; certainly, traditional democratic theorists believed that there was a very close connection.[41]

Contemporary theories of democracy have stressed different ideals.[42] The version that does not rely on civic virtue or a robust version of citizenship is the preference satisfaction model or *subjective welfarism*.[43] Democracy is seen in purely individualistic instrumental terms, as a function of the aggregate of everyone's preferences, the *social choice*.[44] The government is neutral about the quality of those choices, and, as long as individuals' fundamental rights are not violated, the outcome of this process will maximize welfare; welfare simply is a function of the social choice. Politics is not, then, a realm requiring civic virtue, but it is a necessary evil wherein individuals express their preferences. Deliberation about the common good makes no sense on this view, since the good is defined by individuals' preferences; the good is the outcome of the process. Thomas Hobbes argued for such a view of politics. For him, governments are maintained out of self-interest and not out of patriotism or group identity.[45]

Central among the fatal flaws of the social choice conception of democracy is the legitimacy problem discussed earlier. The social choice model makes no attempt at group identification or loyalty. Since political choice is voting my own preferences, it is unlikely that would I see sacrifice for others' interests or national interests as in my interest. I will not see the government's laws requiring me to sacrifice for those others' interests as legitimate. Furthermore, since the theory permits discriminatory preferences to be part of the democratic process, does not question where the preferences come from or the strength of the preferences, and does not put other requirements on the kinds of preferences that go into the calculus, it is probable that the outcomes from the process wouldn't engender wide acceptance. If my preferences are not part of the social choice, then why should I feel allegiance to that outcome? Why should aggregating everyone's uncritical preferences lead to outcomes worth allegiance? If democracy does not entail a process of discussion and deliberation about the various views, including consideration of the reasons for holding one position or another, how can the outcomes of the process have general acceptance?[46]

The republican version of democracy conceptualizes it as instrumental for the best outcome. Participation in the democratic process, as conceived in the republican ideal, has beneficial effects on its citizens and will produce the best outcomes. Citizens, on this view, come together to deliberate about issues for the common good.[47] Rousseau argued that civic virtue and freedom are necessarily connected, since by participating in the democratic process, one is in control of one's freedom. One is participating in making the laws, but one is also then proscribing behavior to oneself.

Rousseau sees "participation as increasing the value of his freedom to the individual by enabling him to be (and remain) his own master." In addition, "the participatory process ensures that although no man, or group, is master of another, all are equally dependent on each other and equally subject to the law."[48] Further, Rousseau suggests that participation has an integrative function: "it increases the feeling among individual citizens that they 'belong' in their community."[49] Rousseau acknowledges that individuals' private interests will not always coincide with the common interests.[50] Nevertheless, to maintain and preserve the state, citizens will sometimes subordinate their own interests for the interests of the common good.

On this republican vision of democracy, we are going to exclude certain kinds of reasons from the deliberative process: those based on narrow self-interest; those based on arbitrary discrimination, hatred, or envy; and those that arbitrarily seek to make it impossible for people to practice certain conceptions of the good. The deliberative democratic process focuses on dialogue about differences of viewpoints and reflection on the issues. This process requires that people listen to the reasons of their opponents and consider the strength of their arguments. That requires civility. It requires treating your opponent with respect even though your opinions differ. It also requires civic virtue, the disposition to further the public good over the private, reflection on the common good, and so on.

Obviously, without civic virtue this version of democracy cannot flourish. Deliberation on the issues is not going to get very far if participants are inclined to advance only their own interests. Some may object that there may be a danger of tyranny in encouraging individuals to subordinate their own interests to some mythic common good. After all, isn't that what the fascists did? I think that the worry of the tyranny of the common good is inflated, particularly with *liberal* republicanism, according to which individuals and their interests are foremost in conceiving the common good.

In modern pluralistic democracies, the cultivation and encouragement of civic virtue allows people to come together as equal members of a common community of citizens to discuss different points of view and find common solutions. Liberal republicanism can find the "common form of life" that gives citizens an identity with their fellow citizens based on a commitment to the values of individual liberty, autonomy, and self-government in the pursuit of the common good. Republicanism commits citizens to certain responsibilities to that political community. Membership in the political community imposes the requirement that individuals participate in the deliberative democratic processes. Participation is not only important for instrumental reasons but also "as a vehicle for the inculcation of such characteristics as empathy, virtue, and feelings of community."[51] Civic virtue as a model of citizenship is an essential condition for the functioning of this vision of democracy. Encouraging the practicing of civic virtue, ideally, would mean that individuals exercise their own freedom through the democratic process and also develop bonds of community with fellow citizens.

Returning to our original concern over the incivility of American society and politics, I suggest that the republican vision of politics and civil society is one that would foster more public spiritedness and less narrow self-interested behavior. Teaching and fostering civic virtue, for example, in the public schools and other areas of public life, might alter the politics of the United States. The sense of community and identity of community might well filter its way into other areas of public life.

Notes

1. The popular press has covered this phenomenon extensively. See, for example, Jill Lawrence, "Excuse Me, But . . . Whatever Happened to Good Manners?" *USA Today*, 16 December 1996, sec. 1A; "The American Uncivil Wars," *U.S. News & World Report*, 22 April 1996, p. 66; Ellen Goodman, "Little Acts Rebuild Civility," *Boston Globe*, 2 January 1997, sec. A15.

2. Presumably, we don't need the same conventions and norms for our family and friends because we are bound to them by affection. Thus, we will likely treat them with respect, although this is where good manners play an important role in telling us exactly how we should behave.

3. Stephen Carter, *Civility* (New York: Basic Books, 1998).

4. For discussion of the duty to rescue under European legal systems, see F. J. M. Feldbrugge, "Good and Bad Samaritans: A Comparative Survey of Criminal Law Provisions Concerning Failure to Rescue," *American Journal of Comparative Law* 14 (1965–1966), 630–57.

5. Aristotle, *Nicomachean Ethics*, trans. Martin Ostwald (Indianapolis, Ind.: Bobbs-Merrill, 1962) and Aristotle, *The Politics*, ed. Stephen Everson (Cambridge: Cambridge University Press, 1988).

6. Richard Dagger, *Civic Virtues* (New York: Oxford University Press, 1997), 14.

7. See T. Pangle, *The Spirit of the Modern Republicanism* (Chicago: University of Chicago Press, 1988); J. G. A. Pocock, *The Machiavellian Moment* (Princeton, N.J.: Princeton University Press, 1975); G. Wood, *The Creation of the American Constitution 1776–1787* (Chapel Hill: University of North Carolina Press, 1969).

8. Shelley Burtt, "The Good Citizen's Psyche," *Polity* 23 (fall 1990).

9. Dagger, *Civic Virtues*, 14.

10. Dagger, *Civic Virtues*, 99.

11. Ibid., 98–99.

12. Will Kymlicka, *Multicultural Citizenship* (New York: Oxford University Press, 1995), 175.

13. See David Miller, "Community and Citizenship," in *Communitarianism and Individualism*, ed. Shlomo Avineri and Avner de-Shalit (Oxford: Oxford University Press, 1992), 96.

14. John Rawls, *Collected Papers*, ed. Samuel Freeman (Cambridge, Mass.: Harvard University Press, 1999), 459.

15. For some of these critiques see Karl Marx, "On the Jewish Question," *Deutsch-Französicher Jarbrucher*, 1844; S. Orkin, "Justice and Gender," *Philosophy and Public Affairs* 16, no. 1; *Justice, Gender, and the Family* (New York: Basic Books, 1989); C. Pateman, "Sublimination and Reification: Locke, Wolin and the Liberal Democratic Conception of the Political," *Politics and Society* 5, no. 4; M. Sandel, *Liberalism and the Limits of Justice* (Cambridge: Cambridge University Press, 1982).

16. Mary Ann Glendon, *Rights Talk: The Impoverishment of Political Discourse* (New York: Free Press, 1991).

17. I am not wholly endorsing these characterizations or criticisms of liberalism. Some of the criticisms inaccurately portray liberal views. Nevertheless, there is some truth to the general claims.

18. Charles Taylor, "Atomism," in *Communitarianism and Individualism*, 29.

19. Marilyn Friedman, "Feminism and Modern Friendship: Dislocating Community," in *Communitarianism and Individualism*, 101.

20. David Gauthier, "The Liberal Individual," in *Communitarianism and Individualism*.

21. See Thomas Hobbes, *Leviathan* (originally published 1651), ed. C. B. Macpherson (Harmondsworth, U.K.: Penguin, 1968) and continuing through the public choice literature, for example, R. Luce and H. Raiffa, *Games and Decisions* (New York: Wiley, 1957) and law and economics literature, e.g., Richard Posner, *The Economics of Justice* (Cambridge, Mass.: Harvard University Press, 1981).

22. Taylor, "Atomism." Sandel makes a similar charge with his idea of the "unencumbered self"; see also "The Procedural Republic and the Unencumbered Self," in *Communitarianism and Individualism*.

23. Charles Taylor, *Philosophy and the Human Sciences: Philosophical Papers, ii.* (Cambridge: Cambridge University Press, 1985).

24. Joseph Raz notes the same problem. He says: "Supporting valuable forms of life is a social rather than an individual matter . . . perfectionist ideals require public action for their viability. Anti-perfectionism in practice would lead not merely to a political stand-off from support for valuable conceptions of the good. It would undermine the chances of survival of many cherished aspects of our culture." *The Morality of Freedom* (Oxford: Oxford University Press, 1986), 162.

25. Of course, libertarians saw this consequence: Robert Nozick, *Anarchy, State, and Utopia* (New York: Basic Books, 1974).

26. Sandel, "The Procedural Republic and the Unencumbered Self," 22–23.

27. Charles Taylor, "Alternative Futures: Legitimacy, Identity, and Alienation in the Late Twentieth Century Canada," in *Constitutionalism, Citizenship, and Society in Canada*, ed. Alan Cairns and Cynthia Williams (Toronto: University of Toronto Press, 1986), 213.

28. Will Kymlicka, *Contemporary Political Philosophy* (New York: Oxford University Press, 1990). Also see William Galston, *Liberal Purposes: Goods, Virtues, and Duties in the Liberal State* (Cambridge: Cambridge University Press, 1991) where he says that with-

out citizens who are willing to show self-restraint, tolerate others with different views, even act from a sense of justice, "the ability of liberal societies to function successfully diminishes" (220).

29. John Rawls, "Justice as Fairness: Political Not Metaphysical," *Philosophy and Public Affairs* 14, no. 3.

30. See M. Friedman, "Feminism and Modern Friendship: Dislocating the Community," *Ethics* 99, no. 2 (1998); A. Gutmann, "Communitarian Critics of Liberalism," *Philosophy and Public Affairs* 14, no. 3 (1985). There are many works criticizing the communitarian model.

31. See Sandel, *Liberalism and the Limits of Justice*.

32. "Community," as Michael Taylor has proposed, is a matter of degree, depending on the degree to which it manifests the following three attributes: "Shared values and beliefs, direct and many-sided relations and the practice of reciprocity." *Community, Liberty, and Anarchy* (Cambridge, Mass.: Cambridge University Press, 1982), 56.

33. Cass Sunstein, "Beyond the Republican Revival," *Yale Law Journal* 97 (1988).

34. Taylor, "Atomism," 30.

35. Dagger, *Civic Virtues*, 12.

36. Ibid., 15.

37. Ibid., 18.

38. Ibid., 15. Republicans also typically defended private property as a way of guaranteeing that a citizen would not be dependent on others for his livelihood. Some, notably James Harrington and Jean-Jacques Rousseau, went further, suggesting that property should be distributed in such a way as to prevent anyone from being so wealthy as to render other citizens dependent. See Thomas Jefferson, *The Papers of Thomas Jefferson*, ed. J. Boyd (Princeton, N.J.: Princeton University Press, 1953), 681–82. Also see Montesquieu's discussion of the importance of equality:

> Love of the republic in a democracy, is that of equality. Love of the democracy is likewise that of frugality. As every individual ought to have here the same happiness and the same advantages, they ought consequently to taste the same pleasures and to form the same hopes; which cannot be expected but from a general frugality. The love of equality in a democracy limits ambition to the sole desire, to the sole happiness of doing greater services to our country than the rest of our fellow citizens. . . . A true maxim it is therefore, that in order to love equality and frugality in a republic, these virtues must have been previously established by law. (*The Spirit of Laws*, bk. v., chaps. III–IV, ed. D. Carrithers, 1977)

39. Philip Pettit, in "Freedom with Honor: A Republican Ideal" (*Social Research* 64, no. 1: 63), argues that for the republican freedom is contrasted with subjection to the will of another. Liberty requires self-mastery and independence. This is contrasted with the traditional liberal view that sees liberty's antonym as interference, specifically by the state.

40. Dagger, *Civic Virtues*, 15.

41. See Alexis de Tocqueville, *Democracy in America*, trans. George Lawrence, ed. J. P. Mayer (Garden City, N.Y.: Doubleday, 1969).

42. For a good survey of theories of democracy, see *Democracy: Theory and Practice*, ed. John Arthur (Belmont, Calif.: Wadsworth, 1992).

43. Cass Sunstein, "Democracy and Shifting Preference," in *The Idea of Democracy*, ed. David Copp, Jean Hampton, and John Roemer (Cambridge: Cambridge University Press, 1993).

44. See Kenneth Arrow, *Social Choice and Individual Values*, 2d ed. (New York: Wiley, 1963) and *Social Choice and Justice*, vol. 1 *Collected Papers* (Cambridge, Mass.: Harvard University Press, 1983); Anthony Downs, *An Economic Theory of Democracy* (New York: Harper, 1957); Mancur Olson, Jr., *The Logic of Collective Action* (Cambridge, Mass.: Harvard University Press, 1965).

45. See Anthony Kronman's discussion in "Civility," *Cumberland Law Review* 26 (1995).

46. Of course, there are technical problems in Arrow's Impossibility theorem.

47. Notice that with these different views of democracy will come different conceptions of property. Two notions are the Jeffersonian and Lockean conceptions. The Jeffersonian view or the republican views see property as important for satisfying individual preferences and also as a foundation for republican government. See Gregory Alexander, *Commodity and Propriety: Competing Visions of Property in American Legal Thought 1776–1970* (Chicago: University of Chicago Press, 1997).

48. Pateman, "Sublimation and Reification," 109.

49. Ibid., 109.

50. Rousseau said,

> Indeed, every individual may, as a man, have a particular will contrary to, or divergent from, the general will which he has as a citizen; his private interest may prompt him quite differently from the common interest; his absolute and naturally independent existence may make him regard what he owes to the common cause as a gratuitous contribution, the loss of which will be less harmful to others than the payment of it will be burdensome to him; and regarding the moral person that constitutes the State as an imaginary being because it is not a man, he would be willing to enjoy the rights of a citizen without being willing to fulfil the duties of a subject. The progress of such injustice would bring about the ruin of the body politic. (Rousseau, op. cit., chap. VII)

51. See Sunstein's discussion of the four central principles of liberal republicanism: (1) deliberation in politics made possible by "civic virtue"; (2) equality of the political actors; (3) the principle of universalism, exemplified by the notion of a common good; and (4) the principle of citizenship. "Beyond the Revival," 1541ff.

Chapter 3

Civic Education in the Liberal State

Emily R. Gill

The principles and commitments of the liberal democratic polity suggest
the self-consciousness of rational deliberation and critical reflection as well
as collective deliberation on policy and the knowing exercise of democratic rights. Such a state, in Yael Tamir's words about citizenship in general,
"is not merely viewed as a gathering of individuals striving to improve their
lot, but rather as a community struggling to preserve its distinctive character."[1] Because liberal societies and governments have traditionally privileged a diversity of incommensurable beliefs and practices, however, sharp
disagreements ensue about the nature of this distinctiveness. I believe that
the liberal polity should be committed both to the maintenance of background conditions for individual autonomy and self-development and also
to a culture of diversity that contains a plurality of options. These values
themselves are often incommensurable, and the tension between them
emerges with particular clarity in conflicts over the proper education of
future citizens.

Commentators like Amy Gutmann, for example, argue that all citizens
should be taught to engage in rational deliberation and critical reflection so
that they can evaluate competing ways of life, including modes different
from those of their parents. This capacity is essential in a liberal democracy
that requires both individual and collective self-government. The pluralism
fostered by diverse families, who may each themselves inculcate an uncritical consciousness, "serves as little more than an ornament for onlookers."[2]
Democratic states should instead facilitate the development of the capacity
"to evaluate competing conceptions of the good life and the good society."[3]

Other commentators, such as William Galston, counter that this type
of public commitment excludes and threatens individuals and groups that
do not place a high priority on rational deliberation and personal autonomy. "Liberal freedom entails the right to live unexamined as well as examined lives."[4] Liberalism, on this view, should protect diversity rather than

43

valorize choice. To champion the latter "is in fact to narrow the range of possibilities available within liberal societies. It is a drive toward a kind of uniformity, disguised in the language of liberal diversity."[5]

I shall argue that the civic respect necessary for liberal democratic citizenship requires a sympathetic and imaginative engagement with other ways of life. Simultaneously, however, I believe that this requirement applies not only to those religious or cultural minorities whose support for liberal democratic principles is suspect in the eyes of some, but to all of us. We must avoid both a cultural complacency that neglects the framework for the perpetuation of liberal values, and also a cultural aggressiveness that, in its zeal to inculcate the virtues of toleration and mutual respect, violates their spirit.[6]

Liberalism: Political or Ethical?

For John Rawls, the political virtues required by a stable liberal democracy include toleration, mutual respect, and a sense of fairness and civility.[7] He rejects the values of autonomy and individuality as too comprehensive and, therefore, too exclusive to be publicly fostered in citizens. Citizens should be educated in their basic rights and should be prepared for social cooperation on terms they want to honor as fair.[8] Citizens may embody these virtues, he suggests, without engaging in the critical reflection on their projects and goals that I see as the hallmark of personal autonomy.

The liberal polity must, indeed, avoid easy conclusions that ways of life that we may dislike cannot represent autonomous choice and that, therefore, we are entitled to exert pressure on citizens to make different choices. This does not mean, however, that the liberal polity need do nothing to influence choice. It cannot legitimately instruct citizens in *what* to choose, but it can and should, I believe, provide instruction in *how* to choose. This should be the focus of civic education. Because a liberal polity should not, I believe, exert pressure at the first-order level of actual choice, its role at the second-order level of how choices are made becomes crucial. Therefore, I do not believe that eschewing civic education for autonomy is compatible with liberalism as I interpret it.

This conclusion leaves untouched the very dilemma that Rawls attempts to solve, that of offering a civic education that does not force the value of personal autonomy on those who would reject it. We then confront three options. The first is to accept a conflation of comprehensive ethical liberalism and political liberalism and to conclude that a stable liberal democracy requires education for autonomy. Gutmann and Eamonn Callan exemplify this option. The second alternative is to backpedal, to decide that, if political liberalism requires education for autonomy, then political liberalism, at least in its Rawlsian incarnation, should be rejected. Galston exemplifies this option. The third alternative is to redefine the requirements of political liberalism in such a way that they do not constitute the constraint on our privately held convictions that some think they are. Stephen Macedo exemplifies this option.

Gutmann's conception of civic education incorporates a specific goal, that of preparation for citizenship in a society in which those who can participate in collective deliberation on public policy have the advantage. She implicitly agrees with Rawls's specification of toleration and mutual respect as political virtues required in a stable liberal democracy. But she is more definite about what these seemingly uncontroversial virtues entail. Mutual respect requires not simply toleration, she argues, but also "a favorable attitude toward, and constructive interaction with, the persons with whom one disagrees." Specifically, mutual respect characterizes "individuals who are morally committed, self-reflective about their commitments, discerning of the difference between respectable and merely tolerable differences of opinion, and open to the possibility of changing their minds or modifying their positions at some time in the future if they confront unanswerable objections to their present point of view."[9]

Although political liberalism intends only to educate for citizenship, not for autonomy, Gutmann admits the near impossibility of teaching the virtues of democratic citizenship without also teaching the skills of personal autonomy.[10] Children should learn to think for themselves, she argues, even about issues with little explicit political content, because only thus will they learn to make judgments about what issues are or are not political. This position is no more partisan, she contends, than the competing one that parents should use their own religious freedom as a basis for preventing their children from learning to think for themselves. For Gutmann, the civic virtue of mutual respect does not deny the value of diversity but instead promotes it by exposing children to the potential value inherent in different ways of life.

Along similar lines, Callan notes that the capacity for a sense of justice requires both a commitment to moral reciprocity and a willingness to recognize the burdens of judgment, or the sources of permanent and irreconcilable disagreement among reasonable persons. From an epistemological standpoint, however, imaginative engagement with other viewpoints will not only develop a sense of justice, but also "profoundly affect" our privately held comprehensive conceptions of the good. Attempting to understand the reasonableness of convictions alien to our upbringing implicitly suggests the hypothesis that these alien convictions might ground a life just as good as our own. As to the latter possibility, Callan says, "That question is unavoidable because to understand the reasonableness of beliefs that initially seem wrong or even repellent I must imaginatively entertain the ethical perspective the beliefs furnish, and from that perspective my own way of life will look worse, or at least no better, than what the perspective affirms."[11] When viewed from the proper perspective, the friction between my way of life and those of many others can lead not to repudiation of those others, but to understanding.

When we examine the components of a way of life, the same mental capacity is at work whether we are evaluating our own lives, on the one hand, or endeavoring to understand our fellow citizens, on the other. "What is required in each case is the ability to envisage a life alien to one's own from the inside so that the goods it makes possible can be understood to some degree in their vivid particularity."[12] This quality of imaginative engagement and sympathy requires a high level of self-reflection and openness. In sum, the educational requirements of political liberalism, suggests Callan, "bring autonomy through the back door of political liberalism . . . [which then] is really a kind of closet ethical liberalism. . . . The partition Rawls labors to erect between ethical and political liberalism has collapsed."[13] Why not exit the closet and admit the centrality of autonomy?

Galston, on the other hand, believes that rational deliberation and self-reflection must, on the practical level, take second place to rhetoric in the formation of future citizens. Because philosophic education focuses on the pursuit of truth, it may have "corrosive consequences" for "structures of unexamined but socially central belief." The focus of civic education, however, is on individual effectiveness within the context of a specific political community, or "education within, and on behalf of, a particular political order."[14] Although the capacity for rationality and reasonable public judgment requires an appreciation of the need for social rules, an ability to respond to rational persuasion, and a disposition to employ public reasons in public deliberation about matters requiring collective action,[15] writes Galston, a Socratic emphasis on the capacity for critical reflection on different ways of life is a controversial notion of the good. It cannot and need not claim the allegiance of all liberal democratic citizens.

For example, adherents of religious doctrines that require close control over individuals' formative social and political environments view the traditional liberal insistence that they forswear this demand as a restriction on their free exercise of religion. Most individuals and groups in liberal society will find expression for "their distinctive conceptions of the good. But for those who are left out, it is hard to see how liberalism can be experienced as anything other than an assault."[16] They experience such inconsonance between their way of life and what they see the liberal state to require that the latter appears as a repudiation of their beliefs. And this experience, in turn, can lead *them* to repudiate the civic education offered or required by the liberal state.

For Galston, then, a liberal society or government that values and tries to inculcate the capacity for autonomy as critical reflection does not promote diversity but undermines it. At the heart of liberal toleration is not critical reflection on various ways of life but, rather, "the refusal to use state power to impose one's own way of life on others. Such refusal need not be incompatible with an unreflective commitment to one's way of life."[17] To refrain from inculcating in all citizens the idea that toleration requires mutual respect among those who practice different ways of life does not contradict the ideal of tolerance but instead exemplifies and instantiates it. Galston doubts, however, "that tolerance, so understood, can be cultivated without at least minimal awareness of the existence and nature of those ways of life." Therefore, the state may pursue "this compelling interest" in tolerance but without explicitly requiring or inviting students to criticize their own ways of life.[18]

But *how* minimal can our awareness be? Apparently it must be minimal enough that we are not encouraged to become skeptical or critical of our own practices, yet comprehensive enough that we find reasons to tolerate other practices. This is a fine line to tread, and it is not apparent that this balance can be achieved easily if at all.

David Johnston makes a useful distinction between *moral autonomy*, which implies the capability of having both a conception of the good and also a sense of justice, and *personal autonomy*, which suggests the capability of subjecting projects and values to critical appraisal and fashioning them into a life that functions as a coherent whole. Personal autonomy, he suggests, is not "an essential ingredient in a good human life in association with others,"[19] and the subjection of one's projects and values to critical appraisal is less important than the simple pursuit of these projects with accompanying adherence to their values. The projects of individuals who discount personal autonomy should be taken seriously; social measures to promote personal autonomy may range from despotic paternalism, at worst, to a disorientation from one's original values, at best, which may undermine effective agency. Yet, just as Galston suggests that liberal tolerance requires a minimal awareness of the nature of other ways of life, Johnston suggests that "*some* degree of ability to appraise or reappraise one's projects and values critically is essential to a good life for human beings in association with others."[20] If, as Johnston argues, moral autonomy requires a sense of justice involving both the recognition of other agents whose claims deserve respect and also an according self-limitation on our own claims, the critical self-appraisal required for personal autonomy should help us to restrain our own claims and recognize others' projects and values. Although Johnston concedes that moral autonomy requires to some degree the skills constitutive of personal autonomy, he still suggests that a society should foster personal autonomy "only insofar as . . . those conditions can be expected to contribute to individuals' capacities to be effective agents."[21] But if effective agency means the imaginative capacity to formulate projects and values independent of our own experiences, as Johnston suggests,[22] then a greater degree of personal autonomy would contribute more to the development of this imaginative capacity than would a lesser degree. Thus, the ability to engage in critical self-appraisal that is characteristic of personal autonomy contributes both to effective agency and to the moral autonomy through which we recognize and respect others' projects and values, facilitating our sense of justice and the cooperation required for a life in association with others.

To place this point in the present context, liberal democracy requires the inculcation of the virtues of tolerance and mutual respect. But in my view, this requires the imaginative capacity to view circumstances as others might, to recognize and respect their claims, and to restrain our own. These dispositions, in turn, require the capacity to understand and evaluate different ways of life. That is, they require the development of the capacity for personal autonomy. This conclusion casts doubt on Rawls's contention that the political virtues of toleration, mutual respect, and a sense of fairness necessary for social cooperation require "far less" substantive civic education than would the inculcation of the comprehensive values of autonomy and individuality. It also impels one to question whether the ability to respond to rational persuasion and the disposition to employ public reasons in public deliberation, crucial elements in Galston's conception of the capacity for rationality, can be fully developed without the corresponding capability of subjecting one's projects and values to critical reflection and appraisal. This process conditions our ability to perceive the value in others' projects and goals as well as to commit to our own. Moreover, the ability to respond to rational persuasion and the disposition to employ public reasons in public deliberation also suggest one of the components of mutual respect for Gutmann: openness to the possibility of modifying or changing one's position in the face of unanswerable objections to the current one.

Galston's first point to which I have responded is that tolerance requires only minimal awareness of other ways of life. Second, he maintains that his "Diversity State" need not imply moral indifference but is also compatible "with engaged moral criticism of those with whom one differs. Toleration means . . . the commitment to competition through recruitment and persuasion alone."[23] Despite his commitment to diversity and pluralism, then, Galston's Diversity State does not practice toleration simply by refraining from interference with objectionable practices. We may criticize constructively the ideas of others whom we believe to be in error, and we may attempt to persuade them that our own beliefs or practices are preferable. But not only does this activity require a greater understanding of other ways of life than Galston admits, it also implies the practice of mutual respect as Gutmann describes it. It would seem to involve constructive interaction, a reciprocal positive regard, and an openness to the possibility of changing our minds—unless, of course, we expect self-reflection and openness to characterize only those whom we criticize, but not us ourselves! All this suggests that the requisite awareness of other ways of life and the inculcation of the competencies and virtues of liberal citizenship demand the sort of sympathetic and imaginative engagement with other beliefs and practices that Callan describes. Galston may want to backpedal from what he sees as the rigid structure of a seemingly perfectionistic Rawlsian political liberalism,[24] but his own, purportedly more inclusive, alternative requires similar political virtues that lead ineluctably to the development of a capacity for autonomy.

Third, Galston advocates decentralized political decision making on many contested issues, pairing a strong freedom of association with an emphasis on a meaningful right of exit. This right requires an awareness of alternatives, a capacity to assess these alternatives, freedom from brainwashing, and the individual ability to participate effectively in other ways of life besides that being abandoned.[25] But these conditions point not simply to a bare awareness of alternatives, but also toward, in Callan's words, "the ability to envisage a life alien to one's own from the inside so that the goods it makes possible can be understood to some degree in their vivid particularity."[26] The capacity to assess alternatives requires the developed capacity to engage in critical reflection on these goods if we are to make the best choices for ourselves.

Fourth, and finally, Galston's concrete policy recommendations do not always protect the diversity that he valorizes, and in some cases they reconstruct practices that seem coercive to some citizens. Among the policies stemming from his advocacy of a functional traditionalism aimed at bolstering beliefs and habits that he associates with the security of liberal rights are measures that privilege intact two-parent families and discourage divorce,[27] that support state law embodying morally traditional attitudes toward homosexuals,[28] and that similarly support state law requiring a moment of silence at the start of the school day.[29] I am less concerned, here, about the intrinsic validity of his particular stands than I am about the combination of his moral traditionalism with his conviction that rational deliberation must take second place to rhetoric in the formation of future citizens. Because disputes about the human good cannot be definitively settled philosophically, Galston maintains, "if children are to be brought to accept . . . commitments as valid and binding, the method must be a pedagogy that is far more rhetorical than rational."[30]

I am extremely wary of what seems to be a recommendation that we paper over moral complexity and ambiguity. I agree with Callan, first, that although Galston cites courage, law-abidingness, and loyalty as fundamental virtues of the liberal state, "law may be enacted or administered in ways that betray the fundamental values of liberal democracy" that Galston is anxious to uphold.[31] Because the historical and political tradition in which we are embedded is subject to varying interpretations, "the pressing question is, What is the best of this tradition? Rather than, what are the dominant or most powerful elements in this tradition?"[32] Second, I agree with Callan in rejecting the consensual conception of common education, according to which "the proper content of common education is given by whatever corpus of substantive educational values can be supported by a highly extensive agreement in our society."[33] Consensus itself is not negative, but "the relevant consensus cannot be complacently identified with the one we happen to have at this moment in history."[34] Galston's rhetorical approach is far too likely simply to endorse the current consensus, rather than requiring "a serious intellectual and imaginative engagement with the plurality of values to which my fellow citizens adhere . . . where the plurality of values is really embodied in the lives of different participants" in this engagement.[35] True openness to cultural diversity, in my view, is grounded not on a consensual conception of common education, but on the basis of equal respect, which in turn requires civic education grounded in more than rhetoric.

I have argued thus far that the solution to discord between different ways of life lies in sympathetic and imaginative engagement with competing conceptions of the good life and the good society. Therefore, I favor the critical scrutiny promoted by Gutmann and Callan over the emphasis on consensus advocated by Galston. His approach may, by papering over rudeness, lessen overt contention, but the price, in my opinion, is the achievement of an artificial consensus that still valorizes some conceptions of the good society over others. Nevertheless, we should not conclude too hastily that we can or should force this sympathetic and imaginative engagement on dissenters across the board. Those who would avoid all invitations to engage in critical scrutiny and self-reflection may repudiate core liberal values, but so also do liberals themselves who are too certain of their own righteousness.

Stephen Macedo's liberalism is a muscular version that is unapologetic in acknowledging that communities or families with totalistic belief systems may be undermined by public policy that advances critical thinking and public argument as appropriate means of political justification.[36] Although freedom is central to liberal politics, "successful constitutional institutions must do more than help order the freedom of individuals . . . they must shape the way that people use their freedom and shape *people* to help ensure that freedom is what they want."[37] Accomplishing these goals "requires liberalism with a spine"[38] and a recognition of "the supreme importance of constituting diversity for liberal ends."[39]

On the other hand, Macedo argues that good citizenship does not require sympathetic and imaginative engagement with rival views. Such a requirement, particularly with regard to religious views, "comes too close to espousing a 'comprehensive' ideal of life as a whole, such as autonomy, and would seem to infringe on individuals' freedom to disagree deeply and vigorously about religious and moral matters. Political liberalism stands for the importance of critical self-examination in politics. Citizens decide on their own what attitude to take toward their religious beliefs."[40] Thus, Macedo believes children should learn that respect for diversity is a part of citizenship, but he argues that schools should avoid the trap of promoting religious skepticism.

Macedo admits that teaching critical thinking about public affairs may spill over unavoidably into critical thinking about spiritual matters. As with Rawls, Gutmann, and Callan, he concedes that education for citizenship may actually constitute education for autonomy. Yet, Macedo still desires a balance. "Explicitly or not, liberal regimes endorse and promote auton-omy. But we still respect the non-autonomous: people have the right to lead lazy, narrow-minded lives, and we minimize and soften interference with their choices."[41] Like Gutmann and Callan, then, Macedo advocates a com-prehensive civic education that develops the capacity for rational deliber-ation and critical reflection about public affairs, but like Galston, he rejects the explicit use of this capacity with respect to citizens' private and more comprehensive religious, philosophical, and moral convictions.[42]

But to maintain this distinction, Macedo relies on a "transformative constitutionalism" in which emphasis on the segmentation of religion and politics tends indirectly to diminish the centrality of religious convictions in tension with liberal democratic values.[43] In fact, he argues that the defenders of those who feel censored or marginalized because they will *not* compartmentalize their political and religious beliefs should realize that the true difficulty is these believers' hypersensitivity. And their defenders are, themselves, mistaken insofar as they regard the marginalization of illiberal views as problematic. As Macedo himself admits, critical thinking about civic concerns readily spills over into critical self-examination about more comprehensive matters as well. And, he maintains that political stability will, of necessity, require the softening of rigidly illiberal views. The mar-ginalized groups whose beliefs are under threat from the wider liberal cul-ture and whose practices are imperiled by the public policies of the liberal state may need to make adjustments, themselves, rather than to petition for exemptions from these policies.[44]

But, these statements do not comport with Macedo's assertion that cit-izens should determine their own attitudes toward the imperatives of their religious beliefs, even if they cannot always carry through these imperatives in a liberal polity. If marginalized groups must make adjustments, his formulation suggests that dialogue between those who support the dominant consensus and those who disagree is a one-way street. The latter must simply adjust when the former declare that atypical practices are illiberal. Those who think I need to alter my supposedly illiberal views *are* in fact challenging my personal moral and religious views when they point to the need for change. And by implication, they are inviting the critical self-evaluation of my comprehensive views, insistence on which Macedo thinks an infringement on religious and moral diversity.

Further, even if Macedo were consistent in his distinction between public affairs and private convictions, there is no inherently clear distinction between the political and the nonpolitical. Practices that stem from my comprehensive beliefs may seem to me to carry political implications that make them fit subjects for political discussion and critical examination. If I may decide what attitude to take toward my beliefs, this includes my deciding to what extent they are political or not, especially if my ability to adhere to them is affected by public policy. Rawls's overlapping consensus is abstracted from religious, philosophical, and moral doctrines that citizens support; even if it is not exclusively political in the sense of having no nonpolitical origins.

Although Macedo contends that it is only illiberal views that must be adjusted or mended, once again, there is no inherently clear distinction between the liberal and the illiberal. Competing sets of social facts may be adduced, each of which points to a different conclusion about the liberality or illiberality of particular beliefs and practices.[45] It is through rational deliberation and critical reflection that we decide what is compatible with the liberal settlement, as we understand it. Macedo says that the mending of intolerant views should occur through open public argument, but it must be remembered that those on both sides of the argument ought to display reciprocal positive regard, self-reflection, and openness to unfamiliar arguments. After all, if I am to mend my views or make adjustments in them, I must be able to enter into sympathetic and imaginative engagement with conceptions of the good other than my own. And you, who want me to make these adjustments, should do the same if you want to determine accurately how radical these adjustments should be. Liberalism makes demands on all its citizens, not only on those liberals regard as illiberal.

What are the implications of my view for practice? I conclude with two examples of cases in which parental religious concerns appeared in conflict with liberal values.

In *Wisconsin v. Yoder*, the Supreme Court in a six-to-one majority upheld Old Order Amish communities in Wisconsin in their desire to terminate their children's formal schooling after eighth grade, in accordance with their fundamental belief that salvation requires life in a church community separate and apart from the world and worldly influence. The Court concluded that the successful preparation for life in separated agrarian communities characteristic of the Amish, the parents' fundamental interests in guiding their children's religious education, and their right to free exercise of religion outweighed any demonstrated state interest in compulsory education.[46] Although parental decisions limit the exposure of Amish youth to alternative ways of life, and although this outcome diverges from core liberal values as I interpret them, I must agree with the Court in *Yoder*.

Separation from the larger community is not instrumental to being Amish, but is intrinsic to and constitutive of what being Amish means. As we have seen, even Macedo holds that, although critical self-examination is required by liberal politics, citizens should be left to decide on their own attitudes toward their religious beliefs. Here, the religious beliefs that the Amish affirm require separation from the larger society. We may hope that enough of the larger society would permeate Amish existence to allow them some awareness of alternatives, but I must reluctantly conclude that we should not force this on them. I also believe that the Amish deserve our full respect, even if we continue to disagree with their views. On some level, a sympathetic and imaginative engagement with these views is what persuaded the *Yoder* Court to grant the educational dispensation. The dialogue between this marginalized group and those representing the dominant consensus was not a one-way street, and the larger society was the entity that made the adjustments. We cannot, ourselves, meet the requirements of liberal citizenship if we deny the possibility of constructive interaction and reciprocal positive regard.

A direct rejection of purportedly illiberal views, on the other hand, is represented by the case of *Mozert v. Hawkins County Board of Education*. In this case, an appellate court ruled against fundamentalist Christian parents in Tennessee who contended that their religious beliefs were violated by the values inculcated in their children through a series of textbooks. The judges, here, argued that exposure to objectionable ideas does not in itself burden the free exercise of religion; that only "a civil tolerance, not a religious one," was required of the plaintiffs; that students must learn to think critically about controversial subjects; and that the teaching of civil tolerance is not a teaching of the religious correctness of other religious views.[47] The *Mozert* parents, however, viewed seemingly neutral exposure to hostile beliefs as a mechanism for undermining religious absolutes in favor of personal opinion, pluralism, and secular humanism. They agreed, in essence, with Callan's claim that political liberalism is a closet ethical liberalism, influencing our conceptions of the good through its promotion of sympathetic and imaginative engagement with other ways of life and causing us to hold our beliefs in a different manner than otherwise.

According to the approach I have developed here, *Mozert* was rightly decided. As citizens of a liberal polity, we may hold the convictions that our own viewpoints are correct, but we must also recognize that this correctness is a matter of belief that is contestable. It is appropriate, therefore, for public education to expose students to ways of life and points of view in such a way that they are "threatened" with the prospect of developing the capacity for critical reflection as a necessary part of their preparation for citizenship. The *Mozert* parents wanted to protect their children from not only the substance of ideas alien to their tradition, but also the process of learning to think about competing belief systems. The liberal polity does not owe this protection to future citizens in its public educational programs. The *Mozert* parents, themselves, repudiated the core liberal value of critical reflection in its challenge, and I think it fitting that the liberal polity responded in kind.

In concluding, however, I want to suggest that the inculcation of the capacity for critical reflection, which in my view requires sympathetic and imaginative engagement with other ways of life, can not only function to sustain the liberal polity, but also to help us to define and understand ourselves. If, as Macedo states, "being a self-critical reason-giver is the best way of being a liberal and a good way . . . of living a life," we should also understand that this is what we are.[48] According to Susan Mendus, we may value education because understanding others "means seeing ourselves as *autonomy valuers* and recognizing the merits and defects of that position by comparison with others"; insistence on either the prescriptive or descriptive "priority of our culture is, somewhat paradoxically, uncritical about the importance we attach to critical evaluation."[49] Humility, for example, is a virtue within Western society, which betokens an accurate assessment of oneself and one's talents; for the Amish, humility is undermined by liberal focus on the primacy of autonomous valuers. The very desire to understand one's proper value would be "a desire which sprang from an inappropriate, indeed morally reprehensible, concern with oneself and one's own moral standing."⁵⁰

From learning this about the Amish, then, we learn that our own emphasis on moral self-assessment is only a partial image of humanity, or of what humility might mean. Sympathetic and imaginative engagement with other ways of life may teach us that "we are prone to identify the oppressive nature of Amish culture. . . . But if we employ education as a means of understanding ourselves, we may come to see that as autonomy-valuers we lack the moral language with which to provide an explanation of their humility as anything other than oppression. In this way, we learn something about the limitations of our own moral world."⁵¹ We may still disagree with Amish views on education, but we may also come to "understand ourselves as the kind of people who may place altogether too much importance on self-understanding." An understanding of the limitations of our moral world should be sought not only by those whose liberal credentials seem questionable, but also by the liberals doing the questioning. Only then can we accommodate the diversity inherent in liberal citizenship and also avoid betraying some of our own core liberal values.

Notes

1. Yael Tamir, *Liberal Nationalism* (Princeton, N.J.: Princeton University Press, 1993), 122; see 124–30.

2. Amy Gutmann, *Democratic Education* (Princeton, N.J.: Princeton University Press, 1987), 33. See also 14, 30, 34, 42–45, and 77–80.

3. Ibid., 33.

4. William A. Galston, "Civic Education in the Liberal State," in *Liberalism and the Moral Life*, ed. Nancy L. Rosenblum (Cambridge, Mass.: Harvard University Press, 1989), 100.

5. William A. Galston, *Liberal Purposes: Goods, Virtues, and Diversity in the Liberal State* (New York: Cambridge University Press, 1991), 329, n. 12. Also see William A. Galston, "Two Concepts of Liberalism," *Ethics* 105 (April 1995): 523–24.

6. See Eamonn Callan, "Last Word," *Review of Politics* 58 (winter 1996): 49.

7. John Rawls, *Political Liberalism* (New York: Columbia University Press, 1993), 122; see also 199.

8. Ibid., 199.

9. Amy Gutmann and Dennis Thompson, "Moral Conflict and Political Consensus," *Ethics* 101 (October 1990): 76; see 76–81, and Amy Gutmann, "Civic Education and Social Diversity," *Ethics* 105 (April 1995): 560–65.

10. Gutmann, "Civic Education and Social Diversity," 563; also see 559–60 and 573–79.

11. Eamonn Callan, "Political Liberalism and Political Education," *Review of Politics* 58 (winter 1996): 17; see 14–18, and also 11–14 on the normative difficulties of the subsequently required bifurcation between public and private selves.

12. Eamonn Callan, "Tradition and Integrity in Moral Education," *American Journal of Education* 101 (November 1992): 22; see also 16–24, and Jeff Spinner, *The Boundaries of Citizenship* (Baltimore, Md.: Johns Hopkins University Press, 1994), 93–94.

13. Callan, "Political Liberalism and Political Education," 22.

14. Galston, "Civic Education in the Liberal State," 90. Also see Galston, *Liberal Purposes*, 242–43.

15. Galston, *Liberal Purposes*, 175–76; see also 253, and Galston, "Civic Education in the Liberal State," 99.

16. Galston, *Liberal Purposes*, 149; see 143–49, 130, 153, 259, and 277.

17. Galston, "Two Concepts of Liberalism," 524; see also 523–24, and Galston, *Liberal Purposes*, 129, 256, and 329, n. 12.

18. Galston, "Two Concepts of Liberalism," 529.

19. David Johnston, *The Idea of a Liberal Theory* (Princeton, N.J.: Princeton University Press, 1994), 91; see 91–99.

20. Ibid., 97.

21. Ibid., 97–98.

22. Ibid., 22–24.

23. Galston, "Two Concepts of Liberalism," 528.

24. Galston, *Liberal Purposes*, 129.

25. Galston, "Two Concepts of Liberalism," 531–34.

26. Callan, "Tradition and Integrity in Moral Education," 22.

27. Galston, *Liberal Purposes*, 280–89.

28. William A. Galston, "Public Morality and Religion in the Liberal State," *PS* 19 (fall 1986): 820–22.

29. Galston, *Liberal Purposes*, 282–83.

30. Ibid., 243.

31. Eamonn Callan, "Beyond Sentimental Civic Education," *American Journal of Education* 102 (February 1994): 203; see 200–3.

32. Callan, "Beyond Sentimental Civic Education," 209; see 205–14.

33. Eamonn Callan, "Common Schools for Common Education," *Canadian Journal of Education* 20 (1995): 256; see 252–64.

34. Ibid., 260.

35. Ibid., 264.

36. Stephen Macedo, "Multiculturalism for the Religious Right? Defending Liberal Civic Education," *Journal of Philosophy of Education* 29 (July 1995): 226; see 224–29.

37. Stephen Macedo, "Transformative Constitutionalism and the Case of Religion:

Defending the Moderate Hegemony of Liberalism," *Political Theory* 26 (February 1998): 58.

38. Stephen Macedo, "Liberal Civic Education and Its Limits," *Canadian Journal of Education* 20 (1995): 304. Also see Stephen Macedo, "Community, Diversity, and Civic Education: Toward a Liberal Political Science of Group Life," *Social Philosophy and Policy* 13 (1996): 240–68.

39. Macedo, "Transformative Constitutionalism," 73.

40. Macedo, "Liberal Civic Education and Its Limits," 308; see 308–9.

41. Stephen Macedo, *Liberal Virtues: Citizenship, Virtue, and Community in Liberal Constitutionalism* (Oxford: Clarendon Press, 1990), 253.

42. Macedo, "Liberal Civic Education and Its Limits," 309.

43. Macedo, "Transformative Constitutionalism," 69.

44. Stephen Macedo, "Liberal Civic Education and Religious Fundamentalism: The Case of God v. John Rawls," *Ethics* 105 (April 1995): 469–70.

45. Kirstie M. McClure, "Difference, Diversity, and the Limits of Toleration," *Political Theory* 18 (August 1990): 361–91.

46. *Wisconsin v. Yoder,* 406 U.S. 205 (1972), 210; see 210–15, 222, and 230–36.

47. *Mozert v. Hawkins County Board of Education, Mozert V,* 827 F. 2d 1058 (6th Circuit 1987), 1069.

48. Macedo, *Liberal Virtues,* 59.

49. Susan Mendus, "Toleration and Recognition: Education in a Multicultural Society," *Journal of Philosophy of Education* 29 (July 1995): 195–96.

50. Ibid., 198–99.

51. Ibid., 199–200.

Chapter 4

Intolerance and Exploitation: Civic Vice, Legal Norms, and Cooperative Individualism

Patricia Smith

The concept that motivates liberal democratic society can be called the ideal of *cooperative individualism*.[1] This is to distinguish *atomistic individualism*, based on ideals of individual self-sufficiency and reciprocal noninterference, from the more general moral view that every individual is uniquely significant and worthy of equal respect and consideration. The latter, alone, is implied in the defining institutions of free societies everywhere. These institutions include constitutional government with limited powers, the private family as a unit to be protected from undue state interference, and cooperative commercial interaction by legal recognition of the private contract. Cooperative endeavor is intrinsic to such institutions, and no free society could survive without them in some form.

Consequently, political theory should represent individuals as cooperative beings interacting within social institutions viewed not only as structures of power, but also as mechanisms to facilitate cooperative interaction. However, individuals and groups are not always cooperative, and social institutions often function as structures of power that propagate injustice and undermine the general welfare by favoring the interests of a privileged minority. Thus, both individual freedom and public utility must be protected. There is no algorithm for doing this; it requires the exercise of practical reason toward the goal of fostering a just and cooperative civic culture.

Two great barriers to the possibility of a society functioning as a just and cooperative culture are intolerance and exploitation.[2] Both of these are violations of the principle that every individual is uniquely significant and worthy of equal respect and consideration.[3] If this principle were truly respected as a basic social norm and the foundation of government, then a society so founded could not consistently be structured in a way that allows intolerance and exploitation to be manifested in overt actions with no governmental mechanism to address the violation.

Human beings are flawed. As individuals, we will always be prone to intolerance and exploitation because we will always be susceptible to such weaknesses as fear and greed. But, social institutions should be structured to counteract these vices or at least to compensate those who are victimized by them. This implies the acceptance of collective responsibility for social conditions that cause harm. To put it another way, it implies an affirmative obligation on the part of all its citizens to maintain social conditions that provide minimally decent treatment for all members of society.[4]

We are not very close to achieving that goal. In fact it may not be a goal that is generally acknowledged at this time, at least in the form suggested here. Such a view may be considered quaintly old fashioned—perhaps the murmuring of an aging liberal, wondering what happened to those ideals of progressive social justice exemplified in the war on poverty and in commitments to civil rights, integration, and the reduction of social inequality. In this paper, I would like to bolster the claim that there is a collective responsibility to maintain minimally decent social conditions for all, at least to the extent of combating exploitation and intolerance, as primary civic vices.

To do this, I will first say a few words about the power and limits of law to combat these civic vices. I will argue that appeal to law and government is not inappropriate for addressing either. Exploitation can be dealt with directly, by prohibiting activities such as loan-sharking, or indirectly, by compensating or assisting those most susceptible to being victimized. Recognizing rather serious limits to the ability of law to directly reduce feelings that give rise to intolerance, I focus the remainder of the paper on considering some requirements for encouraging a civic culture of tolerance.

Law and Exploitation

There are many things law cannot do, and there are many tasks for which government is inappropriate. Some people think that addressing problems of economic exploitation or confronting the poverty that often results from it are among these. There is a long-standing dispute over how such problems should be addressed.[5] Indeed, there is controversy over what sort of economic activity or practice constitutes exploitation.

It is worth noting that whether a situation is identified as a problem at all, and whether the problem is considered appropriate for governmental intervention, depends entirely on how it is perceived and articulated. For example, murder and assault have long been condemned, but dueling and wife beating were once considered private matters, the defense of honor and domestic discipline, and not thought to be civic problems at all. Now, both are viewed as public problems—varieties of murder and assault—to be addressed by criminal law.

Similarly, although exploitation is generally condemned, what constitutes exploitation is open to controversy, and even that which is generally identified as exploitation may be considered a private matter. Are low wages the exploitation of workers? If so, is that always true or only in some circumstances? If only in some circumstances, which ones? What are the factors that make economic activity exploitive? When is it a matter for public concern?

I will argue that the situation faced by the working poor in the United States, today, is an example of economic exploitation that remains generally unrecognized. Many people forced to resort to shelters and soup kitchens today are workers. They are our working poor.[6] They perform a service; they contribute to our national product. They do jobs that need to be done, and for this they are paid less than they need to support themselves. Does this afford them equal respect and consideration? What does it say about how much they count? Why should the bottom of our economic system be so low that workers at that level cannot make a living?

In my view, no society that can afford to do otherwise should allow its economic system to be structured in such a way that those at the bottom are forced to be beggars. We look back on the early days of the industrial revolution, when factory owners paid their workers so little that they could not survive, as a period of economic exploitation. I do not see why we should call it anything else today.

The United States has long been known as the land of opportunity, but the days of the open frontier that purportedly provided free land to anyone strong enough to work it have faded into the distant past. Now, the advice to the young and hungry is to get a good education if you want to live the good life. Thus, the common wisdom is that anyone in this free society who shows sufficient initiative can get trained or educated so as to earn a comfortable living. But this presumption needs examination, since it is somewhat misleading. It may well be true that anyone can earn a living in the sense that no particular person is barred from it, but it is also true that *everyone* cannot earn a living wage, because the structure of the economy precludes it.

Suppose, for the sake of argument, that everyone in the nation pursued an education. If the structure of the economy is such that 10 to 20 percent of the wages for full-time work fall below the poverty level and that an unemployment rate of 3 to 4 percent is necessary to prevent inflation, then 10 to 20 percent of the full-time workers will earn poverty-level wages no matter what they do. Even if everyone in the society had a college degree, some 10 to 20 percent would not be able to earn a living if that is the wage structure of the economic system.

Consequently, the preceding advice presupposes that an educated and aggressive person can succeed, can beat out the competition for better jobs, if and only if others will not be as educated and aggressive. You can win in this game only because others are more likely to lose. This sets up earning a living as a prize that only some members of society can win. This system is unfair because earning a living should not be a prize only for some, but a common benefit available to all. Thus, a wage structure that effectively excludes some members of society from the opportunity to earn a living is unjust.[7] Such injustice can and should be addressed by law.[8]

Exactly how to address this problem is a separate and difficult question, with many possible approaches. Wages and rents could be regulated. Taxpayers could fill the gap between low wages and cost of living by providing vouchers or subsidies, such as the Earned Income Tax Credit, that provide for the difference. The real question is, who should absorb the cost of eliminating extreme inequity that results in destitution? This is a matter of negotiation so long as the solution falls within the minimal requirements of justice.[9]

One major objection to the view offered, here, is the claim that the market is not a moral institution, but a neutral economic force that merely responds to laws of supply and demand by distributing wealth in the most efficient way. If those at the bottom do not earn enough to live, it is because supply exceeds demand for their services. There is nothing personal or immoral about this. It is just the way a free market functions. So long as those on the bottom are free to go elsewhere, to seek training, or to organize themselves to improve their own situations, their lack of resources is not due to exploitation, but to their own failure.[10]

Furthermore, it is often argued, to tamper with the market by regulating hours, wages, benefits, and so forth, ultimately harms *everyone* by disrupting the most efficient distribution of wealth and, thereby, causing problems such as inflation that will also harm the poor and working classes in the long run.[11] Indeed, it is often claimed, the ranting of bleeding-heart liberals over the so-called exploitation of the poor is really an attempt to start a class war based on envy of those who are more successful.[12]

In response to the first point, it is not reasonable to expect ordinary persons to work willingly for less than it costs to live. Since the primary reason for working is to earn a living, it would be irrational to accept work for less than a living wage unless it were either impossible or overwhelmingly difficult to do better.[13] Furthermore, it does not follow that because people are not legally restricted from relocating, or training for a new vocation, or organizing for more bargaining power that they have the resources, strength, or expertise to do so. There is a sense in which this can be characterized as their own failure, since a stronger, more resourceful person might be able to overcome the obstacles that restrict others. Whether it is more plausible to describe this situation as exploitation or as personal failure depends, for one thing, on whether it is reasonable to expect an ordinary person in similar circumstances to be able to overcome such obstacles. The mere fact that an extraordinary person could succeed in spite of any given obstacle tells us nothing about whether it is reasonable to expect people in general to be able to do so. It only tells us that it is not impossible. Clearly, that is not a useful standard for judging the justice or reasonableness of social structures or practices.

If a person were sufficiently resourceful, she could study the relevant law and argue her own case when charged with a legal offense. It does not follow that it is reasonable to expect everyone to be able to do so or that it is, therefore, unnecessary to provide an accused person with legal counsel. By the same token, while some individual might be able to overcome all the obstacles to pulling out of poverty and, thus, out of the position most susceptible to economic exploitation, whether it is reasonable to expect people to be able to do so depends on the odds of succeeding. If very few manage to overcome a given obstacle, this is evidence that it is not reasonable to expect it. Consequently, if most people born into poverty remain in poverty, it suggests that the obstacles are too great and the avenues of escape too few to reasonably expect people in such circumstances to successfully earn a living. If that is the case, it is appropriate to describe the economic situation as structurally exploitive.[14]

Structural exploitation is also suggested if the economic system depends on a reserve workforce of unemployed people or on a workforce that receives less than subsistence wages for services supplied to a privileged class that lives in relative luxury. To excuse such an economic organization as merely a response to supply and demand is, in effect, to endorse as efficient the practice of intentionally excluding some members of society from the means to make a living in order to coerce others into working for less out of fear of losing their jobs. In fact, it is widely recognized in market economics that unemployment is a necessary counterforce to inflation. In several speeches during the spring of 2000, Alan Greenspan, as head of the Federal Reserve Bank, has noted that the level of unemployment cannot be allowed to continue to decline because the job market will become tight, thereby encouraging low-wage workers to demand higher wages, which in turn will produce inflation. The raising of interest rates is a deliberate measure to prevent exactly this phenomenon. It is called "cooling" the economy. What generally goes unmentioned is that accepting this state of affairs as "just the way things are" is to sacrifice some members of society for the good of the rest, and thus, to exploit them.

The market is regulated, boosted, heated up, cooled down, and generally tampered with all the time. To suppose that a market economy is destroyed by any interference whatsoever is not borne out by evidence or history. Although optimal economic conditions may be curtailed or retarded by a sufficiently hostile environment, equalizing mechanisms such as socialized medicine, public schools, and minimum wage laws have been instituted widely and without discernible damage to market economies in Europe, North America, and elsewhere.

To characterize objections to economic injustice as fomenting a class war out of envy is not to give a reasoned argument at all, but simply to portray the position in unattractive terms. What is a class war anyway, if not the objection to unjust treatment of the poor? And, to claim that those who object to working for less than subsistence wages are motivated merely by envy is to ignore the significant fact that they are working for less than subsistence wages. One needn't be envious to object to that, and one is justified in objecting to it whether envious or not. Being unable to make a living is sufficient in itself for complaint. Motive is irrelevant.

If, as is widely acknowledged, a primary function of, and justification for the existence of, a state is to provide for the general welfare, then the burden of justifying deviation from this norm should lie with those entrusted with the common good. If a society is generally poor and unable to address the misfortune of its most vulnerable members, then this may be an excuse or justification for not doing so. But the burden of proof should fall to those in power to show why a society need not provide a realistic opportunity to earn a decent living to all of its members.

Thus, the main point that needs to be rebutted is the idea that it is not the business of law and government to combat economic exploitation. Of course it is the business of government. Who else is going to do it? The poor and the vulnerable, themselves, scrambling for their next meal? They do not have the time to lobby for better wages, medical care, or rent control, nor the leverage to get them. The responsibility is ours, collectively, and we should recognize it in institutions of law and government that address the wrong. A wealthy nation has no excuse for tolerating the indignity and injustice of economic exploitation.

Civic Culture and Legal Norms on Intolerance

Law can be used to address exploitation in several ways, but intolerance is a different sort of problem. Fundamentally, it is an attitude rather than a practice. It may manifest itself in actions, some of which—overt discrimination and violence, for example—can and should be addressed directly by law. But, many of the manifestations of objectionable intolerance are subtle, indirect, and unverifiable.

Intolerance is a complex issue. For convenience I will divide objectionable intolerance into two categories, which, although they may overlap in certain ways, have important differences. The first I will call *group intolerance*. It centers on innate or social characteristics such as race, sex, or nationality that are viewed as signs of inferiority of one form or another. The second type is *moral or religious intolerance*, which focuses on beliefs or practices perceived as wrong. Obviously, these can overlap, homosexuality and ethnicity being obvious examples, but it still may be useful to consider the two types separately.[15]

The easiest to assess morally is the first type, group intolerance, especially if the focus is on immutable characteristics such as race and sex. To characterize an entire race or sex as inferior to another entire race or sex is simply irrational and insupportable.[16] Typically, this form of intolerance involves feelings of revulsion, fear, or suspicion of what is different. These feelings may be exacerbated by long-standing myths, stereotypes, and historical incidents resulting in "blood feuds" and other antagonisms that go into supporting hatred and vilification of the foreign, the dangerous other. Group intolerance is also a crutch, an excuse that provides automatic unearned status and self-respect. "I may be low, but I'm higher than you," says the bigot. "I may not be a big shot, but at least I'm better than them." The nice thing about this form of status is that you cannot lose it, no matter what you do. You are born what you are and so are they, and no one can change that. A white man may not manage to compete well with other men; he may be low man on the totem pole, but he can never fall all the way to the bottom if that position is reserved for women, or blacks, or Puerto Ricans, or whatever groups he identifies as inferior.

The question is, if we take away that position of last resort from the person who relied on it for self-respect, can that person retain self-respect without it? If not, is it possible for such a person to give up that view? Some studies indicate that intolerant white supremacist and militia groups are populated largely by men who are by other measures not doing very well, and by women who are dominated by those same men.[17] For people in these circumstances we need another measure and source of self-respect. This cannot be imposed by law, but it could be addressed in our educational system. Moreover, it might well be alleviated by economic policies that combat economic exploitation, retard cutthroat competition, and promote respect for the dignity of the ordinary worker.

Bigots come in every variety, as we all know, and that is for two reasons: (1) some believe they know the truth, and (2) none of us truly wants full equality. Group intolerance is largely based on the latter. Everybody needs to be better than someone. We say we believe in equality; but we do not really want to *be* equal. We want to be special. What we want is an equal chance for our own intrinsic superiority to shine through. We want to be excellent. Excellence means at least better than somebody, and preferably everybody. Of course, excellence usually refers to some specifiable and measurable accomplishment, and that may be what distinguishes achievement from elitism and prejudice. Yet this distinction is a fine one, and easily confused. Money, just having money, is widely acknowledged as a symbol of excellence, often without attention to how it was gotten.

In any case, all these psychological characteristics, human flaws, and foibles are at the center of group intolerance. It is an irrational and convenient outlet for fear, insecurity, suspicion, or arrogance and a claim of unearned status, privilege, or self-respect for those who have no other bases or outlets available and those who will use whatever stepping stones they can find. It is perpetuated by socialization, indoctrination, and environment.

It is a major feature of individualism to be an antidote for intolerance.

If all individuals are worthy of consideration on their own merits, then you cannot just reduce them to a type or a class or a group of interchangeable digits. If we further recognize that we are all cooperating for the general welfare, not only are we all individuals, we are all contributors to the common good—or at least we could be and should be if societies were structured to allow it to be so. If a society is structured to promote cutthroat competition, then a culture of exploitation is likely to result. In a culture of exploitation, intolerance is fomented both as a mechanism of competition and as an outlet for resentment. Thus, intolerance and exploitation feed on one another. As with economic exploitation, the big question about group intolerance is how to end it. Beyond addressing exploitative policies that feed intolerance and restricting harmful behavior that flows from intolerance, we can barely touch it with law. Education and experience must be our resources for group intolerance.

The second type of intolerance, that which is based on moral and religious disagreement, presents the most difficult philosophical issues. Certainly, all moral intolerance cannot be condemned. I argued that economic exploitation ought not to be tolerated. It is, I claimed, an unjust practice that should be addressed and corrected by law and government, which means that we should all take responsibility for eliminating it.

Some people feel exactly the same way about abortion, homosexuality, working mothers, the spread of atheism, and so on. Dissent over such issues is often regarded as evidence of our moral fragmentation. And, although I feel that all these practices deserve toleration, I must admit that such a view is a logical consequence of not considering the practices immoral. It is hard to be so sanguine if one feels the practice is in fact immoral.

Milton argued that freedom of expression is good even if many disagree with the ideas that get expressed because of it. Locke held the same view concerning religion. Why did they think so? Perhaps Mill put it best: we can all be wrong. Human beings are fallible, always have been, always will be. How many have been stoned, burned, imprisoned, exiled, or persecuted for beliefs and acts that we now consider perfectly legitimate, even good? How many lives have been ruined for no greater offense than deviation from the status quo?

Once again, in the Enlightenment tradition, we presume that the ultimate unit of moral consideration is the individual. The individual is to be respected. Individual welfare is the primary concern, although not the individual in isolation. So, we should agree that clear harm to others can be legally prevented. But where the existence of harm is in dispute, especially where the premises of the arguments relevant to that dispute cannot be verified—a fetus is a person, or conception is sacred, or homosexuality is sin, or ending your life when you are suffering is against God's will—we should leave the ultimate decision to the individuals primarily involved. I have argued that the individual must be considered as a member of a cooperative institution or set of institutions that provide for the common welfare of a given society. Thus, the individual in isolation is not the only consideration. On the other hand, the individual cannot be restricted on institutional grounds unless the institution itself meets basic requirements of justice and utility that form the core of the liberal democratic tradition. I have suggested that an institution is justified if it promotes the common good, distributes benefits and burdens fairly, and respects individual freedom as much as possible. These, I claim, are the implications of a cooperative individualism.

Our government and civic culture do not conform well to the values sketched out here.[18] But they ought to, I think, if we were consistent in the values of the individualist tradition following the Enlightenment. I would suggest that we are making some slow progress toward a society that respects all individuals, although we still have far to go.

If we did achieve this, or approximate it to a reasonable degree, would that solve the problems of moral disagreement and intolerance that are so often taken to be the fragmentation of civic culture? On one level I do not see how it could. Open and unrestricted discourse is the mark of a free society. That may entail a certain level of clamor. I would say that the best human beings in free societies can realistically hope for is respectful disagreement and peaceful coexistence. This itself is a lofty goal but not an impossible one. William Rehnquist and Thurgood Marshall respectfully disagreed about almost everything, as do George Will and Cokie Roberts. Do their ongoing and apparently intractable differences represent fragmentation or merely freedom? In a free society the challenge must be to promote cooperative interaction among diverse groups without oppressing one view or another, one person or another.

Are we doomed to fragmentation and distrust? It depends on what we mean by fragmentation and on what we identify as its cause. If fragmentation is the result of mere disagreement, then there is only fragmentation or oppression from which to choose.[19] But if the source of the problem is not simple disagreement, but intolerance, we could end it by living by the wisdom of Mill's *On Liberty*. I suppose that we cannot do that because we cannot bring ourselves to believe that no one is infallible, that we could all be wrong, and that, consequently, once we raise our children according to our own lights and best judgment, we must then allow all individuals, in the absence of verifiable harm to others, to conduct their lives as they see fit without persecution or harm. Perhaps that is too much to hope for, but, failing that, could we make sure all students read *On Liberty?*

Notes

1. See Patricia Smith, *Liberalism and Affirmative Obligation* (New York: Oxford University Press, 1998).

2. Id. at chap. 9. Following Rawls, I distinguish cooperation from (merely) coordinated activity and presume democratic society to require the former. See Rawls, *Political Liberalism* (New York: Columbia University Press, 1996), 16.

3. Liberal theorists from Kant to Dworkin have held variations on this principle, the point of which is to indicate the centrality of the individual as the fundamental unit of moral commitment. My interest is to consider the political implications of such a commitment, rather than the particular wording of the principle.

4. See Smith, *Liberalism and Affirmative Obligation*, chap. 8, for explication and argument.

5. See, for example, F. A. Hayek, *The Constitution of Liberty* (Chicago: University of Chicago Press, 1960); Henry George, *Progress and Poverty* (New York: D. Appleton, 1882); Burton Weisbrod, *The Economics of Poverty* (Englewood Cliffs, N.J.: Prentice Hall, 1965); Gunnar Myrdal, *Challenge to Affluence* (New York: Random House, 1963).

6. See, e.g., *New York Times*, 21 February 1999; 4 March 1999; 19 December 1999; or 28 March 2000.

7. It may be objected that everyone does have the opportunity to earn a living in the United States. That is false. Everyone has the opportunity to try or to compete to earn a living. Consider this analogy. Most major universities have faculty parking lots for which they give each faculty member a sticker. Since there are always more faculty members than there are spaces, that sticker gives you the opportunity to compete for a space. It does not guarantee a space. So the sticker provides you with an opportunity to try to park, not an opportunity to park. Similarly, the United States provides everyone the opportunity to try to earn a living, but not the opportunity to earn a living.

8. Failing to recognize the injustice of the system was the flaw in George Bush's idea of "1000 Points of Light," which was an appeal to private charity to handle problems of poverty and other forms of desperation. Private charity is important and should be encouraged, but appealing to it to solve problems of justice ignores or denies the nature of the problem. It is not merely that those who are suffering should be helped. It is rather

that those who are victimized by an unjust system are entitled to correction and reparation of the wrong.

9. Nobel Prize–winning economist Robert Solow has recently noted that unless
affirmative measures are taken to prevent it, flooding the job market with low or unskilled workers who were formerly on welfare will lower wages for all low and unskilled
workers with whom they compete for jobs. Thus, the burden of "paying for workfare"
will fall directly on the shoulders of the working poor, in contrast to welfare, which all
taxpayers paid for. Shifting the cost of supporting welfare mothers from the rich to the
poor can hardly be considered a solution that is compatible with justice. This is just one
example of backward and exploitive trends in American economic policy. See Solow,
Work and Welfare (Princeton, N.J.: Princeton University Press, 1998).

10. See, e.g., Hayek, *Constitution of Liberty*.

11. See, e.g., M. Friedman, "Profits Before Ethics," in *Ethics for Modern Life*, ed.
R. Abelson and M. Friquegnon (New York: St. Martin's Press, 1991), 113–18.

12. This is more commonly an informal than a formal claim. But cf. T. Machan, *Commerce and Morality* (Totowa, N.J.: Littlefield, 1988).

13. This point, of course, excludes those who work for charity, for dedication to a
cause, or for the love of the endeavor, since the purpose of such work is not to make a
living and those who choose such work could choose other work and make a living.
Still, the number of people who fall in this category is so small as not to constitute a
counterexample to the general point: most people work in order to earn a living.

14. Intergenerational poverty has been broadly documented in numerous studies,
most commonly focusing on geographical locations—such as various inner city ghet-
tos, Appalachia, southern Mississippi, certain Indian reservations, the rust belt—or on
racial characteristics, such as the concentration of entrenched poverty among blacks,
Hispanics, Native Americans, and so on.

15. For discussion of the second type see, e.g., Thomas Scanlon, "The Problem of Tolerance," in *Tolerance*, ed. J. Hyman (New York: Oxford University Press, 1996).

16. This is not to say that the proposition is never argued for in any form. See R. Herrn-
stein and C. Murray, *The Bell Curve* (New York: Free Press, 1994).

17. See K. Blee, *Women of the Klan* (Berkeley: University of California Press, 1991).

18. For extended argument on this point see my *Liberalism and Affirmative Obligation*.

19. On the other hand, the feeling of fragmentation might be alleviated by recognizing and emphasizing the uniformity of basic moral values across cultures and subcultures. We may not agree on sexual mores, religious beliefs, and codes of etiquette,
but murder, theft, assault, incest, rape, fraud, and other such offenses are condemned
almost everywhere. Basic values are not very fragmented at all.

Part II

Toleration

. . . and diversity not an evil, but a good . . .
—John Stuart Mill, *On Liberty*

It is difficult to imagine any examination of civil toleration being undertaken by a Western philosopher without explicit and frequent reference to John Stuart Mill. Mill's *On Liberty* is a seminal work in liberal political theory and, though the specifics of his argument are not fully endorsed by all liberal thinkers, it is one continuously revisited by those interested in problems of toleration, its grounds, and its limits. Although the preceding quotation brings to mind familiar discourse about diversity and multiculturalism, it is interesting to note that Mill primarily uses the language of *individual liberty* in arguing for toleration. That diversity is a good is certainly part of his utility-based argument for expansive tolerance, and this theme in his work is often emphasized by other advocates of toleration. Still, Mill recognized that the value of individual freedom was an ultimate and necessary element in the logic of tolerance, one without which any further pleading for tolerance would fail.

Diversity and its defense figure more prominently in contemporary treatises on toleration. Discussions of tolerance as a civic virtue typically focus on cultural conflicts, multiculturalism, and value pluralism. With respect to the latter, Leslie Green writes, "it is *because* social groups are conceived as espousing different values that the virtues of restraint, and especially tolerance, are thought to be at the core of modern liberalism."[1] From this perspective, if people of significantly divergent moral outlook are to live together in a civil union, and if the state is not to impose conformity by overtly privileging one set of values, then citizens and their institutions must practice toleration.

The essays in Part 2 ask us to consider what it means to endure, as belonging to the rights of others, views and behaviors of which we may very

71

strongly disapprove and, especially, what this entails by way of legal and political policy. In addressing these questions, the authors explore problems of individual freedom and puzzles generated by principles of equality, as well as the value of social diversity.

Tolerance and Judgment

Rather than taking direct recourse to Mill or other philosophers in considering the nature of tolerance, let us begin with a foray into ordinary language. The following exchange, which occurred in one of my classes, provides us with an anecdotal starting point. "You're being intolerant," one of my students said to another during discussion. The accused student promptly fell silent. I, who had thought all was proceeding well, asked, "Intolerant? How?" "Because," responded the offended party, "She thinks some ideas are better than others." To my dismay, the student described in these terms blushed, mumbled an embarrassed demurral, and refused to participate further. Indeed, no one else was willing to take up the topic, again, and what had been a lively conversation simply ended.

Alarming though this incident may be, it provides what teachers often describe as a learning opportunity. The students could be taught that, far from implying the absence of norms, the concept of tolerance presupposes their existence and applicability. To tolerate something is to bear up under it, to endure it, in a sense that makes no sense if what is tolerated is not already judged to be beyond standards of the approved or acceptable. Tolerance always implies some strain on normal resources, whether we are speaking of tolerance ranges for heated metals or between heated disputants. That which is beyond the limits of tolerance is beyond enduring, and it is judged to be so in terms of norms. Toleration, thus, always occurs somewhere between the limits of the approved and the horizon of the unendurable.

However, the student's complaint and the chastised student's apparent recognition of its validity also teach us something about current notions of tolerance, intolerance, and the requirements of civil interaction. Although many philosophers and careful users of the language might find the linguistic analysis just given trite, a great many people, including many young Americans, do not recognize the correlativity of standards and toleration. They do not regard toleration as conduct or attitude grounded in notions of the acceptable as distinguished from the unacceptable or of the approved as distinguished from the unapproved. On the contrary, to people like the two students, to be tolerant means *to suspend judgment*, to resist any urge to discriminate according to concepts such as good and bad, or even better and worse.

From such a perspective, the old saw that "comparisons are odious" takes on new meaning. It no longer signifies that one ought, in some circumstances, to avoid making public comparisons; rather, it means that one ought to make no comparisons, at all. This, of course, is naïve relativism in all its full-blown, ingenuous, vapidity. All ideas are equally "good," to the extent that such a term of merit may be used. Certainly, all are equally worthy of being entertained, and all beliefs equally worthy of being held. Anyone who imagines that this is but a caricature of the sort indulged in by conservative pundits and religious absolutists need only visit an American college classroom.

Naturally, as a sensible teacher would observe in this situation, no one conducts life in full accordance with such a demand for indiscriminateness. Nonetheless, a great many people believe that the virtue of tolerance must take the form of generalized acceptance. To them, Paine's famous pronouncement of his simultaneous disapproval of a view and recognition of the speaker's right to hold it expresses, at best, a stingy version of genuine toleration. Perhaps they regard it as psychologically improbable that one could both disagree with—even despise—a view and, yet, honestly accept its presentation. Or, perhaps, they think it is simply too difficult for ordinary persons to manage such a psychical trick—better to try to suspend all judgment and to let this stand as the mark of tolerance.

Further, this view is more than a refusal to be judgmental in an obnoxious way. It is, in fact, a moral demand: we *ought* not to comparatively assess anyone's beliefs or ideas, because to do so is to be intolerant. The student's expression of this view is telling in that he faulted his classmate for thinking some ideas *better* than others, not for characterizing anyone's views as inferior or unacceptable. Moreover, it was the student accused of intolerance who was, in fact, silenced: her views were suppressed, her voice not heard, her participation not tolerated. At this extreme, the requirement of tolerance imposes a kind of blackout on the faculty of judgment; whether positive or negative, assessment is forbidden. It is not sufficient to suffer fools, or foolish ideas, gladly.

We might ask how tolerance came to such a degraded state in popular thought, and some suggestions are made in the essays that follow this introduction, but our primary interest lies in achieving an understanding of tolerance and toleration as features of civil relations, particularly legal and political relations. It may well be that some hint of the pop-relativist notion of tolerance has crept into our formal civic relations, and several of these authors struggle to articulate the boundaries of tolerance and suspension of judgment. But, the reader will not find any of these authors recommending individual suspension of judgment. Certainly, none recommends hyperpolite self-censure, or silence, as an element of tolerance among citizens; indeed, several affirm the appropriateness of passionate, provocative engagement. For the most part, the authors hold that tolerance among or between citizens is compatible with strong commitments and pronounced disagreements and that it is the role of liberal democratic institutions to make open discussion of conflicts possible.

The Idea of Civil Tolerance

How, then, should we understand tolerance and the demand for toleration as a virtue in liberal democracies? The story of the two students evinces that toleration is a negative virtue: we are tolerant when we do not silence others, do not preclude their views from being spoken and heard. Closing down a press that offends the ruling party and knocking down a speaker with whom one disagrees are, thus, both instances of intolerance in the largest sense. Of course, one may "be intolerant" in the sense of wishing that people whose views one detests would be quiet. In that sense, avoiding places or media where one could encounter opposing views is a kind of intolerance. However, such internal intolerance, or closed-mindedness, should be distinguished from intolerance as a civic vice, if only to maintain some sense of proportion. It can be argued that civil institutions of a liberal democracy—particularly educational institutions—should encourage individuals to open their minds and sample diverse viewpoints. Nonetheless, it cheapens the currency to classify an individual's avoidance of divergent views as a form of *civil* intolerance. We might say that one practices civil toleration when one does not silence unwelcome voices but that one is truly open-minded when one takes the trouble to hear them out.[2]

The significance of allowing others to speak and be heard, of maintaining an open forum for the expression of ideas, explains, in part, the common association of tolerance with rights of free speech and expression. But tolerance also requires leaving open the possibility for people to live their lives, engage in religious practices, and otherwise conduct themselves in ways of which we disapprove. A low degree of tolerance is exhibited when lifestyles and practices outside the mainstream are permitted on condition of their being kept private. The now infamous "don't ask; don't tell" policy adopted by the U.S. military toward its gay and lesbian members exemplifies this conditional toleration. Clearly, greater tolerance is manifest when governments and individuals allow open demonstration of practices and lifestyles otherwise frowned upon.

We can picture a continuum of degrees of toleration, using homosexuality as an example. At one end, the state does not criminalize, and to that extent allows, homosexuality; at the other end, gays and lesbians are given full legal rights, including legal recognition of lifetime partnerships, protection from discrimination in any form, and so on. Between and beyond these official modes of tolerance, subtler forms and gradations of social tolerance will be found: nonheterosexuals are readily accepted in all professions, open expressions of antipathy to homosexuals are deemed as offensive as racist slurs, the marginal location of homosexuals and those who are intolerant of them is inverted. Here, we note a distinction between *social tolerance* and *political tolerance*. The former is a virtue exhibited in the ways citizens treat one another, their expressed attitudes and interpersonal conduct. The latter is a virtue of government, manifested in laws and policies. Both, again, are virtues of self-restraint rather than virtues of open-mindedness or generous hearts. At some point, being homosexual may no longer mark group membership anymore than does being heterosexual; then, in the absence of strain or perceived improbity, it will no longer be appropriate to speak of toleration.

Although tolerance extends to both expression and conduct, we should note a distinction between toleration of views and beliefs, on the one hand, and toleration concerning differing existential features such as sexual orientation, race, ethnicity, and such. Originally, civil tolerance—political and social—concerned religious disagreement. And, while religious faith incorporates both ideas and behavior, it is a chosen set of beliefs and values, rather than a nonvoluntary characteristic. I am not entering, here, debates as to whether sexual orientation is elective, or whether most people do, in fact, genuinely "choose" their religious perspective. The point to be taken is less controversial: civil tolerance once meant allowing people to espouse and exercise the religious view of their choosing rather than one preferred by the majority or the state. It was out of this context that tolerance came to be understood as involving clashing values or competing "belief systems." This notion of tolerance easily evolved to a concern for more generalized civil rights, including political expression and participation. The extension of tolerance to racial difference also began as a demand for basic civil rights—rights to liberty and full citizenship—but, insofar as race is a characteristic rather than a belief system, racial tolerance naturally came to imply tolerance of the *person* as well as of any divergent ideas or practices.

Let us not oversimplify. The relationship between one's beliefs and values, on the one hand, and one's identity, on the other, is complex. Certainly, those who harbor antipathy to one's religious practice will not always sharply distinguish between one's chosen views and one's person. The connection may be facilitated in the minds of outsiders by appearance, such as a typical manner of dress or speech, or the wearing of beards, shaving of heads, and so on. No doubt the Puritans were as visible on the streets of London, in their day, as Hare Krishna members and Orthodox Jews are on the streets of New York, today. Still, the notion of tolerance *has* evolved from toleration of religious and political commitments to toleration of persons perceived as "types"—the likely coalescence of having a certain perspective and being seen as being of a type notwithstanding. Three consequences of this development bear examination.

First, toleration of persons, of their company and of interaction with them, calls for a considerably higher *degree* of tolerance than does toleration of their beliefs. This doesn't seem a particularly controversial observation. If I must work with someone of a racial or ethnic group I dislike, this demands more of me than does tolerating the occasional expression of views with which I disagree. At a minimum, if I must work with someone whose beliefs displease me, we can agree to keep our political or religious views to ourselves. The person whose racial or ethnic identity offends me can hardly keep that to herself. It's possible that this need for increased tolerance is connected with the emergence of the idea of toleration as suspended judgment. But, it seems likely that the pop-relativist notion of tolerance is more directly associated with the second consequence of the evolution from toleration of beliefs to toleration of persons, as such.

This second consequence is the extension of the prescribed *scope* of tolerance, roughly distinguished from the required degree of self-restraint. Whereas early civil tolerance entailed restraint mostly on the part of the state—permitting a variety of religious and political beliefs—private citizens now bear the burden of tolerating one another in what were regarded as private settings such as work, housing, schools, and so on. Returning to our example of the workplace, we can recall that original religious tolerance did not require anyone to hire, work with, or even do business with those whose beliefs they abhorred. The state was not to outlaw any religious sect, and citizens were not, presumably, to abuse one another on religious grounds, but it was not expected that adherents of the Church of England would have to keep company with Quakers in work or business affairs.

Of course, there have been enormous structural changes, as well. Without a system of public education, it was never supposed that children of antithetical faiths would be schooled together. With the advent of public education, people of differing views *and* of different "types" were increasingly thrown together. Nonetheless, I submit that the extension of tolerance to nonvoluntary, or ascriptive, group membership helped to push the concept of toleration from the requirement of simply enduring the existence of contrarian fellow citizens to that of overcoming one's aversion to them. It required not only *more* tolerance but also a new *mode* of tolerance. In addition, all these developments have been bound up with evolving ideas of equal citizenship and equal treatment, which we will explore in the following section.

Let's turn to the third consequence of the evolution of the concept of tolerance, arguably the most philosophically interesting. As noted previously, tolerance is commonly understood to be called for when values and beliefs are discordant. This, clearly, follows from the original religious and political context in which the need for tolerance emerged. But what, exactly, are the value conflicts between members of different racial groups? What antithetical or even unharmonious belief systems characterize the lives of men and women, Irish Americans and Italian Americans, homosexuals and heterosexuals? Somehow, the notion of doctrinal dispute seems to have been carried over from toleration of beliefs to toleration of persons.

Granted, different values and beliefs may contribute to the strain between persons of different races, ethnicities, sexes, or sexual orientations. Nonetheless, as Leslie Green has argued, we go too far if we assume that all social stresses reduce to value conflicts.[3] Those who regard homosexuality as morally evil do take themselves to be involved in a dispute over values with those who do not share that moral view. But this dispute concerns the relatively narrow matter of sexual morality. This is not a case of fundamental values conflict or incompatible conceptions of the good life; homosexuals do not have a monolithic worldview any more than heterosexuals do. Further, we should note that some who decry the practice of homosexuality on grounds of sexual morality are, in fact, celibate homosexuals and that many who do not morally disapprove of homosexuality are heterosexuals. In other words, whatever values conflict there may be, it is not between homosexuals and heterosexuals; it is between persons holding disparate notions of sexual morality.[4]

Thus, we might say that discrete social tensions call for distinct modes of civil tolerance. The disjunction of ideological conflict and social conflict is yet more evident in the cases of racism and xenophobia. Whatever the racist hates about people of other races, it is not, ultimately, their beliefs or values. Even if she encounters a member of the despised racial group with whose views she is in perfect concert, she will find only this one individual, at best, more tolerable than others of the same race. She still will not want one of "them" as a member of her family. Perceived variations in lifestyle or attitudes are not the core of racism or ethnic antipathy; they merely give the hater something on which to hang her emotional hat.

Nor is the mode of toleration manifest in law and policy, what we have called political toleration, the same as that required between citizens, or social toleration. One important difference lies, again, with the notion of suspended judgment. Although it would be linguistically painful to suggest that government can suspend judgment in the same sense that individuals might attempt, the concept of *state neutrality,* familiar in liberal discourse, implies something akin to individual suspension of judgment. State neutrality entails not privileging, officially, particular religions, political views, and so on. This approach goes beyond simple nondiscrimination.

When a polity does not impose special burdens or restrictions on one set of beliefs or one group of people, it achieves an initial level of toleration. For a period of time such straightforward nondiscrimination marked the extent of political toleration; it was not expected that, for example, a Catholic king would not display a religious preference, but only that his policies not encroach on the practices of Protestant citizens. But, as several of our contributors illustrate, the concept of not privileging one group or one set of views takes us further along the continuum. By abjuring any policy that might appear to *favor* one group or perspective, governments aspire to full neutrality, and this seems to be more along the lines of a suspension of judgment than of a refusal to discriminate. To that extent, the doctrine of state neutrality means that institutions are silent on certain disputed issues; the state, as such, may have no opinion.

Although state neutrality remains a matter of institutional restraint and, hence, a negative virtue, it is also more profound than what is proposed by nonrelativist views of social tolerance. I have argued that the informed conception of social tolerance does not require suspension of judgment. To the contrary, individuals and subnational groups are entitled to have diverse views, and good citizenship entails the airing of those views on appropriate occasions. But, when conjoined with the doctrine of state neutrality, this means that citizens who are openly opposed on specific issues must live with and through political institutions that function so as to give no expression to any perspective whatsoever on those same matters. As several of our authors demonstrate, this degree of political toleration poses significant problems for both citizens and institutional policies.

Equality, Rights, and Freedom

It would be fair to characterize the conception of tolerance just advanced as minimalist, insofar as it suggests that civil toleration does not commit individuals to suspending judgment, nor even to much by way of imaginative engagement with other citizens. This is not intended to foreclose on the claim that civility might require a degree of sympathy among citizens as well as toleration; it is simply to distinguish toleration from other virtues. The nature of tolerance as a civil virtue is, I have argued, minimalist or negative: it demands primarily restraint on the part of citizens and institutions rather than genuine open-mindedness. Other virtues such as sympathy, compassion, and the like may be vital to the health of a society, but they are not, I think, the kind of bedrock civil virtues that tolerance is. An unhappily, even grudgingly, tolerant society can function in the face of deep social divisions; without some degree of tolerance, however, those divisions too easily give rise to uncivil conduct that threatens the ordinary operation of social affairs. Although a disdainful tolerance may be a less communitarian virtue than sympathy or engagement, it is, nonetheless, a necessary virtue for liberal, pluralist societies.

A distinction between sympathetic engagement with others and toleration of them or their views is helpful in examining the relationship between the concept of toleration and principles of equality and individual rights. When we recognize the equality of fellow citizens, it is not necessary that we either agree with them or approve of them; we may even heartily dislike people whose civil equality we would not question. And, however difficult it may be to appreciate someone's right to espouse views we abhor, the virtue of tolerance consists precisely in our honoring that right, no matter what internal turmoil it causes us to hear those views expressed. Obligations of tolerance are, in fact, dependent on the ideal of civil equality and, therefore, on some conception of individual civil rights. The pop-relativist notion of the equal worth of beliefs, itself, flows from an expansion of the idea of equal citizenship. If you and I are equal as citizens and equally entitled to express our views—or equally prohibited from doing so, in some cases—and the state has no business favoring one view over another, then "who is to say" that your ideas are not quite as good as mine? Relativism thus moves from the equal status of citizens who hold divergent beliefs to the equal status of the content of those beliefs.

While not falling into the trap of relativist reasoning, we can observe that civil toleration, even in minimalist form, does place significant constraints on citizens. The undergirding notion of equal citizenship is, after all, fairly abstract, whereas having to endure the presence or the screed of those with whom we are deeply at odds is an unpleasantly concrete experience. Mill was, I think, reasonable in dismissing the concerns of "persons entirely unconnected" with others whose conduct they disdain; such persons are, as he observed, inclined to dismay at nothing more than "the enormity of [someone's] acting or feeling differently" from themselves.[5] Such a low tolerance threshold has to give way in a liberal, pluralist society. But, when citizens are in direct contact with one another or with each other's viewpoints, toleration can be genuinely burdensome. It is here that the recourse to a conception of rights is crucial: to provide not only justification of but also *motivation for* toleration of minority views and marginalized groups.

Whether rights are conceived in Mill's utilitarian fashion or in the more substantive deontological manner,[6] the concept of equal rights grounds the claim that we ought to practice toleration, despite the discomfort it causes us and despite any claim we may have to the support of majority opinion. If we take the notion of equal citizenship seriously, it also obviates the recourse to relativism, even as a psychological device. Equality among citizens entails that whatever rights are recognized, as rights of citizenship, must be afforded to all who are citizens. In a pluralist society, this further entails that disagreement must be tolerated, if only as a practical requirement. We do not need to abandon our own preferences and commitments to appreciate our obligation to be tolerant of persons and ideas odious to us; we need only embrace the principle of equal rights and manifest that acceptance in our conduct toward one another.

There will always be limits, of course; these limits pertain both to what is originally recognized as belonging to the rights of citizens and to the extent of disagreement or social conflict that can be accepted. Often, examining the latter involves reconsidering the former. For example, to determine what minority religious practices are tolerable may require that we reexamine what we recognize as falling under the right of religious practice as it belongs to all citizens, as equals. Undoubtedly, a sense of fairness in reasoning is needed in such reexaminations, but sympathy with those unlike oneself is not.

Principles of equality and respect for rights, however, do only part of the work of justifying and motivating tolerance as a civil virtue. Mill made this clear in placing these words from Wilhelm von Humboldt on the opening page of *On Liberty*: "The grand, leading principle, towards which every argument unfolded in these pages directly converges, is the absolute and essential importance of human development in its richest diversity."[7] Mill's own expression of this principle is particularly moving: "Human nature is not a machine to be built after a model, . . . but a tree, which requires to grow and develop itself on all sides, according to the tendency of the inward forces which make it a living thing."[8] For Mill, it was the ultimate end of free development—of individual flourishing—that warrants toleration within a community. Freedom, rather than equality, was the leitmotif of his argument for social tolerance. In part, this was due to his sense, following Tocqueville, that the spread of social equality produced less tolerance rather than more. But, it was also because he believed intolerance crushed individual development even more thoroughly than it thwarted social progress. Indeed, Mill comes close to ordaining individual development a self-regarding obligation correlative to the other-regarding virtue of toleration. Thus, he derides the conformist as one who "has no need of any other faculty than the ape-like one of imitation," and goes so far as to question such a person's "comparative worth as a human being" relative to those who freely direct their own lives.[9] And, with a lyricism only a utilitarian of Mill's persuasion could manage, he concludes that "among the works of man which human life is rightly employed in perfecting and beautifying, the first in importance is surely man himself."[10]

Those who do not regard individuality and its flowering to be ultimate human goods will not be persuaded to tolerance simply by appeals to equality. A stringently conservative society equally closed to all, or most, of its citizens is not unknown, and citizens of such societies are frequently quite self-aware in choosing homogeneity and parochialism. In Western secular culture, there is a tendency to assume that closed societies of this sort are always religious in nature—either extremist sects or theocratic states. This is a consequence both of our historically based fear of religious factionalism and of what has become a rather unreflective acceptance of political principles of individuality and individual freedoms as applied in religious contexts. But, as Mill observed, the majority of humans are not, by nature, tolerant of diversity in any manifestation nor particularly enamored of individuality where it departs from what is regarded as the norm. And this, of course, is one reason that toleration of persons and beliefs, both in and outside religious contexts, is still an aspiration rather than a fully attained goal even in the most liberal, pluralistic societies.

The difficult history of religious conflict and religious toleration dominates our thinking about toleration, unsurprisingly enough, and this preoccupation with religious tolerance and intolerance is furthered by the apparent intensity of certain religious tensions of today—perhaps especially against the backdrop of largely secular lives. But many apparently religious conflicts are, at bottom, not genuinely about religion; that is, they are not doctrinal disputes in the traditional sense. Whatever its origins, the ongoing civil strife in Ireland is less about Catholicism versus Protestantism than it is a matter of class and political power. The violent clash of Israelis and Palestinians, similarly, cannot be reduced to an incompatibility of Judaism and Islam. Certainly, racism, sexism, heterosexism, class antagonisms, and all the other myriad modes of human antagonism exist and call for the virtue of tolerance entirely absent any religious implications.

What does underlie all these antagonisms are disparate valuations of freedom and individual development and disagreement about the rights of others to equal enjoyment of freedom and individual development. Let us make the point another way. It is not, for example, my conviction that heterosexuality is "best" or that my religious views are "correct" that will cause social conflict between me and those who have divergent beliefs. Rather, it will be my inability or unwillingness to afford them the freedom to have views and engage in practices other than those I elect that will generate discord. With respect to tolerance as a civil virtue, then, the conjoint values of individual freedom and equality of rights form a foundation on which social interaction and political policies are built. It is because liberalism emphasizes those values that civil tolerance is a core liberal virtue in liberal democratic polities.

Ironically, conscientiously liberal societies encounter a particular problem in pursuing their characteristic ideal of toleration, in that they may harbor internal subgroups that reject that ideal and deny the values of individuality and individual freedom. Again, we should note that such groups need not be religious in focus. In the United States, at present, groups that reject the standard liberal principles of individuality, liberty, and civil toleration for their own membership often are both religiously grounded and inegalitarian in some respects.[11] But, there are, as well, groups that aggressively promote intolerance toward nonmembers—for example, racist groups in which hostility toward persons of other races is more salient than control of those within the group. These groups, typically, are secular in cast; any religious pretensions they may have are secondary to the originating racial animus. Whether intolerant subgroups are of religious or secular orientation, and whether their intolerance is primarily inner directed or outer directed, may affect the policies a liberal state adopts in dealing with them. One way or the other, a liberal nation-state can find itself in a political and legal conundrum when it must determine how to tolerate the intolerant among its citizenry.

The Essays

Just as tolerance functions in various modes and to varying degrees, it pertains to different levels of civic life. The first two essays in Part 2, Wade Robison's "Civility and Stability" and Christopher Gray's "Trumping Civilly: Technique in Reference to Secession," illustrate this point by focusing on what might be termed a metaconstitutional level. We often think of tolerance as a virtue called forth in existing political contexts and, hence, we naturally turn to constitutional principles and rules for aid in resolving strife or addressing issues of diversity. In a constitution, after all, we expect to find the basic rights afforded to citizens and those principles of equality and liberty that—in a liberal polity—will enable us to negotiate rival interests.

But, as Robison's essay evinces, constitutions do not drop ready-made from heaven; they must be constructed and consented to, often by people already at odds with one another. Robison focuses on those conflicts among constitution makers that are based on "deeply held interests" and that "reflect deeply compelling as well as competing interests." Such conflicts are not likely to be resolved outside or prior to the constitutional framework. Thus, he argues, constitutions can be expected to reproduce, or in some fashion manifest, those original and deep divisions.

Robison looks to the slavery issue that divided the Northern colonies from the Southern colonies at the time of the American Constitutional Convention as an example of such deep rivalries: the interests of nonslave states in limiting the spread of slavery could be served only at the cost of the political interests of slave-owning states. As he observes, the tensions over slavery were merely "submerged" by the original constitutional agreement, and they resurfaced full fury in the period of westward expansion before the Civil War. A particular problem arose when the Supreme Court, in the *Dred Scott* case, left the North with no constitutional recourse for ending slavery. It did this by appealing to "the nature of the Constitution itself—both to its constitutive conditions and to the conditions of its being adopted." By thoroughly foreclosing the abolitionist case, the Court brought civil dispute to an end.

Robison's diagnosis is just that: an etiology of how profound conflicts infect the framing of constitutions. He does not offer a remedy, and, indeed, makes clear that, after the *Scott* decision, a breakdown in civil union was inevitable unless one side of the dispute had miraculously given up. Are there lessons about toleration to be learned, here? One is that, where interests are genuinely incompatible—where the satisfaction of one set of interests *consists in* the defeat of another set—toleration can be rendered impotent. Northern abolitionists could not be tolerant of the expansion of slavery into the territories that would become new states without abandoning their hopes for abolition. Southern slaveholders could not tolerate federal restriction of slavery in those territories without placing themselves in a politically untenable position. A second lesson is underscored by Christopher Gray's exploration of the Canadian situation. Gray examines a 1998 Canadian Supreme Court case and its implications for civil relations at the level of constitutional confrontations. Like Robison, Gray refers to the technique in constitutional argumentation of "trumping" one position by setting some legal norms or considerations beyond the reach of standard intraconstitutional pleading. Although his prognosis for resolution of the Quebec issue may not be entirely sanguine, he does reveal the importance of avoiding decision procedures that render further civil discourse otiose. This, we might observe, is an example of intolerance in its foundational sense: the silencing of opposing views. That this silencing is achieved nonviolently, through the circumscription of allowable pleading, rather than by violence, makes it no less alienating to those denied the opportunity to press their case.

In making this point, Gray provides a thorough explication of Ronald Dworkin's theory of "trumping" and a comparative assessment of that technique as understood by the Canadian Supreme Court. Using Dworkin's view as a model, Gray argues that the Court misapplied the concept of trumping among equally basic constitutional principles. According to Gray's argument, the Court managed to trump any unilateral secession effort by Quebec by interpreting such a move as an illegitimate attempt to have coequal constitutional principles trump one another. Put another way, the Court trumped secession by the voters of Quebec by charging them with impermissibly trumping absolute principles. In so doing, the Court neither evinced toleration in its decision nor facilitated the continued legal discourse wherein tolerant hearing out of both sides would have been possible.

As did the Taney Court in *Scott*, then, the Canadian Supreme Court has created a constitutional context in which Quebec, like the Northern abolitionists, appears to have no recourse other than to hope that opposing forces will give way. More precisely, it has no civil recourse, and this occasions a third lesson concerning toleration. Tolerance serves stability in two ways: by imposing self-restraint on disputing parties and by providing for continued engagement of opposing views. Useful though the first service is, the second is crucial when conflict is profound and parties are unrelenting. There are genuinely incompatible claims and interests that divide humans, and it is quite possible that certain disputes will never be resolved in the sense of being put to rest. Tolerance on the part of all parties, including institutions that oversee disputes, keeps the disputants talking—in or out of court.

It is sobering to reflect that, even absent the *Dred Scott* decision, the North and the South might not have been able to maintain their union under the pressures of the westward expansion. Of course, we cannot know whether that would have proven true. What Robison and Gray show us is that foreclosing on open discussion, and political combat, at the metaconstitutional level obviates tolerance at any other level. In that respect, it condemns the disputants to finding other modes for continuing the dispute. Toleration will not settle all conflicts, but, to the extent that tolerance keeps people talking about what divides them, it is one means of keeping the peace.

In Erik Anderson's "Liberal Neutrality, Public Reason, and the Religion Clauses of the First Amendment," we encounter a problem of constitutional interpretation, one concerning the familiar issue of religious toleration. Here, the question is not whether the state may favor a particular religious perspective but whether the liberal state can, coherently, establish a religiously neutral position without privileging secularism. As Anderson contends, no state can be expected to preclude absolutely any effective, but unintended and indirect, benefiting of some positions and practices as compared with others. State neutrality, as he defines it, reasonably entails only that the state not *aim* to create benefits or to impose burdens inequitably, and he explores this conception of neutrality in relation to the Rawlsian "ideal of public reason."

Anderson proposes emending the ruling understanding of this ideal so that certain appeals to religious perspectives can be included in the category of genuinely public justifications—their religious references notwithstanding. No one, he suggests, can frame a particularized interpretation of public morality without reference to some background worldview, and religious views are simply one variant of such background perspectives. Thus, he writes, metaphysical or specifically religious "interpretations of *public* reasons, . . . are not claims about the superiority of a particular . . . conception of the good over others. They are claims about what *public morality* requires." He then applies this notion of public reasoning to the Establishment Clause of the U.S. Constitution, so as to relieve religious perspectives of what he characterizes as "a unique disability" regarding state support. Anderson's main thrust is that the position of moderate liberalism unfairly discriminates against religious worldviews as contrasted with nonreligious ones.

We might say that Anderson wants to show the ways in which all worldviews—whether naturalistic or nonnaturalistic, theist or nontheist—are similar in providing grounds for moral and political claims. These grounds are vitally important to those who hold the views and equally "nonpublic," insofar as none has meaning for those holding different comprehensive positions. Thus, he contends that the government should fund programs that serve public interests when administered by traditional religious groups as readily and on the same conditions as when administered by nonreligious groups. A genuinely tolerant, open, liberal state, on this view, can no more be peculiarly nonreligious in character than it can be predisposed to a particular religious view. Liberal toleration ought to extend, Anderson argues, to the differences between nonreligious comprehensive doctrines and religious ones, just as it does to differences among religious ones. Neutrality, it seems, is in the eye of the beholder.

The fourth essay, Thomas Peard's "Regulating Racist Speech on Campus," takes up a controversy that has garnered considerable notice in recent years, both from philosophers and in the popular press. As Peard presents it, the central problem of hate speech regulation for liberal thinkers lies in the aim of ensuring toleration of all persons as a matter of respecting equal liberty. That hate speech is, ex hypothesi, intolerant in its nature and motivation does not relieve liberal doctrine of the burden of toleration with respect to it. As noted in preceding sections, there is no need to tolerate that which does not offend or shock us; toleration is called for when expression or behavior causes outrage, as hate speech does. The recurring liberal concern to determine the "limits of tolerance" simply becomes more poignant when what must be tolerated are open expressions of intolerance.

Peard argues that regulation of hate speech on campuses is acceptable on foundational liberal principles and that, in particular, regulations can be imposed without illegitimate invasion of the personal liberty of those who engage in hate speech. Peard is concerned with those cases of racist speech wherein the insult conveyed and the contempt felt by the speaker are clear and would be generally recognized. Thus, he rules out of his argument those cases in which persons of unusual sensitivity might *perceive* speech as hateful. Further, the instances that Peard has in mind are genuinely interpersonal: that is, they are directed toward identifiable individuals, singly or in a group. Finally, he is interested only in cases of unprovoked verbal or symbolic abuse, not retaliatory expression.

A standard liberal response to hate speech as a general phenomenon could require us to tolerate it just as we tolerate contrarian political or religious expression. This appears to follow directly from the concept of neutrality as it applies to all self-expression. From this perspective, regulating hate speech impermissibly privileges one set of views, nonracist views in this context, and silences divergent—racist—ones. Speech, like conduct, is permissibly regulated only if it can be shown to be harmful. Further, it must be shown as harmful *enough* to meet the normal liberal threshold for harm—which is relatively high, certainly as contrasted with illiberal standards. Moreover, freedom of speech, in particular and as contrasted with overt action, is a special concern of liberalism; liberals of all stripes are typically willing to extend maximum toleration to speech, as such, and are frequently loath to acknowledge that it can cause harm directly.

At this point, most libertarians will have finished assessing the legitimacy of racist hate speech regulation and concluded that it violates liberty interests of the speakers. Peard pursues the moderate liberal approach espoused by Joel Feinberg, through an analysis of the offensiveness and harmfulness of racist hate speech that meets his criteria. His argument is notable in two respects. The first is the highly systematic nature of the analysis. Unlike many on both sides of this debate, Peard first reviews recognized standards of risk, harm, and offense, and then applies those standards to hate speech of the specific kind under consideration. His analysis is well evidenced; in this respect, it fares better than the usual subjective pronouncements about speech, in general, that characterize much of the hate speech literature. Second, while he examines racist hate speech with respect to both its offensiveness and harmfulness, he demonstrates that it *can* pass the threshold of harm, as distinguished from offensiveness, which many liberals and all libertarians prefer to maintain in defending speech from encroachment. Thus, he is able to breach absolutist rejection of all hate speech regulation.

The problem of hate speech regulation, and that posed by civility-oriented antipornography regulations, appears again in Norman Fischer's "First Amendment Morality versus Civility Morality." Fischer believes that recent efforts to limit racist and sexist expression follow from an increase in what he terms *civility morality*—an observation that puts him at odds with the ruling view of our contributors concerning the decrease in social civility. Unfortunately, he claims, where this increased civility leads to censorship, it does so at the cost of First Amendment values. *Pace* Peard, Fischer is willing to consider that some of the proposed regulations have been aimed at "what might be called dangerous speech"; nonetheless, he argues that those proposals undermine their own morality of civility. Further, he makes a substantive bid for the intrinsic superiority of the moral values implicit in a generous free speech doctrine.

With Peard, Mill, and others, Fischer recognizes that regulation of expression implicates important liberty interests, and he embraces explicitly both the consequentialist and nonconsequentialist motivations for free expression that can be found in the work of Mill. Following the lead of Catherine MacKinnon and other procode theorists, he focuses on equality interests. From his perspective, the hate speech debate turns on competing equality claims: that of speakers to equal freedom of expression and that of stigmatized persons to full and equal citizenship. Both sides, in effect, are protesting discriminatory treatment. As Fischer observes, proponents of regulation hold that it is proper to "discriminate between words that stigmatize groups and those that do not"; opponents of regulation claim that such discrimination violates requirements of content neutrality. Fischer is sensitive to the possible criticism that striking down speech regulations is a predictable, reflexive libertarian response—one that simply places liberty interests above equality issues. But, he contends that, insofar as content neutrality and nondiscrimination are equality-based values, speech codes are, or can be, overturned by assessing the equality claims rather than through a simple privileging of liberty over equality.

The problem for hate speech regulation and antipornography ordinances, as Fischer sees it, is that any effort to legislatively articulate a principled identification of proscribable words or images, de facto, bestows upon the listed expressions the crown of moral or political "viewpoint." That is, if we identify certain words or images as forbidden without reference to the context of their use or appearance, our own theorizing creates an assumed theoretical stance on the part of those who employ the forbidden expressions. Expression enjoying the regal status of "viewpoint" is, of course, precisely that which free speech guarantees are intended to protect, first and foremost. For Fischer, thus, both antipornography and antihate speech regulations face a logical paradox, insofar as they elevate what is simply ugly to the level of moral and political expression.

In concluding, Fischer critiques the work of Cass Sunstein and others, whom he characterizes as "civility moralists." Fischer takes the traditional liberal position that open, even offensive, expression is an essential ingredient in democratic discourse. He has little patience with the claim that those who are stigmatized or offended are effectively debarred from full participation in such discourse. Requiring that people give voice only to morally approved views—specifically those that do not reflect animus toward persons based on certain kinds of group membership—is simply the imposition of one's own preferred moral and political view, according to Fischer's assessment. In this light, the civility moralist whom Fischer targets is no more tolerant than the uncivil bigot or the pornographer who depicts women and children as objects of abuse. Indeed, in classic liberal fashion, Fischer seems to have less respect for those who would promote censorship in the name of civility than for those whose hateful or obscene expression he, himself, finds offensive.

In "Rudeness, Rasp, and Repudiation," Jonathan Schonsheck undertakes a conceptual analysis of the varieties of intolerance commonly evident in contemporary American society. This foray into the underbelly of our liberal democratic culture produces an insightful and useful set of distinctions for conceptual clarification. Schonsheck's "three Rs" denote the basic forms of intolerance: (1) *rudeness*, which he describes as simple impoliteness; (2) *rasp*, which is the kind of fractious interaction common in pluralist cultures; and (3) *repudiation*, which is manifest when citizens reject core liberal values of tolerance and mutual respect. Schonsheck contends that it is instances of repudiation that pose a genuine problem for liberalism, because, here, resolution of conflicts cannot be attempted through appeal to those values that liberalism normally employs—values of tolerance, equality, and respect for individual freedom—when citizens have inconsonant views or interests.

Uncivil behavior such as rudeness and civil tensions of the rasp type probably occupy the imaginations and cloud the daily lives of persons in a pluralist, liberal democracy much of the time. On any given day, I am far more likely to encounter a rude driver or to find myself in an awkward moment with a religious proselytizer than to confront someone who wants to dispute liberal metavalues. Rudeness and rasp can make the conduct of ordinary life difficult, unpleasant, or even dangerous, and they are the kinds of events that leap to mind when we speak of incivility. But, repudiation is, as Schonsheck writes, apparently "intractable"—perhaps deeply ingrained in us by our evolutionary heritage—and it can threaten civil stability where pluralism is a nonnegotiable fact. Thus, it is repudiation that demands our civic attention on the macro social and political levels, for it is that which produces deep and enduring divisions within the polity. In other words, as an individual, I may suffer most from rudeness and rasp in my private affairs, but it is repudiation that demands my concern as a citizen.

The paradigm example of repudiation occurs when the conflict between two groups, *itself*, centers on the claim to equal rights of one of the opposed groups—as when racists discriminate against members of the racial group they despise. Yet, there is something puzzling, here. Perhaps whether we are dealing with a case of repudiation of core values is not always clear or can be seen as an interpretive problem. For example, in the conflict between Northern abolitionists and Southern slaveholders, is it accurate to say that either side rejected the values of liberty, equality, and toleration as they were then understood? Abolitionists would have pointed out that the institution of slavery denied exactly those values. On the other hand, proslavery parties might have countered that they only denied the relevance of those values to relations between the two races, on grounds that members of the two races were *not* entitled to the same status according to Nature or under the Constitution. Did the dispute between slavers and abolitionists involve a repudiation of liberal metavalues by the former group, or did it arise from a disagreement—not as to metavalues, but about the application of those values in specific contexts?

Of course, as Schonsheck evinces, there are clear-cut cases of repudiation, and these, however readily classified, seem to defy specifically *liberal* efforts at resolution. The same problem will not occur in a predominantly illiberal polity if a subgroup espousing liberalism begins to contest the ruling metavalues. An illiberal ruling perspective is amply prepared to deal with opposing foundational views; it simply does not tolerate them. Indeed, it might take the same approach to rudeness, and it might preemptively suppress the kind of pluralism that would generate rasp. Like several other contributors, Schonsheck holds out hope for the development of critical faculties, and he looks to the most recent formulation of Rawlsian theory for instruction. Through reason, perhaps, we can surmount ingrained impulses that no longer serve human interests.

The essays in Part 2, collectively, illustrate the ways in which toleration is both a civic virtue and a value for liberal societies. They do not, as I believe Robison, Gray, and Schonsheck suggest they cannot, pretend to argue for tolerance as a universal value or as a virtue of citizenship, *simpliciter*. As the pieces by Peard, Fischer, and Anderson reveal, toleration, like the associated values of equality and mutual respect, has a mirroring effect: it persistently casts its own image—its demands and presuppositions—back upon itself. And, while we need not suspend judgment nor trade passionate commitment for indifference to practice tolerance, there is a sense in which toleration requires transcendence. The tolerant person attempts to transcend specific interests, perspectives, even affective inclinations, in order to recognize the right of others to their own interests, perspectives, and inclinations. The tolerant state attempts to transcend, in its policies, all the disparate interests and perspectives of its citizens or, at the least, to not unfairly privilege or encumber any party.

Tolerance, thus, is both a specifically liberal and a particularly demanding civic virtue. As Tocqueville and Mill recognized, it is not a virtue natural to democratic majorities, however well it may serve democratic interests in the long run. Yet, absent the sincere efforts of citizens and the state to practice the virtue of toleration, contemporary social life would be, on the one hand, less diverse and more dull, or, on the other hand, more confrontational and less secure.

C.S.

Notes

1. Leslie Green, "Pluralism, Social Conflict, and Tolerance," in *Pluralism and Law*, ed. Arend Soetemann (New York: Kluwer, 2001), chap. 6, 87. Green takes issue with those who regard value pluralism as a source of significant political instability.

2. In the same way, being a bigot in one's own head is a personal vice, whereas refusing to employ someone on the basis of race or, even more clearly, to deny them political participation, is civil intolerance. I do not think this difference is entirely one of degree or egregiousness of conduct; rather, it marks the difference between tolerance as self-restraint and open-mindedness as a positive response to others.

3. Green, "Pluralism, Social Conflict, and Tolerance."

4. I suspect that many who do not oppose homosexuality on moral grounds or who, at least, regard sexual orientation as an area for tolerance, often feel some personal distaste toward homosexuals. At the least, we cannot assume that those who are intolerant of homosexuality as sexual conduct are necessarily also those who dislike the company of gays and lesbians.

5. J. S. Mill, *On Liberty* (Indianapolis, Ind.: Bobbs-Merrill, 1956), 103, 113.

6. The utilitarian notion of rights is explained by Mill and others as a shorthand reference to utilities or individual goods that are so universally and consistently desirable as to attain the status of presumed utility. The deontological, particularly the natural rights, perspective asserts that rights are held and are to be respected without regard to utility; persons have certain rights by virtue of being persons, equal citizens, and so on. Thus, on the latter view, even when a right must be "overridden" or set aside by the demands of utility, it remains a right and there has been a significant moral loss.

7. W. von Humboldt, from *The Sphere and Duties of Government*, quoted by J. S. Mill, *On Liberty*, 69.

8. Ibid., 72.

9. Ibid., 71–72.

10. Ibid., 72. It can be argued, of course, that Mill's gift for inspiring language depended on his being a less than strict utilitarian. I prefer to treat seriously his insistence on referring to "utility in the largest sense, grounded on the permanent interests of man as a progressive being." (15)

11. Such a subgroup may privilege males with respect to female members or leaders with respect to ordinary members, and these hierarchies often do derive from the religious views of the group in question.

Chapter 5

Civility and Stability

Wade Robison

For those who, as Hume says, found "government altogether on the consent of the People,"[1] it may seem that a constitution adopted by those it makes citizens provides a way to resolve all disputes within and about the body politic. A constitution is an artifact, of course, and so it may take a study of history to get the details right, or right enough, but, with the right details, with an amending process, and with a commitment by those to be governed, a constitution may seem the ideal solution for how the interests of the state and its citizens are to be furthered and how the inevitable conflicts between citizens and between citizens and the state are to be resolved.

A constitution is a decision procedure, after all. A constitution tells us how laws are to be made, how disputes are to be adjudicated, how even fundamental changes in the constitutional framework are to be achieved.[2] Consenting to this complex decision procedure is supposed to ensure citizens stability.[3] Conflicts are to be resolved civilly, within the constitutional framework—either by appealing to the constitution itself or by appealing to the conditions of their consent. Or so the story goes.

But, a constitution is a contingent arrangement, its acceptance, when it is the explicit foundation of a government, contingent on conditions of compromise between what may be deeply competing interests, conditions that put at risk the supposed advantage of having an adopted constitution. In addition, being contingent arrangements, set within particular and differing social settings, constitutions may have effects not readily foreseeable—effects that may require fundamental changes in a constitution's arrangement of the political framework and that yet may not be possible within the constitutional framework without unsettling the compromise that led to its adoption. We shall see this situation in regard to the United States Constitution and slavery.

Tensed Constitutional Orders

Hume's theoretical attack on the doctrine of consent is well known. As he puts it, "The obligation to allegiance being of like force and authority with the obligation to fidelity, we gain nothing by resolving the one into the other."[4] But, he argues as well, the doctrine faces a practical as well as a theoretical difficulty: "Were one to choose a period of time, when the people's consent was the least regarded in public transactions, it would be precisely on the establishment of a new government. In a settled constitution, their inclinations are often consulted; but, during the fury of revolutions, conquests, and public convulsions, military force or political craft usually decides the controversy."[5] When we look at cases such as the Glorious Revolution of 1688 "where consent may seem to have taken place," he says, it was commonly so irregular, so confined, or so much intermixed either with fraud or violence, that it cannot have any great authority.[6]

In short, Hume argues, the doctrine that government is founded "altogether on the consent of the People" faces two insurmountable difficulties, one theoretical and one practical. But, founding a political order on consent faces a third problem. If a constitution is to be successful and to survive as the founding instrument of a continuing political order, it must either itself resolve any deep tensions that have or can split the body politic or provide a decision procedure that will lead to such resolutions. Yet, to paraphrase Hume, there could hardly be a worse time for creating a constitution than when it is needed to settle the sorts of deep disputes that might be thought to make a constitution desirable. When a state is unsettled by revolution, the conquest of one of its parts by another, or by "public convulsions," fastening upon a constitution would seem more likely to produce the appearance than the reality of stability. In such situations, which party is likely to give up or compromise its deeply held interests for the sake of the interests of another party or of the common good? Even if a people's consent were regular, universal, and free of fraud and violence, the constitution adopted is not likely itself to resolve the deep competing interests that gave rise to its perceived need.[7] It is far more likely to embed them, producing a new political order tensed by those conflicting interests.

Not all tensions are destructive. The tension in the American political system regarding whether it is founded on states or individuals, a tension that gave rise to the Great Compromise of the Constitutional Convention in which states are represented in the Senate, citizens in the House, is arguably a constructive tension. But, the Great Compromise was a solution to competing interests—a way of resolving the conflict—and when a constitution embeds rather than resolves a conflict, and the conflict reflects deeply compelling as well as competing interests, it is purely a contingent question whether a constitution can provide a way of resolving the conflict without the order founded on that constitution being overturned. But, the very conditions Hume argues make consent less than universal and regular also make it likely that a constitution will embed within the constitutional framework a destructive tension that has no easy resolution.

Hume argues that stability within a constitutional order is achieved not through the consent of the governed, but, "as human society is in perpetual flux, one man every hour going out of the world, another coming in, through the new blood conform[ing] themselves to the established constitution, and nearly follow[ing] the path which their fathers, treading in the footsteps of theirs, . . . marked out to them."[8] How such conformation either leads to or justifies allegiance is an intriguing question, raising the issue of how conforming to something creates and justifies it as a norm. Whatever the answer, one condition of such conformity being possible is that there be a stable political system.[9]

Stability can be achieved, however, only if the constitution both provides a decision procedure for handling the inevitable conflicts within a system and finesses, in some way, whatever conditions of potential conflict existed when the constitution was adopted so that they do not come to plague continuously the body politic. For instance, the disparity between the populations of the North and South in the United States at the time of the Constitutional Convention and the foreseeable future was a potential source of conflict and was finessed by the three-fifths rule. The South feared alliance with a set of free states that would both outnumber them, because of the Northwest Ordinance, and outweigh them in population. The former would give the North a majority in the Senate, the latter in the House. Counting each slave as three-fifths of a person would increase the South's representation in the House to a point where they could not be outvoted for major legislation, at least, like the adoption of an amendment, and would be acceptable to the North, or so it was argued, because it was assumed that taxation for federal purposes would be "by the head," and each slave would thus be a source of revenue for the whole, decreasing the contribution otherwise needed from the Northern states.[10]

Yet, even had the process of adoption been regular, universal, and fair in the various states, the Constitution would not have been adopted without some such way of ensuring relative equality between the North and South in Congress—without, more generally, some way of ensuring that over time any political stresses produced by disparities would not fracture the system irrevocably. Or, to make a weaker claim, but one still strong enough for my purposes, a constitution, however adopted, would have failed to take over time, fail to become a founding document of a relatively enduring government, if it did not somehow finesse such deep divisions within the body politic. But, the conditions that make a constitution desirable as a means out of an impasse contribute to deep problems being submerged, not solved, by adopting a constitution, to resurface sometime later to sink the system.

The creation of the U.S. Constitution was somewhat unique in that it was not precipitated by any great internal convulsions or external threats. The creation of the French constitution after the Revolution seems more typical, and the result is that that constitution was anything but revolutionary. Instead, it further entrenched the sort of authoritarian system that was overthrown.[11] But, even the U.S. Constitution did not succeed. It, rather, submerged a deep source of tension that slowly worked its way to the surface, resulting in the Civil War. Examining it will be instructive as to the relations between civility and stability. For, the original Constitution contained within it such tensions between competing interests, without a constitutional means of resolution, that it gave rise to the Civil War. But, we must first get clear on the levels of constitutional appeal if we are to understand how it is that the Constitution failed to provide the resources to resolve the issue of slavery.

Constitutional Disputes

Suppose you are a lawyer arguing before a federal court regarding an issue in which the meaning of a statute is of paramount importance to your success in a case. You are enormously advantaged in terms of the structure of the argument you give, and the subsequent burdens it imposes on your opponent, if you can plausibly up the ante away from the meaning of the statute to the meaning of the Constitution itself, either to one of its constitutive conditions or one of the conditions that made possible its adoption.[12] If your opponent can plausibly argue that the statute could not mean what you claim it means given the meaning of the Constitution itself or one of the conditions of its adoption, then, obviously, you will be on the defensive. For there are three levels of appeal within a constitutional democracy—not levels of adjudication but levels of argument or, perhaps a better metaphor, depths of major premise. First, we may presuppose the basic validity of the constitutional structure and the essential clarity of the Constitution's provisions. We might do that in questioning the consistency of legislative or administrative decrees with constitutional provisions, for instance. Such a dispute would be unproblematic for a political system, its resolution having no serious gravitational effects on the constitutional order since the dispute presupposes the order's essential validity and the clear meaning of at least that portion relevant to determining the consistency of a statute with the constitutional provisions.

Second, however, we might put into question the meaning of one of the Constitution's provisions. A case about affirmative action, for example, would presumably put into question what is meant by the Fourteenth Amendment's equal protection clause. We know that such cases generate a great deal of political heat, but they do so within the existing constitutional order. They do not put into question the order itself but, rather, presuppose the validity of the basic constitutional structure in questioning the meaning of one of its basic provisions.

But, third, the ante could be upped significantly—as high as it can go within the constitutional order—if we argued that the meaning of the particular provision depended on a constitutive condition of the Constitution itself or on the conditions of its acceptance. You as a lawyer defending a particular interpretation of a statute would thus be sitting as high as you can within the set of kinds of arguments created by our constitutional structure if you were to argue that the Constitution would not have been adopted had such and such been meant by one of its provisions or that the very nature of a constitution or the nature of this Constitution requires that a provision mean so-and-so.

The burden that puts on your opponent is that the case now involves what it is to have a constitution and, in particular, this Constitution. So, for instance, you might be able to implicate the equal protection clause, thus upping the ante to the second level, and implicate it in a way that raises the ante even higher by arguing that the statute at issue must mean so-and-so because the equal protection clause at least means that we live under the rule of law, where those who are similarly situated by a law are to be similarly treated by the law. At issue given such an answer is not whether the equal protection clause affords a justification for affirmative action, say, but what it is to live under a rule of law—under a constitution—the claim being, right or wrong, that equality under the law is a constitutive condition of having a constitution at all.

Such a move forces your opponent to the level of argumentation to which you have jumped. The challenge you have created can be met only by finding new premises of greater scope than the ones with which the original argument were met that, yet, still meet your claim about the meaning of the statute and that give a plausible interpretation of the constitutive condition of any constitution you have implicated.

But, your opponent will quickly come up against the limits of the constitutional order. If you have argued from the constitutive principles of all constitutions or the conditions of the adoption of this Constitution, your opponent will be hard-pressed to find a new premise of greater scope without pushing beyond the bounds of the constitutional framework and thus to putting into question the legitimacy of the argument itself. If a constitution is a decision procedure, among other things, for resolving disputes, then it sets the conditions for resolving disputes, and one condition that is arguably constitutive of a decision procedure is that it precludes appeal in making a decision to anything other than what it determines to be relevant. A duel with swords is a decision procedure that precludes one opponent's shooting the other to settle what is at issue between them.[13] The rule that tossing the dice determines the order of play precludes someone's claiming the dice as owner and going first. Just so, a constitution precludes arguments in resolving disputes that appeal to principles or conditions beyond its scope.[14]

So one wins, constitutionally, if the only option one's opponent has in a dispute is to appeal beyond the framework of the constitution. But, resolving a deep tension within a political system in such a way that those on the other side are left with no civil recourse can fracture the political system. The problem is well illustrated by the issue of slavery in the United States and the Dred Scott case (1857).

Dred Scott

The Dred Scott case raised, among other things, the issue of whether a slave was just property. If so, then an owner might carry a slave around the world, like a comb or a shirt, and the slave would remain a slave. Or did a slave have some other status, one that would permit a slave to be free upon entering into a free territory?[15] If the former, then Southern slaveholders could move into free states and continue to hold slaves. If the latter, then Southern slaveholders would need to worry about slaves traveling north to freedom. Neither option was politically viable. Northerners could not accept that their states could be home to slaveholders who decided to move north, and Southerners could not accept that their property could make itself free by walking north.

The Constitution met these competing interests by treating slaves as both persons and property. Slaves were treated as persons by the Constitution insofar as they were counted as three-fifths of a person for purposes of representation. Slaves were treated as property insofar as they were to be returned when lost—a euphemistic way of referring to the Fugitive Slave Law.

Dred Scott raised squarely the issue of what his status really was, claiming to be free because his master had taken him into the free state of Illinois and into the free portion of what had been the Louisiana Territory.[16] Whether the Supreme Court's decision needed to meet the issue squarely is a nice question. Courts always seem to find a way to avoid a difficult choice when they do not want to make it. But, in 1857, for reasons we shall not here explore, the Court made the choice, and it made the choice in a way that precluded further debate within the existing constitutional order.

In the majority opinion, Chief Justice Taney upped the ante as far as it could go. He made an appeal to the nature of the Constitution itself—both to its constitutive conditions[17] and to the conditions of its being adopted—and those appeals trumped all the other arguments and effectively ended all attempts to end slavery constitutionally. Taney argued in the Court's majority opinion that a constitution is between equals, that is a constitutive condition of contracts. But this constitutive condition gives rise, Taney argued, to a compound dilemma.

First, since a constitution is between equals, the U.S. Congress did not act constitutionally when it passed the Missouri Compromise, because that legislative act took away from those states that would be formed from the Louisiana Territory the power to declare for themselves whether to be slave or free. The Missouri Compromise decreed that a portion of the territory would be free and that another portion would be slave. But, such a law was unconstitutional because the new states formed in accordance with that legislation would not be equal to the old states in all their powers. The original states had the power to determine for themselves whether to be slave or free. It was that power which Congress was denying to those states to be formed from the Louisiana Territory. And Congress was, thus, relegating those states to a second-class status, unequal to the original states that formed the United States. So, Dred Scott could not have been made free by going with his master into the free portion of the Louisiana Territory because Congress had no constitutional power to declare any part of the Louisiana Territory free.

This portion of Taney's compound argument depends on the assumption that the original contractors to the U.S. Constitution were states—the thirteen colonies. But, suppose the original contractors were citizens, not states. The same conclusion follows—although for a different reason. Whereas the conclusion drawn from the equality of the states as contracting parties depends on a constitutive condition of what it is to have a contract, the argument Taney sketches—were the contractors citizens—depends on some assumptions about the conditions of the adoption of the Constitution: about what it was reasonable for citizens to have agreed to.

No one could expect anyone to agree to live under a constitutional framework that so arranged relations between the states that if a farmer took a load of tobacco from Virginia to Maryland to sell, the tobacco and the wagon and team of horses ceased to be the farmer's property as soon as the farmer crossed the state line. Just so, no one could expect anyone to agree to a constitutional framework that meant that if the farmer took some of his slaves to help with the unloading of the tobacco, they became free as soon as they crossed into Maryland—ceasing to be the farmer's property. To agree to such a constitutional arrangement would be to license slaves to make themselves free by going north. The consequence would have been chains for the slaves and difficulties for the slaveholders both in maintaining and in using their slaves, difficulties we can reasonably presume they would not willingly bear.

The Fifth Amendment protection against the taking of property without due compensation and the constitutional provision that gave rise to the Fugitive Slave Law were read by the Southerners, on this argument, as a commitment by the other states and by the federal government not to pass legislation that would make slaves free if they went into free states or free territory.[18] It was, thus, a practical condition of the American political system's ever having come into existence through the consent of those individuals who were to be governed by it that precluded Dred Scott from being made free merely by crossing into a free state or a free territory. Even if

Congress could make part of the Louisiana Territory free—even if the Missouri Compromise were constitutional, that is—Scott would not have been made free by coming into it.

Taney's compound dilemma is powerful—with implications that reverberated through the constitutional framework, and so through the political system, far beyond Dred Scott. For instance, if Congress has no power to regulate slavery and freedom in the states, as it tried to do in the Missouri Compromise, was the Northwest Ordinance constitutional? It was agreed to before the Constitution was adopted but made one of the first acts of the First Congress. It took away from the states formed from what was New York and Pennsylvania, among others, the power to decide for themselves to be slave or free.

What we see in this case is one of the fundamental implications of having a constitutional democracy. Having adopted a constitution, a people are bound by its provisions and are likewise bound to settle any disputes that may arise out of it in accordance with the procedures for the settlement of disputes laid out in that constitution. If a people decide that some of the original provisions are troublesome and need to be changed, or that additions need to be made to the original frame, the constitution itself states the conditions necessary and sufficient, and a people are constrained by those conditions. Otherwise, they would change the constitution extraconstitutionally, and that would mean that they had decided not to abide by the constitution and were, to that extent, no longer functioning in a constitutional democracy.

But, when the constitution of a people contains a provision or set of provisions that cannot be changed constitutionally, the only recourse is extraconstitutional. If the provisions are of high moment, rending the body politic, what must follow are not acts of civil disobedience, but acts outside the constitutional order: of refusal in the face of constitutionally founded requirements; of uncivil terror, such as John Brown's raid on Harpers Ferry; or of uncivil war, even if called a Civil War.

What Is an Abolitionist to Do?

We can better understand how such results follow by imagining ourselves just before the Civil War in the position of abolitionists concerned to find a peaceful resolution of the moral crisis that was judged to plague the body politic. What are our options?

In 1842, the Supreme Court ruled in *Prigg v. Pennsylvania*[19] that state legislatures had no jurisdiction over fugitive slaves, declaring the issue a federal matter immune from action by any state legislation. In 1856, when that was the only relevant ruling on the issue, an abolitionist had several options, since it would be arguable that the Constitution, despite recognizing slavery, implicitly if not explicitly also foresaw slavery's end in its provision to end the slave trade and, so, undermined slavery in the presumed commitment to furthering the principles of the Declaration of Independence. An abolitionist could appeal to a plausible reading of the Constitution and make that appeal to the federal judiciary or Congress or to a state judiciary—the executives of federal and state governments having little or no constitutional powers to affect the issue of slavery one way or the other.

But, Dred Scott changed the configuration of options.[20] It cut from the constitutional avenues for change the two federal institutions with any real power to effect change. The Supreme Court declared that Congress had no power to regulate the scope of slavery in the nation, and it made its own position clear. No appeal to the Supreme Court was going to succeed. That still left the state judiciaries, but in 1859 the Court declared in two cases that state judiciaries had no more power over the slavery issue than state legislatures.

The only constitutionally founded avenues of change left were the executive branches of the state and federal governments, the amending process, and the hope that the Court would see the error of its ways. But, it was not likely that the Court would change its views anytime soon. After all, when the issue is as momentous as that before the Court in Dred Scott, where the Court can—or, perhaps, must—choose between two competing and mutually incompatible visions of how the constitutional tensions are to work themselves out, it would require a revolution in the Court's thinking about the nature of the Constitution for a different decision to come about. Such a revolution would, in addition, have to meet the practical objections that the Court would have to declare itself mistaken in declaring an important Act of Congress unconstitutional and, more important, mistaken in having given one faction's vision precedence over the other's. The political complications boggle the imagination.

Appealing to the executives of the states or the United States would be ineffectual. Neither had been ruled unable to change slavery, but neither had any obvious constitutional power by which they could act—which partly explains Lincoln's use of the War Powers Clause to issue the Emancipation Proclamation during the Civil War.

So that leaves only the amending process. But, an amendment requires the agreement of three-fifths of the states, and the free and slave states had been in lockstep since the Constitution's adoption, the distribution of their numbers and the Southern power in Congress ensuring no real possibility of there ever being enough free states to gain the necessary three-fifths of all the states. So, changing the Dred Scott decision through the amending process was not a real possibility in 1859 or any time in even the very distant future.

By 1859, an abolitionist could not be civilly disobedient except with a resigned and unrealistic hope that Southerners would eventually change their views. No real possibility of changing the constitutional structure existed. An abolitionist who chose disobedience thus had no choice but an uncivil disobedience,[21] justified by an appeal beyond the Constitution. The constitutional arrangement precluded any chance of change, provided that the Southern states maintained their unified opposition. In short, the conditions imposed by the Southern states in their agreement to form a union had the effect intended. The disproportionate power of the Southern states in Congress was effective in forestalling any legislation limiting the rights of slaveholders. The pressures for change found no constitutional outlet, and the Civil War was the result.

The Tensions

As the Dred Scott case illustrates, when a constitution contains such deep tensions that working them out puts those on either side in the position of trying to trump the other by appealing to the Constitution itself—to its constitutive conditions or to the reasons for its adoption—and those conditions themselves mirror the original tensions, there can be no ready constitutional way out of this impasse. It is not a necessary truth that those tensions will work themselves out of their constitutional bounds and create a crisis that cannot be met constitutionally any more than it is a necessary truth that tensions in a marriage must break through the bonds of matrimony and sever the relationship. But, as the American experience shows, deep tensions in a system will find a resolution, and they can work themselves out in ways that are destructive of the body politic.

We can illustrate the point through the modern example of the Canadian experience with the Meech Accord. That was a framework for changing the essential constitutional order of Canada so that it would recognize and give special constitutional powers and privileges to Quebec, on the ground that it was a distinct society. The accord required unanimity of the provinces for adoption, and a deadline was set, which several provinces failed to meet. The reason for that failure is pertinent to the point I am making.

A Native American representative in one of the western provinces argued that if Quebec deserved special constitutional treatment as a distinct society, then Native Americans certainly deserved special constitutional treatment. He filibustered in the provincial legislature until the deadline passed. If he had not caused the failure, others would have. It would have been only a matter of time before other Native Americans would have raised the issue of whether their societies were distinct, too. It can certainly be argued with some cogency that Inuit form a distinct society, and if the distinctness of a society is the measure of special constitutional treatment, then granting Quebec special treatment without granting it to the Inuit would be patently unfair. Native Americans in Canada would take the high moral ground whether they had constitutional grounds or not.

The pressure to change a constitutional arrangement in which Quebec alone had special constitutional status would be immense. Either such an arrangement would have to be changed to provide special powers and privileges for other special Canadian societies, such as the Inuit, or the fabric of the civil society would begin to tear as the tensions produced by claims for special powers and privileges began to play through the system, exacerbated, as they no doubt would be, by the unwillingness of the Quebecois to allow other groups to claim the distinct powers and privileges that were meant to mark them out as a special group in Canada. Whether the Canadian constitutional system could handle such stresses without a complete fracture is a good question. But, the tensions in the system are so immense that it is not hard to predict that the issues are going to be raised yet again. The matter seems so deeply divisive and, yet, so central to the Canadian system that it will not take much for it to arise again, blotting out everything else on the political horizon. Indeed, the recent treaty the Canadian government has signed with West Coast Indians giving them legal rights over a large body of land in British Columbia has raised the issue. Opponents argue that "the treaty fundamentally alters the constitution and endangers the country's delicate unity by allowing the Indians a level of self-government denied to French-speaking separatists in Quebec."[22]

The Meech Accord contained the seeds of its own destruction, and the destruction worked itself out in the adoption process. But, it is unclear how the problem can be finessed, how it can be settled constitutionally in a way that meets satisfactorily, in the long term, the competing interests involved. Canada is obviously not unique among modern states in having deep tensions beneath what might appear to be a placid constitutional surface.

Conclusion

The American experience, perhaps more than the Canadian, illustrates the general point I am making. The conditions that made the adoption of the Constitution possible were just the conditions that led to an uncivil resolution to the problem of slavery. Taney's argument is on the point in that regard, at least. Southern states would not have agreed to a union without constitutional provisions that protected their interests: the three-fifths rule for counting slaves, the requirement of three-fifths of the states for a constitutional amendment, the Fifth Amendment, the guarantee of a fugitive slave law and of its control by the federal—not state—governments, and so on. All these features, so essential to the adoption of the Constitution, created a stalemate. There was no constitutional way to resolve the impasse between those who held that slaves should be free and those who held slaves. Or, more accurately, the only ways to resolve the issue constitutionally, deciding either for the one or the other, left those who had lost with no constitutional or practical means of redress.

The point is quite general. When there is the most need for a constitution—to provide for a civil resolution of strife that is pulling a people apart, as in Bosnia or Kosova—the constitution produced is likely to mirror the conditions that led to the strife. Otherwise, it would not be adopted. Parties so willing to go to war to see their interests furthered are not likely to give up those interests in a constitution adopted to allow for a civil resolution of the problem. A people with deeply competing interests are likely to adopt a constitution that mirrors those competing interests, each side jockeying for advantage as they look forward to living together and resolving their disputes civilly. Each side has every reason to try to provide for constitutional provisions that will serve its interests well, and the best that either side can hope for is that a constitutional formula can be found that allows the other party to accept the constitutional order while containing those provisions that allow for it to at least sustain, if not further, its interests.

The Constitution's three-fifths rule, as explained by Madison, is a model for understanding the very best sort of constitutional provision. The provision serves both parties well, giving the South increased representation while lifting, or so he claimed, some of the tax burden from the North. Each party to the dispute about how to count slaves thus gains, and a single resolution thus serves the interests of both. Neither has reason to reject the Constitution because of that provision since both gain by it. But, that provision embeds slavery into the constitutional framework in a way that makes it impossible to eradicate without changing the balance of power in Congress.[23]

Any constitutional framework that everyone who must live under it would agree to is likely to replicate existing tensions. If it did not, that would mean the disputing parties reached agreement on how to create a peaceable kingdom. In the midst of strife, that is improbable. But, in situations where disputing parties need a constitution, the rifts are likely to be too deep, the tensions too high, the interests too different and too important for the disputing parties to compromise. If a constitutional agreement embeds the existing tensions, then those must work themselves out in some other way. Since the justification for a state that rests on a freely chosen constitution *is* that it rests on a freely chosen constitution, there can be no appeal outside the established constitutional order that does not appeal beyond the rule of law, which is what the constitution establishes, and deny the validity of the original constitutional agreement, which is what presumably justifies the constitution. Such an appeal can have no constitutional status. But, as we have seen with the slavery issue in the United States, competing interests of great moment embedded in a constitution are not likely to be resolved constitutionally.

Notes

1. David Hume, "Of the Original Contract," in *Essays: Moral, Political, and Literary,* ed. Eugene F. Miller, rev. ed. (Indianapolis, Ind.: Liberty Classics, 1987), 466.

2. Like all artifacts, a constitution may contain mistakes and may fail to obtain the ends desired. I do not mean to be laying down the conditions for a constitution, or even the conditions for a successful constitution, but marking down some features of relatively successful historical examples.

3. It is one of the features of Rawls's theory of justice that those who are permitted into the original position have a capacity for a sense of justice. It is that capacity which helps ensure the stability of a system of justice. He thus says that "in agreeing to penalties that stabilize a scheme of cooperation the parties accept the same kind of constraint

on self-interest that they acknowledge in choosing the principles of justice in the first place." John Rawls, *A Theory of Justice* (Cambridge, Mass.: Belknap Press, 1971), 576.

4. Hume, "Of the Original Contract," 481.

5. Ibid., 474.

6. Ibid., 474. Hume's claim is that the procedures for adoption historically have not been just: they have been marred by fraud or violence. We should think, here, of the game of Monopoly. The rules for playing the game specify a set of procedures—throwing a die to see who goes first, going in turn, taking only as many steps as the dice show, and so on—and the outcome of the game is just, provided only that the procedure is marred neither by fraud nor by violence. See my "Monopoly with Sick Moral Strangers," in *Reading Engelhardt*, ed. B. P. Minogue, G. Palmer-Fernandez, and J. Reagan (Dordrecht: Kluwer, 1997), 95–112.

7. Such universal consent seems possible only when the parties to the constitution perceive that their interests have been met—to the detriment of the interests of those they oppose. This claim is based on the assumption that the likelihood of a resolution of deeply conflicting interests is small indeed.

8. Hume, "Of the Original Contract," 476–77.

9. Hume's solution will work, in short, only provided a stable political order can be achieved, and, I will argue, the very conditions that Hume cites which prevent consent's being universal and regular make it likely that constitutional stability will not be achieved.

10. See James Madison's No. 54 in *The Federalist Papers*, ed. Garry Wills (New York: Bantam, 1982).

11. See Gordon S. Wood, *The Radicalism of the American Revolution: How a Revolution Transformed a Monarchical Society into a Democratic One Unlike Any That Had Ever Existed* (New York: Alfred A. Knopf, 1992).

12. For a further discussion of these issues, see "Hard Cases and Natural Law," in *Law, Justice, and Culture*, ed. Andre-Jean Arnaud and Peter Toller (Stuttgart: Franz Steiner Verlag, 1998) 49–55. A constitutive condition of a constitution is one without which it would not exist. It is, I think, essentially contestable which conditions are constitutive, but among obvious candidates are that the constitution be public, that it be adopted by some means or other, that it delineate in some way or other the allocation of powers of a government, and so on. Among the conditions that make possible the adoption of a constitution are those contingent features that make any legal act requiring endorsement palatable to those who must endorse it. Among the relevant conditions for the adoption of the Constitution of the United States are those clauses ensuring slavery, such as the rule for counting slaves as three-fifths of a person for representation in Congress.

13. In the film *Indiana Jones*, when Jones is threatened by a heavily armed warrior in a marketplace, ready to slice him to pieces with a sword, Jones shoots him—thus changing the rules of the game the warrior apparently thought he was playing.

14. See in this regard *The Antelope*, 23 U.S. (10 Wheat.) 66 (1825).

15. In *Somerset v. Stewart*, 98 Eng. Rep. 499 (1772), an English court held that slaves transported to free nations became free. Scott's argument can be seen as extending the principle that underlies that decision to transportation from one state within a nation to a free portion of the same nation.

16. Don F. Fehrenbacher, *The Dred Scott Case: Its Significance in American Law and Politics* (New York: Oxford University Press, 1978), 239ff.

17. And perhaps to the constitutive conditions of any constitution.

18. Fehrenbacher, *The Dred Scott Case*, 24–25.

19. *Prigg v. Commonwealth of Pennsylvania*, 41 U.S. (16 Pet.) 539 (1842).

20. Fehrenbacher argues that the decision was not significant because it changed few votes, if any. It is not the measure of even political significance whether something changes votes. Dred Scott changed the constitutional possibilities and in that way was both politically and morally significant.

21. "Uncivil" need not mean violent. Some forms of passive disobedience are uncivil, not recognizing or relying on the constituted civil authority.

22. Anthony DePalma, "Canada Signs Historic Treaty with Indian Group," *International Herald Tribune*, 6 August 1998, p. 3.

23. Of course, one might argue that it would have been to the South's benefit if slaves were set free and given the vote. Then the South's representation in Congress would be augmented by the additional two-fifths of a person each slave would now add to the voting rolls. Of course, the likelihood of freed slaves supporting the Southern agenda is not high, and, as we know, freed slaves did not come to vote in any significant numbers until long after the war was over.

Chapter 6

Trumping Civilly:
Technique in Reference to Secession

Christopher Gray

Civility and Secession

This essay concerns incivility in the breaking up of countries. I argue that one particular technique, namely, trumping, is an uncivil way to accomplish such a break up. *Trumping,* as used by the court under study in this essay, means that one principle is given a determining role in a court's decision, while other principles are not given the same role in the same case. It is not always uncivil to trump others' arguments in order to achieve agreement. If a situation justifies civil force, employing argumentative force will be the more civil alternative, though some parties will go away hurt, resentful, and angry.

Yet, for situations short of violence in a public entity, civility has the sense of a convention; it is a cultural institution defined by schooled resentments, which are not the same as native hurts. In other words, civility occurs in the context of institutions that are *legal persons,* and civility in this context is not the same as neighborliness in regard to natural persons. In particular, the attempt to break up one's country calls for a special sense of institutional civility, since it is called for toward those who foster or who block the attempted secession.

Civility in that setting takes on a purely legal sense, such as attaches to the legal notion of good faith in tabling labor negotiations. Fostering the other's best interest in such negotiations is meaningless. Candor and sincerity have no place. Here, although misstating factual information violates good faith, failing to state facts does not, any more than does fostering deception about one's own values and interests. Truthful candor from a party about its ultimate nonnegotiable demands would be the most disorienting and deceptive strategy of all and most likely to serve as a deal breaker. The civility of keeping legal good faith means no more than seeking an outcome on which both agree, rather than refusing to seek or only apparently seeking an outcome. In fact, hypocrisy in negotiation stimulates long-term civic virtue when, for the sake of success, participants are forced to mouth and then show behaviors in accord with civil virtues whose ideals they despise. The pretenders must act as "good men" if only to achieve the limited goals of Holmes's "bad men."

In this sense of civility, negotiating in good faith is the sole civility required from federalist and separatist participants in the Canadian constitutional debate. And refusal to trump is its name.

The Supreme Court of Canada on Secession

Principles "trumping" each other is the key bit of reasoning in the unanimous and anonymous decision by the Supreme Court of Canada (SCC) in its reference case on Quebec secession in August 1998.[1] The court decided that trumping of one principle of constitutional law by another constitutional principle is not permissible. In the case at hand, the legal validity of a hypothetical, unilateral declaration of independence (UDI) was being decided, and the grounds for decision were a set of four principles in constitutional law. The outcome depended on which principle would govern the decision: federalism, and constitutionalism, in the federalist view of democracy; or minority protection in the separatist view. Excluding the trumping of one principle by another effectively determined the grounds for decision and, thus, the decision itself.

This decision affects the proper characterization of the rights belonging to one sort of minority internal to a nation-state. Here, the minority claims to be people of the province of Quebec, where the nation-state is Canada. The question whether they are a people, and what relevance that has, however, did not need discussion in order to reach judgment, according to the SCC's opinion.[2] The court decided that the province cannot secede unilaterally as long as the country negotiates, in good faith, the province's application to secede.

The court had been asked whether the government of Quebec could effect its secession from Canada unilaterally according to (a) the Canadian Constitution or (b) international law. Further the court had to determine, in case these sources gave conflicting rulings in approving unilateral secession, which would take precedence. If international law permitted unilateral secession but Canadian law did not, or vice versa, which law applied to Quebec's efforts? The court's decision on these questions has the following dimensions: (1) No UDI has legal authorization under Canadian constitutional law; (2) an expressed will to secede places a legal obligation on the federation and its members, and on the applicant, to negotiate a constitutional amendment regarding secession; (3) failure to negotiate delegitimizes either the secession or its rejection, depending on which party is recalcitrant.

The court's reasoning was based on trumping only in this part of its decision, the part in which it answered question (a): whether Quebec has the right under Canadian constitutional law to secede. To a preliminary objection that this is purely a political matter for citizens to decide, the court used different grounds to determine that this reference can be read down to legal issues. The court ignored trumping, as well, in answering its question (b), holding that Quebec has no more right to secede by UDI under international law than it has under domestic law.

On the issue in domestic law, however, the court reached its decision by invoking the technique of trumps. First, the court posited that there are genuine principles of constitutional law. They operate not simply as suggestions, but so as to impose obligations on citizens and governments. The court then identified four such principles: federalism, democracy, constitutionalism, and minority protection. Finally, it read off their features from Canadian constitutional history. The four principles *together* led to the court's answers, because no single principle could be allowed to trump another.

The decision's novelty should be recognized. It is fair to say that, before the decision, all parties and the public predicted the first conclusion, (1) that no UDI is legitimate. In fact, the federal party sought it, to justify a hard line with secessionists, and the separatist party sought it, so as to have an offense that could be used to stir popular sentiment in favor of secession. But few anticipated the obligation to negotiate, or the legitimation crisis that would arise from the parties' failure to negotiate, successfully, in good faith. That negotiation demand was new law.

The Canadian Constitution, as most others, contains no provision for secession, so it is not unreasonable to consider secession unavailable, even outlawed. The court recognized this. Few on either side considered that, at law, the demand for secession amounts to no more than a request for constitutional amendment. Fewer still thought that refusing this obligation would cast the issue outside domestic law and place it into international law, that is, as an issue of whether the applicant could then claim to be exploited and gain entitlement to seek its self-determination by secession.

Trumping

The civility of any technique on which such a significant legal surprise depends is worthy of closer scrutiny, to see whether it can carry that burden. The operation called trumping is a logical relation between principles and other types of legal norms, both policies and rules. The technique of trumping was given recent prominence in legal reasoning by Ronald Dworkin.[3] Dworkin initially defined *principle* in a broad sense that includes policies to identify norms that can trump rules. However, he also used the term in a narrower sense that excludes policy to pick out the norms that, being based in legal morality, can trump those based on legal expediency. In this sense, a principle and a policy can each control the decision, by serving as the determining ground for decision, because principles and policies are not incompatible with each other per se. By incorporation into the reasoning, however, either a principle or policy could lead to a decision incompatible with a decision based on the other.

Within Dworkin's theory, the relations among principles and among policies is different from the relation between either one of these and any other kind of legal norm. This is so because a principle or a policy can "outweigh" another principle or policy, whereas rules cannot outweigh nor be outweighed. When two legal principles appear to give different right answers, one principle must be selected to control the decision. It is to be selected because it "fits" better in expressing the best legal theory wherein both legal principles can be located—as well as all others that operate within that legal system. But, when one legal principle and one legal policy purport to give conflicting right answers, the principle will *trump* the policy with no question of fit or weight.

Once selected, the governing principle does not invalidate the displaced principle or policy, as a dominant rule does the subverted rule. The norm that the principle has displaced continues in force and is available for use in other decisions. The case at hand is not an exception to the displaced principle, as if the exception could have been included into a more complete statement of that principle. Instead, the decision in the case applies the governing principle fully and does not apply or affect the displaced principle at all. This logical relation is captured in the metaphor of *weight*: each principle has a dimension that is its weight, and with this it can outweigh another by reason of having more importance in the given case. Unlike trumping of policies by principles, and unlike the replacement of one rule by another, outweighing is not a type of opposition, much less a contradiction. It may be considered more properly as a deferral.

To express the logic of these relations, let P, with subscript b for its broad or n for its narrow sense, stand for principle; let O stand for policy and R for rules. Then, let T represent the operation of trumping, W that of outweighing, and S that of subverting or replacing.[4] Thus:

If $P_b - (P_n \cdot O)$, then (1) $P_b \, T \, R$; (2) $P_n \, T \, R$; (3) $P_n \, TO$; (4) $P_{n1} \, W \, P_{n2}$, (5) $P_1 \, W \, O_2$, and (6) $R_1 \, S \, R_2$

Dworkin interpreted the notion of weight to have a technical sense in jurisprudence in order to distinguish between how rules and principles function in the law. His purpose in drawing that distinction was to show that legal norms include more numerous types of phenomena than legal rules; legal norms also include principles. The purpose of this, in turn, was to undermine the logic of legal positivism, which, he alleged, once it was allowed to treat all legal norms as rules, could identify their legality with their "pedigrees," or authoritative formulation, and demand that these be shown by any pretender to legality. If a positive norm used in law failed to show this, the legal positivist could claim it to be an extralegal discretionary practice. In turn, Dworkin introduced the notion of fit to keep the choice between competing principles from being reduced to the same sort of extralegal discretion. The notion of trumping is a polemical part of his competing legal theory; in fact, trumping is practically constitutive of the notion of legal principle in his texts.

The civility of trumping by principles is succinctly stated in Dworkin's texts: rights trump policies. These rights are genuine rights, or what he calls rights in the strong sense. Policies are results of utilitarian calculus; they are social concerns or expressions of majority will. The succinct statement is fleshed out into a set of claims:

1. Principles in the broad sense outweigh each other, and rules do not. "The court weighs two sets of principles in deciding whether to maintain the rule; it is therefore misleading to say that the court weighs the rule itself against one of the other set of these principles."[5]

2. Principles in the narrow sense are different sorts of standards from policies. I call a *policy* that kind of standard that sets out a goal to be reached, generally an improvement in some economic, political, or social feature of the community (though some goals are negative, in that they stipulate that some present feature is to be protected from adverse change). I call a *principle* a standard that is observed, not because it will advance or secure an economic, political, or social situation deemed desirable, but because it is a requirement of justice or fairness or some other dimension of morality.[6]

3. Rights are defined by their immunity from being outweighed by policy. "It follows from the definition of a right that it cannot be outweighed by all social goals."[7]

4. Principles go to the very definition of rights. The concept of principles that "underlie" or are "embedded in" the positive rules of law, "define legal rights as a function, though a very special function, of political rights."[8]

5. Rights trump policies. "Most working political theories also recognize, however, distinct individual rights as trumps over these decisions of policy, rights that the government is required to respect case by case, decision by decision."[9]

6. Principles trump policies. "What is in question, in these cases [of the public's interest in disclosure or in justice], is whether the litigant is entitled to a level of accuracy, measured in terms of the risk of moral harm, that must trump these otherwise important and legitimate social concerns. That is a question of principle, not policy."[10]

The metaphor of trumping is derived from card games, where the card of a preferred suit wins a trick over the like-valued card from another suit, and perhaps over even higher-valued cards. To apply this metaphor to jurisprudence fully, the principle and policy might be seen as having equal face value. Thereafter, no matter how better supported the justification of a dismissed policy is, nor how beneficial its results, it cannot prevail over the justified legal norm of a different kind, namely, the principle that has been preferred to govern the case.

This relation also holds for the outweighing of principle by principle. To expand Dworkin's own example in the *Riggs v. Palmer* case of the grand-patricidal inheritor, the principle that no one is to be permitted to use the law to profit from his own wrong outweighs the principle that legitimate expectations are to be upheld. But no matter how well founded is the principle that wills are to be executed as written, nor how beneficial the policy that gifts are to be strictly interpreted in order to secure proprietary interests, they cannot prevail over the principle that no one is permitted to use the law to profit from his own wrong. That principle trumps them, even if its history is rife with cases in which it has been outweighed.

The SCC Judgment

The key reason in the SCC's ruling is an explicit appeal to the device of trumping between principles. This is how the court condemns the incivility of the UDI. The court excludes trumping as a way to discern which among its selection of constitutional principles is to govern the case. But the court does this as though this were unusual, and as though trumping would be the ordinary way to select among principles. In other words, the court does not leave trumping only as the way of selecting principle over policy, as does Dworkin.

1. First, the overall relationship among principles is set out: "These defining principles function in symbiosis. No single principle can be defined in isolation from the others, nor does any one principle *trump* or exclude the operation of any other."[11]
2. Next, trumping by one absolutized principle is dismissed, namely, by democracy over federalism.

   Those principles lead us to reject two absolutist propositions. One of those propositions is that there would be a legal obligation on the other provinces and federal government to accede to the secession of a province, subject only to negotiation of the logistical details of secession. . . . For both theoretical and practical reasons, we cannot accept this view. . . . The democracy principle . . . cannot be invoked to *trump* the principles of federalism and rule of law, the rights of individuals and minorities, or the operation of democracy in the other provinces or in Canada as a whole.[12]

   Notice, however that it is less the principle of democracy than two different applications of it that are maintained.
3. Then, trumping by only the competing principle is rejected, namely, by federalism over democracy.

However, we are equally unable to accept the reverse proposition, that a clear expression of self-determination by the people of Quebec would impose no obligations upon the other provinces or the federal government. . . . This would amount to the assertion that other constitutionally recognized principles necessarily *trump* the clearly expressed democratic will of the people of Quebec. Such a proposition fails to give sufficient weight to the underlying constitutional principles that must inform the amendment process, including the principles of democracy and federalism.[13]

4. Finally, it is held that the two principles are both required to govern the case:

> Is the rejection of both of these propositions reconcilable? Yes, once it is recognized that none of the rights or principles under discussion is absolute to the exclusion of the others. . . . The negotiating process . . . would require the reconciliation of various rights and obligations by the representatives of two legitimate majorities. . . . There can be no suggestion that either of these majorities "*trumps*" the other.[14]

This depends once again on the two settings off of democracy more than on that of democracy and federalism. They are what would, but cannot, trump each other. Nonetheless, this will continue to be treated as a setting off of principles, the way the court interprets it.

Trumping Constitutional Principles

The court's reliance on its rejection of this device calls for examination of at least the following points: (1) Are principles as such resistant to the trumping of one by another? (2) Are these particular principles less amenable to it? (3) Does the context of secession make them so?

(1) On their face, principles are not the sort of things to trump one another, so there appears to be a systematic category mistake here. As seen from the study of Dworkin, whose usage is the uncited source for the SCC's usage, trumping is what characterizes principles as distinct from policies, not principles as distinct from principles.

By leaving their reasoning without an explicit statement of what they take this novel device of trumping or its rejection to be, the justices have let it appear that these principles cannot trump one another. This is so because trumping is the only way they consider as to how one principle could prevail over another; the very idea of one constitutional principle prevailing over another is beyond conceivability. On the other hand, if they meant by "trumping" the relation of outweighing, this is eminently conceivable, as the two absolute propositions they reject exemplify. But these two, and trumping, are not rejected because the propositions are absolute. Instead, the absolute propositions are rejected because they trump each other. And, while trenching of federal and provincial jurisdictions upon each other have had their respective runs over a century, no similar history is available for trumping or its rejection. Why trumping is rejected is never stated explicitly.

(2) Perhaps these constitutional principles are different from other principles, so that no trumping can be made with civility among these four, while it may be among others. An initial unlikelihood for this possibility arises from the fact that few other constitutional principles are identified. Others are hinted at by the court's claim that its enumeration of principles is not exhaustive. But, considering the four "ongoing principles" throughout as a constitutional "architecture"[15] justifies doubt as to whether others could be fitted into the same order of building blocks that these are. The Canadian Charter of Rights requires courts to deal in what are often called moral principles, as inclusive legal positivism has recognized,[16] and the conventions recognized as obligations under the Canadian Constitution but not under its constitutional law are called principles in inexact discourse.[17] But these are not principles in an architectural sense. These four make up a unique set. They are, in fact, generated only now as a unique company. The court refers to few other statements of such principle in case law, upon setting these out. Only one, judicial independence, is mentioned, while only the principles the court regarded as "most germane for resolution of the reference" were the ones "underscored" in its decision.[18] Nor are any others suggested.

As well, none of these four principles is put into a verbal formula; but, while Dworkin does formulate his principles in early writing, his later examples, too, often escape formulation. In addition, none of them achieves unambiguous meaning in the course of the historical précis that is offered to confirm their presence in Canadian constitutional law. Of course, the court's historical sketch is not meant "to be exhaustive, but to highlight the features most relevant in the context of this Reference," and to show that "legality and legitimacy are linked" in Canadian constitutional history; that is, changes in institutions reflect changes in values, by methods that ensure "continuity, stability and legal order."[19]

Although not exhaustive, however, neither is the history very convincing in what it takes to illustrate the principles' centrality.[20] First, what the court takes to illustrate federalism is that the initial constitutional committee proposed a federal model. Without that form of government, delegates would not have agreed; federalism was a legal recognition of diversity to be reconciled with unity. Next, what illustrates democracy is that confederation was initiated by elected representatives, not imperial fiat; continuity in democratic institutions and the rule of law were emphasized in the constitution. Third, what illustrates constitutionalism is that the Quebec Resolution stated that official sanction would be sought. As well, an early attempt at secession by Nova Scotia was rejected by the Colonial Office; rule of law and stability were made the process for evolution to full independence. Finally, what illustrates protection of minorities is that French language and culture are protected. Further, certain religious minorities were given the right of appeal for adverse effects on their denominational school rights. And, 115 years later, the Charter reaffirmed commitment to protection of minority and aboriginal rights. This historical sketch is obviously banal and not the focused revelation of principles in the four formulations, which their centrality to the judgment would require.

Nor is anything different shown in the interaction of the four principles, which is even more essential evidence if the court is to demonstrate that they are inseparable. For example, federalism was considered the dominant principle at the inauguration of the Charter, but only remains a central one by the SCC in its decision, sixteen years later.[21] Federalism facilitates democratic participation by distributing public powers, and it facilitates the pursuit of collective goals by minorities. Quebec, Nova Scotia, and New Brunswick all affirmed their will to protect their individual cultures and their autonomy over local matters, by federating.

Democracy, a baseline not explicitly identified but simply assumed at confederation, was the reason for extending the franchise to minorities unjustly excluded.[22] Democracy is not concerned only with process, but also with substantive goals of promoting self-government and accommodating cultural and group identities. So, expressing the people's sovereign will must be taken in context of other principles: federalism means there are different and equally legitimate majorities, neither more or less legitimate as a democratic expression; it lets citizens participate concurrently in different collectivities.

Nor can democracy exist without rule of law as a framework to ascertain and implement sovereign will. For legitimacy, institutions must rest on a legal foundation; they cannot survive by adherence to law alone, however, but appeal to moral values, many of which are embedded in constitutional structure. Constitutional government, in turn, rests on public opinion, on negotiation to build majorities. Thus "a democratic system of government is committed to considering those dissenting voices."[23]

To provide "a stable, predictable, and ordered society" and "a shield for individuals from arbitrary state action," constitutionalism, or the rule of law, makes law supreme over acts of both government and private persons, embodying the more general principle of normative order.[24] The constitution is entrenched to discourage a majority from ignoring fundamental rights, and from ignoring the right that minority groups have to promote their identities against assimilative pressures. Political representation does not frustrate majority will but defines the majority to be consulted when altering those rules; this assures that amendment occurs through a process of negotiation, which ensures the constitutionally defined rights of all. In this way democracy is harmonized with constitutionalism: constitutionalism facilitates democracy by creating an orderly framework within which to make changes.

Specific protections of minorities, for example, minority religious educational rights and minority language rights, are the product of historical compromises.[25] But, though negotiated, these protections were principled: they reflect a broader principle regarding protection of minority rights. Recently prominent in Charter cases, the principle had a long history before that, even at the time of confederation. It is, itself, an independent principle underlying constitutional order, although the three other principles inform the scope of the provisions that protect minorities.

Treating these four principles as conjoined, while inspiring, and perhaps even cogent, is certainly not determinate enough to rule out selecting only one to govern the reference questions. Indeed, some judges who invoked one of them did not feel compelled to call on all the others at the same time. The principles came into play one by one, historically. Neither trumping nor the more proper device of outweighing invalidates or even diminishes the outweighed principle, as was seen.

(3) Our third question was whether secession is what is uncivil and, thus, makes these four constitutional principles indivisible from one another. Secession is defined as "the effort of a group or section of a state to withdraw itself from the political and constitutional authority of that state, with a view to achieving statehood for the new territorial unit on the international plane."[26] If one principle trumped—or, better, outweighed—the others, that would have rendered secession either unthinkable or a foregone conclusion.

As noted by the court, whatever else secession is, it would profoundly change the constitution of Canada. So profoundly, that it could well be thought to be impossible, and its proposal irreceivable, as it was in an earlier attempt: As the Colonial Secretary wrote in 1868: "The neighboring province of New Brunswick has entered into the union in reliance on having with it the sister province of Nova Scotia; and vast obligations, political and commercial, have already been contracted on the faith of a measure so long discussed and so solemnly adopted."[27] Political representatives of a province have "power to commit the province to be bound into the future by the constitutional rules being adopted."[28]

The court did not say what has changed since 1868. Certainly, it is not the reciprocal reliance of action in view of the responses that have been promised; these have only deepened in a century and a half, as the court recognized. Perhaps it is the diminished luster of sovereignty and the nation-state since the mid-nineteenth century. Perhaps the court felt compelled to do this because both parties had resisted allowing a court to consider a political question like secession, lest the court usurp the jurisdiction of a legislature or, alternatively, of a national collectivity. Whatever the explanation, the court chose to see secession in minimalist legal terms, simply as an amendment to the constitution. The act of secession "would purport to alter the governance of Canadian territory in a manner which is inconsistent with our current constitutional arrangements. The secession of a province from Canada must be considered, in legal terms, to require an amendment to the Constitution, which perforce requires negotiation."[29]

Once reduced to legal terms, what constitutional civility consists in becomes clear. The court rightly identified how constitutional amendment is initiated and how it proceeds under the law, although they gave no explicit references. Amendment begins with a political process undertaken pursuant to the constitution itself, by the initiative from democratically elected representatives of the participants to confederation.

Civility and Repudiation

Subsection 46 (1) of the Canadian Constitution states that "The procedures for amendment . . . may be initiated either by the Senate or the House of Commons or by the legislative assembly of a province."[30] Once this entitlement is in place, and its consequences are spelled out, indeed then "this imposes a corresponding duty on participants to engage in constitutional discussion," as the SCC stated.[31] A referendum, though without direct legal effect, would confer legitimacy on the efforts of the government of Quebec to initiate the Constitution's amendment process in order to secede by constitutional means; such a "clear repudiation of existing order and clear expression of the desire to secede would give rise to a reciprocal obligation on all parties to negotiate constitutional changes to respond to that desire. . . . The corollary of a legitimate attempt by one to seek amendment is an obligation on all to enter negotiations."[32]

This rationale for constitutional civility, using subsection 46 (1), is contained in the four corners of the constitutional document. But, that rationale depends less on the pillars of the four constitutional principles discussed. For those principles operate less to create the obligation of jural civility than to eliminate its antithesis: the arrogant pretension to constitutional absolutism, whether federalist or separatist. Trumping appeared, in turn, as an even less feasible relation among these principles than outweighing. Nevertheless, the high profile given to trumping as the category by which to resolve the question of Quebec today—or those of Prairie and Maritime provinces, tomorrow—is what elicited the court's study of the four principles and their capacity to trump or outweigh. The court's study of those principles clarified when trumping might be uncivil.

The same study of constitutional principles also elicited our examination as to whether the incivility of trumping can bear the weight of the argument laid upon it by the court. Both the court's discussion and that examination may prove advantageous for legal philosophy. Yet, neither is necessary for the resolution of the questions raised. Subsection 46 (1) suffices to resolve them, showing us that legal positivism can sometimes recover its glamour, even for natural law theorists. A straightforward positivist solution, however, would have been less generous in providing a footing for the treatment of constitutional civility, and for putting the body politic on notice of the need to avoid its incivilities.

Notes

1. In the matter of Section 53 of the Supreme Court Act, R.S.C., 1985, c. S-26; and in the matter of a Reference by the governor in Council concerning certain questions relating to the secession of Quebec from Canada, as set out in Order in Council P.C. 1996-1497, dated the 30th day of September, 1996 (indexed as *Reference re Secession of Québec*), (1998) 2 S.C.R. 217.

2. See it discussed by C. B. Gray, "People Who Need Peuple: Politicizing Categories in Quebec Secessionist Discourse," in *The Law vs. The People,* ed. Roberta Kevelson et al. (New York: Peter Lang, 1999), 169–84.

3. Ronald Dworkin, *Taking Rights Seriously* (Cambridge, Mass.: Harvard University Press, 1977); *Law's Empire* (Cambridge, Mass.: Harvard University Press, 1986); *A Matter of Principle* (Cambridge, Mass.: Harvard University Press, 1985).

4. Replacement is due to the implicit repeal of one rule by a later rule inconsistent with it. This is an application of the interpretative doctrine summarized as *expressio unius exclusio alterius,* itself one application of the principle of parliamentary sovereignty, since no legislature is to be taken to have disabled its future actions by its earlier action.

5. Dworkin, *Taking Rights Seriously,* 78.

6. Ibid., 22.

7. Ibid., 92.

8. Ibid., 105.

9. Dworkin, *Law's Empire,* 223.

10. Dworkin, *A Matter of Principle,* 95.

11. *Reference re Secession,* paragraph 49. Emphasis added.

12. Ibid., paragraphs 90–91.

13. Ibid., paragraph 92.

14. Ibid., paragraph 93.

15. Ibid., paragraphs 50–51.

16. W. J. Waluchow, *Inclusive Legal Positivism* (Oxford: Oxford University Press, 1994).

17. *Reference re Resolution to Amend the Constitution of Canada* (1, 2, 3), (1981) 1 S.C.R. 753, 125 D.L.R. (3d), 1.

18. *Reference re Secession,* paragraphs 49–50.

19. Ibid., paragraphs 33–34.

20. Ibid., for these points, see paragraphs 35–39 and 41–46.

21. Ibid., on democracy, see paragraphs 61–66.

22. Ibid., paragraph 68.

23. Ibid., paragraphs 70–77.

24. Ibid., paragraphs 79–81.

25. Ibid., paragraph 82.

26. Ibid., paragraph 82.

27. Ibid., paragraph 76.

28. Ibid., paragraph 84.

29. *Constitution Act 1982*, R.S.C., 1985, being Schedule B of the *Canada Act 1982*, United Kingdom, 1982, c. 11, Section 46 (1).

30. *Reference re Secession*, paragraph 69.

31. Ibid., paragraphs 87–88.

32. Ibid., paragraph 88.

Chapter 7

Liberal Neutrality, Public Reason, and the Religion Clauses of the First Amendment

Erik A. Anderson

Americans commonly think about the relationship between religion and government in terms of the metaphor of a "wall of separation." This metaphor leads political theorists and ordinary citizens to think that only two options exist when it comes to determining the proper relationship between religion and government: either we keep religious beliefs, practices, and institutions entirely separate from the institutions and activities of the state, a position known as *separationism*, or we allow the state to officially embrace and support the religion of the majority, a position that we can call *establishmentarianism*. Since establishmentarianism would allow the state to discriminate in favor of some religions and religious believers and against others, separationism is often touted as the only position that liberal democrats can accept. Thus Isaac Kramnick and R. Laurence Moore suggest that the only alternative to the "Godless constitution" they defend is one that recognizes that "the U.S. was established as a Christian nation by Christian people, with the Christian religion assigned a central place in guiding the nation's destiny."[1]

Kramnick and Moore's appeal to the specter of a Christian America as part of their argument for separationism reflects the overly dichotomous way of thinking promoted by the metaphor of a wall of separation. In his recent study of the Christian Coalition, Justin Watson unearths two distinct and conflicting goals that motivate the political activism of the Religious Right. One is the dream of restoring a lost Christian America through political and legal means—the dream of restoration—that rightly frightens Kramnick and Moore and should frighten anyone committed to maintaining a pluralistic liberal democracy.[2] But it does not follow from the illegitimacy of the Religious Right's theocratic dreams that separationism is correct or that groups like the Christian Coalition possess no legitimate

124

political aspirations that could be satisfied within the framework of a liberal democracy.

In her discussion of the conflict between Muslims and public schools in France, Anna Elisabetta Galeotti claims that what many French Muslims want is to be able to participate in public institutions without bracketing, privatizing, or sacrificing their collectively held religious beliefs, practices, and identities. They do not want to impose Islamic beliefs and practices on their non-Muslim fellow citizens; what they want is to be able to "appear in public without shame" *as* Muslims.[3] Watson finds a similar motivation behind much of the political activism of the Christian Coalition. In addition to the dream of restoration, activists for the Christian Coalition also press "demands for recognition," for an equal "place at the table in the conversation we call democracy."[4] They seek public recognition not only that "individual Christians" have the right "to enter the political realm," but that "Christians as a group" should be able to participate in public institutions and political debate "without . . . having to bracket their distinctive Christian qualities."[5]

I take this second political aspiration to be consistent with the institutional and moral framework of a liberal democracy.[6] The demand for inclusion and recognition within the public sphere as bearers of one particular religious and cultural identity among others is clearly distinguishable from the demand for a Christian America. Separationism, however, fails to mark this distinction. With its firm insistence on a secular public order from which all religious beliefs, values, practices, and institutions have been scrubbed clean, it treats the second and reasonable demand as on a par with the first and unreasonable dream of restoration.

Where the law is concerned, debate over the place of religion in politics centers on the Religion Clauses of the First Amendment. My concern in this paper is with the proper understanding of the Establishment Clause—"Congress shall make no law respecting an establishment of religion . . ."—which limits government's ability to *advance* or *promote* religion. Separationism champions an understanding of the Establishment Clause according to which government is forbidden "to put its imprimatur of approval on religion through any official action—period."[7] The separationist understanding of state neutrality rules out any state action intended to publicly recognize citizens as members of particular religious groups by, for example, providing public funding to schools and social service providers operated by particular religious communities and reflective of their particular religious worldviews.

As an alternative to separationism, I will defend a *pluralist interpretation* of the Establishment Clause, one that eschews both the strict public secularism of separationism and the hostility toward religious diversity of establishmentarianism. The pluralist approach is more congenial than separationism to claims for the public recognition of religious group identities. In the first part of this essay, I determine what both separationists and pluralists should recognize as a forbidden establishment of religion by interpreting the Establishment Clause in the light of recent debates about "public reason." In the second part of this essay, I enter a more specific debate between separationism and pluralism: whether it violates the Establishment Clause to include "pervasively sectarian" organizations that perform recognizably public functions—schools, universities, hospitals, social service providers—in schemes of public financial aid *without* asking them to bracket or suppress their religious character.

Neutrality and Public Reason

The U.S. Supreme Court has repeatedly declared state neutrality toward religion to be the goal of the Religion Clauses of the First Amendment.[8] We can say initially that under the Establishment Clause, state neutrality prohibits the government from passing laws that favor or promote a particular religion or set of religions. But the notion of laws that "favor" or "promote" religion is ambiguous and can be given a more precise meaning in at least two different ways. These two different ways draw on the distinction between the reasons or purposes for which a law is passed and the effects of that law.

The requirement that government pass laws only for reasons or purposes that are neutral toward religion expresses a notion of neutrality that John Rawls has called *neutrality of aim*.[9] Although Rawls voices some reservations about using the term "neutrality," he claims that it is possible for a state to pursue neutrality of aim. He sharply distinguishes neutrality of aim from what he calls *neutrality of effect or influence*. Neutrality of effect requires the state to "cancel" or "compensate" for any effects its institutions and policies have on which conceptions of the good its citizens adopt.[10]

Rawls is right to reject neutrality of effect, so conceived, because it is impossible to identify and control the myriad ways in which the basic contours of a liberal polity influence the religious convictions of its citizens. As he puts it, "social influences favoring some [religious] doctrines over others cannot be avoided in any view of political justice."[11] However, not all the effects that the liberal state has on the religious beliefs and practices of its citizens are as diffuse and unavoidable as the "social influences" to which Rawls refers. We can readily identify effects on religion for which the state is clearly and directly responsible. Moreover, we must do so. The question of state neutrality does not even arise where government actions have no clearly identifiable effects on citizens' religious beliefs and practices.

Since we are investigating to what extent the state may act in ways that benefit religion, we must identify the kinds of beneficial effects that state action can have on religion. There seem to be two primary kinds of beneficial effect. First, state action benefits or promotes religion when it has the effect of forcing people to believe or act in accordance with particular religious beliefs and practices. State actions that have these effects promote adherence either wholly or in part to a particular religion. Second, state action benefits or promotes religion when it has the effect of channeling some public resource such as tax monies or access to public facilities to religious individuals and organizations. State actions that have these effects provide at least indirect support to religious individuals and organizations in the pursuit of their religious ends. The question is whether laws and policies that have either of these two kinds of effect are consistent with state neutrality toward religion under the Establishment Clause, and, if so, under what conditions.

A closer consideration of neutrality of aim will help us to answer this question. Current debates use the notion of *public reason* to make sense of neutrality of aim.[12] A fundamental assumption of the idea of public reason is that reasons for political action that proceed directly from an individual's religious convictions are not publicly accessible, either in that they are unintelligible or nonauthoritative as reasons, to those who do not share them.

Champions of public reason typically contrast religious convictions with reasons for political action drawn from a liberal conception of justice. According to Rawls, a liberal conception of justice can be "worked up" from certain fundamental political ideas that are "implicit in the public political culture of a democratic society" without invoking the nonpublic reasons of any particular religious conception of the good.[13] The resulting conception of justice is supposed to be "religiously neutral" in the sense that citizens can accept it without having to accept any particular set of religious convictions. A liberal conception of justice—or as Rawls now puts it, the family of possible such conceptions[14]—is supposed to provide citizens and public officials with a publicly intelligible and authoritative set of reasons, values, and principles with which to justify their political decisions. These reasons, values, and principles constitute a society's shared public reason.

On this Rawlsian account, neutrality of aim consists in the existence of a justification in terms of public reason for any piece of legislation. We can use this conception of neutrality of aim to distinguish between cases where government actions benefit religion consistently with state neutrality toward religion, and cases where such actions violate this neutrality. Consider the first kind of beneficial effect mentioned earlier, where state action forces people to believe or act in accordance with a particular religious conception of the good. The requirement that all laws and policies possess a justification in terms of public reason rules out state actions with this kind of effect. State actions that force people to believe or act in accordance with a particular religion can be justified only by the view that the religion in question is, as Michael J. Perry puts it, "superior along one or another dimension of value than one or more other religions or than no religion at all."[15] But in that case, the government is guilty of violating the commitment to free religious choice that underlies the commitment to state neutrality. The government is expressing an official preference for one religion rather than allowing citizens to make such judgments for themselves, which is precisely the evil that state neutrality guards against.

Now consider the second kind of beneficial effect previously mentioned, where state action channels some public resource to religious individuals and organizations. Here there are two possibilities. First, the law in question might be justifiable in terms of public reasons and values. If so, then the law is consistent with state neutrality toward religion, despite the fact that it benefits religious individuals and organizations in its operation. It is consistent because, when state action benefits religion as the unintended consequence of pursuing some publicly justifiable purpose, that benefit cannot be seen as the expression of a state preference for any particular religion. Second, the law in question might lack a justification in terms of public reason. In that case, the law violates state neutrality toward religion. This kind of state action can be justified only by the view that the religion in question is worthy of being supported and pursued, which is once again for the government to be acting on the judgment that a particular religion is superior "to one or more other religions or to no religion at all."

According to defenders of public reason, therefore, state action that has beneficial effects on religion must possess a public, that is, a nonreligious, justification to be consistent with state neutrality toward religion. If this account is correct, we can formulate the principle of state neutrality implicit in the Establishment Clause as follows: the state is prohibited from enacting laws that (1) have the effect of favoring or promoting any particular religion or set of religions and that (2) can be justified only by the claim that the favored religion qua religion is true or superior to its rivals.

At this point, however, I believe that the public reason account of state neutrality toward religion requires an important modification. Gerald F. Gaus has recently pointed out that while we may be able to say that certain reasons, values, and principles are publicly justifiable among all reasonable citizens, they are only publicly justifiable when they are specified at an abstract level.[16] Publicly justifiable reasons, values, and principles are *underdeterminate*: they may exclude some political proposals as unreasonable, those that deny or are inconsistent with them altogether, but they do not determine which from among a range of reasonable interpretations of them is the correct one.[17] When it comes to resolving disputes over such controversial issues as abortion, euthanasia, pornography, animal rights, environmental protection, and same-sex marriage, citizens must defend particular interpretations of public reasons, values, and principles that are subject to reasonable disagreement. Moreover, these competing interpretations often and of necessity invoke controversial moral and metaphysical assumptions that are derived from citizens' religious and nonreligious conceptions of the good.[18]

The underdeterminacy of public reasons, values, and principles means that, for many political controversies, there will be no purely public justification for state action. In these cases, the justification for state action will be mixed: it will offer an interpretation of public reasons, values, and principles—such as the principle that all humans possess the right to life—that appeals to controversial beliefs falling outside what is publicly justifiable to all citizens. The upshot of this criticism is that, if the principle of state neutrality toward religion is to be workable, it cannot require the existence of a *purely* public justification as a necessary condition for acceptable legislation.

But, perhaps, we can rescue the public reason account of state neutrality from the perils of underdeterminacy. It seems to me that, even if the resolution of controversial moral issues requires citizens and legislators to stray beyond the bounds of public reason, we can distinguish between state actions that are justified by controversial religious interpretations of public morality and state actions that are justified by the view that a particular religion is superior qua religion to its rivals. The former kind of state action, while anathema to many contemporary political theorists, has played a large role in American political history. Indeed, as Michael W. McConnell points out, the claim that religious interpretations of public morality should be held to violate First Amendment principles "must be understood . . . as a proposal for a change in American political and constitutional culture—and a rather dramatic one at that."[19] Religious interpretations of public reasons, values, and principles are not claims about the superiority of particular religions to their competitors. They are claims about what public morality requires. And since the state cannot remain neutral on questions of public morality, we cannot prohibit the state from acting on religiously controversial interpretations of public morality. Only a bias against specifically religious beliefs and values would exclude them—and not their nonreligious competitors—from the democratic resolution of controversial moral issues.

Thus, we can reinterpret the public reason account of state neutrality toward religion as prohibiting only state actions of the second kind—those that can be justified only by the view that a particular religion qua religion is true or superior to its rivals. Examples of such laws are familiar from the history of societies with officially established religions: laws that channel financial aid and other public benefits to individuals and institutions solely on the basis of their religious affiliation, laws that compel or encourage church attendance, laws that grant a greater degree of civil or political freedom to the adherents of a particular religion, and so on. As long as we take this necessary revision of the public reason approach into account, we can continue to hold that the Establishment Clause prohibits the state from enacting laws that (1) have the effect of favoring or promoting any particular religion or set of religions and that (2) can be justified only by the claim that the favored religion qua religion is true or superior to its rivals.

Pluralism and Separationism in Application

Our discussion so far has proceeded at an abstract level. We have not yet considered how the Supreme Court should go about answering the substantive question of what constitutes state neutrality toward religion under the Establishment Clause. Let us begin by considering the separationist conception of the Establishment Clause. Separationists advocate a *no-aid theory* of the Establishment Clause, according to which "the Amendment's purpose was not to strike merely at the official establishment of a single sect, creed or religion, outlawing only a formal relation such as had prevailed in England and some of the colonies. . . . It was to create a complete and permanent separation of the spheres of religious activity and civil authority by comprehensively forbidding every form of public aid or support for religion."[20] Properly understood on the separationist view, the clause forbids "state support, financial or other, of religion in any guise, form or degree" and "outlaws all use of funds for religious purposes."[21]

Separationism holds that government violates state neutrality toward religion whenever its laws have the effect of channeling public resources to institutions that "teach or practice religion," such as churches, synagogues, and private religious schools. The no-aid theory also prohibits the state from mustering its symbolic or discursive resources in support of religion by, for example, displaying religious symbols on government property or by requiring prayer in public schools. All direct support for religious institutions, doctrines, and symbols must come from the voluntary exertions of the faithful; any benefits that religion derives from the state must be the incidental result of secular measures designed to benefit the public at large. Moreover, even incidental benefits must fall short of "direct public funding" of the "core sectarian activities" of a religious group.[22]

For separationists, religion is subject to a unique disability where state support is concerned. The proper baseline from which to measure departures from neutrality toward religion is the baseline of government inaction.[23] In other words, government is neutral toward religion to the extent that it does nothing to promote religious beliefs, practices, and institutions. Since any form of state support for religion is a departure from the baseline of government inaction, it is impermissibly nonneutral. It can be motivated only by the view that a particular religion or set of religions is worthy of adoption or pursuit, which amounts to an establishment of religion. On the other hand, the state faces no such disability where secular beliefs and organizations are concerned and can support them freely.

What can be said on behalf of the separationist conception of the Establishment Clause? To understand what I take to be the strongest argument in its favor, we need first to unpack the notion of "the secular" as separationists employ it.

Kenneth A. Strike has provided an illuminating account of "the secular" as it is used in American public discourse.[24] Strike describes contemporary religious pluralism in terms of people speaking different ethical languages. He claims that there are three ideal types of ethical language currently in use. First there are *Theological Ethical Languages* (TELs), which make essential reference to the existence of God or some other divine being.[25] Second, there are *Secular, Religiously Antagonistic, Ethical Languages* (SRAELs), which rest on the denial of all religious beliefs, provide "a fully robust view of the ethical and moral life," and present themselves as alternatives to traditional TELs.[26] And, third, there are *Secular, Neutral, Ethical Languages* (SNELs). A SNEL is a form of ethical discourse that seeks to abstract from the disagreements between the rival TELs and SRAELs in a certain political context. It is a religiously neutral ethical language—a form of "moral pidgin"[27]—that seeks to provide "the basics of a civil morality while at the same time allowing people to continue to accept their prior fundamental convictions and to practice the vision of the good life that is associated with them."[28]

Strike's distinctions among TELs, SRAELs, and SNELs are useful for understanding the argument in support of separationism. Suppose that we currently possess a fully adequate Secular, Neutral, Ethical Language, with which we can describe, justify, and pursue any of the activities that it is legitimate for the state to pursue. The state would, then, be able to accomplish all its important purposes—determining the scope and limits of citizens' liberties and providing public goods such as education, medical care, and social services—without departing from the reasons, facts, and values contained in our religiously neutral secular discourse.

If this is an accurate depiction of contemporary American society, and we do indeed possess a SNEL, then it would be a clear departure from state neutrality toward religion for the state to provide public support for viewpoints, activities, and organizations that reflect religious convictions. The state should not provide support for any viewpoints, activities, and organizations unless they are purely secular, in the religiously neutral sense, or unless their secular aspects and religious aspects can be kept separate from one another. Otherwise, public support would reflect an intentional decision to stray beyond society's shared SNEL and provide deliberate support for a particular religious perspective. Such a decision could only be justified by an explicit or implicit judgment that the religion in question is true or in some other way superior to its rivals, which the Establishment Clause clearly prohibits.

Thus, the argument in support of separationism depends crucially on the assumption that we have in our possession a SNEL that is fully adequate for all political purposes. I will contest this assumption. Before doing so, let me give a brief description of the pluralist alternative to separationism.

In contrast to separationists, pluralists embrace a *nondiscrimination theory* of the Establishment Clause. Pluralists argue that, with the rise of the modern welfare state, there is a substantial overlap in the function of many religious and secular agencies in the provision of education, health care, and welfare services. They hold that, whenever religious and secular organizations perform the same public functions, they are entitled to public support on the same terms. Pluralists point out that the activities of educating children, caring for the needy, operating universities, and running hospitals, nursing homes, or hospice care agencies, and so on, are recognizably secular or public in nature even when they are performed by groups in ways that directly reflect their religious commitments. The fact that an activity is performed by a religious group or incorporates a religious perspective does not detract from the underlying public rationale to support the activity. Indeed, the fact that these organizations reflect a particular religious perspective might make them more effective at reaching their target populations than comparable secular organizations, since some citizens may derive more benefit from public services that are provided in ways and in settings that reflect their deepest commitments and religious identities. Therefore, there is, in general, no reason why we should divide up providers of public services into the "religious" and the "secular" and support only the latter.

The pluralist conception of the Establishment Clause thus recognizes "religious perspectives as welcome and legitimate parts of our pluralistic public culture."[29] It does not recognize and support such perspectives and the institutions that reflect them *because* they are religious.[30] But, on the other hand, it does recognize and support them *as* religious, that is, without requiring them to censor, suppress, or mask their religious character as a condition for receiving public aid.

Pluralists argue that the proper baseline for judging whether a religious organization is entitled to public support is the "government's treatment of analogous secular activities."[31] The analogous-secular-activity baseline rules out direct public support for religious organizations that are not engaged in some publicly justifiable activity, but it ensures that religious organizations receive public support on the same basis as similarly situated nonreligious organizations. If a religious organization meets the criteria for inclusion in some scheme of public aid, then it should be included on the same terms as its secular counterparts. To deny public aid only to religious organizations penalizes them for being religious,[32] potentially reduces their effectiveness relative to their secular counterparts, and raises the cost of the services they provide. As a result, religious organizations become either ineffective or prohibitively expensive relative to their secular counterparts, which creates incentives for citizens to use nonreligious providers. Moreover, making eligibility for public funds or access to public facilities conditional on the "secularization" of an organization's activities creates incentives for groups to deny their religious commitments. Therefore, denying public aid to religious organizations on a nondiscriminatory basis skews individual choices *away from* religion, and this violates the goal of state neutrality.

On the pluralist approach, government violates the Establishment Clause when it supports a religious perspective or organization without adequate public justification or when it awards benefits to an individual or organization solely on the basis of religious affiliation. The criteria for inclusion in any public program must be nonreligious; they must not implicitly or explicitly include judgments as to the veracity or relative merits of any particular religion qua religion. The state also violates the Establishment Clause whenever it puts its symbolic or discursive resources exclusively behind the beliefs, symbols, and practices of a single religion or set of religions. But state neutrality is not violated when government opens public forums to the expression of religious views on an equal basis with nonreligious views.

What can be said on behalf of the pluralist conception of the Establishment Clause? The strongest argument in support of the pluralist conception rests on the denial of the assumption that underlies the separationist conception: namely, the assumption that we presently possess a Secular, Neutral, Ethical Language that is adequate for the justification and achievement of the state's important public purposes. I take this assumption to be false, and its falsity to provide us with good reason to prefer pluralism over separationism.

The falsity of this assumption becomes clear when we consider the case of public education. According to separationists, it is both possible and necessary for the state to maintain an entirely secular system of public primary and secondary education. Indeed, the core application of separationism has been to prohibit public aid from flowing to "pervasively sectarian institutions," a phrase that is virtually synonymous with religious primary and secondary schools.[33] But, this position is consistent with a commitment to state neutrality toward religion only if it is possible to conduct public education at the primary and secondary levels without straying beyond the beliefs and values of our shared secular ethical discourse (SNEL).

Can this be done? The most common strategy for designing an entirely secular curriculum is to omit all reference to live religious ideas when instructing students in history, mathematics, health, civics, science, social studies, and so on.[34] The question is, can public education studiously omit all reference to religious perspectives as live options for students' acceptance and nevertheless remain neutral toward religion? The answer is clearly no. The reason is that most religions have their own distinctive teachings on many of the issues that an adequate primary and secondary education must address, and these teachings compete with nonreligious treatments of the same issues. These issues include the origin of the universe and human life, the nature and needs of human beings, questions of public and private morality, and whether human history has some transcendent meaning, purpose, or culmination. Under separationism, state-supported schools can present only nonreligious responses to these questions. But for the state to put its financial and educational resources exclusively behind nonreligious answers to these important questions can hardly be considered neutral treatment of the religious alternatives that are excluded from consideration. If "the core notion of neutrality is not to take sides," then for the state to put all its educational resources behind one set of answers to controversial questions that citizens in the larger society address from a variety of religious and nonreligious perspectives is hardly neutrality.[35]

This criticism can also be stated in terms of Strike's distinctions between the different types of ethical discourse. To be consistent with state neutrality toward religion, a purely secular public education would have to address the religiously and philosophically controversial issues mentioned in terms of a publicly shared Secular, Neutral, Ethical Language, one that does not take sides on questions that are disputed by the adherents of different religious and nonreligious conceptions of the good. But as long as religious and nonreligious voices defend competing approaches to questions of "justice and injustice, human suffering and flourishing, morality and politics, economics and work, love and human relationships, the search for identity and the ways we find meaning in life," whatever nonreligious approaches the public schools present will be forms of SRAEL and not forms of SNEL.[36] They will not be *religiously neutral* approaches to the most important questions that a good education must address.[37]

The falsity of the separationist assumption that we possess a fully adequate SNEL is most evident in the case of public education, but the same point can be made in relation to the other major public services provided by the modern welfare state. Many publicly funded organizations and institutions must deal with areas of human concern that lie beyond the scope of religiously neutral beliefs and values or in relation to which those beliefs and values are radically underdeterminate. For example, hospitals must address religiously controversial questions about the moral and metaphysical boundaries of human life, and social welfare providers must address religiously controversial questions about what personal rehabilitation consists in and how best to achieve it. The areas of human concern that schools, hospitals, and social welfare agencies must address are closely connected to religious questions about the meaning, value, and significance of human life. If this is right, then the idea that the state can support these institutions only as long as they remain religiously neutral in their operation is untenable. Given an official public commitment to secularism, what is more likely to occur is that the demand for religiously neutral answers to these questions will be surreptitiously filled by answers that proceed from nonreligious perspectives that are antagonistic toward and competitive with traditional religion, rather than being neutral.

The separationist conception of the Establishment Clause holds that any intentional public support for religious activities or organizations biases individual choices in favor of religion, while an entirely secular public order is a religiously neutral one that leaves those choices unaffected. Pluralists argue, more persuasively, that in the context of the modern welfare state, the denial of public support to religious activities and organizations on an equal basis with nonreligious ones skews individual choices away from religion. Pluralism explicitly recognizes that many of the areas of human concern in which the liberal welfare state is involved have religious significance for some citizens. The operative principle behind the pluralist approach is that the state is neutral, or more nearly so, when it supports organizations with a wide variety of religious and nonreligious orientations and then allows citizens to choose which ones they will use. By allowing the state to fund a diversity of nongovernmental organizations, pluralism is able to eliminate the incentives to reject religious perspectives that would be created by an entirely secular public order. It is, thus, the superior alternative when it comes to interpreting state neutrality toward religion under the Establishment Clause.

Conclusion

I began this essay by mentioning the worries about religious establishmentarianism that drive many liberals to accept separationism. I hope it has become clear that separationism is not the only position from which one can oppose the use of state power to resurrect "Christian America." Let me conclude by mentioning one further advantage of pluralism over separationism. The separationist demand that government refuse to give citizens' religious beliefs, practices, institutions, and identities *any* public recognition reinforces an equally uncompromising reaction on the part of conservative religionists, who conclude that they must "take back" the government if religion is to play any legitimate public role at all. If the only two possibilities are for "a Christian people to have a Christian government" or for religion to be banished entirely to the private sphere, then each side rightly views the contest over the place of religion in public affairs as a zero sum game. On the other hand, if we were to fully implement the pluralist conception of the Establishment Clause, this contest would not be a zero sum game. Reasonable religious conservatives could rest assured that they will not be asked to suppress the most important part of their identities to participate in the public sphere, and citizens who are leery of conservative religion could rest assured that this form of public recognition, properly understood, does not herald a return to an oppressive religious establishment.

Notes

1. Isaac Kramnick and R. Laurence Moore, *The Godless Constitution: The Case against Religious Correctness* (New York: W. W. Norton, 1997), 13.

2. According to Watson, the "offensive agenda" of the Religious Right "is one of aggressively reasserting, through political and legal means as well as by persuasion, the public authority of evangelical belief and morality." See his *The Christian Coalition: Dreams of Restoration, Demands for Recognition* (New York: St. Martin's Press, 1997), 89ff.

3. Anna Elisabetta Galeotti, "Citizenship and Equality: The Place for Toleration," *Political Theory* 21, no. 4 (1993): 597–98.

4. Watson, *Christian Coalition*, 162.

5. Ibid., 168.

6. As Galeotti puts it, "no one should pay for access to citizenship by denial of his or her identity" as long as he or she is willing to extend a similar recognition and respect to the bearers of other particularistic identities ("Citizenship and Equality," 600–2).

7. Kathleen M. Sullivan, "Religion and Liberal Democracy," *University of Chicago Law Review* 59 (1992): 205.

8. In *Everson v. Board of Education*, for example, the Court held that the First Amendment "requires the state to be neutral in its relations with groups of religious believers and non-believers." This obligation to be neutral forbids government from passing "laws which aid one religion, aid all religions, or prefer one religion over another" (*Everson v. Board of Education*, 330 U.S. 1 [1947], 15). At the same time, this neutrality also forbids government from becoming an "adversary" of religion or from depriving citizens of "the benefits of public welfare legislation" because "of their faith, or lack of it" (*Everson*, 18, 16, italics omitted).

9. Rawls, *Political Liberalism* (New York: Columbia University Press, 1993), 192.

10. Ibid., 193.

11. Ibid., 196.

12. See Rawls, Lecture VI, and "The Idea of Public Reason Revisited," *University of Chicago Law Review* 64 (1997): 765–807.

13. Rawls, *Political Liberalism*, 13.

14. Rawls, "The Idea of Public Reason Revisited," 773–74.

15. Michael J. Perry, *Religion in Politics: Constitutional and Moral Perspectives* (New York: Oxford University Press, 1997), 57.

16. Gerald F. Gaus, *Justificatory Liberalism: An Essay on Epistemology and Political Theory* (New York: Oxford University Press, 1996), 165.

17. On the notion of "underdeterminacy," see Perry, *Religion in Politics*, 15.

18. The disputes over abortion and same-sex marriage are paradigm illustrations of this point. In the case of abortion, it is impossible for the state to avoid taking a religiously and philosophically controversial position on the moral and metaphysical status of the fetus. In the case of same-sex marriage, it is impossible for the state to avoid taking a controversial position on the relative ethical value of same-sex relationships in comparison with traditionally favored and disfavored forms of intimate relationship. For related discussion, see Michael J. Sandel, *Democracy's Discontent: America in Search of a Public Philosophy* (Cambridge, Mass.: Harvard University Press, 1996), chap. 4, and Philip L. Quinn, "Political Liberalisms and Their Exclusions of the Religious," in *Religion and Contemporary Liberalism*, ed. Paul J. Weithman (Notre Dame, Ind.: University of Notre Dame Press, 1997), 138–61.

19. Michael W. McConnell, "Five Reasons to Reject the Claim That Religious Arguments Should Be Excluded from Democratic Deliberation," *Utah Law Review* 639 (1999): 647.

20. Justice Rutledge, dissenting in *Everson*, 31–32.

21. *Everson*, 33.

22. *Rosenberger v. Rector*, 115 S.Ct. 2510 (1995), 2540; Justice Souter dissenting. Separationism has often been expressed in terms of the "*Lemon* test" for the constitutionality of a law under the Establishment Clause, which holds that a law must have a

"secular legislative purpose," a "primary effect" that "neither advances nor inhibits religion," and must not give rise to "excessive government entanglement with religion" (*Lemon v. Kurtzman*, 403 U.S. 602 [1971], 612–13).

23. Douglas Laycock, "The Underlying Unity of Separation and Neutrality," *Emory Law Journal* 46 (1997): 48, 70.

24. Kenneth A. Strike, "Are Secular Ethical Languages Religiously Neutral?" *Journal of Law and Politics* VI (1990): 469–502.

25. Ibid., 470.

26. Ibid., 480–81.

27. Ibid., 479.

28. Ibid., 480–81.

29. McConnell, "Five Reasons," 180.

30. As Michael W. McConnell points out, "When the government provides no financial support to the nonprofit sector *except for churches*, it aids religion. But when the government provides financial support to the entire non-profit sector, religious and non-religious institutions alike, on the basis of objective criteria, it does *not* aid religion. It aids higher education, health care, or child care; it is neutral to religion" (McConnell, "Five Reasons", 184).

31. Laycock, "The Underlying Unity of Separation and Neutrality," 48.

32. McConnell, "Five Reasons," 184.

33. Laycock, "The Underlying Unity of Separation and Neutrality," 54.

34. As Warren A. Nord has noted, the result of this approach has been that "in American public schools and universities students can—and most do—earn high school diplomas, college degrees, M.B.A.'s, J.D.'s, M.D.'s and Ph.D.'s without ever confronting a live religious idea." See Warren A. Nord, *Religion and American Education: Rethinking a National Dilemma* (Chapel Hill: University of North Carolina Press, 1995), 1.

35. Nord, *Religion and American Education*, 165.

36. Ibid., 209.

37. As Strike puts it, "when the state employs an ethical language in an authoritative way, and when that language is inconsistent and competitive with the languages spoken by those with traditional religious beliefs, the state offends those values that motivated the religion clauses of the first amendment" (Strike "Are Secular Ethical Languages Religiously Neutral?" 500).

Chapter 8

Regulating Racist Speech on Campus

Thomas Peard

The number of hate speech incidents on college campuses is staggering. One study found that "serious hate speech incidents have occurred on more than 250 American campuses and involve between eight hundred thousand and one million students each year."[1] According to the same study, one-fifth of minority students experience hate speech during an academic year and one-fourth of the victims face it more than once.[2] In one particularly egregious case, white male students on the campus of the University of Wisconsin followed a female African-American student shouting, "We've never tried a nigger."[3] This incident represents the kind of seriously abusive racist hate speech that I want to address here.

Incivilities may range from mere rudeness to repudiation of fundamental liberal values of tolerance and respect for others. Incidents involving seriously abusive racist speech could hardly be generally characterized as mere rudeness. Nor does it seem appropriate to treat them as conflicts between individuals who subscribe to shared metavalues of tolerance and mutual respect. Those who engage in abusive racist speech reject these metavalues, if not by virtue of consciously held beliefs, at least by virtue of their actions. It is this fundamental rejection of tolerance and respect for others that marks seriously abusive racist speech.

Indeed, this is one reason why the issue of hate speech regulation is so difficult for those of us who endorse liberalism. Individuals who engage in abusive racist speech rely on it to intentionally and brutally express disrespectful and intolerant racist views and attitudes. Regulating such speech, therefore, may constitute impermissible censorship of the speaker's views and this, itself, may be contrary to the liberal values of mutual respect and tolerance.

The liberal is then faced with the difficult moral question of whether regulation of racist hate speech on campus constitutes immoral coercion of university members by virtue of impermissibly restricting the speaker's liberty. This question, which I call the *liberty issue*, is the focus of this paper. The issue is an important one that raises the classical question of the moral limits of social coercion. This issue also underlies commonly raised objections to hate speech regulations on campuses, including the argument that regulation of racist speech inhibits speech and thought and frustrates efforts to achieve intellectual pluralism.[4]

In the first section of the paper, I outline and apply an analytical framework for addressing the liberty issue. In the second section, I consider objections to my analysis. The analysis I propose supports the view that regulation of racist hate speech on college campuses does not *in itself* impermissibly restrict the speaker's liberty.[5] This analysis has the virtue of being both systematic and derivable from plausible general principles of moderate liberalism regarding the moral limits of legal coercion. Despite the significance of the liberty issue, I know of no commentator on racist hate speech who has addressed it by providing an analytical framework of the type I propose—one that is expressly grounded in principles of liberalism. In the final section of the paper, I consider two general objections to hate speech regulation. These purport to show that such restrictions are infeasible or otherwise undesirable, even if they do not constitute undue coercion of the type addressed by the liberty issue. I argue that these general objections are not decisive and certainly do not show, as some may claim, that the liberty issue need not be considered.

The Liberty Issue

We are asking whether regulation of racist hate speech constitutes immoral coercion of university members by virtue of impermissibly restricting the liberty of the speaker. The type of regulation at issue is that imposed by colleges or universities which restricts the use of racist hate speech. We assume that such restrictions are enforced by some form of punishment, which may range from mild—such as censure—to severe—perhaps suspension or permanent expulsion from the university. The liberty issue asks whether regulation of racist hate speech through university or college rules or commands, enforced by penal sanctions, *in itself* constitutes immoral coercion. The expression *in itself* is intended to indicate that the specific form of the regulation is not at issue. In other words, assuming the form of regulation is otherwise appropriate, does the mere fact that the speaker is restricted from using racist speech impermissibly violate her liberty? This issue underlies general objections to hate speech regulation, which hold that all such regulations, however appropriate they may be otherwise, unduly restrict the speaker's liberty.

In addressing the liberty issue, I focus on regulation of *first-strike* racist hate speech, hereafter simply denoted as "racist hate speech." By *racist hate speech*, I mean speech that makes use of racist fighting words or nonverbal symbols and is (1) addressed directly to a minority member or a small, identifiable group of minority members,[6] (2) is intended to insult or stigmatize such individuals on the basis of their race,[7] and (3) is unprovoked and unanticipated. Racist fighting words or nonverbal symbols are expressions that, in addition to their insulting or stigmatizing content, must be commonly understood to convey, in a direct and visceral way, hatred or contempt for an individual or identifiable groups on the basis of their race.[8]

Under condition (1), the speech must be directed to particular individuals. Utterances do not constitute racist hate speech of the relevant type if, for example, they are directed to a large group or appear in writing that does not target particular individuals. Condition (2) ensures that the speech is motivated by an intent to insult or stigmatize the victim. Under condition (3), the victim cannot be blamed for provoking the speech or for failing to mitigate its effects beforehand by avoiding it. Examples of racist hate speech include the Wisconsin example mentioned earlier, as well as other examples involving actual utterances such as "African monkeys, why don't you go back to the jungle?"[9] or "Death Nigger."[10]

The preceding definition is intended to describe exceedingly abusive racist speech. My strategy is to ask whether regulation of such seriously abusive racist speech is unduly coercive. If it is, then according to the analysis I follow, there is little reason for thinking that less abusive speech may be regulated.

Basis of the Analysis

In considering the liberty issue, I will offer an analysis derived from Feinberg's well-known work *The Moral Limits of the Criminal Law*.[11] There, Feinberg argues for a moderate liberal position on the moral limits of criminal prohibitions. On Feinberg's version of liberalism, the only good reasons for criminal prohibitions are those stated in the *harm* and *offense* principles.[12] The *harm principle* states that it is always a good reason in support of penal legislation that it is probably necessary to prevent harm to persons other than the actor.[13] The *offense principle* states that it is always a good reason in support of penal legislation that it is probably necessary to prevent serious offense to persons other than the actor.[14] In applying these two principles, one must determine whether the harm or offense caused by the activity to be prohibited is sufficiently great to warrant its prohibition. Determining this requires, of course, that the importance of the actor's interests in engaging in the activity be considered. Otherwise, prohibition of the activity may cause more harm than allowing the actor to engage in it. Accordingly, the actor's interests promoted by the activity must be balanced against the conflicting interests of those who are harmed or offended by it.[15]

Feinberg's moderate liberalism, which we will incorporate into our analysis, is not only intuitively plausible but has been ably supported by him. Moreover, it is suited to the issue of hate speech regulation that we are addressing. Like criminal laws, to which Feinberg applies his analysis, the hate speech regulations we are interested in are rules or commands enforced by penal sanctions.[16] And, it is assumed that these sanctions are sufficient to coerce (some) individuals into refraining from engaging in racist hate speech.

It may be thought that university regulations are never truly coercive because one has a choice of universities. If a person chooses to attend a university that has a hate speech code, then she assumes the risk of having her speech restricted. However, this objection is based on a misunderstanding. We are asking whether, as a matter of social policy, university regulation of racist hate speech is unduly coercive. The analysis is intended to be universalized, subject to its assumptions. Thus, it applies regardless of how many universities regulate racist hate speech. If regulation of racist speech is permissible, then it is permissible for *all* universities to adopt such regulations.

The Analytical Framework

As we have seen, under Feinberg's principles, we should balance the actor's interests against the interests of those who are harmed or offended by the conduct at issue. I propose that, in addressing the liberty issue, the interests of the speaker who engages in racist hate speech should be balanced against the hearer's interests. On one scale of the balance is the seriousness of the harm or offense caused by the speech. This is weighed against the reasonableness of the speaker's conduct.[17]

The seriousness of the offense or harm is determined by (1) the *magnitude* of the risk of harm, if any, compounded out of *gravity* and *probability* of harm; (2) the *intensity* and *durability* of the offense, if any; (3) the ease with which the victim can avoid the offensive or harmful conduct; (4) whether the victim assumed the risk of harm or offense; and (5) whether and to what extent the harm or offense can be mitigated. Factors determining reasonableness of the conduct are (6) its personal importance to the actor and its social value generally; and (7) the extent to which the conduct is motivated by spite, malice, or the intent to harm or offend the victim.[18]

Following Feinberg, we understand *harms* to be wrongful setbacks to significant interests, such as interests in mental and physical health, intellectual acuity, and so forth.[19] *Offense* encompasses various disliked mental states caused by wrongful conduct.[20] The principal offended states of mind relevant here are shame, embarrassment, anxiety, fear, resentment, humiliation, and anger.[21]

Applying the Analysis

Principal *harms* that may be caused by racist hate speech include those resulting from (i) racial subordination, (ii) group and individual defamation, and (iii) breach of the peace.

(i) Racial subordination: Racist speech is a pervasive means for conveying discriminatory attitudes. It is a severe dignitary affront that may cause immediate emotional and physical distress and impair an individual's self-worth. In some cases it is an integral part of assaultive conduct. A single incident of racist hate speech typically causes incremental harm that builds on past discrimination and increases the victim's susceptibility to future harm. Racist speech on campus may also result in educational inequalities: intimidated minority members are less likely to participate fully in academic and extracurricular activities.

Richard Delgado has presented substantial evidence of the harmful effects of repeated discriminatory treatment that include psychological, sociological, physical, and economic harm, and even harm to the victim's children through the effects of racism on parenting practices.[22] Mari Matsuda cites studies indicating that hate speech can cause "physiological symptoms and emotional distress ranging from fear in the gut, rapid pulse rate and difficulty breathing, nightmares, post-traumatic stress disorder, hypertension, psychosis and suicide."[23] Matsuda further notes that to avoid hate speech some victims leave college, avoid public places, and otherwise alter their behavior.[24]

(ii) Defamation: Full consideration of harms caused by defamatory hate speech requires a theory of defamation that is beyond the scope of this paper. However, under standard defamation law, it is unlikely that racist hate speech typically constitutes provable individual or group defamation.[25]

(iii) Breach of the peace: Racist hate speech can both *provoke* the victim and *challenge* the hearer to fisticuffs or even more severe forms of physical violence.[26] Accordingly, such conduct may pose a significant risk of harm from breach of the peace. Delgado cites studies indicating that permitting hate speech increases the risk of violence.[27]

As commentators have observed,[28] the *offense* caused by racist fighting words is often intense and durable. It is varied as well and may include shame, embarrassment, anxiety, fear, resentment, humiliation, and anger.

In assessing the seriousness of the offense or harm—factors 1 and 2—we may find the disvalue of harms and offenses compounded. The total disvalue—the risk of harm plus the offense given—of an act of racist hate speech generally exceeds the disvalue of the harm or offense alone. For example, where the incident causes a setback to educational equality *and* immediate offense, the total disvalue of the act is greater than that of either addendum. Regarding factors 3 through 5: typically, the victim of racist hate speech does not assume the risk of the conduct, cannot avoid it, and cannot mitigate the harm or offense, for example by "more speech" or by steeling herself against the conduct.[29]

With respect to the reasonableness of the conduct, factors 6 and 7, the Supreme Court has recognized that fighting words are "no essential part of any exposition of ideas."[30] Racist hate speech has little to do with discovery of the truth; rather it impedes robust discussion and debate through intimidation of minority members. Such speech primarily consists in emotive utterances intended to express and vent animosity and to personally vilify the speaker's audience. Undoubtedly, the speech may have propositional content—often indeterminate—but the essential cognitive content of the propositions can be communicated without the use of racist hate speech.

It may be thought that racist hate speech has value to the extent that it plays a role in *emotive advocacy*—persuasion through the venting or expression of emotions and attitudes. However, the purpose of such advocacy is usually to weaken the opposition through intimidation, harassment, and similar means and, perhaps, to issue a rallying cry to others perversely motivated by the personal vilification of minority members. Emotive advocacy may allow the individual to avoid repressing what is shameful or sinister,[31] but there is little evidence of a social benefit from allowing speakers to vent emotions that might otherwise be expressed in violence.[32] Moreover, there are ways to reveal one's sinister side even through the use of racist speech that does not fall under our definition of racist hate speech. Although emotive advocacy also may be used defensively to counter advocacy of opponents, this has little bearing on first-strike utterances.

The social value, if any, of emotive advocacy through intimidation and similar conduct is low, owing to the risks of multiple harms such as racial inequality, divisiveness, and incivility. As Richard Delgado has noted, racist speech is a principal means for expressing discriminatory attitudes.[33] It is inconsistent with according even minimal respect to members of other races or cultures. Likewise, emotive advocacy in the form of racist hate speech deters efforts to attain a sense of community among university members. Furthermore, advocacy of this type is likely to be malicious conduct intended to harm and offend others. The reasonableness of such conduct must then be *further* reduced under factor 7 of our test.

The personal value of racist hate speech is also low. The conduct hardly promotes the speaker's interests in acquiring information or making considerate judgments—interests sometimes associated with the value of free speech.[34] Certainly, the speaker's interests in communication are implicated. But base impulses to deprecate others often play no significant role in the speaker's network of interests and may be self-defeating, as where the conduct results in debilitating guilt. There are extremists for whom such conduct plays a more integral role, but even this may be relatively minor. In any case, whatever its *personal* value for the speaker, the reasonableness of such conduct must be drastically reduced under factor 7. Further, any interference with speaker interests such as liberty and autonomy due to speech regulation is wholly offset by the speaker's interference with correlative victim interests. Finally, it would be unfair to require an innocent party harmed or offended by the actor's conduct to pay the costs of promoting the actor's interests, especially where the harm or offense is intentional. In such cases greater weight should be given to the innocent party's interests. Call this the *fairness principle*. Its applicability to racist hate speech requires us to give additional weight to the victim's interests.

In sum, the offense caused by racist hate speech may be extreme, and there is typically a substantial risk of incremental harm. There is also risk of serious harm, as where the victim is especially vulnerable to discriminatory treatment. On the other side, the personal and social value of racist hate speech is typically low and must be further reduced under factor 7.

The foregoing analysis, thus, supports the view that regulation of racist hate speech does not in itself impermissibly interfere with the speaker's liberty. The speaker's interests in such speech are relatively trivial compared to those victim interests that may be frustrated by racist hate speech. Additionally, the fairness principle applies, requiring more favorable treatment of the victim's interests. Thus, in the absence of significant empirical evidence to the contrary, we may plausibly conclude that the speaker's interests, rather than the victim's, should be put at risk and that regulation of racist hate speech in itself does not impermissibly interfere with the liberty of the speaker.

Before turning to objections, we should avert misunderstandings about the scope of our conclusion. We have been considering whether regulation of racist hate speech *in itself* constitutes immoral coercion of the speaker, independently of the form the regulation may take. It is possible, of course, that some types of regulation may constitute immoral coercion because of factors other than the mere prohibition of the use of racist hate speech. For example, a regulation may constitute immoral coercion of the speaker because it *unfairly* restricts the use of racist hate speech, say, by giving proponents of egalitarianism an unfair political advantage. Or a regulation may be unnecessary or ineffectual such that it constitutes immoral coercion by virtue of being a pointless restriction of the speaker's liberty. These results are not inconsistent with our conclusion. Our analysis assumes that the form of regulation is appropriate—effective, morally permissible—and asks whether otherwise appropriate regulation nevertheless constitutes immoral coercion solely by restricting the use of racist hate speech. In the two examples just mentioned, this assumption is not satisfied and the regulations are impermissible for reasons not addressed in the analysis.

The conclusion of our analysis is a significant one precisely because of the general moral concern it addresses. It is assumed or believed by many that any regulation of racist speech, however effective or otherwise appropriate, impermissibly interferes with the speaker's liberty to engage in such speech. The analysis challenges this view and indicates that moral doubts about hate speech regulation would be more properly directed to issues relating to *the form a regulation takes*, rather than to the mere prohibition of racist hate speech.

Objections and Responses

Three objections to our analysis should be considered. The first is that racist hate speech has *propositional* content that cannot be effectively conveyed through other forms of expression. Regulation of racist hate speech may, then, threaten impermissible content censorship, thereby limiting the liberty of the speaker and hampering the university's principal mission of promoting knowledge and searching for the truth.

This objection assumes without argument that the propositional content in question is individuated by its form of expression. Even if that is true, the *essential* propositional *and* emotive content necessary for robust discussion of opinions and ideas is surely expressible without using racist hate speech, as we have defined it. In addition, propositional content may be restricted where it threatens sufficient harm or offense. Spitting in another's face can be proscribed even if the conduct conveys an otherwise inexpressible proposition. Undoubtedly, our liberties include expression of disrespect.[35] But this liberty is limited by the harm or offense caused by the form of expression. Shooting another person in the kneecaps can be an expression of disrespect, but we are permitted to impose sanctions for this conduct.

The second objection is that racist opinions—not their forms of expression—are the principal cause of the harm or offense just described. It is claimed that racist speech without fighting words may be just as painful as racist speech that makes use of them.[36] For example, the utterance "You know what we'd call you if we weren't prohibited from doing so" may be as painful as what would be conveyed by using racial epithets.[37] If that is so, would colleges and universities be allowed to regulate all painful racist speech, even if it contains no fighting words?

This analysis does not entail that it is permissible to regulate all painful racist speech. One reason racist hate speech has so little value is that there are other ways to communicate racist opinions. If we also regulate "civil" forms of racist speech, those that do not contain epithets, we would more significantly infringe on the speaker's liberty. The preceding analysis, thus, does not establish that all painful racist speech may be regulated, only that which includes fighting words or racial epithets.

The third objection is that racial epithets are just words and that the best antidote is not to regulate them, but to repeat them until they become banal.[38] This objection assumes that mere words do not cause significant harm, contrary to substantial evidence.[39] Moreover, it is far-fetched to suppose that repetition of hate language by *members* of oppressed groups will always mitigate the harm caused by racist hate speech directed *against* them. The contexts and speech acts are wholly different. In addition, victims of racist hate speech could not be required to repeat such language; many would consider such conduct callow, humiliating, and demeaning.

Objections

Even if regulation of racist hate speech does not itself impermissibly violate the liberty of the speaker, it may have other immoral or undesirable consequences, depending on the form it takes. Such consequences were not considered in our discussion of the liberty issue. Indeed, some may hold that the liberty issue need not be addressed at all, because all forms of regulation are infeasible or otherwise undesirable, apart from that issue. In this section I consider two such general objections to hate speech regulation. My aim in doing so is the modest one of convincing the reader that these general objections are not decisive and, thus, do not render the liberty issue irrelevant.

First, there is the claim that hate speech regulation is *inequitable*. The objection is that any viable hate speech regulation is fundamentally unfair because it constitutes impermissible *content discrimination*. Consider the former Stanford speech code, which regulated insulting or fighting words "intended to insult or stigmatize an individual or a small group of individuals on the basis of their sex, race, color, handicap, religion, sexual orientation, or national and ethnic origin."[40] This regulation apparently constituted subject matter and viewpoint discrimination, because it regulated fighting words only on matters specified in the regulation.[41] It did not regulate, for instance, hate speech directed against bigotry. Egalitarians, thus, were permitted to use the most virulent language available to them to support their viewpoints while their opponents were not.[42]

This argument assumes that Stanford-style regulations are inequitable and skew political debate by taking weapons from the communicative arsenal of opponents of equality without a proportionate taking from the communicative arsenal of egalitarians. But, there is no showing that egalitarians have like weapons in their arsenal—those that cause substantially the same offense and harm. If they have no like weapons, then it is the use of fighting words hate speech that unfairly skews debate.

Moreover, the preceding objection may not apply to "hostile environment" speech codes that are based on Equal Employment Opportunity Commission regulations developed to protect civil rights under Title VII of the 1964 and 1990 Civil Rights Act.[43] Such codes would restrict hate speech that is so severe or pervasive as to constitute a hostile or abusive academic environment. The focus would not be on directly banning specific forms of hate speech, but on prohibiting conduct that uses speech to create a hostile environment.[44] Arguably, hostile environment codes would address much of the harm or offense caused by racist hate speech. Further, from both a legal and moral standpoint, such codes may not constitute impermissible content discrimination. For if they did, it is argued, the Civil Rights Act on which they are based would be morally and constitutionally suspect as well because, as one author states, "the categories and justifications of Title VII campus codes are drawn straight from Civil Rights law."[45]

A second general objection to hate speech regulation is that effective regulation can never be accomplished without unduly restricting protected speech. Such restriction, it is argued, may occur in various ways, including overzealous enforcement and overbroad or vague language that results in an undue chilling effect. A regulation may be drafted so narrowly that it will not chill protected speech, but then, the argument runs, it will not be effective in preventing the harm or offense caused by hate speech.

It is unlikely one could ever establish that *all* effective hate speech regulation improperly restricts protected speech. That would require a showing that such measures as careful drafting, cautious enforcement, and strict construction of the regulation are *always* ineffective in reducing the chilling effect on protected speech. Moreover, the objector has a dual burden. In addition to establishing the chilling effect of such regulations, she must also show that *in every case* the costs associated with chilling protected speech outweigh the benefits of the regulation in question. The general argument we are considering does not meet the objector's burden.

Conclusion

I have offered an analysis of the liberty issue that is expressly grounded in principles of moderate liberalism. The analysis supports the view that regulation of racist hate speech on college and university campuses does not *in itself* impermissibly restrict the liberty of the speaker. That is to say, if such regulations are otherwise appropriate, the analysis indicates that the mere restriction on racist hate speech imposed by them does not constitute immoral coercion of the speaker.

I say "indicates" because so many issues relating to hate speech regulation are empirical. In the case of racist hate speech, for instance, additional empirical evidence would be helpful in drawing more definite conclusions about the harm or offense specifically attributable to this form of hate speech on campus. Nevertheless, there is substantial evidence of the harm or offense caused by racist speech, generally, and, as we have seen, the value of such speech to the speaker and society is typically low. So, it is plausible to conclude under our analysis that the mere restriction of such speech does not impermissibly invade the speaker's liberty. It does not follow from this conclusion, of course, that regulation of *less* egregious forms of hate speech constitutes immoral coercion. A separate analysis would be required to determine that.

Our conclusion challenges the often espoused view that any regulation of racist speech, however effective or otherwise appropriate it may be, constitutes immoral coercion. We have shown that this position is at best questionable. Accordingly, if regulation of racist hate speech is not itself unduly coercive, moral concerns about hate speech regulation may be more properly directed to issues relating to the form a regulation should take. We have also considered two general objections to regulation of racist hate speech that purport to show that, even if such restrictions are not unduly coercive, they are unacceptable for other reasons. We have seen that these arguments do not establish the general conclusions they are offered to support. Certainly, they do not show that regulation of racist hate speech is so infeasible or otherwise undesirable that we need not address the liberty issue on which our analysis has focused.

Notes

1. Timothy C. Shiell, *Campus Hate Speech on Trial* (Lawrence: University Press of Kansas, 1998), 2, citing Howard Ehrlich, National Institute against Prejudice and Violence, *Campus Ethnoviolence . . . and the Policy Options* (Baltimore, Md.: National Institute, 1990). Shiell reports that this study was redone in 1995 and reported in the *Higher Education Extension Service Review* 6, no. 2. (Shiell, *Campus Hate Speech,* 165).

2. Shiell, *Campus Hate Speech*, 2, citing Ehrlich, *Campus Ethnoviolence*.

3. Thomas C. Grey, "Civil Rights versus Civil Liberties: The Case of Discriminatory Verbal Harassment," *Social Philosophy and Policy* 8, no. 2 (1991): 81–107; reprinted in *Philosophy of Law*, ed. Joel Feinberg and Hyman Gross, 5th ed. (Belmont, Calif.: Wadsworth, 1995) 294–310, at 296.

4. For arguments along these lines, see, e.g., Jonathan Rauch, "In Defense of Prejudice: Why Incendiary Speech Must Be Protected," *Harper's Magazine*, May 1995, 37–46; reprinted in *Taking Sides: Clashing Views on Controversial Moral Issues*, ed. Stephen Satris, 6th ed. (Guilford, Conn.: Dushkin/McGraw-Hill, 1998), 148–56.

5. When I speak of hate speech regulations on college or university campuses, I mean regulations that would be generally applicable throughout the campus, as opposed to regulations that apply only to a particular location or type of location, such as a classroom.

6. See *Cohen v. California*, 408 U.S. 15 (1971).

7. This language is derived from The Stanford Discriminatory Harassment Provision quoted in Grey, "Civil Rights versus Civil Liberties," 307.

8. This language is derived in part from a model hate speech code proposed by John T. Shapiro in "The Call for Campus Conduct Policies: Censorship or Constitutionally Permissible Limitations on Speech?" *Minnesota Law Review* 75 (1990): 201, 230–31, quoted in Shiell, *Campus Hate Speech*, 112. I have also used language from The Stanford Discriminatory Harassment Provision quoted in Grey, "Civil Rights versus Civil Liberties," 307.

9. This example is in Shiell, *Campus Hate Speech*, 114. The utterance was scrawled on a mirror inside the room of two African- American college students.

10. This example is in Charles R. Lawrence III, "If He Hollers Let Him Go: Regulating Racist Speech on Campus," *Duke Law Journal* 431 (1990); reprinted in *Social and Personal Ethics*, ed. William H. Shaw, 3d ed. (Belmont, Calif.: Wadsworth, 1999), 266–75, at 266. The utterance was scrawled on a counselor's door.

11. Joel Feinberg, *The Moral Limits of the Criminal Law*, 4 vols. (New York: Oxford University Press, 1985; Oxford University Press Paperback, 1987).

12. Joel Feinberg, *The Moral Limits of the Criminal Law*, vol. 2, *Offense to Others* (New York: Oxford University Press, 1985, Oxford University Press Paperback, 1987), xiii.

13. Feinberg, *Offense to Others*, xiii. This formulation ignores refinements that we need not address.

14. Ibid. This formulation also ignores refinements that are not relevant to our purposes.

15. See Feinberg, *Harm to Others* (New York: Oxford University Press, 1985), 202–6.

16. Ibid., 7–10.

17. Ibid., 25–26.

18. This test is derived from Joel Feinberg's mediating maxims for application of the harm and offense principles. See Feinberg, *Offense to Others*, chap. 8, and *Harm to Others*, chap. 5.

19. See Feinberg, *Harm to Others*, chap. 1.

20. Feinberg, *Offense to Others*, 1–5.

21. See ibid.

22. This paragraph is an exceedingly brief summary of Richard Delgado's comprehensive discussion of harms caused by racial insults in "Words That Wound: A Tort Action for Racial Insults, Epithets, and Name-Calling," *Harvard Civil Rights-Civil Liberties Law Review* 17 (1982): 133, 135–49.

23. Mari Matsuda, "Public Response to Racist Speech: Considering the Victim's Story," *Michigan Law Review* 87 (1989): 2320, 2336, quoted in Shiell, *Campus Hate Speech*, 32.

24. Matsuda, "Public Response," 2340, quoted in Shiell, *Campus Hate Speech*, 32.

25. See, for example, Delgado, "Words That Wound," 157–59; John Arthur, *The Unfinished Constitution: Philosophy and Constitutional Practice* (Belmont, Calif.: Wadsworth, 1989), 90–91.

26. See Feinberg, *Offense to Others*, 226–36.

27. Richard Delgado and David Yun, "Pressure Valves and Bloodied Chickens: An Analysis of Paternalistic Objections to Hate Speech Regulations," *California Law Review* 82 (1994): 871, cited in Shiell, *Campus Hate Speech*, 118.

28. See, e.g., Charles R. Lawrence III, "If He Hollers," 272–80.

29. See Delgado, "Words That Wound," 146.

30. *Chaplinsky v. New Hampshire*, 315 U.S. 568, 571–72 (1942).

31. This statement of the argument and its elaboration are from Diana Tietjens Meyers's "Rights in Collision: A Non-Punitive, Compensatory Remedy for Abusive Speech," *Law and Philosophy* 14 (1995): 221. For additional comments on this and other arguments for permitting abusive hate speech that Meyers raises, see my "Diana Tietjens Meyers's Remedy for Abusive Speech: Objections," *Law and Philosophy* 18 (1999): 1–12, at 9–10.

32. See Delgado, "Words That Wound," 140.

33. Ibid., 135.

34. See, e.g., Joshua Cohen, "Freedom of Expression," *Philosophy and Public Affairs* (1994): 207–63 at 224, 228–29; Kent Greenawalt, *Speech, Crime, and the Use of Language* (New York: Oxford University Press, 1989), 26–27.

35. This point is made by Larry Alexander in his unpublished "Free Speech, Racist Speech, and Respect." Alexander's paper is a response to an earlier draft of this paper. Both my paper and Alexander's response were discussed at the 1998 conference of the American Section of the International Association for Philosophy of Law and Social Philosophy (AMINTAPHIL).

36. This objection is based on one of Alexander's arguments in his "Free Speech, Racist Speech, and Respect," 4.

37. Ibid.

38. See Meyers, "Rights in Collision," 221.

39. See, e.g., Lawrence, "If He Hollers"; Delgado, "Words That Wound"; Matsuda, "Public Response."

40. Quoted in Grey, "Civil Rights versus Civil Liberties," 306–7. The Stanford Discriminatory Harassment Provision was adopted as a disciplinary rule at Stanford University. It was subsequently held to be unconstitutional by the California Superior Court, Santa Clara County, in *Corry v. The Leland Stanford Junior University*, No. 740309 (1995).

41. See Grey, "Civil Rights versus Civil Liberties," 302.

42. See ibid.

43. Shiell, *Campus Hate Speech*, 98–100.

44. My discussion of hostile environment speech codes in this paragraph is from Shiell, *Campus Hate Speech*, chap. 5.

45. Shiell, *Campus Hate Speech*, 109–110.

Chapter 9

First Amendment Morality versus Civility Morality

Norman Fischer

Within the last two decades the U.S. Supreme Court and other federal and state courts concerned with the First Amendment have dramatically limited censorship of what might be called dangerous speech, by striking down hate speech ordinances and codes as well as antipornography legislation. At the same time, a new *civility morality* theory has emerged that attacks judicial decisions limiting censorship of hate speech, pornography, and other forms of dangerous speech, thus showing the link between civility morality and a contemporary "cabin'd, cribb'd, and confined" view of free speech and the First Amendment. The key First Amendment victories over civility-based censorship occurred in *R.A.V. v. City of St. Paul*, prohibiting hate speech ordinances; in *Corry v. Stanford*, prohibiting campus hate speech codes; and in *American Booksellers Association v. Hudnut*, prohibiting antipornography ordinances.[1] The first part of this paper shows the unified First Amendment morality behind *R.A.V.* and *Corry*, and *Hudnut*. The second section delineates how the moral attack by civility theorists on these First Amendment victories undercuts their own enterprise and actually highlights the superior morality of expansive free speech and First Amendment ethics.

First Amendment Morality versus Hate Speech Restrictions

The striking down of the Stanford University hate speech code on 27 February 1995 logically concluded a strong animus in U.S. First Amendment decisions against such restrictions. Judge Peter Stone, applying *R.A.V.*'s striking down of a city ordinance three years earlier, ruled, first, that the Stanford code was overly broad and, second, that the state cannot censor content and viewpoints by picking out some "fighting words" to prohibit.[2]

155

Corresponding to the two legal arguments are two separate moral arguments for striking down antihate ordinances and codes. The moral basis for banning ordinances and codes because they are overly broad combines a nonconsequentialist emphasis on the value of liberty with a consequentialist analysis of what happens when liberty that should be protected is swept up in codes and ordinances aiming at liberty that should not be protected. In contrast, the moral basis for content and viewpoint neutrality does not depend on consequentialist thinking, but shows that the very search for a moral basis for banning the purest acts of hateful speech logically makes the speech in question protected by elevating it to a viewpoint. Both the illegality and the immorality of the codes and ordinances arise out of their morality.

In June 1992, *R.A.V.* struck down a hate speech ordinance in the city of St. Paul, Minnesota, which had prohibited certain words and symbols that were commonly held to stigmatize individuals on the basis of their membership in groups, characterizing these words and symbols as "fighting words." The St. Paul ordinance went back to the famous *Chaplinsky* Supreme Court case, which held that some words were unprotected by the First Amendment because their sole purpose was to make people fight. Edward Cleary, who successfully argued *R.A.V.* in front of the Supreme Court, clearly stated its meaning: that it brings to fruition the line of legal thought that limits fighting words to a purely contextual definition. In contrast, Cass Sunstein and Thomas Grey—the latter an architect of the Stanford hate speech code struck down under *Corry's* use of *R.A.V.*—have both defended hate speech restrictions; for them, *R.A.V.* represents a constitutional aberration that blocks the full development of U.S. antidiscrimination law. Grey has extended the same argument to *Corry*.[3]

In *R.A.V.*, the majority opinion, written by Justice Scalia, struck the ordinance down for violation of content and viewpoint neutrality. Not only did he strike down censorship because of the offense-to-groups aspect of the ordinance, but he also identified this aspect as the core of the ordinance, hidden under the shell of fighting words. Beneath that shell, Scalia made clear, was the unjustified extension of Fourteenth Amendment equality rights to the idea that a predefined group of words can be censored. After *R.A.V.*, hate speech restrictions can more easily be seen to censor a certain content or viewpoint, even when hidden under the shell of a fighting words concept bloated far beyond a contextual definition of them.[4]

The minority also struck the ordinance down, but for overbreadth and chill. Grey's and Sunstein's answer is that overbreadth can be gotten around by a precise appeal to the constitutional concept of equality and nondiscrimination.[5] This begs the question of whether a general ban on fighting words as broad as the one Grey and Sunstein are considering as a possible answer to the majority opinion can really overcome the chill and overbreadth problems raised by the minority and in all probability accepted by the majority in *R.A.V.* Scalia's majority opinion stops this tactic as an answer to the minority opinion. Scalia's ban on selective governmental restrictions against certain fighting words logically implies that the more proponents of hate restrictions attempt to define the hate they want to get at by appealing to nondiscrimination in the Fourteenth Amendment, the more the U.S. judiciary will want to throw out the hate speech restriction because it is censoring content or viewpoint.

The most obvious constitutional problem of hate speech restrictions is overbreadth and chill, which were key to the minority opinion. But the insuperable barrier to such restrictions, key to the majority opinion, is that the more critics of *R.A.V.* try to get around overbreadth and chill by defining fighting words in terms of group stigma, the more these predefined terms become protected as viewpoints. The political theory that opposes hatred based on fixed characteristics creates a theory behind the opposed words. The more defenders of hate speech restrictions theorize, the more they elevate hate speech to the status of protected viewpoint. In contrast to the political theorizing about hate speech and fighting words found in the St. Paul ordinance, the original fighting words case of *Chaplinsky* was, arguably, a case of pure insult—one in which the fighting words were defined entirely by the context.

Scalia was able to employ the very elaborate theorizing that made hate speech ordinances emblems of Fourteenth Amendment morality to bring about the downfall of those ordinances. Sunstein and Grey never state the full strength of Scalia's opinion, which shows that the more critics such as they theorize against *R.A.V.*, the more they prove Scalia's point. For them, one can accept the restriction on even well-intended viewpoint discrimination and argue that the cross burning dealt with in *R.A.V.*, and other acts of hate, are not viewpoints.[6] But in making this argument, they lose the basis for defending landmark extensions of the concept of viewpoint to acts such as flag burning and refusals to salute the flag or recite the pledge of allegiance.[7] The bold message of *R.A.V.*, when added to those earlier cases, is that left and right cannot censor each other in the United States.[8]

Beyond the question of their constitutional correctness as interpretations of the First Amendment, *R.A.V.* and *Corry* raise the question of their *moral* implications for free speech and for group interests in equality. The common defense of hate speech restrictions is that the restrictions increase the equality and, hence, liberty of stigmatized groups. The moral defense of constitutional bans on such restrictions must address this claim. It must also address Grey's question as to whether, since the equal protection clause of the Fourteenth Amendment demands nondiscrimination in equal access to university facilities, it cannot also limit liberty of speech that stigmatizes groups, thus allegedly violating their equal access.[9] Neither *R.A.V.* nor *Corry* provides a morally adequate account of this issue. Before we can understand the strongest moral argument against hate speech restrictions, we must understand the strongest moral argument for them. We can tease such an argument out of the claims of their defenders such as Sunstein and Grey.

The moral claims for group equality contained in St. Paul–type ordinances and Stanford-type codes must center on the inegalitarian element that these restrictions aim to stop. But, what is the core inegalitarian element in hate? This question has not been adequately addressed by ordinance or code advocates such as Sunstein and Grey. At present, the answer to this question is elusive, at best, and this is why the restrictions have and should have been struck down for overbreadth, vagueness, and chilling effect. It is, hence, easy to provide a moral argument against the restrictions: in the interests of stopping speech that is unworthy, there is too great a danger of stopping speech that is worthy. Indeed, Grey accepts that overbreadth is an issue but differs with *R.A.V.* and *Corry* as to how much of an issue it is.[10] Certainly, in his ruling, Judge Stone dashed Sunstein's hope that the *R.A.V.* ruling against city ordinances would not be extended to campus speech codes.[11] The difference between Stone and Sunstein and Grey on the question of overbreadth thus charts the familiar moral territory both of liberty versus social interest and of consequentialist concerns for harmful effects of overly broad laws. The moral issues in the first, overbreadth, argument are thus traditional.

In contrast, what is elusive is the moral issue, itself, in the second aspect of *R.A.V.* and *Corry*—that most commonly criticized as merely libertarian: the idea that hate speech codes and ordinances constitute content and viewpoint discrimination. Further analysis, however, of the difficulty in finding the core of hate can lead us to a nonconsequentialist defense of striking down the codes and ordinances because they violate content and viewpoint neutrality. Of course, the moral defense of these restrictions is precisely that they *should* discriminate between words that stigmatize groups and those that do not, that only in that way can they protect the equality of members of the stigmatized group, including their equal right to liberty.[12] To the opponents of *R.A.V.* and *Corry*, what *constitutionally* defeats the restrictions as content- and viewpoint-based discrimination is what makes them *morally* worthwhile. This is a paradox that the moral defenders of *R.A.V.* and *Corry* must answer; my defense of banning such restrictions is precisely that it is their morality that makes them immoral.

To get at the core of hate and group stigmatization that these codes and ordinances are after, and thus at their alleged moral basis, it is best to begin by getting at what even the defenders of the ordinances and codes might admit is at their periphery. If we show the moral weakness of the periphery, we are better prepared to see the moral weakness of the center. What is this periphery? The answer is that many hate speech restrictions go far beyond restricting hate against a protected core of gender and race, and go on to add a peripheral laundry list of group stigmatization. To pick one example from this laundry list, why do strictures on speech against veterans' status—found sometimes in campus speech codes but unlikely to crop up in a city ordinance—stick out like a sore thumb? The reason is that, from the standpoint of liberty of speech, citizens have the right to strongly criticize moral choices, and veterans' status seems to represent, at least in part, a moral choice. Religion and sexual orientation can also be seen as another part of the periphery. Although some may dispute that either is primarily a matter of choice, others claim that they are, and the issue is certainly one of legitimate debate. If religion and sexual orientation are moral choices, then a liberal state must respect the right of a person to make these moral choices. But, it must also respect the right of others to criticize those choices. Further, the state must respect the right of citizens to *dispute* as to whether religion and sexual orientation are moral choices.

R.A.V. and *Corry* do respect the right of citizens to make choices on veterans' status, religion, and sexual orientation. But they do not demand, indeed they disallow, mandating something further: namely, that citizens refrain from criticizing the group to which any person comes to belong by exercising the right to make choices on these matters. Here, it is helpful to distinguish between strong and weak conceptions of respecting a right. On the *strong* conception, even though we may disagree with what is chosen, we respect, first, the exercise of the right and, second, the autonomy shown in the exercise of it. On the *weak* conception, even though we may disagree with what is chosen, we respect the exercise of the right just because it *is* a right and not because autonomy is shown in its exercise. This distinction can be applied where someone criticizes the moral choice of becoming a veteran, joining a religion, or adopting a sexual orientation. Thus, these choices could be respected in a weak sense because the right to make choices is respected; or they could be respected in a strong sense because, as well, they exhibit autonomy. Also, the right to *criticize* these choices can be respected in a strong or weak sense.

We now see the clear difference between the moral defense of the content and viewpoint neutrality aspect of *R.A.V.* and *Corry* and the moral critique of such neutrality as applied to hate speech ordinances and codes. The critic of these two case decisions, particularly of the content and viewpoint neutrality aspect as opposed to the overbreadth aspect, will say that advocates of the decisions do not distinguish between the strong and weak sense of respecting a right. For, if they did, they would certainly choose to rate hate speech against groups at a lower value than the expression of group membership being stigmatized. These critics of *R.A.V.* and *Corry* would say that the former deserves respect, at most, in the weak sense, whereas the latter deserves respect in the strong sense. On that basis, the critics would be willing to justify censoring the content and viewpoint of hate speech directed against groups, in the interest of both the equality and liberty of the stigmatized group. In the case of peripheral group stigmatization, where membership seems to involve some choice, the critic will hold that any choices made to join a stigmatized group should be respected in the strong sense, whereas the choice to stigmatize that membership should be respected in no sense. To this, the moral defender of *R.A.V.* and *Corry* asks how we can make such a sharp distinction between choices and still preserve that choice which is free speech.

The logical answer for the critic of the decisions is to say that the hate speech restrictions in their essence are not directed to the stigmatization of the peripheries that give rise to the dilemma, but to stigmatization of a core group identity that the legal history of the United States and many other countries has established as particularly worthy of protection. The defender of the codes and ordinances will say that gender, racial, and ethnic identity are not subject to choice in anything remotely like membership in the groups that could be classified as of peripheral moral and constitutional interest might be said to be—that stigmatizing people because of membership in the groups made up of racial, sexual, and ethnic identity constitutes a pure act of hate. The argument would be that these are pure acts of discriminatory and inegalitarian hate because it is directed to fixed characteristics. Thus, they will argue that it is such pure acts of hatred that the codes and ordinances aim to punish.

Following this line of argument, the purest acts of hate directed toward groups would have to be picked out by the defenders of hate speech codes and ordinances, and the attempt to stop purely peripheral expressions of hate toward moral choices to belong to a group would have to be put at the periphery of the moral defense. The fundamental problem, here, for someone who wants to morally defend content- and viewpoint-based hate speech codes and ordinances, would be to limit the restrictions to speech clearly expressive of pure hate. What is it about "pure hate" that the defenders of hate speech restrictions want to get at? The answer has to be that it is hate directed toward aspects of a person not the result of moral choice.

The first problem in explicating the idea of pure hate is ascertaining whether the expressers of hate think there has been a moral choice in the group membership concerning which they are expressing their hatred. Consider expressions of hatred found in the writings of Rudyard Kipling and Friedrich Nietzsche. Kipling's hatred of Americans after he gave up his attempt to settle in Vermont, and Nietzsche's hatred of women in his late writings on Wagner—like his hatred of Christians throughout his later writings—are all based on the idea that moral choices have been made to act as Kipling and Nietzsche thought typical of members of those groups.[13] Would the defenders of hate codes and ordinances want us to censor these passages from Kipling and Nietzsche if read aloud to women and Americans on a campus with a hate speech regulation? The difficulty in deciding this question will plague defenders of hate speech codes and ordinances, since pure expressions of hate toward fixed characteristics of gender, race, and ethnicity will often be mixed with less pure expressions directed against what the speaker regards as moral choices.

The second problem in explicating the idea of pure hate is to determine whether an *expression of pure hate* must be *purely an expression of hate*. A similar problem has been the Achilles' heel of obscenity and pornography legislation. There, the issue has always been whether the alleged obscene or pornographic expression in question is *only* that, or whether it is more, such as a politics based on or intermingled with such expression. Similarly, we can ask what to do with an expression of hate when it intermingles with a politics based on hate. Parts of Kipling's diatribes against Americans and Nietzsche's diatribes against women may well be based on hate, but they also express a *politics of hate* directed toward certain moral choices.

It may seem that these two problems about defining the pure hate which should be the object of moral opprobrium are still primarily problems of overbreadth and consequentialism, but in fact they also begin to define the nonconsequentialist moral debate over whether restrictions on group stigmatization constitute content- and viewpoint-based limits on liberty of speech. These problems in defining pure hate suggest that hate codes and ordinances face a paradox. The more they attempt to define the hate they want to get at in terms of pure animus leading to group stigmatization, and thus to alleged violation of guarantees of nondiscrimination and equality of groups such as are found in the Fourteenth Amendment, then the more the U.S. judiciary will want to throw out the hate restriction because it is censoring content or viewpoint. The first problem of hate speech codes and ordinances is their bad consequences, overbreadth and chill. But the second problem is that independent of consequences, logically, as soon as fighting words become defined, as in the Stanford code and St. Paul ordinance, in terms of group stigmatization that allegedly violates constitutional rights to equality, then they can no longer be censored, because they have become viewpoints, theories, and political statements. If these codes and ordinances are directed at impure acts of hate against groups at the periphery of moral concern, in which membership may be the result of moral choice, then they stop political discussion. This leads to the search for pure acts of hate. Aside from the difficulty of disentangling pure acts of hate from impure acts, shown by the examples of Kipling and Nietzsche, even if those pure acts of hate are defined, they are then defined by the legislative political theory of pure acts of hatred against fixed characteristics of race, gender, and ethnicity. In contrast to this political theorizing about hate and fighting words found in the Stanford code and St. Paul ordinance, the original fighting words case of *Chaplinsky* was arguably a case of pure insult precisely because it was defined entirely by the context. The moral paradox that emerges from *R.A.V.* and *Corry* is that it is the hate restrictions themselves which elaborate fighting words into political stigmatization of groups, thus showing that the words they want to censor must be protected by the First Amendment. Hence, they are not pure expressions of hate. The moral defenders of hate speech restrictions fail, because the more they argue against

R.A.V. and *Corry* the more they prove them. We will now see that the same moral issues arise with antipornography ordinances.

First Amendment Morality versus Antipornography Ordinances

Hudnut v. American Booksellers overthrew an Indianapolis ordinance based on Catherine MacKinnon's concept of pornography as hate against women as a group. MacKinnon and Ronald Dworkin have disputed over exactly how the decision addressed the use of equality claims against liberty claims, but they agree that the use of equality to trump First Amendment liberty failed to triumph legally.[14] *Hudnut* thus feeds into *R.A.V.* and *Corry*, both of which show that a Fourteenth Amendment group equality claim cannot prevail over the First Amendment. But ethically and legally, the latter two go beyond *Hudnut* because they address group hate restrictions that had been defended using an unusually elaborate moral basis.

In *Hudnut,* more work had to be done to discern the moral basis of the censorship ordinance. In 1985 Judge Frank Easterbrook of the U.S. Court of Appeals, Seventh Circuit, affirmed *Hudnut,* a Federal District Court ruling striking down the Indianapolis pornography ordinance. In 1986, the U.S. Supreme Court unanimously affirmed Easterbrook's decision without comment. The essence of *Hudnut* was that the proposed ordinance was (i) overbroad and (ii) violated content and viewpoint neutrality. The parallels with the hate speech cases are, thus, obvious.

Overbreadth (i) was simple: indeed, it should have been obvious to anyone familiar with the long march from *Roth v. U.S.* in 1957 to *Miller v. California* in 1973, to rescue Joyce, Lawrence, Miller, Nabokov, and other heavily censored modern writers from obscenity charges, that the Indianapolis ordinance would have to go for overbreadth. The ordinance opened the floodgates to censorship that had been closed by the *Miller* requirement that "a work on the whole have no serious artistic, literary, social, or scientific value." Because the Indianapolis ordinance potentially opened all works to civil law suits for their alleged pornographic content without regard to their other merits, it achieved with one stroke an overbreadth that the U.S. courts had worked for decades to deflate. Its unconstitutionality on grounds of overbreadth was a foregone conclusion.[15]

What is more difficult to explicate in *Hudnut* is (ii) the content and viewpoint neutrality ruling. Easterbrook had at his disposal little of the First

Amendment–bashing moral and legal theory that Stone and Scalia could use later. Still, MacKinnon had provided a significant amount of rope by which to hang the ordinance, and enough of that material had entered the ordinance itself, so that Easterbrook was able to bring out the paradox of high moral viewpoint censorship, by linking it with other examples from U.S. constitutional history. The result is that *Hudnut* is a preliminary version of *R.A.V.* and *Corry*.

R.A.V. and *Corry* deflate the range of fighting words so that theorizing about moral principles of what fighting words would be censored would be seen as tilting toward content and viewpoint censorship. This deflation left fighting words defined contextually. So, too, Easterbrook had to deflate an attempt to build, out of then current obscenity law, some sort of moral principle by which obscenity could be theoretically redefined as pornography. *Hudnut*'s doctrine that obscenity should remain contextual thus parallels *R.A.V.*'s and *Corry*'s doctrine that fighting words should remain contextual. U.S. obscenity law's focus on context is clearly depicted in Edward De Grazia's account of the historic progression from *Roth* to *Miller*.[16]

Easterbrook saw clearly how the Indianapolis ordinance left the contextual *Miller* behind and substituted political censorship of viewpoint and content.[17] It thus could be argued that in 1985 Easterbrook laid the foundation for *R.A.V.* and *Corry*: when well-meaning people theorize morally about what hate is, whether in a pornography ordinance or a hate speech ordinance or code, and try to censor what corresponds to that definition, they block the constitutionality of their own censorship by their own moral theorizing. By developing elaborate moral theories about what they want to censor, they elevate it to a viewpoint and thus make it uncensorable.

Civility Morality versus First Amendment Morality

Legally, hate speech ordinances and codes have fallen along with antipornography ordinances. But Grey and Sunstein have a second line of argument for hate speech restrictions, and Sunstein and Michael Sandel extend the argument to antipornography ordinances.[18] The argument is that such restrictions are necessary for the morality of civility. Sunstein has presented what amounts to a unified argument for watering down First Amendment rights in the interest of civility in cases of both hate speech and pornography.[19] Indeed, Sunstein has become the spokesperson often cited by journalists discussing the viability of procensorship views.[20] But, this unified civility argument reveals a hidden moral weakness in the civility position and hidden moral strengths in the anticensorship position.

The views of Sunstein and Sandel anchor censorship in a theory of democracy that stresses two key ideas. The first idea is that defense of public reasoning is necessary for First Amendment law and for democracy, itself; this is a view with which many anticensorship advocates agree.[21] The second idea is that civility, in the form of restrictions on hate speech and pornography, is necessary for the defense of public reasoning.[22] By contrast, opponents of hate speech and pornography bans such as Dworkin hold that the imposition of civility based on such restrictions is contradictory to democracy.[23] Yet, civility democracy theorists have cited little or no evidence that an emphasis on active participation, based on public spiritedness and public reasoning as represented in the civic republican tradition, should envisage passive, fearful citizens for whom the paternalistic state must censor expression that would offend their sense of civility.[24]

Sunstein claims that the primary concept for building a procensorship position is a two-tiered speech theory of core and periphery. Speech serving democratic deliberation is at the core of protected speech, but everything else is at the periphery.[25] Sunstein and Sandel argue that if U.S. constitutional law had consistently followed Felix Frankfurter in *Beauharnais*, when he found a law prohibiting group libel constitutional, then the hate speech ordinance struck down in *R.A.V.* would have been constitutional. Sandel defends *Beauharnais*, and Sunstein defends much of the reasoning behind it.[26] The reason for *Beauharnais*' isolation in First Amendment law is that it is based almost exclusively on civility-grounded avoidance of words that offend groups.

Sunstein also argued that a university or college, because of its special educational mission, has a broader right to censor speech than does a city like St. Paul, and thus is less subject to *R.A.V.*'s proscriptions. Sunstein appeals primarily to civility ethics, rather than an ethics of democracy or liberty. For Sunstein, because of its special concern to avoid offense to members of its community, a university should be allowed more room to maneuver than *R.A.V.* gave cities. He argues that the mission of the university allows extensive censoring by and of teachers. He also appeals to the right of managerial university elites to control their purely administrative employees at many levels of speech, including the coherence of their speech with diversity talk. "Colleges and Universities are often in the business of controlling speech."[27]

Sunstein's civility critique of *R.A.V.* in terms of how it tolerates offensive words is paralleled by his critique of *Hudnut*. *Hudnut* attacks the very idea of pornography legislation as an alternative to the relatively settled area of obscenity law. Sunstein announces that he prefers to defend the narrower and more limited approach of censoring only pornography that causes violence to women; he claims that this distinguishes his position from those who would censor pornography because its images subordinate women, discriminates against women, or treats them unequally.[28] In fact, much of what he says supports the latter type of censorship. Yet, in accepting censorship on the former grounds, Sunstein is still at odds with *Hudnut*. Even in the bad old days, Joyce and Lawrence were censored for what was allegedly *in their work*, not for what their work allegedly *might cause others to do*.

Sunstein claims that the community standards appealed to in obscenity law are a less neutral basis for censorship than those provided by Fourteenth Amendment equality claims, because the former endorse existing prejudices and the latter attempt to implement principles of equality. He writes, "Obscenity law takes existing social consensus as the foundation for decision, whereas antipornography law is directed against that consensus. . . . Obscenity law, insofar as it is tied to community standards, is deemed neutral, but only because the class of prohibited speech is defined by reference to existing social values. Antipornography legislation is deemed impermissibly partisan because the class of speech is defined by less widely accepted ideas about equality between men and women."[29] But Sunstein's defense of antipornography ordinances actually validates *Hudnut*'s critique of them.

First, Sunstein makes clear what is left vague in the Indianapolis ordinance, namely, that a defensible antipornography ordinance could censor even art with "serious social value."[30] Hence he wants to retreat to pre–*Roth* and *Miller* days.

Second, homosexual material will not be proscribed under Sunstein's model antipornography ordinance. Even the makers of the proscribed Indianapolis antipornography ordinance felt responsible enough to Fourteenth Amendment consistency that they did not require that the harm and degradation that the ordinance was after be of exclusively heterosexual origin. Sunstein's limitation to heterosexual harm and degradation narrows the politics of his censorship even beyond what Easterbrook found in the Indianapolis ordinance. "We might find it an exceedingly strange artifact of current legal and popular thinking that an attack on material featuring sex and violence against women should be believed simultaneously to endanger art relating to homosexuality. The antipornography argument, rightly understood, calls for fierce protection of speech that complains explicitly or implicitly about discrimination against homosexuals, because that speech is 'high value.' "[31] Sunstein's argument here appeals only to a vaguely defined civility and is neither egalitarian nor democratic in any obvious sense. And if Easterbrook ever read Sunstein's claim that only heterosexual viewpoints would be prosecuted under his proposed law, the judge might have wished that he had possessed this extra rope before he hung the Indianapolis ordinance with what rope he already had. Easterbrook might well also have enjoyed the proof Sunstein supplied that antipornography ordinances would be used for political censorship, when Sunstein, the defender of homosexual pornography in 1993, lent his voice to the crusade against Milos Forman's 1996 film, *The People versus Larry Flynt*. For Sunstein, "A lot of press reports have treated this as though Larry Flynt . . . is a kind of hero of the First Amendment. It's as if there are these evil people who are really moralistic and punitive and then there are freedom lovers. That's really a congratulatory, complacent way for movie makers to see the conflict. . . . Flynt isn't really a political dissident; he's basically a pornographer."[32]

Sunstein's willingness to censor pornography whatever its serious social value, and his willingness to so politicize the ordinance that it is directed against heterosexual but not homosexual pornography, demonstrate that, as in his civility-based defense of hate speech restrictions, he elevates what he wants to censor to a viewpoint protected under the First Amendment. Furthermore, in the moral contest it is First Amendment morality that is linked not only with liberty, but also with democracy, whereas civility morality remains fixated on stopping offensive words.

Notes

1. *R.A.V. v. City of St. Paul* 505 U.S. (1992); *Corry v. Stanford*, no. 740309, California Superior Court, Santa Clara County; *American Booksellers Association v. Hudnut*, in *Philosophical Problems in the Law*, 2d ed. ed. David Adams (Belmont, Calif.: Wadsworth, 1996).

2. *Corry*, 10–11; *R.A.V.*, 306. For the history behind the former, see Nat Hentoff, "The Final Nail in the Coffin of College Speech Codes," *The Village Voice*, 25 April 1995, pp. 18–19. For the effect on college and university codes, see Jon Gould, "The Precedent That Wasn't: College Speech Codes and the Two Faces of Legal Compliance," *Law and Society Review* 35 (2001): 345–93.

3. *R.A.V.*, *Corry*. Edward Cleary, *Beyond the Burning Cross* (New York: Random House, 1994), 172–90; Thomas C. Grey, "How to Write a Speech Code without Really Trying: Reflections on the Stanford Experience," *U.C. Davis Law Review* 29 (1996): 917–23; Cass R. Sunstein, *Democracy and the Problem of Free Speech* (New York: Free Press, 1993), 189–93: *Chaplinsky v. New Hampshire* 315 U.S. (1942).

4. *R.A.V.*, 323.

5. Ibid., 327; Sunstein, op. cit., 193; Grey, op. cit., 899–911.

6. Sunstein, op. cit., 189; Grey, op. cit., 817–23.

7. *Texas v. Johnson* 491 U.S. (1989); *W. Virginia v. Barnette* 318 U.S. (1943).

8. For left and right censorship, see Nat Hentoff, *Free Speech for Me but Not for Thee* (New York: Harper Collins, 1992).

9. Grey, op. cit., 919.

10. Ibid., 918.

11. Sunstein, op. cit., 203; and "Liberalism, Speech Codes, and Related Problems," in *Philosophical Problems in the Law*, op. cit.

12. Grey, op. cit., 922–23.

13. Rudyard Kipling, *Something of Myself* (London: MacMillan & Co., 1937), 108–32; Freidrich Nietzsche, "The Case of Wagner," in *The Birth of Tragedy and the Case of Wagner* (New York: Vintage, 1967), 185.

14. Ronald Dworkin, *Freedom's Law* (Cambridge, Mass.: Harvard University Press, 1996), 227–44; Ronald Dworkin and Catherine MacKinnon, "Pornography: An Exchange," *New York Review of Books*, 3 March 1994, 47–48.

15. *Roth v. U.S.* 476 U.S. (1957); *Miller v. California* 413 U.S. (1973).

16. See Edward De Grazia, *Girls Lean Back Everywhere: The Law of Obscenity and the Assault on Genius* (New York: Random House, 1992), 551–76.

17. *Hudnut*, 205–6.

18. Michael Sandel, *Democracy's Discontent* (Cambridge, Mass.: Harvard University Press, 1996).

19. Sunstein, *Democracy*, 180–93, 210–26; "Liberalism," 190–94; Grey, op. cit., 901–7, Sandel, op. cit., 70–90.

20. See Nina Bernstein, "A Free Speech Hero? It's Not That Simple," *New York Times*, 22 December 1996, sec. 2, 1, 36; Neil A. Lewis, "Switching Sides on Free Speech," *New York Times*, 26 April 1998, Sec. 4, 4.

21. Sunstein, *Democracy*, 120–24; Sandel, op. cit., 80. And see Dworkin, op. cit., 202–8.

22. Sunstein, *Democracy*, 223–26, "Liberalism," 190–94, Sandel, op. cit., 74–80.

23. Dworkin, op. cit., 222–24.

24. Sandel, op. cit., 83–90; Sunstein, "Liberalism," 190–94.

25. Sunstein, *Democracy*, 23–27.

26. *Beauharnais v. Illinois*, 343 U.S. (1952): Sunstein, *Democracy*, 185–87; Sandel, op. cit., 83–85.

27. Sunstein, "Liberalism," 190, 192, 191, 193–94. Also see Sunstein, *Democracy*, 203.

28. Sunstein, *Democracy*, 212.

29. Ibid., 223–24.

30. Ibid., 225.

31. Ibid., 226.

32. Cass R. Sunstein, cited in Nina Bernstein, op. cit., 1.

Chapter 10

Rudeness, Rasp, and Repudiation

Jonathan Schonsheck

It has been said that trying to achieve consensus among philosophers is like trying to herd cats. And yet—although the evidence adduced is informal and anecdotal—there is a consensus among the philosophers who have contributed to this volume that, of late, the incidence of incivility has increased. No matter how incivility is specified, we are encountering more of it. But then the cats scatter. *Incivility* denotes a vast array of actions, attitudes, and values; there are many distinguishable ways in which we encounter departures from civility.

In this essay, I distinguish three broad categories of incivility—and shall term them rudeness, rasp, and repudiation. Very generally, *rudeness* is essentially impoliteness. *Rasp* is the friction of jostling political, moral, religious, and ethnic groups that is inevitable in any multicultural "liberal democracy"— a system, or theory, or philosophy of government that cherishes the values of toleration and mutual respect. Not everyone, however, subscribes to toleration and mutual respect; the *repudiation* of these values generates the third, and most serious, category of incivility.

Although distinguishable, these categories are hardly unrelated. Indeed, the victims of incivility may not be able to determine, at least initially, the sort of incivility to which they have been subjected. Both rasp and repudiation may be experienced, at least initially, as simple rudeness. Furthermore, the infliction of unpleasantness may be precisely the intention of the perpetrator: the forceful assertion of a particular political or religious or ethnic value; the forceful rejection of a particular political, religious, or ethnic value.

I begin with brief discussions and illustrations of rudeness and rasp. The next sections are devoted to tolerance and intolerance. In the former, I discuss liberal democracy; I offer a brief historical sketch, and then discuss in more careful detail the most powerful contemporary formulation, John Rawls's just-published *Justice as Fairness: A Restatement*.[1] Even in historical texts such as Mill's but especially prominent in Rawls's recent work is the importance of "groups," incivility as clashes between individuals *as members of groups*. I then look to our evolutionary past: the prerational attractions and aversions that would have proved advantageous for our hunter-gatherer ancestors, in their environment. We have inherited their impulses, but not their environment; indeed, we find ourselves in a very different environment. Consequently, acting on these impulses puts us in peril. In the last section, I bring these together to highlight the deep tension between prerational impulses and cool rationality: the sorts of actions we must elect if we are to live in a Rawlsian "well-ordered society," and the urges that must be constrained if we are to elect those actions.

Incivility as Rudeness; Incivility as Rasp

Some incidents of incivility seem to be manifestations of a general, globalized impoliteness or *rudeness*, a lack of manners. People are curt, or abrupt; they do not exhibit the appropriate social graces. For example, they use their cell phones—whether incoming or outgoing—in ways that are intrusive and disruptive. Another example of this sort of incivility is aggressive and inconsiderate driving in general, and "road rage" in particular. No account with which I am familiar attempts to explain "road rage" as a behavior that naturally arises from an identifiable set of deeply held values. Rather, it seems to be the result of increased traffic congestion, an infrastructure in need of repairs or actually undergoing repairs, as one negotiates lane shifts and reductions, uneven pavement, and interminable delays, and a rise in the basal level of stress in our lives. A contributing factor may well be self-centeredness, a heightened sense of self-importance: my time is valuable; I can't afford to be stuck here, or to wait my turn, or to stay off the shoulder or the sidewalk, or to wait for you to finally pass that slow-moving truck. But that is hardly a *value commitment*. And few would disagree with the proposition that the quality of our driving lives would improve considerably if there were greater reliance on the smile and the brake pedal, less reliance on the accelerator and the extended middle finger. A public campaign to enhance driving courtesy could hardly be considered an affront to anyone's core values.

And more generally, as the United States becomes more multicultural and moves from a "melting pot" in which ethnic and cultural heritage are effaced to a "stew" or an amalgam, with roughly identifiable subcultures and ethnic groups maintaining religious and cultural practices, there are increased opportunities to quite inadvertently offend others: to thoughtlessly exhibit behaviors that are, unintentionally, offensive to others.

Incivility as *rasp*, I believe, reached its zenith—or nadir—during the Clinton presidency. For whatever reasons of policy, style, comportment, or political chemistry, William Jefferson Clinton and Hillary Rodham Clinton ignited and fueled continuous political conflagrations. Whether one considers the ill-fated attempt at health-care reform, the $65 million decade-long Whitewater investigation that came to naught, the extraordinary sequence of events leading to the impeachment and acquittal of the president, or the parting pardons, one finds acrimonious and divisive political battles.

There is no controversy in claiming that the media played a significant role in all this. The questioning and investigating were unprecedented in both scope and depth; no predecessor had been subjected to such withering scrutiny—especially of that which, heretofore, had been considered one's "personal" life. How did this come about? Perhaps contemporary reporters have had an inadequate upbringing and education; neither their mothers nor their elementary school teachers nor their journalism professors taught them manners. Perhaps the demands of competition overrode a decent upbringing and education: the advent of twenty-four-hour-a-day cable television news shows enlarged the need for "content," whether genuinely newsworthy or not. Something had to be put on the screen—hence, the Clintonian omnipresence. All this can be said without taking sides; my goal here is simply to illustrate rasp.

Tolerance, Democracy, and Reason

The United States is a liberal democracy. The Founders, in writing the Declaration of Independence, and the Constitution of the United States, relied heavily on John Locke's *Second Treatise of Government*.[2] Many of the most basic ideas of those founding documents were first articulated by Locke; some of their most memorable language first appeared in Locke's *Second Treatise*. Of central importance for Locke and his philosophical successors is the idea that each *individual* possesses a set of *individual* rights. These individual rights, and additional legal rights, are guaranteed by the U.S. Constitution, either in the text of that document or as key provisions that have been interpreted by the Supreme Court. Prominent among these rights is the quite individual right of freedom of conscience.

Toleration and mutual respect constitute the essential values of liberal democracy; the state is to function as a "safe haven" for people to lead the life they choose, despite the various individuals' being committed to a diverse array of other, core values. Indeed, mutual respect and toleration are more accurately characterized as *metavalues* in liberalism; they constitute the framework within which people of diverse or even conflicting values can coexist—and even flourish. In a liberal democracy, then, it is to be expected that there will be "friction" between individuals due to their subscribing to different core values. I have called this friction the "rasp" within liberal democracy, the inevitable grating of different sets of core values. However, despite subscribing to various—inconsistent, conflicting—core values, political liberals share a commitment to the overarching metavalues of liberal democracy: tolerance and mutual respect.

Despite the hallmark "individualism" of liberal democracy, many of the rights guaranteed by the Constitution, and defended by subsequent liberal democrats, are most perspicuously viewed not as individual rights per se, but as rights exercised by people *together with other people*—that is, in groups. Freedom of assembly and freedom of the press are the most obvious rights of this sort; freedom of religion, insofar as religion is conceived as an institution rather than a matter of conscience, falls into this category too. John Stuart Mill, in specifying "the appropriate range of human liberty," first argues for "liberty of conscience in the most comprehensive sense," and then for "liberty of tastes and pursuits, of framing the plan of our life to suit our own character." But then, he writes, "from this liberty of each individual follows the liberty, within the same limits, of combination among individuals: freedom to unite for any purpose not involving harm to others; the persons combining being supposed to be of full age and not forced or deceived."[3]

For most people, membership in groups is essential to one's identity—indeed, to one's life. Typically, we are members of many different groups. People belong to groups of varying size, ease of entrance or exit, purpose, and so forth. We may well "belong" to a family, a church, a school district, a race, an ethnic community, a neighborhood, a city, a state, a region, a Cub Scout Den, a Brownie Troop, a political party, a profession, professional associations, and so forth. And we may well "identify" with these groups: when we think about "who we are," we specify our roles in these groups. Additionally, we view our prospects as inextricably intertwined with theirs: if the group prospers, then we prosper. If the group languishes, then we languish.

Civic virtues tend to be exhibited within such groups. We support these groups with our time, talents, and resources: we pay taxes to the city, county, and state (as well as to the nation); we tithe to the church; we pay dues to the Troop, the union, the American Philosophical Association; we pay membership fees to clubs; we bake cookies and cakes for the school Parent Teacher Association; we coach T-ball and soccer; we make charitable contributions, and so forth. Furthermore, some of these groups are the "contraries" of other groups; no person could be a member of both: one is a Republican or a Democrat, a Protestant or a Catholic, and so on. And some of these groups are competitors, in the sense that one group's flourishing means that other groups languish. In a casual sense, it's a zero-sum game.[4] These facts—that our identity and prospects depend so heavily on group membership and that some of the groups to which we belong are in competition with other groups—are essential to an adequate understanding of incivility as rasp—and, ultimately, incivility as repudiation.

In *Justice as Fairness: A Restatement*, John Rawls focuses on a certain kind of group/group membership. He invokes a technical term, appropriately vague: a "comprehensive view" that is a philosophical or religious position, including "the moral and aesthetic values to be sought in human life."[5] Those who subscribe to the beliefs and values of a comprehensive position thereby constitute a community; "by a community I mean a body of persons united in affirming the same comprehensive, or partially comprehensive, doctrine."[6] Because of "profound and irreconcilable differences" in its citizens' "comprehensive positions, ... a democratic society is not and cannot be a community." However, a liberal democracy can be, and ideally is, the structure of governance for numerous communities of this sort—that is, a contemporary multicultural nation-state. "It is a serious error not to distinguish between the idea of a democratic political society and the idea of community. Of course, a democratic society is hospitable to many communities within it, and indeed tries to be a social world within which diversity can flourish in amity and concord; but it is not itself a community, nor can it be in view of the fact of reasonable pluralism."[7]

An important task of political philosophy—its "practical," and arguably its most important, role—is to delineate a structure of governance that accommodates this pluralism, this multicultural, multiracial, multiethnic "stew." Toleration and mutual respect among the citizens is essential. We suppose, then, that one task of political philosophy—its practical role, let's say—is to focus on deeply disputed questions and to see whether, despite appearances, some underlying basis of philosophical and moral agreement can be uncovered. Or if such a basis of agreement cannot be found, perhaps the divergence of philosophical and moral opinion at the root of divisive political differences can at least be narrowed so that social cooperation on a footing of mutual respect among citizens can still be maintained.[8] To achieve such social cooperation, we must find common ground on which to build a secular system of government:

> Political liberalism neither accepts nor rejects any particular comprehensive doctrine, moral or religious. It does allow that it belongs to these doctrines to search for religious, philosophical and moral truth. . . . To realize this aim we try to work up, from the fundamental ideas implicit in the political culture, a public basis of justification that all citizens as reasonable and rational can endorse from within their own comprehensive doctrines. If this is achieved, we have an overlapping consensus of reasonable doctrines.[9]

Of course Rawls believes that the *contents* of that overlapping consensus ought to be justice as fairness. Whether he is right in this is not our concern. Our concern is this: agreement on an overlapping consensus on constitutional issues, despite a plurality of diverse and even antagonistic comprehensive positions, is a sine qua non of a stable, well-ordered society. And achieving that overlapping consensus is not possible without toleration and mutual respect.

> The idea of an overlapping consensus is introduced to make the idea of a well-ordered society more realistic and to adjust it to the historical and social conditions of democratic societies, which include the fact of reasonable pluralism. While in a well-ordered society all citizens affirm the same political conception of justice, we do not assume they do so for all the same reasons, all the way down. Citizens have conflicting religious, philosophical, and moral views and so they affirm the political conception from within different and opposing comprehensive doctrines, and so, in part at least, for different reasons. But this does not prevent the political conception from being a shared point of view from which they can resolve questions concerning the constitutional essentials.[10]

As regards these "constitutional essentials,"

> The role of the principles of justice (as part of a political conception of justice) is to specify the fair terms of social cooperation. . . . These principles specify the basic rights and duties to be assigned by the main political and social institutions, and they regulate the division of benefits arising from social cooperation and allot the burdens necessary to sustain it.[11]

In sum,

> Given the fact of reasonable pluralism, a well-ordered society in which all its members accept the same comprehensive doctrine is impossible. But democratic citizens holding different comprehensive doctrines may agree on political conceptions of justice. Political liberalism holds that this provides a sufficient as well as the most reasonable basis of social unity available to us as citizens of a democratic society.[12]

Rawls's claim here, which I endorse, is more starkly on point when put in the contrapositive: if we *fail* to achieve an overlapping consensus despite being members of diverse communities, committed to antagonistic comprehensive doctrines, then we will *not* have a well-ordered and stable society, the sort of society that is essential to our collective survival. If the core metavalues of liberal democracy, toleration and mutual respect, are *repudiated*, then the members of the competing communities, each drawn together and energized by the comprehensive doctrine that defines their respective communities, will be in conflict. Incivility escalates to insurrection, to civil war.

Thus, there are powerful reasons—engaging the critical, reflective faculties—for practicing one's comprehensive doctrine in the political structure of a liberal democracy.[13] There are powerful reasons for respecting, or at least tolerating, those who subscribe to different comprehensive doctrines. Failing to do so leads to a life that is still best described as "poore, solitary, nasty, brutish and short."[14] With such good reasons, with so much at stake, how can reason sometimes fail?

Tolerance, Evolution, and Prerationality

The best way to understand the powerful forces working *against* toleration and mutual respect is to investigate the evolutionary past of our species, the deep emotional impulses that literally predate our critical, reflective faculties.

The argument begins with the simple yet profound observation that for more than 99 percent of our species' history, our ancestors lived in hunter-gatherer bands. For hundreds of thousands of generations, they were subjected to the selection pressures of the hunter-gatherer environment.[15] We are descended from those who succeeded. And what proved successful for them: the interrelated phenomena that R. Paul Shaw and Yuwa Wong have nicely termed "in-group amity" and "out-group enmity."

There can be little doubt that the *capacity* to fight has evolved through natural selection. *Homo sapiens* have evolved the capacity to respond aggressively to threats just as they have evolved the capacity to learn culture and language. Such capacities become operative when prompted by appropriate stimuli and environment.[16]

Note that this is not a "decision":

Humans, like other animals, are endowed with physiological and neurochemical responses which underlie their capacity for aggression . . . researchers have identified specific brain mechanisms implicated in aggressive behaviors, the role of stimuli which act as triggers for aggression, and different goals served by aggressive behaviors.[17]

Writing a decade earlier, sociobiology's founder Edward O. Wilson wrote that "primitive men cleaved their universe into friends and enemies and responded with quick, deep emotion to even the mildest threats emanating from outside the arbitrary boundary."[18] And later,

Human beings are strongly predisposed to respond with unreasoning hatred to external threats and to escalate their hostility sufficiently to overwhelm the source of the threat by a respectably wide margin of safety. Our brains do appear to be programmed to the following extent: we are inclined to partition other people into friends and aliens, in the same sense that birds are inclined to learn territorial songs and to navigate by the polar constellations. We tend to fear deeply the actions of strangers and to solve conflict by aggression.[19]

This "cleaving" is a crucial phenomenon; the argument too divides here, between in-group amity and out-group enmity. Let us consider these in turn, noting the selection pressures and evolutionary mechanisms that explain each—and then consider their potentially lethal conjunction.

In-Group Amity

The key to understanding in-group amity is the mechanism of kin selection, or inclusive fitness.

The *evolution* of much contemporary social behavior has originated during the past one to two million years when our ancestors lived in small, tight-knit kin groups. We call these groups "nucleus ethnic groups." Numbering approximately 100 individuals at most, a nucleus ethnic group comprises one's offspring, one's siblings' offspring, and one's parents and their siblings and their offspring.[20]

"Survival of the fittest" means, in this context, survival of the fittest *family*.

> Inclusive fitness differs from traditional notions of survival of the fittest in two respects. First, according to inclusive fitness, natural selection favors the ability of individuals to transmit their genes to posterity. Fitness is thus measured by this ability rather than fitness in terms of health, strength, beauty, or other physical traits. Second, an organism's inclusive fitness can be increased by assisting others who are genetically related (nepotism). It is in this later component that an ultimate explanation for allegiances and sacrificial altruism—and thus, the origins of sociality—can be found.[21]

Selection pressures would favor those who contributed to the survival of the nucleus ethnic group—even the contribution of self-sacrifice:

> Inclusive fitness and, more specifically, kin selection also provide an ultimate, evolutionary rationale for anticipating origins of "self-sacrifice to the death." As individuals are motivated to maximize their inclusive fitness rather than personal survival and reproduction alone, sacrifice to the death can still have a genetic payoff; it can enhance reproduction and survival of close relatives who share the same genes by common descent. That is, an individual's genes—the units of natural selection—can still be propagated though personal fitness is lost in the process.[22]

Over time, we would see some refinements in-group amity:

> High costs of within-group aggression would act to change the character of the dominance system. Insofar as dominant individuals could not afford to be injured in rank-order fighting, there would be an increased selection for social skills in attaining and maintaining status, and decreased emphasis on overt aggression. These would combine to produce a more effective internal ordering of power relations to the extent that groups could be more quickly mobilized to meet challenges from outsiders. In the process, intergroup conflict would select for greatly increased human capacity to establish and accept group hierarchy as well as to recognize enemies versus relatives and friends.[23]

Membership in these nucleus ethnic groups had many benefits:

> In early hominid evolution, it is likely that membership in an expanded nucleus group (50–100 individuals) would have increased each individual's access to scarce resources and the ability to manage others. Hunting in numbers, for example, would have enabled primitive man to overcome larger game. Numbers would also have reduced the susceptibility of individuals to attack from dangerous animals. To facilitate hunting and to prevent attack, groups would almost certainly have served as information centers about the nature of both resources and predators. The more these features of group membership enhanced inclusive fitness (the rate of reproduction,

quality of offspring, survival), the more group members would have been deterred from splintering off.[24]

According to inclusive fitness theory, then, the genetic endowment for pre-rational dispositions favoring in-group amity would, over generations, spread through the species and become a characteristic of the species. Nucleus ethnic groups that were cohesive, and motivated, would win the struggle for survival against nucleus ethnic groups that were not cohesive and motivated.

Out-Group Enmity

Altruism and cooperation within the group would enhance inclusive fitness. And fitness would be enhanced by hostility toward outsiders, especially in competition for scarce resources. In some contexts, the "tie that binds" is a shared animosity toward some other group or groups. Here the argument moves from in-group amity to out-group enmity:

> Kin selection has formidable implications for anticipating origins of cooperation and conflict among early man. It implies that assistance, favors or altruism would be directed at individuals who were genetically related enough to give the common gene pool greater survival advantages. Genetic relatedness would be greatest with members of one's lineage and one's own kin or nucleus ethnic group. It would be less between members of neighboring groups, less again between members of groups even farther removed from each other, and so on. As the degree of genetic related-ness declines, we would expect offerings of altruistic or socially cooperative acts to decline as well. Indeed, we might expect zero cooperation or blatant aggression to be directed towards strangers.[25]

Broadly, the struggle for survival is also a struggle between groups—in this case, between different "nucleus ethnic groups." Here the relevant mechanism is group selection.

> It is highly plausible that the sociobiology of ethnocentrism was reinforced during humanity's past due to important changes in always hostile environments. The crucial change would have involved an increased prevalence of other human groups competing for scarce resources. To counter this competition, groups of tightly related kin (nucleus ethnic groups) would have begun to ally and merge through inter-marriage. Failure of nucleus ethnic groups to cooperate in fending off competition or threats from a larger group might have meant reduced access for the individual for scarce resources, subjugation, and perhaps eventual extinction.[26]

A consequence of this:

> Resource competition and resulting warfare were thus among the major forces which stimulated tribal formation and acted to maintain tribal organization. In similar fashion, they were among the major forces which stimulated and maintained chiefdoms (amalgamation of tribes), and so on. It is by this process that out-group enmity and ethnocentrism have been reinforced and carried over from nucleus ethnic group to band, to tribe, to chiefdom, to nation-state.[27]

Here Shaw and Wong endorse Wilson's position, that "with the rise of chiefdoms and states, this tendency became institutionalized, was adopted as an instrument of policy of some of the new societies, and those that employed it best became—tragically—the most successful. The evolution of warfare . . . could not be halted by any people, because to attempt to reverse the process unilaterally was to fall victim."[28] And later, Wilson writes, "These learning rules are most likely to have evolved during the past hundreds of thousands of years of human evolution and, thus, to have conferred a biological advantage on those who conformed to them with the greatest fidelity."[29] One important way of referring to those who "conformed to them with the greatest fidelity": *our ancestors*.

So, we have inherited strong emotional impulses. We tend to bifurcate the world into "us" and "them." The "us" typically includes kin; we are prepared to cooperate with them, to make sacrifices for them—including the ultimate sacrifice. We view "them" with suspicion, and that suspicion can quickly escalate to hostility and violence.

But now it is essential to remember Wilson's term *arbitrary boundaries*, together with the observations made at the outset about groups: we belong to many groups, in many different social contexts. Thus, there is no fixed "us" versus a fixed "them." It's not as if we belong to just one group of "us" in competition with one group of "them." In different social contexts, in different social roles, different individuals count as members of "us," different individuals count as members of "them." A given person could well be a friend in one social setting, a foe in another. What endures in any particular social context is some identifiable "in-group" requiring amity, and some identifiable "out-group" requiring enmity.

Of course the degrees of both amity and enmity vary widely. Some are pretty trivial, such as *Den One versus Den Two* in a tug-of-war, or the competition of the Pinewood Derby, or sports rivalries generally.[30] Far more serious degrees of amity and enmity are to be found in the conflicts between those "comprehensive positions" known as religions. Wilson writes on this issue quite perceptively:

> The highest forms of religious practice, when examined more closely, can be seen to confer biological advantage. Above all they congeal identity. In the midst of the chaotic and potentially disorienting experiences each person undergoes daily, religion classifies him, provides him with unquestioned membership in a group claiming great powers, and by this means gives him a driving purpose in life compatible with his self-interest. His strength is the strength of the group, his guide the sacred covenant.[31]

This can result in extraordinary motivation for out-group enmity:

> This extreme form of certification is granted to the practices and dogmas that serve the vital interests of the group. The individual is prepared by the sacred rituals for supreme effort and self-sacrifice. Overwhelmed by shibboleths, special costumes, and sacred dancing and music accurately keyed to his emotive centers, he is transformed by a religious experience. The votary is ready to reassert allegiance to his tribe and family, perform charities, consecrate his life, leave for the hunt, join the battle, die for God and country.[32]

It is not difficult to devise a contemporary instantiation of Wilson's incantation: Prepared by *madrassas*, consecrated by mullahs, promised virgins in the afterlife, the votary reasserts allegiance to al-Qaeda, proclaims *Allah Akbar*, and flies a hijacked airliner into the World Trade Center. But, now, Wilson argues that the "learning rules of violent aggression are largely obsolete. We are no longer hunter-gatherers who settle disputes with spears, arrows, and stone axes. But to acknowledge the obsolescence of the rules is not to banish them. We can only work our way around them."[33] How can we "work around them," or at least attempt to work around them? By the use of our critical, reflective faculties. By affirming the possibility of a better life for oneself, and one's children, and one's children's children, by exerting rational control over the prerational impulses and responses that lead to social disintegration.

This brings us to the confluence of Rawlsian liberal democracy and sociobiology. We have inherited the propensity for bifurcation, for in-group amity and out-group enmity. It benefited our ancestors, for hundreds of thousands of generations, in the hunter-gatherer environment. In our environment, it threatens us with extinction.

Multicultural Park and the Three Rs

The distinctions among rudeness, rasp, and repudiation—as well as the potential consequences of these three sorts of incivility—can be illustrated by considering, with modifications, a well-known philosophical quarrel between Raymond Gastil and Joel Feinberg. So let us look first at that argument in its original and then commandeer it for our purposes.

Gastil likens the "moral environment" to a public park and claims that "everyone's likes and dislikes cannot be accommodated in the same square." Feinberg rejects Gastil's claim, arguing that

> Gastil's "public square" analogy will not survive scrutiny long. To be sure, you cannot have a band concert, transcendental meditation sessions, carnivals, six-day bicycle races, automobile traffic, and public promenades all at the same time in the same small public square. . . . But there is plenty of room, even in a small public park, for an unlimited variety of thoughts, beliefs and attitudes. Catholics take up no more room than Protestants, Republicans no more than Democrats, blacks no more than whites. And if we find it easy to accommodate religious, political, and ethnic pluralism, indeed pluralism of every *other* kind, why not moral pluralism too?[34]

Of course Feinberg's rhetorical question is to be understood as the assertion that we can, do, and *ought*, in a liberal democracy, to "easily accommodate" diverse religions, political positions, and ethnic and racial groups, and also diversity in moral commitments—again, in Rawls's language, diverse and even antagonistic comprehensive positions.

As I have argued, a significant portion of contemporary incivility is best understood as animosities among people in their roles as members of particular groups. In some instances, the groups with contrary value commitments nonetheless subscribe to the liberal ideals of mutual respect and tolerance. Because of the different value commitments, interactions between the members of the two groups may well be uncivil, but because of a deeper commitment to mutual respect and toleration, these flare-ups can—at least in principle—be quelled. Appeals can be made to those bedrock metavalues that are necessary for coexistence. And coexistence makes possible a better life for all. When groups with incompatible value commitments nonetheless subscribe to the liberal democratic metavalues of mutual respect and toleration, then the public park will indeed accommodate us all. So Feinberg's rejection of Gastil's public park analogy is wholly successful—provided that the members of the various groups, despite their subscribing to different and even antagonistic comprehensive positions, nonetheless subscribe to mutual respect and tolerance. In sharp contrast: if the people in the park *repudiate* tolerance and mutual respect, if their actions are not constrained by a shared commitment to those liberal metavalues, the incivility can become explosive.

For ease of reference, let us name the public square "Multicultural Park." And let us investigate: what sorts of incivilities might erupt in Multicultural Park, and how might those eruptions come about? Of course we can expect to encounter *rudeness*. Led Zeppelin, R. Kelly, or Rachmaninoff being played at ear-splitting volume. Careless bicycle riding; skateboarding and roller blading in inappropriate venues. Footballs and soccer balls and baseballs and Frisbees repeatedly invading the picnic area. And, of course, escalating reactions and overreactions to all of the above.

In addition, we can expect to encounter *rasp*. Even if it is unlikely that Catholics and Protestants could identify themselves and the others in Multicultural Park, Hasidic Jews can be identified—by others, and by one another—from quite some distance. Republicans and Democrats might be able to make the identifications: buttons, bumper stickers, placards at an organized political rally. Other "political" affiliations would be recognizable: Ku Klux Klan robes, burkas, Nazi insignia, skin heads. Race—in the casual sense of color—is obvious and easy even if fallible. Ethnicity—one's own and that of "the other"—might be determined on the basis of color, traditional clothing, or language. In most cases, gender and age can be observed, and public displays of affection could reveal sexual orientation.

This is, of course, but a small sample of the ways in which we divide ourselves into groups of (potentially) differing comprehensive positions— but these are ways in which members and nonmembers could identify themselves and the others, even in a public park. Incidents of rasp between individuals, or more to the point, *groups* of individuals, could break out. But so long as it is rasp merely, there is the in-principle constraint on that incivility of the shared commitment to toleration and mutual respect.

The observable features just enumerated could, however, serve as the basis for the people in Multicultural Park to divide themselves into the in-group, for amity, and the out-group, for enmity.[35] So the incivilities of *repudiation* are possible, too. No doubt the reader has anticipated this: contemporary multicultural societies are Multicultural Park writ large. Some members of some races do not want to share the park or any other part of the *civis*, for that matter, with at least some members of the other perceived races. Some of the devotees of one religion do not want to share the park or any other part of the *civis* with the blasphemers who worship false gods. What if the practices of some group are considered, by another group, abominations in the eyes of the true Supreme Being—and that the first group's very *existence* is a stench in His nostrils? What if those (sub) humans are descended from the barbarians who murdered and raped our ancestors, and stole our sacred lands? In such extreme cases, the "others" are considered to be the infidels, the heathens, the barbarians, the unclean, the blasphemers, and worse. Mutual respect is inconceivable; toleration is unthinkable. Aggression is appropriate; violence will be rewarded in this world and the next.

As argued, Feinberg's rejection of Gastil's analogy is successful—provided that all parties subscribe to the liberal metavalues of tolerance and mutual respect. But if the groups do not subscribe to those metavalues, then Feinberg's rejection of Gastil's analogy is wholly unsuccessful and incivility is precisely what one ought to expect when the members of one group just don't want to commingle with the members of another group, or groups. If the incivilities arise from repudiation, the *civis* cannot be big enough for all.

I believe that incivility as *rudeness* is philosophically unproblematic. Our lives would be more pleasant with less of it; calls for greater sensitivity and more politeness do not threaten individuality or freedom of conscience. Incivility as *rasp*, as the friction between antagonistic comprehensive positions, does raise some issues of philosophical interest. Membership in a community as defined by Rawls is essential to one's identity and one's expectations. Nonetheless, the events of 11 September 2001 are a powerful and sobering reminder of the value of living in a liberal democracy and the centrality of toleration and mutual respect.

Incivility as *repudiation* is, philosophically, the most interesting. It is the most complex and of course the most dangerous. It merits our closest scrutiny: the deep-seated causes of our emotional impulses and reactions, and the dire consequences of our failure to constrain them with sweet reason.

Notes

1. John Rawls, *Justice as Fairness: A Restatement*, ed. Erin Kelly (Cambridge, Mass.: Belknap Press of Harvard University Press, 2001).

2. John Locke, *Second Treatise of Government*, ed. C. B. Macpherson (Indianapolis, Ind.: Hackett, 1980).

3. John Stuart Mill, *On Liberty*, ed. Currin V. Shields (Indianapolis, Ind.: Bobbs-Merrill, 1956), 16.

4. It is also possible that the groups are not, in point of *fact*, "competitors"—mutual prosperity is possible—but that their members *perceive* the groups as competitors.

5. Rawls, *Justice as Fairness*, 3 (internal cites omitted).

6. Ibid.

7. Ibid., 21. The passage continues, "For that would require the oppressive use of government power which is incompatible with basic democratic liberties. From the start, then, we view a democratic society as a political society that excludes a confessional or an aristocratic state, not to mention a caste, slave, or a racist one."

8. Ibid., 2.

9. Ibid., 28–29.

10. Ibid., 32. Internal cite omitted.

11. Ibid., 7.

12. Ibid., 9.

13. Rawls writes, "Political philosophy, as a work of reason. . . ." (*Justice as Fairness*, 3).

14. Thomas Hobbes, *Leviathan*.

15. "Most genetic evolution of human behavior has occurred over a span of hundreds of thousands of years prior to civilization. This means that a legacy of aggression and lethal conflict has adapted to serve humans for 99% of their existence. During that same period, structures of the brain and processes of cognition that are attuned to aggression/warfare have evolved." R. Paul Shaw and Yuwa Wong, *Genetic Seeds of Warfare: Evolution, Nationalism, and Patriotism* (Boston: Unwin Hyman, 1989), 14.

16. Shaw and Wong, *Genetic Seeds of Warfare*, 6.

17. Ibid., 8–9.

18. Edward O. Wilson, *On Human Nature* (Cambridge, Mass.: Harvard University Press, 1978), 116. I shall have more to say about the concept of the "arbitrary boundary" in what follows.

19. Ibid.

20. Shaw and Wong, *Genetic Seeds of Warfare*, 14.

21. Ibid., 27.

22. Ibid., 31.

23. Ibid., 53.

24. Ibid., 47.

25. Ibid., 27.

26. Ibid., 45. "First, all definitions of warfare imply that conflict involves a group. Second, group formation requires altruism and cooperation among individuals" (24). "Weapons would have altered the costs and benefits of aggressive behavior since they could be developed faster than physiological protection against them would evolve. Weapons could also be thrown, thereby removing the need for the attacker to be in close proximity to the attacked. Thus, the development of arms would have lowered

the cost of attacking while increasing the costs of being attacked. In doing so, xenophobia and antagonism toward strangers would likely have increased as well. . . . Outgroup enmity would be strongly reinforced in the process" (53).

27. Ibid., 45. Italics deleted.

28. Ibid., 116.

29. Ibid., 118.

30. Although sometimes sports take on an exaggerated importance for some, leading to violence.

31. Wilson, *On Human Nature*, 188.

32. Ibid., 183.

33. Ibid., 119.

34. Joel Feinberg, *The Moral Limits of the Criminal Law: Harmless Wrongdoing* (New York: Oxford University Press, 1988), 51.

35. It is also possible that the fact that some of "the others" can be identified by the briefest of visual inspections, or so it seems, has contributed to the increase in general impoliteness. Return to "road rage," and consider the following hypothetical "confessions." "I *hate* being cut off in traffic—but I *especially* hate it when it's by: a goddamned yuppie in a BMW, yakking on his cell phone; a rag head who hasn't learned how to drive in America; an absent-minded professor obviously visiting an alternative world; a welfare queen with a passel of kids in a blue-smoking wreck; a forlorn hippie in a psychedelic VW microbus; a J.A.P. in an S.U.V. with Jersey plates, "PINKI"; indistinguishable slant-eyes of all sorts; geezers with blinking turn signals indicating the *other* way." It is interesting to ask: how much of everyday friction is exacerbated upon noticing that another is "an other," a disrespected other?

Part III

Cultural Fragmentation

Culture is a sort of theatre where various political and
ideological causes engage one another. Far from being a
placid realm of Apollonian gentility, culture can even be a
battleground on which causes expose themselves to the light
of day and contend with one another.

　　　　　　　　　　—Edward Said, *Culture and Imperialism*

I hear that melting-pot stuff a lot, and all I can say is that we
haven't melted.

　　　　　　　　　　　　　　　　　—Jesse Jackson

Culture and Society

The contrast between two senses of "culture" noted by Edward Said is
nicely captured if we compare our grandparents' notion of "exposing oneself
to culture" and the more contemporary injunction to "expose oneself to
differing cultures." Culture in the former sense—often rendered with a capital C—was something unquestionably admirable, an area of human activity above the common, and to become a cultured person was a recognized
form of self-improvement. This Culture was, generally, limited to the arts,
literature, theater, and so on. It was high Culture and was widely taken to
transcend the particularities of time and place. Low culture, or what we
now call mass culture, wasn't cultured, at all.

On the other hand, the culture that *is* theater, in Said's metaphor, includes not only the heights of human expression but also the grittiest facts
of ordinary life. It is nothing less than the totality of the ways in which a
people lives. At first blush, it is an elastic concept, easily extended from
national to transnational cultures or narrowed from civic culture to subculture. In this volume, we have made mention of Western liberal democratic

187

culture and noted the existence of various subcultures, and academics discuss fraternity or campus "culture" while popularizing psychologists explore the "culture" of an individual family. Although I will argue that at least some of these are extended metaphorical usages, the basis of the metaphor is evident. In all these uses, the "culture" in question is a life context specific to time and place. Culture, in Said's second sense, is the context and all the modes of our living taken as a whole; it is something one can neither pursue nor escape. Further, culture is a fact of life; it cannot be said of any person or group that they "lack culture," however un-Cultured they are. The extended usages we have noted either take this notion out to its furthest reach or take it piecemeal, but the relationships they reference always exist within a larger social culture of which they are subcategories.

In some circles, recognition of the equal importance, or "validity," of the world's diverse cultures has been taken to signify the demise of the honorific conception of Culture. It is probably more accurate to say that recognition of the diversity of cultures has led open-minded people to appreciate the high Culture of cultures other than their own. That is, it is catholic tastes rather than indiscriminateness that awareness of diversity inspires. Although there is no single, transcendent body of human achievement—frequently misrepresented by a list of books or great works of art—that eclipses all others, the idea of diverse cultures incorporates rather than eliminates the distinction between high and low cultural expression. Every culture has its excellences, its failures, and its mundane features; cultural diversity teaches us to appreciate this fact. Today, to be truly Cultured requires that one be interested and versed in several high Cultures and, possibly, be familiar with some low cultures, as well.[1]

However we understand Culture, it is "culture" in the second sense, culture as totality of modes of life for a particular group of people in a given time and place, that we have in mind when we raise questions about cultural fragmentation.[2] The essays in Part 3 all deal with questions about the purported disintegration of individual national cultures, the cultures of Western nations being the object of most concern. Reverend Jesse Jackson's remark about the situation of American blacks provides an example of the cultural disjunction that the authors address. Characteristically pithy, in one image he confronts us with both awareness of alienation from white culture and a refusal to be subsumed—melted—within it. Cultural fragmentation of this kind most often occurs where groups endorse and seek to maintain different, possibly incompatible, modes of life. Granted, a social subgroup may be rejected by the dominant cultural group, despite individuals' willingness to be assimilated. In those cases, the dominant group imposes its own sense of difference and may force the rejected group to live in conditions that effectively create cultural inconsonance. The many devices that relegated African Americans to inferior educational and employment opportunities effectively prevented most blacks from integrating within the white culture, even when they tried to do so.

Nonetheless, a distinctive feature of the last half-century has been increased resistance to assimilation and cultural homogeneity on the part, especially, of previously oppressed cultural groups. Such intergroup antipathy is what we usually mean when we speak of cultural fragmentation in contemporary contexts. The resistance of certain cultures to foreign influences similarly manifests rejection of homogeneity. In those cases, however, it is a homogeneous "global culture" that is rejected, and it is the foreign influences that threaten to bring cultural fragmentation where none is recognized currently.[3] In either case, when a subgroup refuses to be assimilated and when a society rejects global homogeneity, the aim is to maintain some degree of cultural integrity for the group threatened with loss of a distinctive form of life.

Where the primary dividing issue is religious worldview, this resistance is often pronounced and readily comprehended.[4] Those whose worldviews are at odds, either by pronouncement or de facto, might be said to have good reason for their experiences of incompatibility. At the least, they have reasons for resisting integration and interaction more visible to outsiders than those separated by less life-defining matters. The complete weltanschauung given by many theologies explains the depth of such differences. Perhaps, recognition of the foundational character of a profound religious perspective accounts for the historic tendency of U.S. courts to tread lightly where cultural clashes are religiously grounded. Certainly, we are more ready to demand that citizens compromise where social divisions are seen as being "merely" racial, ethnic, and so on. Indeed, we believe that individuals should try to *overcome* their racial and ethnic antipathies, to the extent that these feelings are regarded as both irrational and damaging to social unity. Laws preventing racial and ethnic discrimination in housing, employment, and education force a measure of social congress on all who would live an ordinary, mainstream, American life. Those who identify with a racially or ethnically defined subculture are expected, for the most part, to accommodate social norms. By contrast, we are less willing to argue that any group should abandon its cherished religious perspective to facilitate social functioning, and American courts commonly seek ways in which the larger society can accommodate religious subgroups.[5]

The familiar reference to religious views as "cherished" is revealing: outside racist circles, who would describe potentially divisive racial views in the same terms? The very suggestion that white identity constitutes a culture comparable to religious cultures—much less one with cherished tenets—is disconcerting. Such language works only if we are employing the piecemeal meaning of "culture," according to which there is a drug culture, an Internet culture, a playground culture, and so forth. Often, this extended usage implies disapprobation, and what is disapproved of in many instances is not, or not solely, the conduct and attitudes of the subgroup's members, but also the effort to elevate mere prejudices or narrow tastes and interests to the level of culture. A culture as the totality of a people's way of life is not a single idea or set of ideas, nor is it a simple collection of habits and mores. Culture, in the strictest sense, is both comprehensive and coherent; it provides a complex worldview having its own internal logic. The sense that only exaggeration and artifice could transform something on the order of racial identity—far less racism—into a full-fledged culture is the source of the extended, ironic, and vaguely disapprobative use of a term that normally designates an impressive human accomplishment.

I do not mean that history presents us with a parade of equally admirable cultures, by any means. Yet—as encompassing the worldview, activities, morality, and aspirations of a group of people over time—any culture, properly so called, is an example of an essentially human enterprise. Individual cultures may be destructive, oppressive, or mediocre; the activity of culture building may be valuable only from a species-specific vantage. Nonetheless, the complexity and magnitude of culture creation is impressive enough to warrant use of a special term, one distinctive to the activity and its product. Those other "minicultures," as Jacques Barzun characterizes them,[6] even those we deem harmless or appealing, are but snippets of culture, in the full sense. Barzun writes: "These small groups are not independent. Their 'culture' consists only of local customs and traditions, individual or institutional habits, class manners and prejudices, language or dialect, upbringing or profession, creed, attitudes, usages, fashions, and superstitions; or, at the narrowest, temperament."[7]

His point, as I take it, is not that these matters are not elements of a culture but that they are, individually, no more than elements.[8] Race, ethnicity, gender, political affiliation, profession, religious denomination as distinguished from worldview—each of these is an important feature of individual and group identity, but none is a culture. Thus, while there is nothing intrinsically objectionable in the idea of a race culture, a corporate culture, a television culture, or a youth culture, these are of insufficient scope and cohesiveness to constitute a culture in the fullest sense. In particular, none of these, nor even a simple aggregation of them, could suffer from cultural fragmentation as that phrase is normally intended and of the sort the authors have in mind.

Fragmentation

What does it mean to say that a society, or a society's culture, is fragmented? "Fragmentation" implies that a whole has been broken into bits—that something which was of a piece is now in pieces. This is why we do not speak of the global variety of cultures as an example of fragmentation. Every national society can be expected to have a relatively distinctive culture, and, so, there is nothing surprising nor alarming in the plurality of the world's cultures. Fragmentation, by contrast, is the condition of what we expect to be unified, such as a national culture.[9] Moreover, the language of fragmentation connotes truly fundamental problems and the peril of full-blown social breakdown. At the least, the context of ordinary life is shaken by fragmentation, as though the backdrop on a stage were to wobble or collapse during the performance. The consternation and confusion—the sense that the action was losing its point along with its setting—would be palpable. Mere plurality does not cause fragmentation, although it is frequently a precondition of it and can be confusing in its own way.

Then, what sense is there in applying the imagery of fragmentation to a functioning national society so long as that society, indeed, continues to function in relatively orderly and stable fashion? Here, there are no pieces lying about, like shards of smashed pottery or shredded fabric. Perhaps it would be more apt to say a society is "cracked" or, like one of the faux finishes currently so popular, "crackled." Neither conveys the actual breakage carried by the metaphor of fragmentation. The former does seem to threaten breakage or loss of function but holds out hope that the damage can be mended. The latter term suggests superficial lines of division, something that can be rendered harmless and aesthetically interesting with a coat of adhesive. Is one of these what we mean when we describe a society as culturally

fragmented? It may be, then, that we are too quick to perceive disintegration where there is only detachment and disassociation. And why do we
believe so many existing societies *are* fragmented? Not only liberal Western societies such as the United States, Canada, France, or Britain, but also
more homogenous, less open, societies such as those of Saudi Arabia, Japan,
or former Soviet Block nations, are now characterized as suffering from
social fragmentation. Apparently, neither internal cultural diversity nor liberal tolerance is a necessary precondition for social disintegration; nor can
conservatism and antidemocratic processes fully guarantee its prevention.
One might suspect that social disunity is the plague of our time, infecting
not only those societies that encourage cultural pluralism but also those
that seek to preclude it. Even if we substitute the less dramatic metaphor
of dissonance for fragmentation, social disunity of various forms appears
widespread. As Barzun observes, the proliferation of "minicultures" can be
read as a response to the fracturing of culture in the full sense.[10] What is
now called identity politics provides an example: individuals and groups
seize on elements of self-identification such as race, gender, or ethnicity as
substitutes for a disintegrating comprehensive culture. Often, the extended
application of "culture" for these minicultures expresses someone's hope
that a genuine culture can be generated out of these small beginnings.

In addition to pluralism, many of the other usual suspects blamed for
loss of civility and deterioration in civic virtues figure, again, in the diag-
noses of sociocultural fragmentation; these include modernism, capitalism,
declining religious practice, value diversity, and so on. Yet, many commentators also name opposed forces: thus, antimodernism, nascent or too-
fettered capitalism, religious fundamentalism, and cultural stagnation are
frequently faulted for social stress in certain parts of the world. Of course,
it is usually the clash of these latter forces and conditions with their an-
titheses that are cited. Thus, fragmentation is said to result from abrasion
of unfamiliar economic, social, and cultural forces against traditional modes.
Often, the new modes are regarded as foreign in origin so that the forces of
change seem to constitute an attack on existing conditions. The most
familiar scenario depicts Western influences, particularly liberal pluralism
and creeping capitalism, as a relentless global tide, eroding older patterns
to which some groups desperately cling. In these cases, Western liberal observers argue that it is resistance to modernism, pluralism, and so on that
leads to social fragmentation. On the other hand, communitarians and conservatives cite ready accession to the same forces and conditions as con-

tributing to social fragmentation in our own, Western, societies—thus lending some credence to the claims of those who seek to preserve their less liberal traditions. From this perspective, one more sympathetic to existing modes and traditions, it is oppressive or violent reaction to change that causes fragmentation, not the clinging to the old.

But this raises another question: where oppression smothers all outcroppings of pluralism and dissent, is the society fragmented in the same sense as a society of diverse, disengaged subcultures or minicultures? It might be useful to distinguish between two forms of social fragmentation, which we can call (1) cultural and (2) civil fragmentation.[11]

Cultural fragmentation is manifest where divergent groups compete for the heart of the society; intolerance and value conflict mark this condition. In the United States, many claim that hate crimes, the emergence of the militia movement, rising fundamentalism, as well as ugly and debased political discourse are symptoms of cultural fragmentation. In the political arena, we have even given this condition an appropriate name: the culture wars—the "cultures," in this case, being minicultures based on sociopolitical perspective. Violence by students is also cited as evidence of cultural alienation, and it is common to hear our young people referred to as constituting a youth culture. In both examples, a subculture or movement is regarded as so alienated from the mainstream national culture as to warrant the extended appellation. Here, the proliferation of subcultures is both a symptom of and self-treatment for fragmentation.

The idea of *civil fragmentation*, by contrast, better represents those societies wherein cultural divisions are few, if only because they are effectively suppressed by nondemocratic political and social institutions. It does seem accurate to characterize Afghanistan under Taliban rule as a fragmented society—rather than a unified one—even though the Taliban either eliminated or silenced those who disagreed with their cultural vision. Enforced cultural uniformity is no more a condition of healthy social integration than is intracultural estrangement; it simply substitutes the hegemony of one group for the disarray of many. Further, as is frequently observed of those countries that reemerged after the dissolution of the Soviet Union,[12] imposed cultural unity may but disguise real conflicts. Whether the peace-enforcing powers fail because of external pressures or through the persistent corrosion of those repressed internal divisions, the cultural disunity only needs an opportunity to resurface—perhaps tragically.

This brings to mind Ronald Reagan's unfortunate remark that "we" didn't know there was a race problem in the United States when he was a young man. Widely decried as manifesting historical ignorance, racial insensitivity, or both, his comment illustrates an important fact: social rifts can be hidden, at least from the eyes of those who belong to the dominant group. I think it's fair to claim that, in the 1940s and 1950s, the majority of white Americans were not fully aware of the mechanisms that kept racial disunity hidden from them. Culpably or not, they did not perceive racial disunity as social fragmentation until the civil rights movement put both the misery of African Americans and the brutal mechanisms of their oppression on display on the nightly news. Should we say that the society was fragmented but that many did not know it, or that it became fragmented only when racial conflict surfaced in demonstrations, violent reprisals, and the clash of federal and state authorities?

If the former, then effective repression precludes significant cleavage, and we must reverse our earlier judgment that Afghanistan under Taliban rule was a fragmented society. Surely, this is a mistaken reading of social realities. For, where government and social institutions conceal social fissures from the consciousness of the dominant group, those whose alienation is thus masked nonetheless experience it for themselves. African Americans knew they lived in a divided society before the civil rights movement whether most whites recognized the fact or not, just as those who managed to survive Taliban violence continued to suffer the effects of estrangement and social conflict while pretending otherwise. It isn't plausible to argue that the relatively peaceful methods of African American oppression in the United States—excepting outbursts of both official and unofficial violence against blacks in certain localities that could be dismissed as aberrations by an inattentive public—somehow exempted the nation from social fragmentation. Perhaps the Taliban, too, would have managed with time to so thoroughly silence all dissidence and complaint that violent repression would no longer be required.

Thus, although it would be too extreme to say that fragmentation is, entirely, in the eye of the oppressed beholder, the dominant group's ignorance of or indifference to social disunion neither precludes nor mends it. There is another lesson, here: fragmentation is painful. Dominant groups, by virtue of their privileged position, do not suffer the pain of fragmentation until alienated groups make their own condition known. Ignorance being bliss, natural resistance on the part of dominant groups often requires that this knowledge is made evident to them—painfully. Thus, the dominant group may feel doubly stricken: first, by the fact of fragmentation where they had seen, or chosen to see, none; and second, by the agitations of disadvantaged groups to bring the message home. From their vantage point, the discontent of subgroups may be seen as self-perpetuating. If only "they" would fit in, let bygones be bygones, try to get along, not tell if we don't ask, and so forth. Resistance to assimilation is understood as refusal to accommodate reasonable social norms of the dominant group or groups, and all parties accuse one another of intolerance and narrow-mindedness.

The nature of complaints made by alienated subgroups can vary, depending on the facts of social history and current conditions. A history of explicit and immediate discrimination may have forced a subgroup to exist *as* a subgroup, as alienated, despite the readiness of some or most of its members to live in harmony with the dominant group. Once that history is generally acknowledged, the oppressed group might not be willing to forgive and forget and may, reasonably enough, be nonplussed by the dominant group's conversion to social unity. The African-American experience is the most dramatic example of this sort of history in the United States.

Sometimes there are longstanding cultural divisions or ideological conflicts, and a subgroup will have grounds for complaint based either on the actual repression of their cultural modes or on the indifference of the dominant group to the special requirements of those modes. Here, we can compare the treatment of Mormons in the early days of their movement with the current situation of fundamentalist religious observers in the United States. The first Mormons were, literally, driven out of their homes and towns, forbidden entirely from practicing polygamy, which they regarded as a duty rather than a privilege, and subject to violent attacks by fellow citizens and government officials, alike. Many religious observers, today, feel that their need to express their religious views—for example, by public prayer, through participation in school clubs, and in their own discrimination against those who deviate from their moral code—is dismissed by a secular society and its institutions. Although the brutal treatment of early Mormons imposed alienation of a different order, it cannot surprise us that religious fundamentalists living in an officially secular society would also feel themselves significantly at odds with the larger culture.

At present, much cultural dissonance is the consequence of emerging ethnic pride or newly valorized group identity. My sense is that this occurs most often where the dominant culture has historically denigrated diversity, in general, or manifested negative attitudes toward the specific features of personal identity at issue. In the first instance, there is reaction against an excessively hegemonic national culture, a denial of intracultural homogeneity. From the perspective of many, the much vaunted American melting pot ideal required that some groups be assimilated, not into a genuine admixture of cultures, but within a predominantly white, Christian, European cultural heritage. But, even to the extent that the American culture was something novel—the product of multicultural amalgamation and frontier spirit—emphasis was placed on becoming part of that culture as distinguished from holding to traditions from native lands.[13] The melting pot was not supposed to celebrate diverse cultures as they previously existed in distinction from one another; it was to dissolve them all into a novel brew. For an example of the second variant, we need only look to the gay and lesbian pride movement and the proclaimed gay and lesbian subculture in light of historic and continuing mistreatment of nonheterosexuals. The often-expressed wish of straight Americans that their gay and lesbian fellow citizens would not "flaunt" their sexual orientation nicely completes the picture of incompatible demands: on the one hand, "let us be ourselves"; on the other hand, "keep it to yourselves."

Frequently, the cynosure of a miniculture is a marker for more profound differences. Thus, preserving linguistic identity may become the lodestar of a group's struggle to retain broader cultural distinctiveness. The importance, for example, of Spanish to Hispanic and Latino Americans depends on its symbolic connotation of cultural and religious roots as much as on their valuation of it simply as a language. Language use, in and of itself, is not the heart of the matter. In turn, dominant or otherwise opposed groups will also focus on the issue of language—as though that, alone, embodied all the sources of conflict among the relevant groups. The English-only movement in the United States attracts many advocates whose interest lies less with linguistic unity than with expressing group dominance and imposing a degree of cultural hegemony. They are not concerned that some Americans speak Spanish, as a rule; they are concerned that the inclusion of Spanish in public documents, on signs, or at the voting place bestows equal status on the Hispanic elements in American culture. The tortured, if amusing, lengths to which certain European governments go in preventing the encroachment of foreign-language terms and usage into their native language is another example of this phenomenon. No one can seriously claim that the mere use of foreign terms—such as my use of *weltanschauung*, earlier—could despoil one national culture with features or characteristics somehow specific to another. Loss of a native language may be part of cultural dilution, but it is neither a necessary nor a sufficient condition of it. Yet, as symbolic of cultural drift, perceived loss of purported linguistic purity is a ready marker, especially useful for purposes of political and social agitation.

Thus, we find several etiologies of cultural fragmentation. The underlying disputes always concern accommodations: accommodations made to subgroups in the name of diversity or denied in the name of unity, accommodations made or rejected to preserve national character from foreign influences, accommodations between competing needs and conflicting values. Who will accommodate whom, in what ways, to what extent, and on what grounds—these are always the fighting issues of cultural rift.

Accommodation, Multiculturalism, and Individualism

It is tempting to claim that prevailing cultural groups are naturally disinclined to change or universally unwilling to accommodate the demands of dissident subgroups, but such a claim overstates the facts. Although it is true that few dominant groups happily permit significant inroads on their own values and mores, all culture is fluid. Said's metaphor of the theater of conflict should be supplemented with one that is more organic. Culture is not simply the arena of intentional human activity; it is also the process and product of all our endeavors and interactions. It is a sea of intersecting tides that sweeps us up in its currents, and we often feel unable to direct or to fully comprehend our own cultural wash. Cultural forces appear to have a life of their own, one that sometimes resists avowedly objective external analysis as much as internal comprehension. For, as Said also observed, "All cultures are involved in one another; none is single and pure, all are hybrid, heterogeneous, extraordinarily differentiated, and unmonolithic."[14] This is what makes reductive cultural analyses so patently unsatisfying; we simply know that there is more—that the whole matter is more complicated, more disorderly, more dynamic.

And so, whether we are fish in our own body of water or oceanographers attempting to explain it all from a drier vantage point, any given culture presents itself always in motion and as deeply complex. Thus, every culture admits of alterations. The most aggressive efforts to maintain a culture as it exists at one point in time necessarily fail, sooner or later, and no culture is a seamless whole at any point in its history. When we speak of homogeneous cultures, as when we speak of cultural disunity, we are always speaking relatively. There are degrees of unity and dissonance, degrees of harmony and friction, degrees of hegemony and plurality. It is for this reason, in part, that cultural fragmentation is, itself, a matter of dispute, turning on the diagnostician's perspective. Further, it is partly this that accounts for the disparate perceptions typically experienced by conservatives and liberals making cultural assessments. There is more to the disagreement than is suggested by the old saw that conservatives are pessimists and liberals optimists; in fact, they have very different responses to sociocultural plurality. People of a conservative bent do not simply foresee danger in diversity; they find it discomfiting. The liberal-minded are likely to be comfortable with diversity and difference, even if they recognize an element of destabilization. These are caricatures, of course. Still, a good caricature conveys some truth, and the divergence in liberal and conservative temperaments is reflected in the history of politically liberal and conservative societies.

We should be careful, here, for there is no necessary relation between type of political structure and diversity of culture. Consider the Roman Empire, particularly the city itself, with its remarkable jostling of cultural influences, cults, ethnicities, and occupations. Clearly, the empire was not politically liberal, however culturally tolerant—or libertine—it may have been. We can also imagine politically liberal institutions governing a fairly homogeneous cultural milieu;[15] postcolonial America and present-day Holland both come to mind. It is quite possible for those who embrace liberal political institutions to prefer relative cultural homogeneity and for those who favor conservative political order to be indulgent toward cultural clutter. But, having said this, we can acknowledge the norms: political liberalism tends to be accompanied by cultural pluralism, and political conservatism tends to be associated with cultural homogeneity or the appearance of it. This seems to be true of most contemporary societies, bearing in mind that diversity and homogeneity are relative concepts. Principles of democracy, equality, and tolerance, as well as lenient immigration and travel policies, serve to increase variation in cultural modes and allow for open expression of differences. Pluralism will flourish where it is tolerated.

These factors, and others,[16] have contributed to the United States becoming one of the most culturally diverse nations in all history. Its multicultural profile is both heralded and decried, as the several uses of the term reveal. *Multicultural* denotes a society in which many cultural modes are manifested and celebrated; this is its descriptive meaning. But it is also used

normatively—both in recommending acceptance of cultural heterogeneity and in disparaging it. Thus, the movement known as "multiculturalism"
actively promotes heterogeneity in education and other sociopolitical institutions, while its critics deny that the United States is or should be multicultural. The multiculturalists assert that whatever dominant culture once
existed in the United States is now fading or vanquished, and they hail the
coemergence of varied subcultures in its place. The melting pot, they claim,
was an oppressive concept, not an ideal to be pursued in a free society. Critics of multiculturalism contend that loss or rejection of a dominant national
culture is an evil to be avoided by any healthy society. Multiculturalism,
they argue, *is* cultural fragmentation, and it is the cause of numerous social
ills, including failing schools, street violence, moral ennui, and the decline
of patriotism.

Here, we arrive at issues of accommodation. Even within a theoretically
liberal society such as the United States, where individual liberty and official tolerance are respected values, capacities for managing diversity will
vary. They will vary, moreover, not merely among individuals or groups but
also within single institutions and the state as a whole. History, national
temperament, and accidents of time and place determine each society's ability to accommodate cultural diversity and change. In the United States,
the original and powerful concern for religious tolerance has proven inadequate to overcome contemporary official hostility to recreational drug use.
Thus, Rastafarians and others who have sought dispensation from the government to use mood-altering drugs, as their religious traditions dictate,
have been rebuffed. By contrast, the Amish, whose aims conflict with
American commitments to educating the young and furthering individual
autonomy, have largely succeeded in preserving their own cultural modes.
So, too, in America every type of political advocacy is permitted, while sexual orientation continues to be a basis for overt discrimination and sup-
pression. This dichotomy puts us in the culturally awkward position of
being officially more accepting of neo-Nazis than of gays and lesbians, to
the perplexity of our Western allies.

Such vagaries are evident not only with respect to the substance of cultural divides, the nature of the issues that divide us, but also in the modes of
accommodation that a given society or group is ready to make. An interesting example is the peculiarly American fixation on the distinction between
expression, or speech, and practice, or action. That there is a distinction is
an important principle of all liberal societies, but it is one that is made to bear

unusual weight in American legal and cultural debates. In a famous free-speech case, *Cohen v. California,* the U.S. Supreme Court upheld Cohen's right to enter a courtroom wearing a shirt with the bold proclamation "F-k the Draft." Although the majority and dissenters quibbled over the correct categorization of this moment in Cohen's life, the Court concluded that this was speech, not conduct, and therefore must be protected. We may say what we will, but not always do as we please, and marking the difference is an American art to which other equally liberal societies are less devoted.[17]

There are many other possibilities for divergent accommodation of pluralism. For example, while some states are inclined to enact and preserve laws they do not enforce, others will refuse to legislate unless enforcement is intended. The material effects of these approaches may be much the same, but the cultural milieus must differ dramatically in the experience of those whose lives are officially circumscribed. So too, some states proscribe or prescribe conduct with a heavy hand, while others prefer to use education and persuasion. Here, disparate effects on the lives of the citizenries and for each society as a whole can be materially significant. Imagine an America in which money and official energy were channeled into treatment programs rather than into the "drug war" and where recreational drug users were counseled rather than imprisoned. Further, citizens in some nations expect one another to observe decorum in public although they are indifferent to liberties enjoyed in private, whereas citizens of other nations deride any freedom that does not extend to full disclosure. The supposedly unique degree of freedom enjoyed by U.S. citizens may be exaggerated by the extent to which individual Americans feel free to engage in public displays of self-expression.

With respect to this last point, it is difficult to gauge the relative roles of genuine idiosyncrasy and mere self-display in our notion of individualism. But, we do recognize that these are often distinct. American adolescents, for example, are loath to differ from others in their identity group although individually compelled, it appears, to announce themselves to the larger public. Two teenaged girls—identical in dress, speech, and manner—can easily attract the attention of an entire room of shoppers with their exuberant presence. And what reason could we have to ascribe a genuinely individual outlook to the "Pink Lady" of my youth, who promenaded in the downtown district each Saturday, hair, clothes, and poodle all similarly tinted? Exhibitionism signifies one's wish to stand out, but persons of ordinary, even conformist, natures may have that wish from time to time. A culture that valorizes individualism need not, in fact, produce many genuinely unique personalities.

Certainly, the tendency of a people to appear much the same in dress and other outward modes does not entail their lack of individuality *as* individuals nor that their culture suppresses diversity of viewpoint, values, or conduct. On the other hand, public self-restraint undoubtedly minimizes cultural friction by allowing citizens to remain unaware of what otherwise separates them, at least until they actively engage one another. It is here that the cult of individualism bears import for cultural plurality and cultural fragmentation. When the desire to "strut your stuff" is armored in a sense of individual right, anyone may be prone to defy the sensitivities and wishes of others. Indeed, their dislike of our self-expression is an offense against our individuality. In this way, with all clamoring to be heard—not simply to speak—resentment breeds resentment, and accommodation becomes increasingly difficult to achieve. Individualism, to the extent that it links being true to oneself with being inconsiderate of others, fosters cultural conflict where there might have been no more than plurality.

Moreover, emphasis on the individual and the individual's discreteness can lead to social fragmentation where there is no meaningfully *cultural* division at all. Where individual independence is part of the cultural value system, as it is in the United States, alienation between citizens may be as much cause for concern as conflicts between groups. Here, what is at issue is not the uniqueness of one's viewpoint or personality, nor divergent values and beliefs. Individuality in the sense pertinent to interpersonal alienation is perfectly compatible with cultural uniformity, so long as the culture in question permits persons to be indifferent to one another's interests or welfare. This is the context in which the language of "rugged individualism" takes its special meaning. The rugged individual, who may be quite ordinary in tastes and outlook, is self-sufficient and self-reliant, and the ethos of rugged individualism requires that others be equally so. The rugged individual "goes it alone" insofar as he or she seeks no help from others, and a nation of rugged individuals is a nation of citizens who neither seek aid from nor proffer it to those with whom they are not closely associated.

Another caricature, admittedly. Nonetheless, when everyone aspires to be a John Wayne film character, interdependency is neither necessary nor desirable. And so, social fragmentation reaches its point of ultimate alienation where there may be no cultural division whatsoever. The distinction between cultural rifts and extreme individualism is important, because it gives the lie to those slippery-slope predictions that antipluralists some-times make. Cultural pluralism is not the death knoll of public conscious-ness and community spirit; nor is homogeneity a guarantor of interpersonal closeness and communal interdependence. Shared values and interests do not bring us together as a matter of course. We may share the values of competition, independence, and self-sufficiency as easily as those of coop-eration, interdependence, and care. And our interests, for example in accru-ing wealth, may be the same even as they pit us against one another. In sum, although it may be easier to care about the well-being of those who are like us, cultural familiarity and interpersonal concern are, unfortunately, causally discrete.

The Essays

The contributions to the concluding part of this volume center on social fragmentation of the types just discussed. The first four, by Joseph Ellin, Heidi Malm, David Reidy, and myself, are also examples of what is com-monly known as "applied" philosophy: that is, they present normative posi-tions regarding concrete legal and social problems. Here, each of the problems addressed arises from or points to social fragmentation of a par-ticular variety within the United States. With an eye to the applied char-acter of the essays, they are offered in pairs, each pair dealing with a single issue; in this way, the reader is provided with two contrasting views on each concrete problem. The final piece, by Lester Mazor, is a description and analysis of the condition of contemporary German society and, thus, pro-vides a glimpse into issues of cultural fragmentation outside the United States. Mazor does not focus on a single issue; rather, his commentary dis-closes the several sources of the social disharmony currently afflicting the German people, institutions, and culture.

We begin Part 3 with two pieces, Heidi Malm's "Civic Virtue and the Legal Duty to Aid" and Joseph Ellin's "The Mind of a Bad Samaritan," on a subject that has occupied many legal philosophers, including this editor, for some time.[18] Generally, the issue is the reluctance of Anglo-American legal systems to impose criminal liability for omissions, or failures to act. The most commonly discussed instance of such liability is that for what is popularly known as "Bad Samaritanism," or failure to aid others in peril. By consensus, based on notions of fairness and reasonableness, possible lia-bility for failure to rescue is presumed limited to cases in which a rescuer might provide aid without "significant" risk to herself. The idea, here, is simply that the law ought not to require ordinary citizens to be heroes. Concern that law not be unduly onerous is heightened insofar as heroism attempted by ordinary persons may well increase the number of lives lost or injuries suffered. As television shows often warn us, heroic stunts are better not tried "at home." All parties to the debate over duties to rescue agree that preventing loss of life or serious injury is, ceteris paribus, a social good. This is the one aim of Bad Samaritan liability that can be embraced by both opponents and proponents.

Other aims, implicit or stated, are very much at issue. A particular worry of many opponents, including those to whom Malm refers as libertarians, is that the law should not be used to make people good. This reflects standard liberal wariness of *legal moralism*: that is, the view that conduct may be controlled by the state simply on the grounds of its "immorality" but absent a causal connection with actual harm.[19] Immorality as such, according to liberalism, is not a warrant for criminal liability; some specifiable harm to others caused by the agent's conduct must be the basis for liability. And, although Mill himself believed that failure to act could be a cause of such harm to others, he cautioned that "to make anyone answerable for doing evil to others is the rule; to make him answerable for not preventing evil is, comparatively speaking, the exception."[20]

It is interesting and important to note that neither Malm's, highly provisional, advocacy of Bad Samaritan laws nor Ellin's opposition to them is grounded directly in the legal moralism debate. Granted, Malm does not object to any possible ameliorating effect that liability might have on the character of those currently indifferent to the well-being of others, and Ellin questions the wisdom of using Bad Samaritan liability to effect moral improvement in the citizenry. However, Malm does not recommend Bad Samaritan liability on moralist grounds, and Ellin's objection is that such liability is unlikely to have the effect of improving anyone's moral character. To the contrary, he asserts, it is more likely that people will act—if they do—simply out of fear of liability; mere compliance with the law, he reminds us, is not a genuine form of moral motivation.

What does divide Malm and Ellin, who share a fundamentally liberal perspective on the limits of the law, is the *extent* to which Bad Samaritan legislation represents encroachment on individual liberty and the *amount* of social advantage to be gained by such encroachment. From a liberal viewpoint, the latter is as important as the former; the liberal assumption is always that liberty is a basic good and that any limitations on it must be justified by a *greater* good. Thus, Ellin can admit that Bad Samaritan laws might achieve some social benefit, but nonetheless argue against them on grounds that the benefits cannot outweigh the evil of liberty restriction. In countering such a claim, Malm can, and does, seek to both emphasize the good that can be achieved and minimize the seriousness of the liberty infringement. I am suggesting, then, that these two essays are best read as liberal analyses of a possible form of criminal liability aimed at reducing social harms, rather than as a communitarian/libertarian debate about the legitimate extent of the law or the use of legal coercion to make citizens become morally better persons. Although Malm does reference some arguments for a duty to rescue that she, herself, characterizes as legal moralist or communitarian views, her own provisional defense of Bad Samaritan legislation seems to rest on grounds that would suit Mill and, possibly, even Ellin. In fact, she concludes her essay by arguing that current Bad Samaritan laws are *not* fully justifiable, precisely because they impose on individual liberty without assurance of an appreciable reduction in social harm. So, too, Ellin concludes his piece by forcefully denying the social value of Bad Samaritan laws as weighed against the encroachment on individual liberty and the practical difficulties attendant on framing them. No doubt, Malm is more sympathetic to the idea of positive duties to aid than is Ellin, but what finally distinguishes their positions is their estimation of just how surmountable such practical difficulties might be. Malm suggests that legislation and enforcement *could be* designed that would serve the justifiable ends of Bad Samaritan laws, while Ellin clearly does not. In particular, Malm is more comfortable relying on prosecutorial, judicial, and jury discretion than Ellin, who warns us of the dangers always attendant on such discretionary powers. Yet, even Malm is not persuaded, finally, that the dangers of such laws outweigh the goods they might secure for us.

Underlying Malm's and Ellin's dispute concerning the use of a legal duty to rescue are issues of social alienation that exercise liberals and nonliberals alike. Malm and Ellin, in different ways, evince their disapproval of those who are indifferent to the welfare of others, and Malm, at least, affirms the existence of a moral duty to render easy aid. But, given their focus on the possible concrete effects of Bad Samaritan laws and the troubles inherent in legislation and enforcement, the authors cannot address what might be the salient question for many of us: what is it that makes some individuals so unwilling to help others? Put another way, the question that remains for the reader is how civilized people, and Americans in particular, can become so alienated from their fellow humans, and citizens, that they will not act on behalf of others even when there is little or no cost to themselves.

The second pair of essays in Part 3, David Reidy's "Hate Crimes Laws: Progressive Politics or Balkanization?" and my "Hate Crime and Social Fragmentation," also take up the legitimacy of a form of criminal liability: that imposed by a group of laws jointly known as "Hate crimes" law. Hate crimes legislation and the conduct it is intended to control are directly related to the issues of social fragmentation discussed in this Introduction. To that extent, hate crime liability is, perhaps, the sort of legal problem that comes to mind most readily under the rubric of social—especially cultural—fragmentation. Here, we have both conflicts between cultural subgroups and questions as to the use of social power to support diversity where it is opposed by some members of the society. As was the case with the essays by Malm and Ellin, these two pieces take a broadly similar position on the use of criminal liability—in this case, both are in favor of hate crime liability of some form or other—but there are significant disparities in approach. The crucial issues that separate us regarding hate crimes law are the justificatory purposes of liability and the specific forms of liability in light of those purposes; that is, Reidy and I disagree both as to the legitimate ends to be served and the legitimate means to be employed.

Although a number of contributors to this volume might characterize their own views as progressive, communitarian, or the like, Reidy presents a perspective that is, arguably, farthest from mainstream liberalism. As his title suggests, he argues from a "progressive" or left-of-liberal standpoint, and much of his criticism is directed toward what he describes as "standard liberal" arguments for hate crime liability. Reidy contends that those standard arguments are flawed—and are flawed in pretty much the ways opponents of hate crime liability claim.[21] He distinguishes between three lines of arguments: (1) those based on claims that hate crimes cause greater harm than other crimes of the same type; (2) those that claim the culpability of hate crime offenders is greater than that of other offenders of the same type; and (3) those that contend for expression of liberal values of tolerance and nondiscrimination, values that hate crimes typically affront.

Reidy assesses and rejects each of these lines of argument, finding them to be weak, contrary to the intuitions that underlie hate crimes law, or both. I find the argument from greater harm and the evidence of it to be more cogent than does Reidy. But, this is an empirical issue, as he notes, and may be one on which we must agree to disagree, statistics and statistical interpretation being what they are. Further, I suggest that, in addition to physical and psychological harms suffered by individuals, hate crimes inflict a serious social harm particularly worrisome to liberal pluralist societies— societies in which social bonds tend to be tenuous in the best of times. Thus, I offer what might be called an "argument from social disunity." And, although I do not employ the argument from greater culpability, per se, I do argue that the hate crime offender's motivation *as a causal factor* warrants special legal concern. Finally—while, again, I do not rely on an argument from liberal values as he depicts it—I am not persuaded that expression of social outrage at specific types of criminality is unwarranted or unjust, even prima facie.

As an alternative to such liberal defenses of hate crime liability, Reidy recommends an argument "from oppression." Fundamentally, this defense of hate crime liability turns on the claim that members of certain social groups—notably African Americans and other nonwhites, Jews, gays and lesbians, and people of non-European ethnic heritage—have been historically oppressed by the social structures of the United States and, therefore, merit special protection from crimes that effectively "reconstitute" that historic mistreatment. In making out this argument, Reidy provides two insightful and highly useful analyses. The first gives us a taxonomy of types of social groups and their divergent situations; the second evinces the specific features of vulnerability to structural oppression. Based on these analyses, Reidy argues that the purpose of hate crimes law is to redress, to some extent, the history of oppression and to prevent further abuse of those most vulnerable to discrimination and group hatreds. It is here that Reidy and I come into sharpest disagreement. Granting the importance of history and social facts as historically constructed, I reject the argument that specific groups of persons should be provided special protection from hate crimes or hate-crime-like offenses. The difficulties attendant on any such effort at victim specification are, I believe, evinced by Reidy's own need to add "and the like" or "and so on" each time he tries to list the groups for whom he thinks special protection is required.

In my essay, I offer more detailed analysis of problems consequent upon such attempts at specification, but the reader will recognize that Reidy and I are at odds about more than the practical difficulties of crafting workable legislation. From my perspective—one perhaps more standardly liberal than

Reidy's—the practical problems follow directly from the illegitimacy of designating certain groups of persons as more worthy than others of protection under law. As I argue in the essay, the special protections offered by law to children, police officers, and so on, are not—at least not most cogently—based on their being persons more deserving of legal concern, not even more vulnerable to criminal activity. Our affection for children and respect for those who perform services to the state may be quite real; in and of themselves, however, those feelings are not sufficient ground for enhanced liability for criminals who victimize them.

Reidy is quite correct in citing our historically informed intuition of a moral difference between a case of white on black hate-motivated crime and a case of black on white hate-motivated criminality. But, my own sense is that this moral difference is not one to be dealt with in the definition of offenses. Like Malm, I am inclined to leave some of these matters to the discretion, if not the wisdom, of prosecutors, judges, and—especially—juries. And, as to the worry that liability for hate crimes will fall equally on the shoulders of members of historically oppressed and oppressing groups, I fear that we are far from the day when whatever ahistorical impartiality the law can muster will be reflected in the conduct of all our citizens. In other words, members of historically oppressed and marginalized groups will continue to be the majority of hate crime victims, however evenhanded legal liability for such offenses may be.

Our final piece, Lester Mazor's "Contemporary Germany Faces Multicultural Society," also addresses cultural fragmentation grounded in intergroup antipathy, as distinguished from alienation among individuals. It provides our one look into a European nation's efforts to deal with cultural pluralism, efforts that the author reveals as being, themselves, a significant cause of social fragmentation. Mazor is a sometime resident of Germany, and he brings that direct experience to bear on German cultural fragmentation in combination with both historical and philosophical analyses. The resulting essay is, in many ways, unique among those in this volume and, so, provides a fitting end to the collection.

Many readers will be struck by the openly xenophobic attitudes common to many native Germans, as Mazor reveals them. Indeed, the fact that legal status *as* a German was restricted to those who can claim German bloodlines until quite recently is likely to be a startling revelation to Americans, accustomed as we are to the idea that there are—and should be—several paths to obtaining full citizenship. The traditional German fixation on "blood," or ancestry, as the sole determinant of true citizenship may seem shocking to us and disturbingly reminiscent of the kind of thinking promoted by the Nazi myth of "Aryanism." On the other hand, Mazor warns us against being too quick to condemn the German people as a group or to assume that the genocidal history of World War II fully captures the possibilities of German thought. He provides several anecdotes to illustrate recent German racism and ethnophobia, but the astute reader will recognize that most of these stories involve Germans—perhaps as background figures—who reject those prejudices. And, we must remind ourselves that distressing instances of hate crime, discrimination, and inflammatory anti-immigration politics can be found in our own culture.

Although Mazor's piece is primarily historical and descriptive in character, he suggests two main theses. The first is that Germany is heading toward a crisis point in its dealings with immigrants and residents who are not of German ancestry. One cause of this looming threat is the rise of multiculturalism currently experienced in all the Western nations. Economic opportunities and political freedoms—even if less than fully realized for immigrant groups—draw people from other parts of the world to the Western democracies to study, work, and live. This trend, of course, is facilitated by the increasing mobility of all peoples; it is further accelerated by the tragedies of war and famine suffered by people in many poor and undemocratic nations, to whom the West offers the only available escape. As Mazor notes, Germany's participation in the European Union introduces new pressures for multiculturalism and toleration; Germany as a state has embarked on a course that xenophobic groups and individuals were unable to halt and will likely be unable to reverse. Borrowing from Hegel and Marx, we might say that history is against the xenophobes, both ideally and materially.

This reference to Hegel and Marx brings us to Mazor's second thesis: that German philosophical thought has played and can continue to play an important role in Germany's search for social harmony and stability. Mazor contests the view that Germany failed to enjoy the full fruits of Enlightenment thought and, therefore, did not learn to deal with the stresses of modernism. Rather, he argues, Enlightenment themes of rationality, universalism, and progress abound in the work of Kant, Hegel, and Marx. I take Mazor to be claiming that the problem for German thought is not a lack of liberal or rationalist moral and social theory, but the collapse of modernism. In this, the German situation is similar to that of many other

Western nations, including the United States: they seem to be left with what Mazor characterizes as an arid and abstract liberalism—one that is no more than the best available option among an array of failed sociopolitical experiments. What distinguishes the German situation is that Germans, themselves, have never become fully acclimated to the liberal style. For them, toleration and pluralism have never been facts, not even imperfectly actualized as they are in the history of other Western nations. Therefore, liberalism as a mere modus vivendi, with its half-hearted tolerance and purely formal respect for rights, is inadequate to meet the demands of a multicultural German society.

Mazor concludes his article with a tantalizing prospect: the rehabilitation, so to speak, of Nietzsche and Schopenhauer as sources of German sociopolitical thought. He tempts us with the notion that social connectedness might be achieved through human empathy rather than through either the abstractions of Enlightenment philosophy or the tribalism of ancient peoples. The result, should it be achieved, would be a society in which pluralism could fully flourish along within genuinely human social bonds.

C.S.

Notes

1. The failing of the list wavers is not their insistence on a distinction between high and low—better or worse—but on the reasons they employ for purposes of discrimination. Put another way, their lists are typically parochial and, thus, too short. And *that*, of course, is the problem with lists.

2. It might be noted that extreme disassociation between consumers of high and low culture could be an indication of cultural fragmentation, particularly if the gap is due to severe disparity in wealth, education, and so on.

3. Concerning ignorance or denial of existing cultural rifts, see the section entitled "Fragmentation" in this Introduction.

4. The same can be said of metaphysical perspectives, in general. Theistic worldviews differ from other metaphysical perspectives as held by ordinary members of a group, insofar as specific tenets of belief are enunciated; this allows enemies and heretics to be clearly identified. Also see note 9.

5. Of course, the courts do not always or reflexively *decide* in favor of groups seeking special accommodations on religious grounds. Accidents of history, prejudice, and social tolerance have bequeathed us a legal record that jurisprudence must sometimes strain to render theoretically lucid.

6. Jacques Barzun, *From Dawn to Decadence; 500 Years of Western Cultural Life* (New York: HarperCollins, 2000) xiv–xv.

7. Ibid., xv.

8. Here, I understand "creed" to be something far narrower than "religion" or "religious viewpoint." The many Christian denominations espouse a variety of creeds, but I would argue that all participate in one religious culture. Further, that culture is usually named Judeo-Christian, which widens the creedal scope considerably.

9. This raises the intriguing question of whether the idea of a single global culture is meaningful. Does the concept of culture entail plurality? On the one hand, it should not do so; if humanity should ever become sufficiently unified, and ways of life sufficiently homogeneous, a worldwide macroculture is possible. On the other hand, history has ingrained in us the notion that culture has some boundaries, typically signified by the existence of other, differing, cultures. Thus, we conceive of Western culture in contrast to Eastern cultures and of Judeo-Christian cultures as distinguished from cultures grounded in ancestor worship and polytheism. Certainly, absent these and similar contrasts, talk of cultural identity would lose import, because we would all have the same cultural identity. In that case, minicultures and subcultures might become the primary and appropriate denotative objects of the language of culture, all else becoming simply "human."

10. Barzun, op. cit., xv.

11. For those who wish to make the comparison with Gramsci's distinction between *civil* and *political* society, according to which *culture* is a feature of the former, only, in nontotalitarian systems: I, too, take "society" to be the generic term, within which I distinguish between two forms of fragmentation, cultural and civil. Although there is clearly overlap between "civil," in my usage, and "culture" in Gramsci's, I do not distinguish as sharply between institutions of the state and "voluntary" institutions as Gramsci did. Therefore, while I think oppressive state rule creates or signifies a special type of social fragmentation—which I call civil fragmentation—I do not think culture, in general, exists altogether apart from (nonoppressive) political institutions.

12. It can be noted that the nation of Russia, as it exists post–Soviet Union, is a society that is disintegrating but not clearly suffering from social fragmentation of either sort discussed here. Culturally and civilly, Russia appears to remain a relatively unified nation, but its economy is moribund, crime has increased greatly, and the social institutions that formerly served to protect the most vulnerable citizens have been eliminated. Social pathology includes more than our two modes of social fragmentation.

13. The importance of "the new" in American culture should not be underestimated. Naturally, many immigrants arrived with the hope of creating new lives and new identities for themselves. This, combined with the expectations of those already in place, transformed the opportunity to begin anew into a duty to leave old ways behind.

14. Edward Said, *Culture and Imperialism* (New York: Knopf, 1993).

15. We can remind ourselves of Mill's claim that what we call cultural homogeneity

was a mark of a healthy society; this from one who championed experimentation as well as democracy and individual rights.

16. Exactly what brings most immigrants to the United States is a question that merits a more complex answer than I can offer, here. In particular, the comparative appeal for immigrants from culturally conservative nations of economic opportunity and democratic institutions, on the one hand, and cultural liberality, on the other, bears some examination. We are accustomed to saying that all people come to the United States in search of freedom. However, this is also said of the Puritans, whose affection for cultural pluralism was not renowned.

As to the claim itself—that the United States is highly multicultural—I have some hesitation. First, there is a recognizable American culture, or style, that is manifest even amid our diversity. Second, many critics of American culture observe that our mass culture is stultifyingly homogeneous, making ours a nation of strip malls, smooth-voiced television news anchors, and fast-food restaurants with little regional or local distinction. On the other hand, there is evident truth to the claim of our pluralism. And, at any rate, it is such a commonplace observation that I feel compelled to accept it for present purposes.

17. In fairness, the case was correctly decided on liberty grounds, and the majority probably would have decided it that way without the distinction between speech and conduct. The point, here, is that reliance on that distinction was understood to secure the decision, as though the distinction rather than the liberty was the crucial issue.

18. See, for example, C. Sistare, "In the Land of Omissions: An Opinionated Guide," *Criminal Justice Ethics* 14:1 (1995).

19. See Malm, chap. 11, this volume. The tradition is usually traced to Mill's elaboration of his "simple principle," that is, that the individual "cannot rightfully be compelled to do or forbear because it will be better for him to do so, or, in the opinion of others, to do so would be wise or even right." J. S. Mill, *On Liberty* (Indianapolis, Ind.: Hackett, 1978), 13.

20. Mill, *On Liberty*, 15.

21. Reidy is to be commended, in my opinion, for contending against claims that hate crimes laws are the product of resentment and mean-spiritedness—rather than simply dismissing such arguments as the ad hominem smokescreens they are.

Chapter 11

Civic Virtue and the Legal Duty to Aid

Heidi Malm

In the concluding episode of the long-running television series *Seinfeld*, the famous foursome witness a roadside robbery, but, instead of trying to interrupt the robbery, aid the victim, or use a cell phone to call the police, the foursome stood by mocking the victim's weight and pondering his general worthiness as a human being. Unbeknownst to the foursome, such failures to aid were illegal in the state in which this one took place, and they were arrested and brought to trial. The evidence phase of the trial provided the show's writers with an excuse to highlight comedic moments from past episodes that showed the characters' extreme shallowness and self-absorption and, thus, further evinced the characters' callous disregard of the welfare of others. In the end, the members of the foursome were sentenced to a year in jail for their conduct.

Unfortunately, appalling failures to aid are not limited to television sitcoms. In May 1997, David Cash saw his best friend, Jeremy Strohmeyer, struggling with a seven-year-old girl in the men's room of a Nevada Casino. Cash returned to the casino without trying to stop Strohmeyer, aid the little girl, or report what he saw to hotel security or the police. Strohmeyer subsequently raped and strangled the child, then returned to the casino to continue gambling with Cash, whom he told about the murder. Strohmeyer has been sentenced to life in prison with no possibility of parole for the kidnap, rape, and murder of the child. But Cash, having violated no law in Nevada, remains unpunished and has returned to his studies at University of California-Berkeley. Cash's freedom so enraged society that more than twenty thousand persons signed a petition in California demanding that the courts find some way to punish him for his heinous disregard of the little girl's life. But, in the absence of a preexisting prohibition, nothing could be done.

More recently, in August 2000, two men allegedly saw a stranger lying on a restroom floor in a Michigan train station alive, but having been the victim of a brutal beating. They are said to have told an official that there was a man in the restroom needing aid, but they didn't aid the man themselves nor impress upon the official the urgency of the need. Another stranger, a young boy, finally summoned aid, but the victim was already dead.

As a means to curb such shocking displays of indifference and incivility, many have argued for the enactment or increased enforcement of so-called *Bad Samaritan laws*. Bad Samaritan laws subject persons to criminal penalties for failing to provide easy rescue or other aid for persons in grave peril when they could have provided the aid with minimal risk, cost, and inconvenience to themselves. The laws have a long tradition in European countries—Sweden, Belgium, Denmark, and Germany, among others, have the laws—but they are seldom found in English-speaking parts of the world. In the United States, only a handful of states have enacted the laws, and the ones enacted are exceedingly modest.[1] For example, the Vermont law, which was the first in the United States, treats a violation as a misdemeanor punishable by a one-hundred-dollar fine, and a law in Minnesota treats a failure to render aid as a civil-petty misdemeanor, on a par with failing to return a library book on time and cross-country skiing without a valid pass. Moreover, although the state laws have been in effect for a cumulative total of more that fifty years, it appears that only one person has been convicted of a violation. That case was atypical in that the convicted Bad Samaritan helped to create the peril that ultimately harmed the victim; others who also stood by and watched the harm occur were not even charged.[2]

Proponents of Bad Samaritan laws hope that the renewed attention to enactment and enforcement will provide a deterrent to future Bad Samaritans and help instill the disposition to aid—part of the general virtue of civility—by teaching people that helping behavior is what society expects of its citizens. Critics respond that failures to provide easy rescues, though morally abhorrent, are simply not the business of the criminal law and that even if they were, it would be impossible to draft a law that isn't intolerably vague. Moreover, they claim, enforcing the laws will require that we pass judgment on the values of others in the course of determining whether the aid could have been provided at what we perceive as no significant risk, cost, and inconvenience to the accused. This risks discouraging the virtue of toleration in a liberal democracy to the degree that it encourages the virtue of civility.

I adopt, here, the modest aim of showing that although proponents of Bad Samaritan laws can adequately respond to the most common objections, their favored "middle-ground" option of drafting mild, safeguard-laden laws with minimal enforcement is the least desirable alternative and cannot achieve the desired ends. The first section explores some of the ways that proponents of Bad Samaritan laws can argue for their moral legitimacy— that is, can argue that the legal enforcement of the moral duty to aid is a legitimate aim of the criminal law. In the second section, I examine some of the more traditional objections, which typically take the form of line-drawing objections, that have been offered against the laws and argue that those objections can be adequately met. I'll then expose some often overlooked but nonetheless important objections that are not so easily met and that arise from the need to enforce the laws within a diverse and pluralistic society. In the third section, I argue that neither of the two main objectives of Bad Samaritan laws—that of deterring future Bad Samaritans and helping to instill a disposition to aid—can be met through the currently popular, middle-ground approach and that achieving those objectives requires that we adopt laws that are far more serious in content and enforcement than the ones that are currently in place or envisioned. Yet, I argue, doing so will exacerbate the previously mentioned problems, and I suggest that the benefits of the laws may not be worth their societal problems and costs.

A few points of clarification are in order. First, I assume throughout this discussion that persons *morally* ought to aid others when they can do so at minimal risk, cost, and inconvenience to themselves. Therefore, I focus on whether this moral obligation ought to be backed up with the coercive power of the criminal law and whether our moral condemnation should be expressed through legal punishment. I do not address questions of civil liability.[3] Second, I assume the duties that would be engendered by Bad Samaritan laws are ones that would fall on us simply because we are members of the moral community and find ourselves in a position to provide easy aid. They do not require any special role on the part of the Samaritan or special relationship between the Samaritan and the potential victim. Potential rescuers in these cases are clearly obliged to provide aid, but the source of the obligation is whatever it was that created the special role or relationship, and not merely the need for aid on the part of the victim. Further, rescuers in these latter cases are typically required to go to much greater lengths to provide the aid than would be required of the Samaritan, who is only obliged to provide minimal acts of aid.[4]

Finally, Bad Samaritan laws should not be confused with a related set of laws that have come to be called *Good Samaritan laws*. The latter protect persons from liability if, in the course of providing aid, they nonnegligently cause a harm to the victim. For example, they protect the Samaritan who accidentally breaks the victim's rib while competently administering the Heimlich maneuver. Good Samaritan laws have been enacted in more than forty states and are not controversial because they merely encourage people to provide aid by removing a psychological impediment to the aid—the fear of being sued. In contrast, Bad Samaritan laws create a psychological impediment for persons who are *not* disposed to provide aid by threatening punishment for the failure.

Moral Legitimacy

Questions about whether we ought to enact Bad Samaritan laws are otiose unless we already know that we can enact them legitimately. Thus, proponents of the laws have the burden of showing that the omissions of the Bad Samaritan are properly the law's business. More precisely, they must show that Bad Samaritan laws are legitimate candidates for enactment insofar as they are consistent with the basic principles and commitments of the legal-political system in question, even if they turn out not to be desirable, all things considered.

Of course, whether one will be persuaded by any particular argument for the legitimacy of the laws depends, at least in part, on the other principles and commitments that one is willing to accept. Libertarians, for example, are not likely to be persuaded by any argument for legitimacy except, perhaps, one that presumes that the Bad Samaritan actually *caused* the harm that befell the victim. But such a defense would be fatally flawed in several other ways. For example, if the failure to aid were the cause of the harm, there would be no basis for the standard limit on the amount of effort or risk that could be required of the Samaritan. After all, persons can be expected to incur great risk to avoid causing a harm to an innocent other. Also, if the failure to aid were the cause of the harm, not just as morally bad as causing, then there would be no need to create a special type of law and no need for the present discussion. Finally, if one responds to these points by invoking some version of the *responsibility thesis*, which entails that whether the failure to aid counts as a cause of the harm depends on the agent's moral culpability for the failure, then the attribution of causal status would be irrelevant. That is, it could serve no function in determining the moral status of the act because the moral status must be known before the causal status can be determined.[5] Libertarians are not likely to endorse any view entailing that the moral status of an act determines its criminal status.

The fact—assuming it is a fact—that there are no arguments that would establish the legitimacy of Bad Samaritan laws within libertarianism is not likely to disappoint the libertarians. They do not seem to be among the law's advocates. The more interesting question is whether there are arguments that establish the moral legitimacy of the laws within the political-legal systems favored by those who *want* to enact the laws. In what follows, I will sketch a few of the defenses offered by proponents of the laws. My aim is not to argue that any one of them is preferable to the others, but only to show that there are many ways to argue for the legitimacy of Bad Samaritan laws within a number of political-legal systems.

Legal moralists, at least some communitarians and others who have no principled objection to enforcing morality per se, have no trouble establishing the legitimacy of Bad Samaritan laws. Given that the failures of the Bad Samaritan are agreed to be immoral, their prohibition by the criminal law is thereby a proper function of the state. Other proponents of Bad Samaritan laws may hold that enforcement of the duty to aid is legitimate even though the general enforcement of morality per se is not. Christopher Wellman argues that political society is itself legitimate only if we accept a benefit principle—that is, a principle asserting that the state may legitimately limit liberty to get people to benefit each other.[6] Once that principle has been accepted, the legitimacy of Bad Samaritan laws is obvious. Yet, this view does not commit one to holding that other immoral acts can be punished on the ground of immorality.

Liberals and others who maintain a prima facie principled objection to the enforcement of morality must offer a more detailed defense. Patricia Smith offers such an account when she argues that although liberals value autonomy and liberty, they also value justice.[7] And justice requires that we show a basic respect for persons *as persons*. The actions of the Bad Samaritan are inconsistent with this requirement, she argues, because they imply that the victim's life is worthless. That is, by choosing to do nothing when you could have saved a life at no cost to yourself, you imply that the victim's life is worth less than nothing. Thus, the foundational values of liberal theory sanction legal duties to aid, she argues, and the legitimacy of the laws is not in question. Utilitarian liberals can also advocate Bad Samaritan laws. Mill explicitly lists the duty to aid as one of the obvious exceptions to the claim that acts should be prohibited only if they cause harm to others. Since providing the required aid would not, by definition, significantly limit the agent's efforts to pursue her own conception of the good, and since preventing a death allows that person to continue to pursue her good, Bad Samaritan laws would foster Utilitarian aims without implying that the state is a better judge of our good than we are.

Other defenses also work within general liberal constraints but focus more on practical matters. Bruce Landesman notes that in other areas of the criminal law persons are obliged to perform positive acts that aid others. For example, they can be required to serve on a jury, as well as to testify in court, to help ensure that the accused has a fair trial.[8] By analogy, we shouldn't object to laws that require us to do other minimal acts that can prevent a significant harm. Finally, Feinberg argues that the legal duty to aid is merely an extension of our already accepted societal duty to provide a safety net for those in need. Our taxes benefit others in numerous ways by funding fire departments, schools, and various welfare programs. The coordinated efforts and social programs provide much of the needed aid and distribute the burden among us all, but they can't do everything. Bad Samaritan laws are needed for those problems that, because of their unpredictable nature, cannot be addressed through coordinated efforts.

Traditional Objections

Of course, establishing that Bad Samaritan laws are morally legitimate in principle establishes only that the laws are proper *candidates* for enactment. It doesn't show that they ought to be enacted, all things considered. To answer that question, we need to determine the practical moral costs of the laws and balance them against the expected benefits.[9] By "practical moral costs" I mean the morally undesirable consequences that would accompany efforts to implement the laws and that arise from a practical problem or limitation as opposed to a theoretical one. For an analogy, consider the risk of killing the innocent in connection with capital punishment statutes. That risk is a practical moral cost that arises from the problem of human fallibility in assessing guilt. Unlike the claim that intentional killing is inherently wrong, it does not try to show that capital punishment is itself morally illegitimate. Critics of Bad Samaritan laws—even those that share the same political or legal commitments as the proponents—often argue that because of the practical difficulty of defining just *when* a legally enforceable duty to aid exists and *when* that duty has been violated, Bad

Samaritan laws cannot be fairly drafted or enforced. As a result, the critics maintain, the laws should not be enacted even if they are morally legitimate in theory. In this section I'll discuss three such objections, each of which is offered as a line-drawing objection.

Line-drawing objections can take a variety of forms. They may be offered as (1) a problem of theory, that is, as where to draw the line that distinguishes conduct that may be legitimately required of the Samaritan from conduct that may not; (2) a problem of draftsmanship or how to define the line in a criminal statute; or (3) a problem for the courts, how to enforce the line. Although they are open to different responses, these forms share the basic claim that because of the practical difficulty of defining, drafting, or enforcing the line, significant moral or legal problems will accompany enactment of Bad Samaritan laws.

Two of the three versions of the line-drawing objection that I will discuss begin with the same premise, namely, that it is impossible to draw a nonarbitrary line that distinguishes conduct that may legitimately be required of the Samaritan from conduct that may not.[10] Support for this premise typically takes the form of a sorties argument: If the law can legitimately require a person to take one step to aid another, then surely it can legitimately require her to take two steps, because the difference between one step and two is far too insignificant to mark a moral difference between them. And if the law can legitimately require a person to take two steps to aid another, then surely it can require her to take three steps. For again the difference is too small to mark a moral difference. And if the law can legitimately require a person to take three steps to aid another . . . and so on, until it seems that the law can legitimately require a person to run five miles in the noonday sun or "cross the desert of India" to render needed aid.[11] But surely this is more than can legitimately be expected.

Given this starting point, the first version of the line-drawing objection takes the form of an empirical slippery-slope argument—the kind one reads regularly in the "Letters to the Editor" section of a newspaper. It combines the difficulty of drawing a principled line with the fear that, without such a line, initially minimal duties to aid would develop in time into very demanding ones; what begin as simple obligations to call an ambulance or toss a life preserver, for example, develop into grander obligations requiring us to stand watch for persons we could aid and to sacrifice our own important aims. Thus, accepting requirements to provide even simple acts of aid will, in time, undermine our liberty.

As are most slippery-slope arguments, this version of the objection is weak. It presupposes that the drafters of the laws want to, or would be willing to, sacrifice significant amounts of individual liberty in an effort to maximize the prevention of harm. It also ignores the fact that a legal system can recognize multiple values and endeavor to strike a balance between them. In that vein, Anthony Woozley responds to the objection as follows:

> If [bad] Samaritan law cannot be introduced without undermining the foundations of individual liberty, how is it that it is alive and well in Denmark, France, Germany, Holland, and Norway? What seems to lie behind this objection is fear of vagueness, that we cannot put limits on the scope of a duty to aid. But we can; that is what skilled legislative draftsmen are paid for. . . . Any new law is some restriction on liberty, but not all restrictions are threats to it.[12]

Still, this response is less than ideal, because the worry behind the objection is one of time—of what the skilled draftsmen may do in the future. A more satisfactory response would show that the limits on the duty *can* be defined in a principled way. That would show that the slope is not slippery. It would also respond to the second version of the objection, which assumes, as does the first, that a principled line cannot be drawn. But, rather than worrying about future developments, it argues that problems of justice and fairness arise wherever we currently do draw the line. For, if the limits on the duty to aid cannot be defined in a principled way, then they must be defined arbitrarily. And, if they are defined arbitrarily, then it is not fair, for example, to hold Art criminally liable for refusing to spend a quarter to call the police, but not Bert for refusing to donate a quarter to Oxfam, or Charles for refusing to buy a doughnut for a starving beggar.

To respond to this objection, advocates of Bad Samaritan laws need to be able to define *and defend* the limits on the duty to aid. That is, for each limit set, they need to be able to show that there is a morally relevant difference between cases falling on one side of the limit and cases falling on the other. This includes not only the limit on the *amount* of effort, risk, or cost that can be required of the Samaritan, but also, for example, the limit on the *types* of peril to which the Samaritan is obliged to respond. Thus, we should be able to resolve the difference between the Vermont law, which limits the duty to aid to cases in which the potential victim is exposed to "grave physical harm," and claims by Wallace Rudolph asserting that the relevant peril should include significant property loss or damage as well.[13]

Patricia Smith offers the first half of this sort of response when she proposes that a legitimately enforceable duty to aid exists when

(a) the agent is *"directly confronted"* with a peril,
(b) the peril creates a *"clear, immediate need"*—an "emergency" as opposed to a chronic condition,
(c) the peril threatens "serious bodily harm or death,"
(d) the needed aid is "minimal," and
(e) the duty is *"individual,"* meaning both that "an individual (as opposed to society) has it" and it is "owed to an individual."[14]

Although Smith's conditions are clearly plausible, her account does not provide a complete response since she does not include a defense of each condition as a proper limit.[15] Still, defenses for some of the conditions can be found elsewhere, and the general strategy for providing the defenses gleaned from these examples. For instance, in a discussion about one of Lord Maculay's examples, Feinberg argues that there is an important difference between perils that can be addressed through coordinated efforts and social programs, such as starvation, and perils that, due to their nature as unforeseeable emergencies near at hand, cannot, such as a potential drowning at a private beach.[16] Since coordinated efforts and social programs, in contrast with individual acts of aid, better distribute the burden of the aid among us all and better ensure that those needing aid receive it, they are to be preferred when the type of peril permits it. As noted earlier, Bad Samaritan laws are restricted to perils that either slip through the cracks or are immune to coordinated relief. This supports condition (b) and perhaps (e) as well—the conditions of "clear, immediate need" and "individuality of the duty."

Feinberg also offers partial support for condition (c)—that the "peril threatens *serious* harm or death"—when he responds to a different objection. The objection asserts that Bad Samaritan statutes are more invasive than ordinary criminal prohibitions because legal duties to aid may "drop on us out of the blue," with no relation to our current activities; "Consequently, they weaken our control over our own affairs."[17] He responds by conceding the greater invasiveness of Bad Samaritan laws and arguing that it is the reason why legal duties to aid should be restricted to cases in which the harm threatening another is severe. In that way, we strike a principled balance between the values of individual liberty and the prevention of harm to others.

This reasoning about individual liberty also supports condition (d)—the restriction on effort and risk. However, a complete account of this value, of its nonderivative nature and its proper balancing with other values, would be needed to explain why the line should be drawn at "minimal" rather than "moderate" risks. Also remaining to be defended is that part of condition (c) which limits duties to aid to cases in which the harm threatening another is a serious *physical* harm. Why shouldn't the threat of emotional or psychological harm, or of tremendous property loss, engender a duty to provide minimal assistance in preventing it?[18] I will leave these and other defenses aside, noting only that the preceding discussion indicates the means for defending the limits on the duty to aid.

Once proponents have defended the limits, they face the task of defining those limits in a criminal statute. This brings us to the third version of the line-drawing objection. It takes the form of a dilemma. The two horns arise from the fact that it is impossible to anticipate all the cases in which a legitimate duty to aid might arise and, thus, impossible to draft a law that correctly states just when and how much aid is required. Thus, on the first horn, we do the best we can to draft a precise law. The problem is that however we define the conditions for a duty to aid, we know that we will exclude some cases that should have been included and include other cases that should have been excluded. Thus, some persons will unfairly escape prosecution, and others will be unfairly convicted. On the other horn, we draft the law using vague terms, such as "minimal" or "reasonable" effort or risk, and "serious" or "grave" harm to another. We then allow judges and jurors to determine whether a given agent's conduct violated the law. The problem with this horn is that it would "permit prosecutors and juries unbridled, and indeed unprincipled, discretion in deciding whether a given omission is criminal."[19] Thus, again we face the problem of improper conviction.

Feinberg offers a solution to this dilemma. He proposes that we "grasp (but gingerly) the second horn of the dilemma and formulate Bad Samaritan statutes in relatively vague terms that allow juries the discretion to apply standards of reasonable danger, cost, and inconvenience."[20] But rather than requiring jurors to draw the line between reasonable and unreasonable aid, thereby running the risk of improper conviction, he proposes that they draw the line between *clearly* reasonable and *questionably* reasonable aid. That is, we should divide up the spectrum of hypothetical cases into three segments: (1) clear cases of opportunity to rescue with no unreasonable risk, cost, or inconvenience whatever; (2) cases of opportunity to rescue but only at clearly unreasonable risk, cost, or inconvenience to the rescuer or others; and (3) everything in the vast no-man's-land of uncertain cases in between the extremes. To err on the side of caution, we would hold no one in the uncertain category liable. . . . That would be to hold everyone liable who *clearly* deserves to be liable, while exempting all those who do not clearly deserve to be liable—both those who clearly deserve *not* to be liable, and those whose deserts are uncertain.[21]

In short, jurors would be instructed to vote for conviction only if the conduct needed to aid the victim *clearly* involved no unreasonable risk, cost, or inconvenience.

The virtues of Feinberg's proposal are clear. By employing standards of reasonableness with respect to risk, cost, and inconvenience, we bring a wider range of objectionable conduct under the scope of the criminal law than if we either reject the laws altogether or draft them with very precise standards. Second, by instructing jurors to vote for conviction only when the needed aid was *clearly* reasonable, we provide a strong safeguard against the risks of prosecutorial abuse and of convicting persons who were not actually Bad Samaritans—because the needed aid was more than could reasonably be expected—but merely nonheroic. Third, since jurors are expected to make judgments of reasonableness in many other sorts of cases, such as assessments of whether an accused suffered provocation that even a reasonable person could not bear, Bad Samaritan laws should not be significantly more difficult to enforce than a variety of other laws.

To sum up thus far, proponents of Bad Samaritan laws seem to have adequate, even if not perfect, responses to the worries raised in the traditional versions of the line-drawing objection. The first version's slippery slope and the second version's concerns about justice and fairness are addressed by defending the intuitively plausible limits on the duty to aid in the ways just sketched. The problematic aspects of each horn of the third version are avoided by drafting the laws so that they include these intuitively plausible but only vaguely definable limits, and then instructing jurors to vote for conviction only if the conduct needed to aid the victim clearly fell within these limits. This cautious approach thus allows us to recognize a difference between legitimately and nonlegitimately required aid while avoiding the problematic consequences of attempting to draw a precise line between them. In turn, it helps make Bad Samaritan laws attractive to the population at large.

However, other, less obvious, dilemmas must be resolved before we can implement Bad Samaritan laws in the way outlined.[22] I'll mention a few of them in an effort to show that the trade-offs involved between protecting the innocent and deterring the evil, or the merely callous, entail that the currently popular approach of drafting laws with ample safeguards and minimal punishments is not a tenable option.

Before jurors can determine whether the conduct needed to aid a victim was "clearly reasonable," they need to know whether the degree of risk involved in that conduct should be determined from the perspective of the particular Samaritan or from a more neutral "reasonable person" perspective. Both options are problematic. The former option assesses the risk of cost or inconvenience relative to the beliefs of the agent. Sincere but false beliefs, or sincere but atypical beliefs, entailing that the needed conduct was more than minimally risky would preclude liability for failing to aid. For example, if the agent believed that the AIDS virus is easily transmitted through CPR, or believed that summoning medical help as opposed to relying on the power of prayer would doom the victim to eternal damnation, then she would not be subject to punishment. The same would be true of a timid agent who is deathly afraid of water and believed that if she ventured near enough to the pier's edge to toss in a life preserver she would have fallen in herself and drowned. From the perspective of the agent, the needed conduct in these cases was more than minimally risky, and the agent would not have violated the law.

This alternative seems to be favored by our cautious approach to enacting the laws, given its efforts to place the margin of error on the side of protecting the questionably innocent from conviction. After all, the agents in these imagined cases did not intend to violate the law and did not knowingly do so. They believed that the needed conduct was more than minimally risky and thus that it wasn't required. It also seems favored by a respect for pluralism and diversity because it would not force persons to learn, hold, or act on views that the majority find reasonable in order to avoid criminal liability.[23] The problem is that, if we accept this alternative, we increase the difficulty of ever convicting anyone of a failure to aid. Almost any accused person could *claim* that she held some atypical belief that, in her eyes, rendered the needed conduct unreasonably risky; the prosecution would have a difficult time proving, beyond a reasonable doubt, that she did not in fact hold this belief. As a result, the laws on the books would be merely *symbolic*, since there would be little hope of actually convicting someone.[24]

The other alternative is to assess the risk from an abstract "reasonable person" perspective by asking whether the needed conduct could be expected from an average citizen. This alternative seems in keeping with our other laws that require jurors to make judgments of degree from the perspective of a reasonable person. It also would allow the laws to be applied more uniformly than the other alternative and would make convictions more likely, thereby increasing the deterrent effect of the laws. But along with these benefits come the costs of increasing the likelihood of convicting persons who, because of their atypical beliefs, were not actually morally culpable. Whether one finds these costs acceptable, or prefers the other alternative, depends on the degree to which one wants to gain a deterrent effect from the laws, or is instead content with having the laws be primarily symbolic, that is, on the books as a sign of society's condemnation of Bad Samaritanism, but not routinely enforced. I'll return to this point in the next section.

Other decisions that need to be made before Bad Samaritan laws can be enforced boil down to similar trade-offs between costs and benefits. For example, before we can determine whether an accused Samaritan is guilty, we need to determine the *types* of risks that jurors should take into account when assessing whether the degree of the risk that they would incur is clearly reasonable. Physical risks clearly matter, and financial risks have been agreed to matter too. But what about emotional risks (e.g., suppose that stopping to aid would make one late to one's mother's funeral) or risks to objectively worthless but subjectively prized possessions? If persons can't be legally obliged to spend an additional two hundred dollars to save a life, or be obliged to donate blood or even bodily organs after they are no longer needed, should they be obliged to sacrifice a personal possession that, for whatever quirky reason, they regard as even more valuable? (Suppose that, to provide needed aid, one would have to get blood all over a sweater knitted by one's dead grandmother.[25]) We also have to determine whether persons should be as culpable for ignorance surrounding their failures to save (e.g., "I didn't know how to do the Heimlich maneuver," or "I didn't know I couldn't get AIDS from CPR") as they are for commissions that end up causing harm ("I didn't know the gun was loaded"). In each case we face a trade-off between rendering the laws merely symbolic and risking convict-

ing persons who weren't actually Bad Samaritans. But rather than addressing these particular issues directly, I'd like to expose a problem that underlies the current efforts to balance these concerns by adopting cautious,
safeguard-laden laws, with minimal punishments and little enforcement.
To do so, I need to turn to the apparent reasons behind the efforts to criminalize the failures of the Bad Samaritan.

Objectives

Two main objectives seem to lie behind efforts to enact Bad Samaritan laws.
One is to create a deterrent effect for the would-be Bad Samaritans, and
the other is to provide a public statement of society's condemnation of the
acts of the Bad Samaritan and a corresponding expression of what society
expects of its citizens. This expression, it is argued, is supposed to help persons internalize the norm and foster a disposition to aid. (Retribution might
also seem to be an objective, but it is more accurately viewed as a reason
for punishing particular offenders than as a separate reason for enacting the
laws themselves. I'll discuss the need for punishment in connection with
the other options.) My primary aim in the remainder of this discussion is
to suggest that if we are going to have laws that fulfill either of these two
objectives, then we can't continue with the current practice of drafting very
weak, safeguard-laden laws, with minimal punishments and no serious efforts at enforcement. And if we are not willing to draft and enforce far more
demanding laws, and bite the bullet with respect to their practical moral
costs, then we should not advocate the laws at all.

Consider the objective of deterrence. Most of us do not need the threat
of criminal punishment to get us to aid another when we can do so at minimal risk to ourselves. If we do omit to aid another in emergency situations
it is likely because we thought that the risk to ourselves was significant or
that others were taking care of the aid. The deterrent threat of punishment
is instead needed for the minority of persons who, due either to a callous
disregard for the welfare of others, or to some psychological perversity or
dislike of the particular victim that makes the Samaritan want to see the
victim suffer, won't provide the minimal aid. But small fines such as those
we have now aren't likely to deter the Bad Samaritans who want to see the
victim suffer. And although they may be able to deter the merely callous
Samaritans by having the inconvenience of the fine outweigh the inconvenience of aiding, this can happen only if the bystander believes that there

is some reasonable chance of being arrested, prosecuted, and convicted. The lower the probability of conviction, the greater the threatened punishment must be.[26] To put it in another way, if deterrence is what we want, then, in comparison to the laws that are currently enacted, we need to *dramatically* increase the threatened punishment as well as the efforts made to impose it. We need to be willing to spend the resources needed to enforce the laws as well as to interpret and apply the laws in ways that don't allow easy excuses (e.g., we should adopt the reasonable person perspective). But of course, one consequence of dramatically increasing the size of the penalty and ease of conviction (including the risk of mistaken conviction) may be decrease in society's general willingness to accept this new kind of law or to vote for conviction (which, of course, would decrease the deterrent effect).

The other option is to defend the laws in terms of their symbolic, expressive, or educative value. (The differences between these need not concern us here.) That is, one might argue that the central benefit of the laws lies not in their deterrent effect on would-be Bad Samaritans, but instead in their ability to express, solidify, and educate citizens about society's moral condemnation of the acts of the Bad Samaritan and its expectations of citizens. As Aristotle said, the state is charged with the continued development of virtue in the adult population.[27] Thus, the enactment of Bad Samaritan laws helps confirm that the duty to aid is an important societal norm and helps educate citizens about the boundaries of the norm and the situations in which it applies. This in turn fosters or supports a disposition to aid such that once this social norm is internalized, citizens won't need the threat of punishment to get them to do the right thing. Thus, on this view, we don't need to worry about the problems that would arise were we attempting to defend Bad Samaritan laws on the basis of their deterrent effect.[28] Robinson and Darley explain the underlying point in more detail as follows (though they are not focusing on Bad Samaritan laws in particular):

> Given the weak deterrent threat facing people, why do the vast majority still act in a way consistent with the law? Social scientists have a preliminary answer: More than because of the threat of legal punishment, people obey the law (1) because they fear the disapproval of their social group if they violate the law, and (2) because they generally see themselves as moral beings who want to do the right thing as they perceive it. . . . Criminal law in particular can influence the norms that are held by the social group and that are internalized by the individual. Criminal law's influence comes from being a societal mechanism by which the force of the social

norms is realized and by which the force of internal moral principles is strengthened. That is, the law has no independent force, the way that social group norms and internalized norms do. It has power to the extent that it can amplify and sustain these two power sources; it has power to the extent that it influences what the social group thinks and what its members internalize.[29]

Thus, it would seem that even if we draft the laws with broad safeguards and minimal punishments, we can still gain a significant benefit from the laws without incurring significant moral costs.[30]

But this view is mistaken. Enacting the laws initially may help solidify the social norm and promote its internalization. But enactment without serious and sincere efforts at enforcement can actually harm the norm in the long run by sending the message that we don't really mean it—that we are just paying lip service to duty to aid. Feinberg gives the following analogy. "It is murder in Mississippi, as elsewhere, for a white man intentionally to kill a Negro; but if grand juries refuse to issue indictments or if trial juries refuse to convict, and this is well understood by most citizens, then it is in a purely formal and empty sense indeed that killings of Negroes by whites are illegal in Mississippi."[31] Clear expression that the social group doesn't take the duty to aid seriously may diminish the recognition of the duty by individual citizens and thus leave us worse off than if the duty to aid were left solely within the moral arena with strong social sanctions given for violations.

Furthermore, enforcing the laws with the minimal penalties that we have now is also problematic. For again as Robinson and Darley argue, people

> are likely to attend to the comparative liabilities that are assigned by sentencing provisions of legal systems; people intuit that more morally serious offenses should command greater penalties. As Cook remarks, "The legislated (and actual) severity of penalty for a particular offense may influence the public's feeling for the seriousness or moral repugnance of this offense." In the long run, for those crimes in which "moral inhibition" plays an important role, announcing the high severity of punishment may be an important communication; more important than ensuring high probability of punishment.[32]

Thus, current laws that assign the same penalty to a failure to save a life as for parking in a handicapped zone, and less severe than for petty theft, won't send the message that proponents are trying to send.

In short, if we are going to achieve either of the two main objectives of Bad Samaritan laws, we need to draft the laws with serious penalties and make serious efforts at enforcement. But this will also increase the risk of mistaken conviction and the significance of that risk. Yet, this, in turn, may lead some heretofore supporters of the laws to withdraw their support on the ground that the benefits of the laws—which may be achievable in other ways—are not worth the costs.[33]

To sum up, I have argued that proponents of Bad Samaritan laws face few obstacles with respect to establishing the *moral legitimacy* of the laws. They also seem to be adequately able to meet the traditional line-drawing objections. But further discussion and argument is needed regarding the means for enforcing the laws, both with respect to resources expended and the instructions to jurors, and regarding the penalties assigned to violations. I've argued that the apparent compromise position of enacting the laws but drafting and enforcing them in cautious ways that almost guarantee that no one will suffer a significant punishment is the least desirable option of the three. It won't deter those who need deterring, and it sends the message that a violation of the duty to aid is only a minor moral offense. Thus, we need to either bite the bullet with respect to the moral costs, or find way other ways to encourage people to aid.[34]

Notes

1. The laws in Vermont and Wisconsin require people to render aid, when possible, as well as notify the relevant authorities. The laws in Florida, Massachusetts, and Rhode Island merely oblige persons to notify the relevant authorities. In Massachusetts the duty to notify is limited to crimes involving bodily harm. No notification is required in non-crime situations. In Florida, the duty is further limited to specific kinds of criminal conduct (e.g., sexual assault but not attempted murder). See David C. Biggs, "The Good Samaritan Is Packing," *University of Dayton Law Review* 22, no. 2 (1997): 225–64, 230.

2. One cannot claim with certainty that there were no other convictions since it is possible that a charge was made and a conviction obtained with no broadly accessible public notice. It is much easier to determine that there were no other cases that underwent appellate review. See John Pardun, "Good Samaritan Laws: A Global Perspective," *Loyola of Los Angeles International Comparative Law Journal* 20 (1998): 591–613, 597 and 598 for an account of his means for determining that there have been no arrests or prosecutions under Minnesota's law and apparently no successful convictions under Vermont's law. He also discusses *Wisconsin v. LaPlante*, which was the case that withstood appellate review.

3. For discussions of civil liability for failing to aid, see Anthony D'Amato, "The 'Bad Samaritan' Paradigm," *Northwestern University Law Review* 70 (1976): 798–812;

James A. Henderson, Jr., "Process Constraints in Tort," *Cornell Law Review* 67 (1982): 901–48; and Arthur Ripstein, "Three Kinds of Duties," *Law and Philosophy* 19, no. 6 (2000).

4. Indeed, the Samaritans in question are not really required to be *good* Samaritans at all, but only minimally decent ones. The good Samaritan of the Bible, recall, went way out of his way to help the stranger in need. Of course, using the biblical parable as our guide, the laws would have more aptly been named "bad Levite laws" since it was the Levite who walked by the stranger in need. But "Bad Samaritan laws" is the name that caught on.

5. It also has the odd result that there can be nonculpable causings by positive action but not nonculpable causings by omission. For a discussion of the responsibility thesis, see Eric Mack, "Bad Samaritanism and the Causation of Harm," *Philosophy and Public Affairs* 9, no. 3 (1980): 230–59.

6. Christopher Wellman, "Liberalism, Samaritanism, and Political Legitimacy," *Philosophy and Public Affairs* 25, no. 3 (1996): 211–37.

7. Patricia Smith, "The Duty to Rescue and the Slippery Slope Problem," *Social Theory and Practice* 16, no. 1 (spring 1990): 19–42.

8. As noted in Feinberg, *Harm to Others* (New York: Oxford University Press, 1984), 165.

9. One could also object to the financial costs, but I won't pursue that here.

10. See, e.g., Richard Epstein, "A Theory of Strict Liability," *Journal of Legal Studies* 2 (1973): 198. "Once one decides that as a matter of statutory or common law duty, an individual is required under some circumstances to act at his own cost for the exclusive benefit of another, then it is very hard to set out in a principled manner the limits of social interference with individual liberty."

11. The reference to India is from Lord Thomas Maculay, "Notes on the Indian Penal Code," in *Works*, 8 vols. (New York: Longmans, Green and Co., 1897). He argues that, because of the difficulty of drawing a nonarbitrary line, liability for omitting aid ought to be restricted to cases in which the omissions "were on other grounds illegal" (e.g., the agent had a special duty to aid) (495). Also, Feinberg discusses Maculay's view, as well as the argument just cited in the text, but he does not classify the versions of the line-drawing objection in the way that I do. This affects neither the plausibility of Feinberg's proposal, nor my response.

12. A. D. Woozley, "A Duty to Rescue," *Virginia Law Review* 69 (1983): 1229–30.

13. Wallace Rudolph, "The Duty to Act: A Proposed Rule," *Nebraska Law Review* 44 (1965): 508. Rudolph also argues that the "circumstances placing the person in a position to act must be purely fortuitous," so as not to overburden the wealthy.

14. Smith, "The Duty to Rescue."

15. Initially Smith claims only to be setting out the conditions of properly enforceable duty to aid "*as it is generally accepted*" and with the *hope* that this will "yield some *clues* about limits" (emphasis added, "The Duty to Rescue," 24). Yet in her concluding

section she claims that the proposed conditions "enable us to distinguish the duty to rescue from all other positive duties . . . which allows us to avoid the slippery slope to oppressive obligations to aid everyone in need" (37). But to avoid the slippery slope one must do more than point to differences between the duties. One must also explain *why* those differences are relevant—one must defend the limits.

16. Feinberg, *Harm to Others*, 158–59.

17. Ibid., 64. However, in further support of such laws, he notes that other positive legal duties can "drop on us out of the blue," such as the duty to testify about a crime one has witnessed. This is weak, it seems to me, because it is possible to argue that our courtroom duties are an extension of our negative duties not to cause harm. If one views judges, jurors, and the like as representatives for society at large, then, when a criminal is punished, it is society that causes the harm. Our duties to participate in the criminal proceedings are part of our duty to ensure that we do not cause harm *unjustly*.

18. Smith argues that the general reason for not including property loss or damage, as such, is that harm to property does not in itself incapacitate the victim in a way that necessitates external intervention by a random stranger" (op. cit. 31). But this leaves the initial question unanswered: *Why* is (physical) incapacitation a necessary condition for obliged external intervention?

19. Feinberg, *Harm to Others*, 154.

20. Ibid., 156–57.

21. Ibid., 156.

22. I develop each of these dilemmas and its implications in more detail in "Liberalism, Bad Samaritan Laws, and Legal Paternalism," *Ethics* 106, no. 1 (October 1995): 4–31.

23. Making exceptions for recognized minorities such as Christian Scientists or Orthodox Jews would not solve the problem. We'd only be paying lip service to pluralism if we made exceptions for the atypical beliefs of some minority groups but not others—assuming that none is trying to impose its views on others by causing harm.

24. One way out of this dilemma that seems worth exploring requires that we treat defenses based on atypical or sincere but false beliefs along the lines of the insanity defense. That is, jurors would assess the risk of the needed conduct from the perspective of a reasonable person, and individuals who are claiming innocence on the basis of atypical or false beliefs would have the burden of proving that they held them.

25. Of course, the important question isn't whether persons *ought* to provide aid under such circumstances, but whether and on what ground this sort of risk can be judged clearly reasonable while risks of money and significant inconvenience not be judged to be clearly reasonable.

26. Within limits. After a certain point, the probability of conviction is more important than the size of the threat.

27. Aristotle, *Nichomachean Ethics*, 1179a30–1180a5.

28. Note that in Bad Samaritan cases, the bystanders rarely have anything to gain by failing to aid. There is no pull away from doing what is right as there is in cases in which

one might be tempted to steal, cheat, and so forth. Thus the lack of need for a deterrent in these cases need not transfer to other prohibitions.

29. Paul Robinson and John Darley, "The Utility of Desert," *Northwestern University Law Review* 91, no. 2: 453–500, especially 486 and 471.

30. Thanks to Janice Nadler for enlightening discussions on this matter.

31. Feinberg, "The Expressive Function of Punishment," in *Philosophy of Law*, 5th ed. (Belmont, Calif.: Wadsworth, 1995), 595.

32. Robinson and Darley, "The Utility of Desert," 472.

33. I develop these arguments in more detail in "Bad Samaritan Laws: Harm, Hype or Help?" *Law and Philosophy* 19, no. 6 (2000).

34. I'd like to thank Alex de Miranda, Dan Hefter, Bev Kracher, Joan McGregor, Janice Nadler, Pat Smith, and Kit Wellman for the various ways in which they contributed to this manuscript. I'd also like to thank the participants of the AMINTAPHIL conference, at which a draft of this manuscript was presented, for the very helpful discussion that ensued.

Chapter 12

The Mind of a Bad Samaritan

Joseph Ellin

The argument in favor of Bad Samaritan laws is simple. Presumably, helping people in trouble or danger is morally desirable. The more people are helped, the better, one might well think. In the absence of Bad Samaritan laws, some bystanders help voluntarily. Were rendering assistance made mandatory, those who help voluntarily would continue to do so, and some few others would, or anyway might, render help because of the legal obligation. Therefore, the number of assistances could not decrease and might increase. So it would seem that there is nothing to lose and possibly something to gain by enacting Bad Samaritan laws.

This is a powerful argument, and, like many powerful arguments, it should be suspected of oversimplification. Thinking about Bad Samaritans, like much thinking about capital punishment, is impelled by the "emotional monster" syndrome, where it is assumed that the targets of law would be the clearly worst cases for whom no one has a merciful word. I am not arguing that the goal of assuring uniformity and limiting liability to the worst cases is impossible. I simply want to point out some of the difficulties inherent in Bad Samaritan statutes. My suggestion is not that these problems are insoluble, but that they are sufficiently difficult to give us pause as to whether the gain from having such laws would be worth the risks involved in interpreting and enforcing them.

Criminal liability normally requires a particular state of mind or mens rea, but Bad Samaritan proposals have not paid much attention to the question of what frames of mind would impose liability and what would excuse failure to rescue. This is not a simple question. In this paper, I give fifteen accounts, varying only by the actor's state of mind, of a single failure to rescue. Do any of these reasons for the failure excuse it? The goal of the essay is to suggest that, in view of the problems of formulating mens rea, the necessity of resolving some or all of them by fiat rather than reasoned policy, and the opportunities for abuse these ambiguities present, the rationale for Bad Samaritan laws is weak. Given the range of possible cases, the cases in which people clearly may be punished for failure to rescue may be few. This observation reinforces the claim that forcing people to do good, even if there are some very clear cases where such a policy is justified, inhibits character development, restricts the scope of individuality, opens the door to arbitrariness and unfairness, and should not be imposed without significant social gain. Such gain does not seem to exist in the case of Bad Samaritan legislation.

Mens Rea

So-called "Bad Samaritan" laws would create a kind of crime relatively new to the United States: the crime of failing to rescue or assist. In principle it may seem that there is much to be said in favor of enacting such laws; and, perhaps, in principle there is. When, however, it is kept in mind that, aside from strict liability, there can be no criminal liability without criminal intent, interesting difficulties present themselves. What is the appropriate mens rea for the crime of Bad Samaritanism? In what frames of mind might one fail to rescue a person in trouble? Should any mental states excuse the failure? Discussions of Bad Samaritan laws have not paid adequate attention to this question. Let us imagine some scenarios.

First, suppose I am walking in the woods when I pass a lake. You are in the water some distance from shore, thrashing about and calling for help. I am a good swimmer who could easily swim out and rescue you. I do not do so, and you drown. This would seem to be a standard case in which one is liable under Bad Samaritan laws. But is it? Consider the following more detailed accounts:

a. I mistake your thrashing about for having fun in the water, and take your cries of "help me, help me" to be "yippie, yippie." I continue walking. You drown.

b. I understand that you are thrashing about and crying "help me," but I think you are playing a practical joke. I say to myself, "You can't fool me, friend." I continue walking. You drown.

c. I understand that you are thrashing about and crying "help me," but I know the water is only four feet deep. I think you are not really in trouble and will soon right yourself. I continue walking. You drown.

d. I mistakenly believe the water is only four feet deep and that you will be able to right yourself. In fact the water is twelve feet deep, and you drown.

e. I understand that you are thrashing about and crying "help me," but

I immediately identify you correctly as Ted Kaczynski, who has recently escaped from prison and is the subject of a ten-state manhunt. I think to myself, "Society is better off without him." I walk out of the woods and phone the police. You—Ted—drown.

f. I recognize you to be my next-door neighbor. I happen to know that you beat your wife, cheat at cards, and keep four mistreated dogs who howl all night and chase my cats. I think to myself, "I wouldn't walk across the street to save his life." I continue walking. You drown.

g. You are the dean of my college, who, I believe, has just maliciously and wrongfully denied me tenure, for which I am suing the college and you personally. I think to myself, "Should I save the life of the man who has tried to ruin my career?" I continue walking. You drown.

h. From many signs I determine that you have been drinking heavily and have swum out beyond your depth. I think, "Should I rescue a man from the consequences of his own folly? Let him save himself, if he is able." I continue walking. You drown.

i. Although I am a good swimmer and could easily swim out and save you, I am dreadfully afraid of hidden water animals such as water snakes, snapping turtles, and large fish, because I was once bitten painfully by something while swimming in a lake. Consequently, I confine my swimming to swimming pools. To complicate proof at the subsequent trial, I am deeply ashamed of my fear and have never told anyone about it. I think I ought to swim out and rescue you, but the water is dark and murky, and I cannot bring myself to go into the lake. You drown.

j. Although I am a good swimmer and could easily swim out and save you, I unaccountably panic and start to run back and forth on the shore yelling, "help, help." No one comes. You drown.

k. Although I am a good swimmer and could easily swim out and save you, I remember the old water rescue adage, "throw, row, go." Fortunately there is a life preserver on the shore. Unfortunately, my repeated attempts to toss it to you fall short. You drown.

l. Again I remember the old adage. There is a heavy timber rowboat upside down on the shore. By the time I right it and push it into the water, you have drowned.

m. This time there is also an aluminum canoe. I recognize that I could easily paddle out, but I am afraid that the lightweight canoe might upset itself as I try to haul you into it. I try to right the rowboat instead. Same result as before.

n. I am a student of philosophy. Years ago, I read *Sextus Empiricus* and became sincerely and truly converted to Pyrrhonian skepticism. Although it seems to me that you are drowning, I do not believe I can be certain, due to mistrust of the senses. I follow Pyrrho's counsels and believe nothing. You drown—or so it appears.

o. I am a student of philosophy. Years ago, I read Ayn Rand and became converted to strong ethical egoism. I sincerely and truly think it is morally wrong to help anyone without an expected return. I continue walking.

Now, all these examples involve failure to accomplish the required rescue, but for interestingly different reasons—each of which raises mens rea questions.

Intention, Mistake, and Negligence

Whenever there is a duty to perform, we must ask what counts as discharge of the duty. Typically, the law does not require that "affirmative" duties be successfully performed, but only that a good faith effort be made. But what is a good faith effort? Examples k, l, and m involve mistakes of judgment about *what should be done*. Even before deciding whether the good faith requirement is satisfied in these instances, we must decide whether liability is to be objective or subjective. Suppose we consider whether the mistakes were "reasonable." If only unsuccessful efforts based on reasonable mistakes count as good faith efforts, then an unreasonable mistaken belief about what to do would be mens rea sufficient for liability, even if an honest effort were made. This is an example of (i) *objective liability*. If unsuccessful efforts based on objectively unreasonable mistaken beliefs also count as good faith, then any honest effort would excuse. In that case, the mens rea for the duty to rescue would seem to be limited to intentional, or as we might say deliberate, failures to perform; here we have an example of (ii) *subjective liability*.

Suppose we opt for (i) *objective liability*: only failures to perform due to mistaken beliefs that are reasonable will count as good faith efforts. Honest but foolish effort does not excuse, so an unreasonable belief is adequate mens rea, and the unreasonably mistaken nonperformer is guilty of failing to rescue. So, if what you tried to do was unreasonable, you are liable for failure to succeed and a Bad Samaritan under the law—no matter how hard you tried to perform the rescue. But this may seem unfair, since it may be assumed that a Bad Samaritan is one with wrong intentions, not unreasonable beliefs.[1] A Bad Samaritan is one who does not care to rescue, not one who is mistaken about *how* to rescue.

Another problem with the objective standard is the question of how to determine what is reasonable. What is reasonable for one person to do might not be reasonable for another, depending on their abilities. Throwing or rowing might be reasonable for the weak swimmer, but not for the strong. In example (1) for instance, the weak swimmer is going to be excused for trying the rowboat; but arguably the strong swimmer should not be, under a reasonableness standard. But this raises the objection that if standards of reasonableness are individualized to the capacities of the actor, the competent would be put at greater jeopardy of culpability than the less competent. Weak swimmers are excused in examples k, l, and m; strong swimmers very likely are not; and moderate swimmers take their chances with the jury's opinion about what is reasonable for them. Incidentally, this gives each of us an incentive to conceal his capacities, or even not to acquire them in the first place.[2] On the other hand, if a common standard of reasonableness—what would be reasonable for the person of average capacities to do—is adopted, the less competent may be treated too harshly, the more competent, not harshly enough. In example m for example, it may be unreasonable for the average swimmer not to take the canoe, since should it tip he can always save himself by swimming away. But, then, under an average person standard applied to all, even the poor swimmer is punished, which is clearly unfair. On the other hand, in example k, the average swimmer may be excused for futilely throwing the life preserver because, being only an average swimmer, he should not be required to rescue by swimming, while, again arguably, the strong swimmer should not be.

Under the (ii) *subjective standard*, where good intentions and honest effort are sufficient to excuse, any honest attempt, no matter how stupidly planned or executed, defeats liability. Mens rea for Bad Samaritans would be restricted to deliberate failure to perform. Against this it might be argued that if we are to impose a duty to rescue, we ought to require not merely that the rescue be attempted, but that it be performed with at least minimum intelligence, so as to stand a fair chance of actually succeeding. Otherwise, Bad Samaritan legislation risks deteriorating into tests of good intentions rather than being a stimulus for actually saving lives. And proof of culpability would be difficult, since it is easy to claim and hard to refute that you honestly believed that what you were doing would succeed.

But, let us look at examples i and j. Would someone be guilty if they fell into a panic, or were seized with a real but neurotic fear? Presumably panic, fear, confusion, and so on are fairly common reactions to life-threatening emergencies, although Bad Samaritan proposals typically seem to assume a movie-hero-like presence of mind in the average passerby. Should they excuse failure to perform? If so, should they do so on grounds that the failure was involuntary? Liability generally requires a voluntary act or omission, and examples i and j arguably involve omissions that are involuntary. On the one hand, there is a deterrent argument that these excuses should not be allowed, since to allow them would encourage people who tend to panic not to try to control their fear. On the other hand, this seems unduly harsh toward those whose panic and fear are not only real but a source of shame to them. Whether, in a given case, these conditions could have been controlled and whether it is right to punish someone who failed to control them, are questions that, for their philosophical perplexity, we should be very reluctant to give to juries. Nor should we be complacent that the fate of real human beings might be made to turn on how some random set of people answers them.

A way to avoid this inquiry is to opt for (ii) *subjective liability*, holding that panic excuses because a person who falls into a panic may have the intention to perform, but lacks the presence of mind to do so. If the Bad Samaritan is one who does not care, then the panic-stricken rescuer is surely far from a Bad Samaritan. This observation tends again to push us to saying that the only mens rea for rescue omissions is specific intent. Therefore, so long as you sincerely *want* to help, failure for whatever reason will not make you liable, even if, through panic, you utterly fail to do anything helpful. But that, first, may seem unduly forgiving to the weak spirited; second, it once again opens the door to every kind of unprovable imaginative excuse, which in turn raises interesting questions about the burden of proof in Bad Samaritan cases.

Let's turn to examples a, b, c, and d. These all involve mistake of fact as to *whether rescue is needed*. Are these mistakes reasonable or unreasonable? Does this matter? According to the point made earlier, if the Bad Samaritan is one who does not care to perform the rescue, the actor in these examples has not shown himself to be a Bad Samaritan and should be excused. In other words, any honest mistake of fact, no matter how avoidable or simply silly, defeats mens rea. And there are the usual reasons to resist this proposal: the general deterrent loss from such a broad and unprovable exception and the problem of reducing liability to a test of intentions. In addition, there is the unfairness to the wise and discerning of allowing the foolish and simple to be excused from a duty to which they are held. Nevertheless, the argument for the subjective test is fairly compelling. It cannot be that I become a Bad Samaritan just because I make a mistake, even a stupid mistake.

Of course a *negligence standard* might be proposed as a compromise. Suppose, as in example a, I fail to take steps that the person of ordinary prudence would take to confirm my assumption that you are simply horsing around. For example, I could yell out to you, "are you OK?" Or, in example c, I could shout to you about the depth of the water and wait until you succeeded in righting yourself. If you did not do so, as in example d, I would know you needed help. Not having done this, I would be guilty of negligent, as opposed to intentional, failure to rescue.

There are questions however about what constitutes the negligence. In example a, I do not have any initial perception that there is a problem; that there might be any problem is a purely theoretical possibility, as far as I notice. So what is it that triggers my duty to call out? After all, huge numbers of people thrash about playfully in the water all the time, and virtually none of them drown. Must I assure myself that everyone who conceivably might be in trouble, is not? If not, then it is not clear that my conduct *was* negligent. And in examples c and d, where I recognized that you were in trouble, based on what I believed I did not think the trouble was acute enough to warrant intervention. To allege negligence here invites after-the-fact judicial scrutiny and a legitimate danger of prosecution based on hindsight and bad outcomes.[3]

The practical joke case, example b, is interesting for another reason. If my belief is correct, then nothing I do—as I might reasonably suppose— would cause you to admit the truth. As a result, nothing you do can count as a sign of real drowning so as to alter my belief that you are playing a joke on me. Hence, given my belief that you *are* joking, I am logically unable to reasonably conclude that you are actually in trouble. Under these circumstances, it seems a bit excessive to punish me for not saving you.

Motivation

Now what about examples e, f, and g? Here we have clearly intentional failures to perform. But that does not end the tale. In these cases the excuse that is being offered is morally acceptable motivation. It is true that motivation is normally a jury argument, and that liability goes to intent, but this is not necessarily so in cases where we are enforcing a *moral* duty. First, of course, it has to be shown that it *is* a moral duty. And it's not so clear that saving the lives of—as opposed to refraining from actively killing—the Ted Kaczynskis of this world is even so much as morally condemnable.

It is even less clear that it may properly be demanded; would it be right to demand that someone save the life of a convicted serial killer such as Ted Bundy? It is certainly arguable that the rescue of known monsters, or even of one's real or imagined personal enemies, is a *supererogatory* act and not a moral *duty,* and so not suitably required by the law. And, since it *is* arguable, and therefore the moral question is open, it seems that we ought to grant an exemption for those who take this view of the matter. But this excuse creates another loophole and an incentive for bogus claims, for example, of mistaken identity. Then, the deterrent issue posed may well be whether we are willing to legally require people to do things that morally we may not demand of them, to prevent other people from getting away with not doing what we think we may legally require.

The two philosophical cases, examples n and o, are not as fanciful as they may seem. Doubtless the practical legal mind will brush these examples aside with the observation that people ought to act as common sense, rather than off-the-wall philosophical theories, dictates. Perhaps this is the judicial equivalent of the pragmatic argument against Pyrrhonian skepticism: that it cannot serve as a guide in life, and hence is refuted not by our logic but by our practice. This as it may be, the examples test the limits in an interesting way of *the right of conscience*. It is true that Pyrrhonianism and egoism are more likely to be regarded as dangerous right-wing delusions than as matters of conscience worthy of protection. But, perhaps pacifism— which is classically deemed worthy of legal exemption—is also a dangerous delusion, as one might conclude after reading criticisms by notable philosophers.[4] Someone must decide which of these "matters of conscience" is a morally acceptable basis for inaction. Heidi Malm shows herself sensitive to less recognized minority groups and acknowledges that religious beliefs—including what are by conventional standards far-out ones—and even badly erroneous medical beliefs, should be grounds for exemption. It is doubtful that there is some principle with which to resist the spread of this exemption to *all* sincerely held beliefs.[5]

Further, which beliefs are worthy of protection is not the only issue raised by these philosophical examples. Another is what are the social goals that would justify denying protection to those matters of conscience that *are* deemed worthy of protection? Those who support a limited right of conscience admit that the right must give way before social interests that are clearly compelling. In time of dire national emergency, a pacifist may be sent into combat; during a time of revolutionary civic disruption, the right to assemble and demonstrate may be curtailed. Whatever balance is struck, these are social goals that are easily defended. In the concluding section, I argue that Bad Samaritan laws advance social goals that are, at best, morally questionable, socially problematic, and historically inconsequential. They do not meet the standard of compelling social concern we would expect partisans of conscience to uphold.

Justifying Bad Samaritan Law

One conclusion that might be drawn from Malm's discussion is how unconvincing are the arguments in favor of Bad Samaritan legislation. Christopher Wellman, she reports, "argues that the moral legitimacy of political society itself requires the acceptance of a benefit principle. . . . Once that principle has been accepted, the legitimacy of Bad Samaritan laws is obvious." What is obvious to this author, on the contrary, is that Wellman's conclusion is a non sequitur. What he has to show is that a "political society" is not morally legitimate *unless* it enacts Bad Samaritan legislation. This is a tall order, and, if it is correct, American political society is not morally legitimate. Patricia Smith is quoted as saying that the Bad Samaritan's actions "imply that the victim's life is worthless." But, this is an exaggeration, if not false. My failure to save you may imply only that I do not think that the burden of saving you falls on me. In itself, it implies nothing of what I think about the value of your life. If I thought your life were truly worthless, I would give myself the right to kill you, like an insect.

Malm also cites two analogies used in favor of Bad Samaritan legislation. Bruce Landesman makes an analogy between the duty to rescue and duty to serve on a jury. Joel Feinberg makes an analogy between the duty to pay taxes and duty to rescue. Both the duty to serve on a jury and the duty to pay taxes are affirmative duties, as would be a duty to rescue. But these are weak analogies, at best, because the former two duties are also basic social duties. Their performance is necessary for the operation of the society. The jury system, after all, is an essential part of our legal system; thus, failure to serve violates a basic social duty. So, too, paying taxes—even redistributive taxes—is essential in the same way. Neither Landesman's nor Feinberg's example establishes a duty to rescue that is a basic social duty analogous to those cited.

More interesting is the utilitarian case Malm suggests. Would utilitarians support Bad Samaritan laws? It's difficult to say, given the wide variety of utilitarianisms. Character utilitarians such as myself might argue that more good character occurs if rescues are allowed to be voluntary. Legal requirements tend to suppress good character traits and replace them with enlarged motives of personal prudence. Even if the goal is to produce overall social well-being directly, and not through good character, it is arguable that we would have more rather than fewer rescues if people are encouraged to rescue voluntarily, rather than told that they will be punished if they don't. One ground for this hypothesis is that punishment generates avoidance rather than compliance; avoiding being caught as a Bad Samaritan does not seem all that difficult. And, we should remember that Mill's argument that the duty to aid may be required, is not an argument that it *ought* to be, on utilitarian grounds.

Unlike Malm and many others, I think there is little to be gained from Bad Samaritan statutes. The gain is virtually confined to allowing us to punish in egregious cases, as when a few people witnessing a crime in progress fail to call the police from the security of their homes. Even in those cases, we must be able to identify them to prosecute. Most of the mens rea problems defy principle and, so, will have to be answered more or less by arbitrary judicial fiat. Opening the door to arbitrary judicial legislation is not something we should do unless we have in view an honestly foreseeable and fairly significant social gain. In this case, we most certainly do not.

One good reason not to have Bad Samaritan laws is that we should always be suspicious of laws that force people to do good. Such laws restrict people's space to determine their own personal morality, within the generally accepted limits. As the limits close in, our individuality is more and more confined. Malm, at one point in her excellent piece, defends broad exemptions to Bad Samaritan laws out of "respect for pluralism and diversity." In a comparable vein, out of respect for integrity and independence of mind, we simply should allow people to decide for themselves how much good they will do in the world and at what cost to themselves. Scrooge is better dealt with by the Spirit of Christmas than by the shadow of the hangman. Do we want a society populated by cautious do-gooders—doing good not from conviction but out of enforceable social mandates? This prospect evidently pleases some people more than it pleases me.

Notes

1. I ignore what is fairly obvious and often discussed, that agents may err in assessing the risk to themselves as well as the danger to the victim or the best means of effecting the rescue.

2. Feinberg has proposed a "clearly reasonable" standard of risk to the rescuer, but this seems merely to shift the bar, relieving some of uncertainty while imposing it on others. It may be not "clearly reasonable" to expect the moderate swimmer to "go" when a "row" alternative presents itself, but is it clear what is clearly reasonable for the strong swimmer? See Feinberg, *Harm to Others* (New York: Oxford University Press, 1984), 155–57.

3. Patricia Smith holds that the duty to aid exists when the actor "is close enough to be aware of the problem, identify it as a problem, and act on it" (Smith, "The Duty to Rescue and the Slippery Slope Problem," *Social Theory and Practice*, 16, no. 1 [spring 1990]). But this is ambiguous between the actor's *in fact* identifying the problem, and the actor's being in a position to identify the problem. This has to be cleared up before an enforceable duty has been specified.

4. Such as Anthony Kenny. See Kenny, *The Logic of Deterrence* (London: Firethorn Press, 1985), 5–7.

5. Heidi Malm, "Civic Virtue and the Legal Duty to Aid," this volume: note 22. Orthodox Jews, however, do not need the protection of a religious exemption; they would not refuse to call the police on the Sabbath, since for them saving life takes precedence over religious observance, even on the most sacred holidays.

Chapter 13

Hate Crime and Social Fragmentation

Christine Sistare

In the past decade, several state governments and the federal government of the United States have developed forms of criminal liability commonly referred to as "hate crimes."[1] The forms of liability employed are of three types: distinct offenses, penalty enhancement, and offense-grade enhancement. Penalty enhancement appears to be the dominant approach, and the phrase *penalty enhancement* is used to incorporate increases in grade of offense as well as additional sentencing. Many penalty enhancement statutes include provision for alternative additional sentencing such as community service, reparation to victims, or antibias education for young offenders. Among distinct offenses, statutes proscribing arson or vandalism at places of worship are the most familiar.

These legal developments are a response to what legislators perceive as the unique problem of bias-motivated criminal conduct, that is, criminal acts motivated by the offender's negative prejudices against certain groups of people. Such conduct ranges from threats and vandalism to arson and homicide. The most common types of bias-motivation are antiblack racism, misogyny, anti-Semitism, and antihomosexual (gay or lesbian) hostility. Bias-motivated crime is atypically personal injury crime and often displays particular brutality. It is also atypically likely to be a "stranger crime," rather than being committed by persons in any way associated with the victim.

In this essay, I explore some of the arguments surrounding bias-motivation liability. In particular, the essay addresses questions about the nature of liability for bias-motivated criminal conduct. I believe that much of the debate concerning "hate crimes" law can be resolved by attention to the definition of offenses and the description of liability standards. Put another way, I believe that much of the debate is mired in confusion and conceptual red herrings. When some of this is clarified, a justification for hate crimes legislation specific to liberal, pluralistic societies emerges. Although this justificatory argument does not undercut standard liberal values of toleration and openness, it does point to the critical role that the sense of social connectedness plays in a highly diverse, pluralist culture. To that extent, the argument turns some traditional notions of the relation of toleration, diversity, and openness on their heads.

Punishment for Thought

Although bias-motivated offenses and penalty enhancement are employed by most of the state governments and the federal government, they are the subject of ongoing political controversy. It is sometimes suggested that bias-motivated liability creates classes of persons who receive either "special rights" or "special protections" based on their group membership. But, it appears that the root of opposition to bias-motivated liability is the conviction that it constitutes or verges on liability for unpopular political and social perspectives. Some critics convey this belief by characterizing bias-motivated liability as "viewpoint crime"—liability for one's viewpoint—and many deny the need for bias-motivated liability on the grounds that the problem of bias-motivated criminality is invented or inflated for political purposes.

Why, or whether, bias-motivated conduct merits special attention is a matter for later discussion. What should be noted, here, is that "hate crimes" legislation that affixes liability to beliefs or attitudinal states, per se, can never be legitimate. There must be conduct that is legitimately proscribed on its own terms; typically, these will be actions that threaten or impose harm on persons or their property. *To be* biased or hate filled or prejudiced is not sufficient grounds for liability. Conduct that violates the rights or offends against the protected interests of other persons is a fundamental and necessary condition for criminal liability in a free society. Legally just liability for bias-motivated crimes must, therefore, be clearly grounded in the criminal conduct that is the occasion for liability.

Thus, although penalty enhancement laws and newly created bias-crime offenses direct legal attention to a class of crimes resulting from distinct classes of motive, it must be the criminal conduct itself that is the object of attention and the basis for liability. If bias-motivated crime *is* a legitimately distinct category of liability, it must be so because it constitutes a distinct category of conduct, not because the offenders are particularly unlikable persons. We can compare such liability with that for child molestation, assault on police officers, or assassination of high government officials.

No doubt child molesters have especially despicable desires and attitudes; still, it is society's interest in protecting those who are among the most vulnerable of its members and who represent its future that grounds special legal concern. Similarly, however much we admire them, it is not our special respect for police or presidents that warrants distinct offenses for criminal threats or violence against them. On the strictest terms, we single out criminal harm against children, police officers, and presidents because these acts are particular threats to society, not because we especially disapprove of the views or thoughts of the agents.

Bias Motivation, Prejudice, and Hatred

A feeling of hatred, as such, should not be a required element of new bias-motivated offenses or bias-motivated penalty enhancement. This would, as critics suggest, make "hate crime" akin to punishment for character. It is not the perpetrator's feelings that are central in bias-motivated offenses, but his motivations *as productive of proscribed conduct*. Feelings are often factors in motivation, but they are not dispositive of bias or prejudice as motivators. It is quite possible for someone to engage in illegal conduct for *reasons* of bias without any particular *feeling* of hatred. Indeed, coolness in the course of violence against members of despised groups has characterized some of the most heinous historical instances of hate crime. The image of efficient, dispassionate genocide is as much part of our human inheritance as is that of the enraged bigot with burning torch in hand. Some might even regard the perpetrator carried away with hatred as less culpable than the one who acts on his prejudices with little feeling.

Such comparisons of culpability are not central where our concern is the basic definition of bias-motivated illegal conduct. Some offenders are more in control, and, so, more culpable than others; variant culpability is always a feature of criminal conduct. In defining an offense, however, the law looks to the common features of the undesired conduct; it is these that we wish to address through liability. For bias-motivated crime, it is the fact that prohibited conduct was engaged in primarily or substantially because of the offender's biases (against certain types of persons or institutions) that is, or should be, the definitive element. Those who burn a church *because* of antireligious views or who assault other persons *because* of their victims' perceived sexual orientations are hate-crime offenders in the only legally defensible sense.

What must be stressed is the significance of the causal link between the illegal conduct and the bias that motivated it. Despite the purported difficulty of explicating the requisite linkage,[2] the relation of motivation to criminal acts is explored in many categories of offense, as well as in the sentencing stage of criminal trials. Bias motivation is no more mysterious than motivations of material gain, jealousy, or fear. Indeed, to the extent that we set aside questions as to the offender's feelings of hatred, and so on, bias motivation may be more easily determined than some of the more emotion-laden motivators. An informed trier of fact should be able to make reasonable determinations as to the motivational link between an offender's *proven* bias and his or her *proven* criminal conduct.[3] Let us consider two representative cases.

Some years ago, New York City was the site of several murders in which all the victims were homeless people; in each of these unrelated cases, the offenders said the vagrant status of their victims was "the reason" for the killings. Most of these crimes were exceptionally violent, typically including the burning alive of the victims where they were found sleeping or intoxicated. In the original and highly publicized case, the offenders came upon their victim in an alleyway after they were forced to leave a bar where they had been in an altercation. In the subsequent copycat killings, the offenders apparently went out looking for vagrants to murder.

In the copycat cases, we have clear instances of bias-motivated crime. Although it might be true that the killers were all "violent people," it is evident that they undertook to murder homeless people because of antipathy toward such people as a group. They would not have committed these murders but for their bias against "bums," as several of them described their victims. But, what should we make of the original crime? It appears that dislike of homeless persons inspired the actual killing, although other factors might be said to have contributed to the actors' violent course of action. If the trier of fact determines that the offenders would have gone on their way without harming anyone had they not encountered a homeless person, it is plausible to hold that the murder itself was largely bias motivated. The causal linkage is not of the same "but for" type as in the copycat cases; that is, in other terms, the crime was not premeditated. Yet, the victim's being a homeless person and, thus, an object of contempt for the attackers, played a substantial, perhaps decisive, role in their directing their anger toward him with violent abandon.[4]

Now, consider a different case. A thief acknowledged choosing his victims because of their race and gender. He was African American; his victims were white males. The thief said he robbed white men because they usually carried money and because he, like all black men, was a victim of racial oppression. Thus, white men made fruitful victims, having money, and he felt gratified in harming their interests. Let us assume that the offender was quite sincere in his beliefs about racial inequity and, hence, in his antipathies toward white men. Is this a bias-motivated crime? Rejecting the spurious suggestion that only members of dominant racial groups can be biased in the relevant sense,[5] we, nonetheless, should also reject classification of this as a bias-motivated crime. What is missing, here, is a genuine causal link between the bias and the criminal conduct. This is a thief who may very well be biased against people of another racial group. He is not the victimizer of people of another racial group who happens to use theft as his preferred mode of victimization. Even if we were to sympathize with his justification for selecting white male victims, this would not lead us to describe his criminal conduct as bias motivated. On the contrary, that he can find victims of the oppressor group would be regarded as a happy fortuity. Note, as well, it is not because his acts of theft were self-serving—crime typically is—that we would not treat them as bias-motivated offenses. Nor, again, are his feelings of hatred, which might have been quite intense, relevant. These are not bias-motivated crimes because they were not substantially the result of, or produced by, his bias toward his victims. He was a racially biased thief, but not a thief because of bias motivation.

Some critics of bias-motivated offenses and penalty enhancement observe that concepts such as "bias" and "prejudice" are inherently vague or subjective in meaning. On this ground, they argue that to base liability on the causal linkage of bias and conduct is no more legally defensible than to punish people for feelings of hatred. Jacobs and Potter, for example, observe that the word *prejudice* has many meanings, both positive and negative, and that prejudice of the "negative" variety can range from the fairly innocuous to the most virulent and dangerous.[6] Noting that prejudice and bias, in these broad senses, characterize much human interaction, they write:

> If practically everyone holds some prejudiced values, beliefs, and attitudes, every crime by a member of one group against a member of another group might be a hate crime; at least, it ought to be investigated as such. Moreover, since criminals, as a

group, are usually less tolerant and respectful of others than noncriminals, they are disproportionately likely to be motivated by prejudice. Indeed, in one sense, all (or at least most) violent crimes could be attributed, at least in part, to the offender's prejudice against the victim, based on the victim's race, gender, age, size, looks, perceived wealth, perceived attitude, and so forth.[7]

Further, they claim,

> There is every reason to believe that a high percentage of male violence against women is motivated, at least in part, by anti-female prejudice, especially if prejudice is broadly defined. Practically every act of male violence and intimidation against women is a potential hate crime. Should all crimes by men against women be counted twice, first as generic crimes (murder, assault, rape) and second as hate crimes?[8]

Setting aside the curious contention about the intolerance of criminals, as a group, and the controversial depiction of intersex relations, defenders of bias-motivated crime legislation must respond that an overly broad definition of *prejudice* or *bias* is as much to be avoided as an overly generous conception of the required causal linkage between motive and conduct. Indeed, the two conceptions should function cooperatively. One's low-level or unconscious biases against members of a specific religious or racial group are not likely to *generate* criminal conduct against such persons. Thus, it is legally irrelevant whether we treat the antiwhite views of the thief, in the preceding example, as not being of the correct "type" of prejudice or as not a sufficiently powerful motivator in his conduct. Whether we see this as a matter of defining "prejudice" or of delimiting causal linkage, the conclusion will be that his was not bias-motivated criminal conduct. The possible breadth of natural language concepts such as bias and prejudice is not a bar to liability for bias-motivated crime. Judge or jury will seek to answer this question: "Did the offender's (i) negative feelings, views, attitudes, expectations, or beliefs (ii) directed against a group or groups of persons, as conceived by the offender, (iii) primarily or substantially cause (iv) the criminal conduct of which the offender has been accused or found guilty?" Undoubtedly, there will be a variety of lucid and perspicacious ways of phrasing this question so as to convey the relevant issues to the trier of fact. Not all cases will be paradigm cases; there will be hard cases and borderline cases. If contemporary legal philosophy has taught us any lesson, it is that human law can never be made mathematically precise. Our language and concepts are, at the least, fuzzy around the edges, and very usefully so. Therefore, if we find liability for bias-motivated criminality indefensible, it cannot be because humans do not know, a priori, how to craft perfect laws.

Specification versus Nonspecification

Let us recap: It is not that the offender had certain feelings or feelings of a particular intensity, nor that he or she is a person of specific character or personality, that is the basis for just bias-motivation liability. It is the offender's conduct as motivated by negative ideas, feelings, and so forth, about a group of persons that grounds criminal liability or penalty enhancement. Bias as motivator of proscribed behavior, not as object of contempt or distaste on the part of society, is the foundation of liability.

A further problem concerning bias-crime legislation is the description of victims according to their real or perceived group membership. Most bias-crime law originated in response to racially and religiously motivated crimes. Yet, racial and religious prejudices are not the only forms of crime-productive bias. The dilemma is: should specific groups or forms of bias be identified in bias-crime legislation? If categories of victims or grounds of bias are to be identified, which ought to be included and why not others? On the other hand, if biases or groups of victims are not specified, the law may be seen as dodging historical realities for the sake of a specious neutrality.

The specification approach is the more commonly used. Critics argue that it creates, or may appear to create, "specially protected" groups of persons by identifying as bias offenses only (bias-motivated) crimes against members of those groups. The undesired implication is that persons not belonging to the protected groups do not receive equal protection under the law. For example, legislation prohibiting vandalism of places of worship or enhancing penalties for crimes motivated by religious prejudice effectively distinguishes victims of religious bias from those of racial, sexual, or ethnic prejudice. Atheists and agnostics, in particular, might claim that religious practice or membership was being granted elevated status or that their own status as citizens was, at least symbolically, denigrated. Similarly, in the United States, there is some sentiment against the "special" protection of gays and lesbians through bias motivated offenses and penalty enhancement. Those who take this view oppose the inclusion of bias based on sexual orientation because they believe it gives gays and lesbians "special rights," demonstrates social approval of nonheterosexuality, or both. Conversely, some spokespersons for the disabled oppose listing of disability bias because they fear it will increase hostility against and alienation of disabled citizens.

Specification may be made in any of three ways: (1) by features of the persons against whom bias is directed; (2) by type or category of bias; (3) by reference to places, institutions, or activities that are targets of bias crime. These distinctions are not conceptually pure, but they do help to illuminate some issues. Examples of the first are identification of women, persons of color (nonwhites), disabled persons, or gays and lesbians, as unique targets of bias crime. Examples of the second are proscription of crimes motivated by gender, racial, or religious bias. Examples of the third approach are protection of voting places and churches, of activities such as voting or union meetings, or of institutions such as schools.

There are instances in which the choice between the first and second approaches is of little import. So, to proscribe violence against "disabled persons" or violence motivated by "disability bias" is the same, so long as the language of the offense does not appear to require that the victim *be* what the perpetrator believes him or her to be. On the other hand, there is an evident danger inherent in the first approach, precisely because it does suggest special concern for or protection of some groups of persons. The second approach, by contrast, avoids the patent difficulties of protecting members of only some racial, religious, and so forth, groups and not others.

I rejected, above, the notion that bias motivation is intrinsically an oppressor against oppressed or dominant group against minority group phenomenon. Whatever the frequency of offenses motivated by one bias or the other, it is in fact possible for women to be biased against men, for gays to be biased against heterosexuals, for people of color to be biased against whites. To deny this, as a political statement, is to confirm the suspicion of opponents of bias-crime law that some groups or persons are being afforded special status. This is not to say that specification creates "special rights," as that term is normally used. To enhance penalties for or create special offenses of male on female crime does not permit women to commit crimes against men with impunity—which would be a special right. However, the first approach to specification does appear to signify that some victims are more important or are objects of greater concern than others. It gives this appearance to the extent that the offense turns on their identities or group membership rather than on features of the crimes committed against them. For this reason, the bias-specification approach is preferable to the victim-specification approach.

The third approach functions as an additional basis for liability. Certain activities, locations, and institutions are favored targets of bias-motivated crime. In the United States, churches have long been a symbol of African-American community and have provided both safe haven and civil rights leadership. As a result, racial bigots seeking to intimidate or simply injure black Americans have targeted churches for arson. Schools and daycare centers populated by minority racial or ethnic children have also been targeted for attack. Intimidation of or assaults on people trying to vote, to attend labor or community organizing meetings, or simply to worship, are also familiar bias-motivated acts.

Although addressing these forms of frequent criminal conduct is defensible on public safety grounds, the third approach to specification does raise interesting issues. First, we may note that violence against parties to a labor dispute or against union meeting places, like violence against government agents or property, are often not bias motivated in the primary sense employed here. Often, these acts are more aptly described as terrorism. The terrorist intends to bring about changes in policy or some other result in the conduct of others with whom he or she is in conflict, either by directly influencing those others or by creating a general atmosphere of public insecurity. It seems likely that parties to a labor dispute are not biased against one another for their group memberships, at all. The same may be said of crime that targets government officials or buildings: the offender seeks to achieve some result—if only violent self-expression—and that is the motivation, not attitudes or beliefs about persons of a certain type.

The lines of distinction between bias-motivated crime, in the strictest sense, and terrorism narrowly defined may be blurred in many cases. Still, it does seem to be a conceptual feature of bias-motivated crime that it is, so to speak, *self-contained*. We might say that the offender achieves his goal in acting on his motivations. This point of distinction follows from the fact that the "true" terrorist is largely indifferent to the identity of his victims, whereas the identity (real or imagined) of the victim is a primary feature in bias crimes. Timothy McVeigh, who bombed the Federal Building in Oklahoma City, referred to the 168 dead in that event as simply the necessary "human toll" and as "collateral damage." He did not set out to harm them and had no interest in any of them; he set out to "take revenge" on the government of the United States.[9] Bias is person oriented; terrorism is not. Of course, it is quite possible that a crime is both bias motivated and terroristic in intention; some church bombings appear to have been both intended to interfere with civil rights activism and motivated by racist antipathies.[10]

Finally, we come to the nonspecification approach to bias-crime legislation. This is, as noted, a minority approach among current bias-crime laws. Penalty-enhancement statutes in Texas and Georgia define bias motivation simply as prejudice aimed at any person or group, without specification of protected groups or bias type. Nonspecification enjoys the obvious advantage of precluding worries about unequal protection. No doubt, it also allows passage of legislation without surfacing politically awkward controversies such as those surrounding homosexuality and gender conflict.

On the other hand, the nonspecification approach may appear to dodge social and historical realities. That is, by addressing bias motivation, *simpliciter*, these laws fail to reflect the social facts that members of certain groups are more often the targets of bias-motivated crime than others and that this divergence in victimization is, itself, the product of significant social tensions. Further, collection of data under nonspecific bias-crime laws might not reveal changes in social relations, such as those resulting in the recent increase in bias-motivated crimes against Asian Americans or gays and lesbians. In the latter event, we would not only be obscuring the social realities with which we live, but also preventing ourselves from learning more about them or foreseeing potentially critical changes.

Finally, there is the possibility that nonspecification "trivializes" what are perceived as genuine—historically and culturally significant—bigotries and prejudices. Some proponents of specification may regard the enunciation of types of bias or classes of victims as recognition of the oppressed or marginalized status of certain groups in the society. Put another way, they may regard nonspecification as an attempt to revise, minimize, or distort histories of oppression and abuse. Something like this sentiment may also motivate those who want to define certain biases unidirectionally, claiming that only white on nonwhite crime or male on female crime can be bias motivated.

Despite these difficulties, concrete and symbolic, the nonspecification approach does reach the heart of legitimate bias-crime liability. For, although it is undeniable that women, blacks, Jews, and nonheterosexuals are the most frequent victims of bias-motivated crimes, it is their being targets of criminal conduct that is the concern of the law, not their being members of certain groups. The law seeks to address a category of crime, not classes of victims as defined by their group membership. What makes bias-motivated crime a unique category of crime is the motivational role of the *offender's perception* of the victim's identity and the *offender's* conduct.

Perhaps it is this close relationship of the victim's perceived identity and the offender's conduct that leads some opponents of bias-crime legislation to speak in terms of "victim selection." The language of victim selection is employed to suggest that bias-motivated crime is, in fact, no different from any other form of crime. All criminals, it is claimed, select their victims according to some characteristics or other; bias-motivated crimes, therefore, should not be treated as more serious than other instances of the same conduct type—for example, murder or threat not motivated by bias. What the language of victim selection obscures, however, is the causal or motivational relation of the victim's perceived identity and the offender's criminal acts. The bias-motivated offender does not pursue criminal conduct and, then, select a victim to fit the conduct. Rather, the bias-motivated offender engages in criminal conduct because of his or her perceptions of the victim. So too, where the bias-motivated conduct is aimed at places, activities, or institutions rather than at individuals, it is the problem posed by the type of crime that is of legal concern. Churches and meeting halls are not places more worthy of protection than homes or businesses, any more than women and Jews are more worthy of protection than men and Christians. Unfortunately, churches and meeting halls are places that some persons target for criminal conduct in which they would not or would be less likely to engage elsewhere.

Nonetheless, the law should not be crafted so as to mirror the offender's motivational valances. Nor should offenses be defined for purely political or symbolic purposes. If "special" liability for bias-motivated crime is justified, it must be grounded in the special nature of the criminality involved. The nonspecification approach does this most effectively. Further, it ensures that the law will be ready to deal with the social and cultural realities of an unknown future—one in which targeted persons and places may change.

Justifying Liability

Some critics of bias-crime legislation observe that human nature has ineradicable features, many of them ugly and socially disruptive. Among these, they suggest, we may have to recognize not only violence and dishonesty but also prejudice, bigotry, and bias. If this is so, however, it is a fact that undergirds special attention to bias-motivated criminality, rather than undermining it as they contend. Law cannot eliminate bias anymore than it can eliminate greed or anger. What it can and should do is promote control over conduct resulting from these human failings and, so, protect the legitimate public safety interests of citizens. Wherever society perceives a particular issue of legitimate security, criminal law may be employed. It is recognition of this that accounts for our acceptance of "special" liability for criminal conduct targeting police, children, government property, and the exercise of important rights such as voting. *If* there are reasonable grounds for increased or focused legal attention, then the law has a legitimate role to play, in accordance with existing standards and practices.

Liability under specifically created offenses or to increased penalties for carefully defined bias-motivated criminal conduct can be an instance of the law's proper operation in defending protected interests. Supporters of such liability argue that bias-motivated criminality is worthy of special legal concern because it poses a unique threat to protected interests of citizens and society alike. The greater incidence of physical injury to persons and higher levels of brutality in bias-motivated crimes than among crimes, in general, do give cause for concern. Also, bias-motivated crimes produce retaliatory offenses and widespread social disturbances more commonly than do non-bias-related crimes; this is sometimes described as their "epidemic effect."

Reportedly, the emotional and psychological harms following bias-motivated victimization are unique and profound. That bias-motivated victimization is so often perpetrated by persons unknown to the victims may be a factor in this heightened psychological effect. Although it is true that anyone may be the victim of crime at any time, there is something particularly disturbing about the curiously unpredictable character of much "hate crime." What is unpredictable is not within our control. Although the contrast, or our normal sense of control over what befalls us, may be exaggerated, the feeling of being an open target is particularly disturbing to people. And, as bias-motivated crime often takes distinctive forms, such as vandalism and intimidation, the sense of being more vulnerable to victimization may be quite real. Recognition of this special threat to our sense of control may partly account for the protection that bias-crime law frequently affords to particular places and activities. Schools, places of worship, the voting place: all these are places in which we might expect, or hope, to be especially safe and in control of our immediate lives. That they are chosen targets of bias offenders is, thus, especially disturbing.

Moreover, it is claimed, bias-motivated offenses threaten and cause alarm to all persons who regard themselves as members of the targeted group or groups. These other persons are often referred to as "the victim's community" in the sense that they share in the outrage and fear suffered by the victim. They experience the crime as one aimed at them as much as at the actual victim. Here, it should be noted that members of the larger community, not just those who belong to the subgroup that was the object of the offender's prejudices, may experience suffering unique to bias-motivated disruptions in the social fabric.[11] Particularly in a liberal society, any citizen might be more distressed by bias-motivated crime than by "ordinary" criminal acts. Although not themselves targeted, other citizens often express unusual discomfort when bias-motivated crimes occur. They may be disturbed by the very fact that some persons try to alienate and isolate fellow citizens.

There is a great deal more that can be said about both the nature and justification of bias-motivated liability. I do not hope to have addressed all the relevant matters in this essay. However, I believe it has been demonstrated that wisely crafted liability for bias-motivated criminal conduct is possible and that such liability can be justified on grounds of legitimate public interest. When we set aside the political rhetoric and posturing, we face a familiar set of questions: Is there a problem of sufficient weight to merit the use of criminal law? If so, can legitimate and workable law be fashioned? In the case of bias-motivated criminal conduct, the answer to the first question perhaps remains open for discussion. The answer to the second question is "Yes."

Notes

1. The data employed in this article come from the following sources: American Prosecutor's Research Institute, Anti-Defamation League, Bureau of Justice Statistics, Federal Bureau of Investigation/Hate Crime Data Collection, National Criminal Justice Association, and the Uniform Crime Reporting Program of the Department of Justice.

2. James Jacobs and Kimberly Potter, *Hate Crimes: Criminal Law and Identity Politics* (New York: Oxford University Press, 1998). Despite their worries, the authors provide a chart of degrees of causal linkage using examples they apparently think are clear.

3. And, of course, evidentiary standards and burdens should not be other than those required in any criminal case.

4. The point might be made in the antiquated, and itself troublesome, language of "specific intent": the perpetrator's intent was to injure, abuse, or otherwise victimize per-

sons or institutions associated with membership in *this* group *because* of that association. The natural route to determining such intent, of course, is the actor's bias motivation.

5. Although I sympathize with arguments that "sexism" and "racism" are structural phenomena dependent on distinctions between dominant and oppressed groups, I do not think this alters the psychological reality of bias as an equal opportunity motivator.

6. Jacobs and Potter, *Hate Crimes*, chap. 1.

7. Ibid.

8. Ibid. It is difficult to know if this claim of male bias is politically grounded or based on data the authors cite showing that male perpetrators commit the majority of crimes against women. Of course, men are also the perpetrators in most cases of crimes with male victims.

9. I cannot explore, here, the conceptual question of whether one can be biased against a government or institution, in the same sense that one can be biased against persons. Thus, although one can be biased against members of the military, it is not clear that one can be biased against "the military" as such. So, too, one may be prejudiced against members of certain religious groups, but can one be biased against the religion, as such? Bias seems to be a fundamentally person-oriented phenomenon, even where its originating grounds—political conflict or religious disputes—are detachable, as it were, from the persons involved.

10. This difference between policy-oriented terrorism and person-oriented bias crime may explain the fact that very little reported bias-motivated crime is carried out by or through ideological groups such as Aryan Nation or other white supremacist organizations. Individuals acting as individuals, rather than as members of organized political groups—however bigoted the underlying ideologies—commit the great majority of bias-motivated crimes in the United States. Of course, it is probably the case that many of these individual offenders are "consumers" of hate speech promulgated by organized groups.

11. I have not encountered this suggestion elsewhere; it is based on supposition rather than on sociopsychological studies.

Chapter 14

Hate Crimes Laws:
Progressive Politics or Balkanization?

David A. Reidy

In 1981 the Anti-Defamation League of B'nai B'rith published the model for what have now become known as hate crimes laws. Hate crimes laws are "penalty enhancement" laws. They enhance the penalties for a variety of crimes—most commonly assault, homicide, arson, trespass, and vandalism—provided certain triggering conditions are met. Some hate crimes laws apply to specified crimes any time the perpetrator selects a victim because of race, ethnicity, religion, sexual orientation, or other specified characteristic. Others apply to specified crimes *only* if the perpetrator selects a victim out of a special animus toward a racial, ethnic, religious, or other specified group to which the victim belongs. So, a law of the first sort but not the second would apply to a criminal who commits one of the specified crimes against a black victim not out of any particular hostility toward blacks as a racial group, and not randomly, but because he believes the police less likely to investigate crimes committed against blacks and thinks judges sentencing those convicted of such crimes less likely to impose harsh sentences.[1]

Hate crimes laws of one or another sort are now common in the United States; they have even worked their way into federal law.[2] Notwithstanding significant public and academic support, these laws have been subject to strong, serious, and persistent criticism.[3] Much of this criticism has been aimed at the standard arguments offered as justification for these laws. And much of it is well deserved, for the standard arguments in favor of hate crimes laws are either unsound or weak. Demonstrating as much is the first aim of this essay.

Its second aim, however, is to offer a nonstandard argument for hate crimes laws that is neither unsound nor weak. This argument I call the *argument from oppression*.[4] It captures and expresses better than any of the standard arguments the moral basis for the sentiments or intuitions many people have in favor of hate crimes laws, and its structure is such that most of the objections to the standard arguments do not apply. But one objection, or family of objections, must still be addressed. This objection, or family of objections, posits hate crimes laws—along with, perhaps, affirmative action policies, the expansion of sexual harassment laws, slavery reparations initiatives, and the like—as the balkanizing result of an identity or interest group politics of resentment inconsistent with progressive liberal democratic values. This paper's third aim is to assess whether this objection, or family of objections, is telling against hate crimes laws as justified by and revised suitably in light of the argument from oppression. At the risk of ruining an otherwise suspenseful read, a bit of foreshadowing would seem apropos: I argue that the objection, or family of objections, is not telling when directed at hate crimes laws justified by and revised suitably in light of the argument from oppression.

The Standard Arguments

There are three standard arguments for hate crimes laws. The first is the argument from greater harm. The second is the argument from more culpable mental states. The third is the argument from liberal democratic values. Each of these arguments is either unsound or weak.

The Argument from Greater Harm

Whether crimes satisfying the trigger conditions of hate crimes laws cause greater harm, physical or psychological, either to victims or nonvictim third parties, than similar but nonhate crimes is, of course, an empirical question. This is often forgotten, and a priori pronouncements regarding the greater harmfulness of hate crimes are not uncommon. Unhappily, as prima facie plausible as these pronouncements may be, they are not supported by the available empirical evidence.[5]

Crimes said to be hate crimes do often cause physical harm to their direct and immediate victims. But that is because they are very often assaults and homicides, not because they are committed by perpetrators who satisfy the relevant statutory trigger conditions for hate crimes penalty enhancements. As a class, the crimes that satisfy these conditions are no more violent or physically harmful to their victims than the class that does not. And, in any event, existing laws already scale punishment to reflect the greater physical harm of assaults and homicides to victims as compared to the physical harm of other crimes to victims, and of the physical harm of aggravated assaults and homicides to victims as compared to the physical harm of assaults and homicides generally to victims.

Because there is little evidence to support the claim that crimes falling within the scope of hate crimes laws are more *physically* harmful to victims—or, for that matter, to nonvictim third parties—than those otherwise similar crimes that do not, the argument is often made that these crimes, those that fall within the scope of hate crimes laws, cause greater *psychological* harm to their direct and immediate victims, or to nonvictim third parties, than those that do not. This greater psychological harm justifies, so the argument goes, the additional punishment imposed by hate crimes laws.

Crimes said to be hate crimes do cause psychological harm both to their direct and immediate victims and to nonvictim third parties. But so do virtually all crimes. The question is whether candidate hate crimes cause greater psychological harm than otherwise similar non-hate crimes. With respect to direct and immediate victims, the available empirical evidence suggests that they do not. Indeed, it suggests that candidate hate crimes may cause their direct and immediate victims marginally less psychological harm than similar crimes that would not count as hate crimes under typical hate crimes laws.

This evidence is admittedly counterintuitive. There is, consequently, a temptation to dismiss it in favor of armchair psychological speculation. But the evidence ought not be dismissed, although pending further studies it ought to be regarded as tentative. Most candidate hate crimes are committed against persons belonging to historically oppressed groups: blacks, gays, Jews, ethnic minorities, and the like. It is not implausible to suppose that many of these victims will possess preferences and other psychological mechanisms adapted to their condition and that these may mitigate their subjective experience of psychological distress when made victim to a candidate hate crime. It is also not implausible to suppose that the nature of many candidate hate crimes makes it clear to the victim that she was targeted because of her race, or sexual orientation, or religion, and so forth, thus giving her a way of making a kind of sense of the crime committed against her that she would not be able to make were she randomly victimized. These suppositions, admittedly unconfirmed, are sufficiently plausible as explanations of the admittedly counterintuitive empirical evidence regarding the psychological harm caused by candidate hate crimes to their direct and immediate victims that that evidence ought not be simply dismissed.

As with direct and immediate victims, there is little evidence to support the claim that candidate hate crimes cause nonvictim third parties greater psychological harm than similar crimes that fall outside the scope of hate crimes laws. The psychological harm of any crime to nonvictim third parties is determined primarily by the proximity and visibility of the crime to such parties.[6] This, of course, does not preclude additional psychological harms to nonvictim third parties arising from the fact that the victim was selected because of or out of animosity toward her membership in a racial, religious, ethnic, or other specified group. Or, at least it does not preclude such additional psychological harms when the crime visibly manifests an animosity toward a group with which the nonvictim third parties strongly self-identify. Although there is no substantial body of empirical evidence to confirm the claim that candidate hate crimes cause such harms to nonvictim third parties, the claim that, for example, obvious gay bashings "terrorize" the gay community generally, is prima facie plausible. Of course, even if there were empirical evidence confirming the claimed psychological harms, it would still be necessary to argue that those harms are serious enough to justify the relevant penalty enhancements. It should not surprise, then, that this argument has been made to do much of the justificatory work in the case for hate crimes laws. Given the absence of compelling empirical evidence establishing the claimed psychological harms, however, it is at present a weak argument. It is also just the sort of argument that invites the characterization of hate crimes laws as the fruit of a balkanizing, identity group, politics of resentment. But that is a matter the discussion of which must be temporarily postponed in the interest of completing a review of the standard arguments. The upshot here is that the best version of the argument from greater harm is the argument from psychological harms to nonvictim third parties, and that that argument is, as things stand, not very compelling.

The Argument from More Culpable Mental States

The criminal law in the United States already scales punishment according to whether an offender acts intentionally, knowingly, recklessly, or negligently. Thus, if hate crimes laws are to be justified by appeal to the more culpable mental states of those who commit crimes satisfying their trigger conditions, it must be that those who commit such crimes act from a more culpable mental state than those who commit crimes otherwise identical but outside the scope of such laws.

This is straightforwardly implausible with respect to those hate crimes laws that apply to perpetrators who simply select their victims because of their race, or religion, or ethnicity, or sexual orientation, and so on. Recall that hate crimes laws of this sort would apply to a criminal who selects only Protestant victims because he believes only Protestants will in fact enjoy the sort of salvation that might redeem their suffering here on earth. He selects his victims because of their religion. But does he act from a mental state more culpable than the criminal who randomly selects his victims just because he likes the experience of anonymous power, or the criminal who carefully selects his victims based on who is most likely to suffer the most from his crime? Obviously not.

To be sure, it may be that some criminals who commit crimes against victims selected because of their race, religion, ethnicity, and so on, act from mental states more culpable than those who commit otherwise identical crimes against victims selected for other reasons. But this is not true of all criminals who commit crimes against victims selected for such reasons. It follows that where the mental state of a criminal who selects a victim because of race, religion, or ethnicity is in fact more culpable than it would be had he selected his victim for some other reason, the additional culpability must be a function of something beyond the fact that he selected his victim because of race, or religion, or ethnicity. What that something else is I will turn to later. For now, it is enough to note that the argument from more culpable mental states fails as an argument for those hate crimes laws that enhance penalties whenever the criminal selects a victim because of race, religion, ethnicity, sexual orientation, or similar features.

The argument from more culpable mental states is perhaps more plausible as a justification for those hate crimes laws that apply to perpetrators who select their victims out of one or another specified group-based animosity. After all, to act from racist, anti-Semitic, homophobic, or xenophobic hatred or animosity is clearly to act from a very culpable mental state, indeed a mental state more culpable than many still significantly culpable alternatives. And this greater culpability can be explained by reference to the evil of targeting individuals solely out of a group-based animosity.

But, is it obvious that the mental state of a criminal who selects his victims out of racist animosity is more culpable than that of the criminal who selects his victims out of a desire to see the weak suffer, or to impose the greatest harm possible on a nonvictim third party, or to display his superiority to the ordinary run of humanity, or to salve an ego all too easily bruised? That is less clear. Indeed, once adequate attention is given to the range of vicious and evil reasons that lead persons to commit crimes against others, it is not obvious that racist, anti-Semitic, homophobic, or xenophobic reasons are significantly more vicious or evil than other familiar reasons criminals have for selecting victims that the law largely ignores when it comes to scaling punishment for crimes. In fact, the whole idea of correctly scaling criminal punishments to reflect the culpability of the reasons for which the criminal selected his victim looks to be beyond the reach of ordinary human abilities once the full range of reasons that lead people to commit crimes against particular victims is fully in view. It is, perhaps, no accident that for the most part the criminal law has limited its inquiry into the culpability of mental states to whether the act in question was done intentionally, knowingly, recklessly, or negligently.

Like the argument from psychological harms to nonvictim third parties, the argument from the greater culpability of racist, anti-Semitic, homophobic, xenophobic, or similar mental states has been pressed into active and regular service by proponents of hate crimes laws.[7] But it too is a weak argument. The problem is not that an empirical premise remains unconfirmed, but rather that an axiological premise—that to select a victim out of racist animosity, say, is worse, ceteris paribus, than to select a victim for virtually any other reason—appears either dubious or unjustifiable through argument available to ordinary human intellect. And this weakness renders the argument from more culpable mental states vulnerable, like the argument from psychological harms to nonvictim third parties, to the charge that it arises out of and affirms an undesirable balkanizing, identity group, politics of resentment. What else, the objectors ask, could explain the vigor and confidence with which proponents of this argument assert the greater culpability of selecting a victim because he's black, or gay, or Jewish, or Latino as compared to selecting a victim for any number of other reasons? This charge aside, the upshot here is that the argument from more culpable mental states is not very compelling for either of the two sorts of hate crimes laws in force in the United States today.

The Argument from Liberal Democratic Values

Hate crimes laws are sometimes defended on the grounds that they are needed to give adequate public and symbolic expression to the fundamental liberal democratic values of nondiscrimination and tolerance.[8] Crimes committed against particular victims because of or out of a group-based animosity for their race, religion, ethnicity, or sexual orientation violate these values in a manner and to a degree calling for special public condemnation. Or so the argument goes.

There are many difficulties with this argument. The first is that it is a weak argument for hate crimes laws that apply just in case the criminal selects his victim because of but not necessarily out of animosity toward the victim's race, religion, ethnicity, and so forth. The criminal who decides just to assault Catholics, not because he has any group-based animosity toward them, but rather because he wants to systematize his victims in some fashion and attacking only Catholics enables him to do so, does not violate the liberal democratic values of nondiscrimination and tolerance in any significant way, or at least he violates those values no more so than does any other criminal guilty of assault. So, the argument is best taken as an argument for hate crimes laws that apply just in case the criminal selects his victim out of one or another specified group-based animosity.

But even so taken the argument is not strong. Even if a criminal who so selects his victim violates the liberal democratic values of nondiscrimination and tolerance, and even if that violation calls for a special and visible public condemnation, it does not follow that that condemnation must take the form of enhanced criminal penalties. A special concern with and condemnation of such conduct may be publicly and visibly expressed in a variety of ways within and through public political culture. Given the seriousness of enhancing criminal penalties—which is a limitation of liberty, after all—the argument from liberal democratic values is weak as an argument for hate crimes laws unless it can be shown that enhancing penalties is the only or the best way publicly and visibly to express a special concern with and condemnation of such conduct.

But suppose this can be shown. Is the argument from liberal democratic values then a strong argument for hate crimes laws, or at least those laws triggered when a victim is selected out of a specified group-based animosity? Well, yes and no. It all depends on what we mean when we speak of the liberal democratic values of nondiscrimination and tolerance.[9]

Suppose we mean that persons ought not impose avoidable harms on others for irrational, irrelevant, or indefensible reasons. Employers ought not deny jobs to otherwise qualified persons solely because of their race. Children ought not exclude from their circle of friends perfectly kind and fun but very heavy or bespectacled peers. And the like. If this is what we mean when we speak of the values of nondiscrimination and tolerance, then the argument from liberal democratic values justifies hate crimes laws applicable not only to criminals who select their victims because they are black or gay or Jewish, but also to criminals who select their victims because they are fat or skinny or ugly or exceedingly beautiful or socially awkward or socially adept, and so on, including all irrational, irrelevant, or indefensible reasons for which criminals might select their victims. But if this is what we mean, then it is hard to see how to limit hate crimes laws to any manageable list of specified group-based animosities the selecting of a victim from which will trigger the laws' application. And if the list of group-based animosities triggering the application of hate crimes laws is to include hatred of the fat, the skinny, the ugly, the tattooed, the homeless, the socially awkward, the excessively wealthy, and so on, then what is the point of having hate crimes laws? Why not simply enhance the penalties for all crimes of the targeted type, for example, all assaults, all vandalisms?

Suppose what we mean by the values of nondiscrimination and tolerance is instead that persons ought not impose avoidable harms on others because of some attribute or trait that either cannot be changed or can be changed only at an unreasonable cost. Employers, again, ought not deny jobs to otherwise qualified persons solely because of their race, religion, or ethnicity. And children, again, ought not exclude from their circle of friends perfectly kind and fun but very heavy or bespectacled peers. But, again, if this is what we mean by the values of nondiscrimination and tolerance, the list of specified group-based animosities the selecting of a victim from which will trigger the enhancing of criminal penalties will be long indeed. Those who target the tall, or the exceedingly intelligent, or the stutterers ought to be subject, on this understanding of nondiscrimination and tolerance values, to the penalty enhancements of hate crimes laws.

If hate crimes laws of the sort proponents advocate are to be justified by the argument from liberal democratic values, then the values of nondiscrimination and tolerance must be tied specially to race, religion, ethnicity, sexual orientation, and the like. After all, the sentiments and intuitions felt by the supporters of hate crimes laws are aroused by lynchings and cross burnings, gay bashings, vandalisms of Jewish businesses or cemeteries, arsons in Latino neighborhoods, and the like. These are the paradigmatic hate crimes that call for enhanced penalties—not attacks against the fat, the skinny, the tattooed, the shabbily dressed, the ugly, or the glamorous, even when they are specifically targeted out of a generalized animosity for such persons.

266 David A. Reidy

So, suppose what we mean when we speak of the values of nondiscrimination and tolerance is just that persons ought not impose avoidable harms on others because of their race, religion, sexual orientation, ethnicity, and the like. If this is what we mean, then we might be able to argue from these liberal democratic values to hate crimes laws of the typical sort. The question is whether this is what we do, or should, mean by these values.

The advantage of this account of nondiscrimination and tolerance values, or at least of these values as they are invoked as part of a justification for hate crimes laws, is that it captures the idea that there is something special about race, ethnicity, religion, sexual orientation, and the like and, thus, something special about imposing avoidable harms on others because of their race or ethnicity, and so on. If I refuse to date tall people or to purchase goods from persons who bear tattoos, I irrationally and indefensibly impose an avoidable harm on others, perhaps even because of a characteristic or trait that cannot be easily altered. But it would be a stretch at best to say that I violate the fundamental liberal democratic values of nondiscrimination and tolerance, at least insofar as we are talking about those values as violated by paradigmatic hate crimes. To be sure, my conduct may be rightly criticized, perhaps morally criticized, through a loose use of the language of nondiscrimination and tolerance. But the basis of that criticism cannot really be that I violate the values of nondiscrimination and tolerance insofar as we take those values to be essential to a just and stable liberal democratic order. But, if we substitute blacks for tall people or Jews for persons who bear tattoos, then the picture changes, at least for those of us living in the United States, with its history.

It is tempting here to say that what the core values of nondiscrimination and tolerance demand is that we ignore race, religion, ethnicity, or sexual orientation in our interactions with others. That we be color-blind, and so forth, when it comes to social life and even in our criminal conduct, should we endeavor such conduct. But this is a view that many if not most proponents of hate crimes laws will have reason to reject. It implies that there is no significant moral difference between a white criminal who selects victims because they are black and a black criminal who selects victims because they are white, or between a Protestant criminal who selects victims because they are Jewish and a Jewish criminal who selects victims because they are Protestant. But many if not most proponents of hate crimes laws begin with the intuition that there *is* a moral difference, even if there are also moral similarities, between these cases. In each example, the prior but not the latter case reflects, expresses, and arguably serves to reconstitute existing historical patterns of structural, group-based oppression. To treat the two cases as if they are not morally distinct in any significant way is to fail to attend to the realities of long-standing, structural, group-based oppression at which hate crimes laws are aimed as a partial remedial social response. It is to view the issue of hate crimes from the point of view of the nonoppressed.

It is racially motivated crimes against blacks, and not racially motivated crimes generally, religiously motivated crimes against non-Christians, and not religiously motivated crimes generally, that generate the intuitions and sentiments many feel in favor of hate crimes laws. It is crimes against members of already oppressed groups precisely because they *are* members of already oppressed groups that call for enhanced penalties. Given the realities and history of structural, group-based oppression, a racially motivated murder committed by a black man against a white man is, for the purposes of punishment, not very different from any other murder, or at least not very different from a murder motivated by a hatred of brunettes committed by a blonde. But a racially motivated murder committed by a white man against a black man is different from other murders. It connects with those realities and presses that history forward in ways other murders cannot.[10]

At their core and as affirmed and protected by law, the values of nondiscrimination and tolerance must be understood in terms of race, religion, ethnicity, sexual orientation, and the like. There is indeed something special, morally speaking, about these specific kinds of social groupings: they point us toward some of the most pressing historical cases of structural group-based oppression that call for a remedial social response. What we mean, then, when we speak of the fundamental values of nondiscrimination and tolerance is not that race, religion, ethnicity, or sexual orientation ought always to be ignored in social life, but rather that social life ought to be reorganized so as to eliminate the real, specific, long-lived, structural, group-based oppression of blacks and other nonwhites, Jews and other non-Christians, gays, lesbians, and other nonheterosexuals, and non-European ethnic groups. These are the great, structural, and evil instances of discrimination and intolerance we want to end, not the more general fact that we notice and sometimes are moved in our social interactions by the race, religion, ethnicity, or sexual orientation—or height, IQ, handsomeness, for that matter—of others. The intuition or sentiment that racially motivated assaults on blacks, for example, deserve more punishment than other assaults in the United States arises out of a strong desire to end a real, particular case of structural group-based oppression and an awareness of how such crimes affirm and threaten to reconstitute that very oppression.

The argument from liberal democratic values, then, is strongest if the values of nondiscrimination and tolerance are understood not just to be specially connected and limited to race, religion, ethnicity, sexual orientation, and the like, but to be so connected and limited in a particular way—proscribing the imposition of avoidable harms on blacks because they are black, or Jews because they are Jews, and so on, where the imposition of those harms reflects, expresses, or serves to reconstitute the real, historical oppression of blacks, Jews, and so forth.[11] Of course, this version of the argument, like the strongest versions of the arguments from greater harm and from more culpable mental states, invites the objection that those who advocate hate crimes laws are engaging in a balkanizing, identity-group, politics of resentment.

There is, consequently, a temptation to retreat to the position that while it is not true that a murder is always just a murder, it is true that a racially motivated murder is always just a racially motivated murder. All racially motivated murders violate the liberal democratic values of nondiscrimination and tolerance equally, and, thus, if any call for enhanced penalties, all call equally for the same enhanced penalties.

This version of the argument from liberal democratic values is weak, however. It presupposes a basic social structure within which blacks and whites, gays and straights, non-Christians and Christians are situated or positioned symmetrically as groups. But this presupposition is false. Indeed, it is from an awareness that this presupposition is false that the moral intuitions and sentiments that most strongly favor hate crimes laws arise. Even if this presupposition were true, however, this version of the argument from liberal democratic values would still be weak insofar as it offers no account of why selecting a victim on the basis of race, religion, ethnicity, or sexual orientation is so bad as to merit enhanced penalties, rather than some other sort of special public condemnation, as compared to selecting a victim on the basis of height, weight, IQ, or occupation. Only one such account is plausible, of course, and that is that some of the most dramatic and damaging cases of oppression in the United States have involved specific races, religions, ethnicities, and sexual orientations. But to admit this is to admit that not all racially motivated crimes, for example, are morally equal, for not all racially motivated crimes reflect, express, or potentially reconstitute such oppression. Oppression is always asymmetric. So, racially motivated attacks by whites on blacks connect with historic and ongoing oppression in ways that racially motivated attacks by blacks on whites never could.

The upshot then is twofold. The strongest version of the argument from liberal democratic values invites the same balkanization objection as the strongest versions of the other standard arguments for hate crimes laws. And the strongest version of the argument from liberal democratic values rides piggyback on, indeed is perhaps best understood as an imperfect articulation of, a deeper argument from oppression. It is that argument to which we turn now.

The Argument from Oppression

The argument from oppression goes like this:

P1: Structural group-based oppression is a fact of history and contemporary life in the United States;[12]

P2: Those who belong to oppressed groups are disproportionately and systemically more vulnerable to a wide range of structurally and socially produced but avoidable harms;[13]

P3: Those who by virtue of their social positioning vis-à-vis the vulnerable members of an oppressed group enjoy a special capacity to protect them from the harms to which they are vulnerable, or to help to reorder social life so as to minimize—and eventually eliminate—their structurally produced, group-based vulnerability, have a special moral obligation to do so;[14]

P4: Those who intentionally select a member of an oppressed group, because they are a member of that group, but not necessarily out of a group-based animus, as their victim for a crime the harm of which reflects, expresses, or contributes distinctively to the social reconstitution of the disproportionate vulnerabilities from which members of that group suffer, and who do so notwithstanding their being positioned socially such that they enjoy a special capacity to protect or aid the members of that group, fail to live up to a special moral obligation they owe to their victim;[15]

P5: It is the violation of this special moral obligation that makes paradigmatic hate crimes morally worse than otherwise similar crimes;

P6: In general levels of criminal punishment should be scaled to reflect degrees of moral wrongfulness;

(D) The additional moral wrongfulness of paradigmatic hate crimes justifies the extra punishment imposed by hate crimes laws of a suitably revised sort.

This argument differs from the standard arguments in important ways. Although it appeals to the place of hate crimes in a social order that systemically works a certain kind of harm on members of oppressed groups, it is not an argument from the greater harm caused by hate crimes to direct and immediate victims or nonvictim third parties. And although it appeals to the greater moral culpability of hate crimes offenders, it is not an argument from the greater culpability of motives grounded in one or another group-based animosity. And finally, although it rests ultimately on and aims at the vindication of liberal democratic values, it casts itself fundamentally as an argument from structural group-based oppression, not from the values of nondiscrimination and tolerance as values applicable to interactions between individuals assumed to be symmetrically positioned as group members by and within their basic social structure.

Central to the argument from oppression are the ideas of oppressed groups, disproportionate vulnerabilities, and special moral obligations to protect or aid. Explicating some of these ideas may help to avoid misunderstanding. And so it is to that task I turn now.

Oppressed groups are, first, social groups.[16] *Social groups* are more than mere aggregates. Insurance companies may aggregate persons with one or another genetic trait for actuarial purposes. But, taken together, persons so aggregated do not constitute a social group. To constitute a social group, members must stand in determinate relations with one another constituted through their interactions with one another and with those at the margins or outside the group. There are many different kinds of social groups, including associations, cultural or identity groups, and structural groups. Oppressed groups are necessarily structural groups, although as such they sometimes overlap with cultural or identity groups, or with associations.

Associations are social groups within which the determinate relations group members stand in, with respect to themselves and to those at the margins or outside the group, are a function of the group's shared aims, purposes, or ends—for example, families or the Catholic Church. *Cultural* or *identity groups* are social groups within which the relevant relations are a function of how group members construct their identity or self-understanding at its most basic levels—for example, Chicanos and Southerners. Cultural or identity groups need not share any aim, purpose, or end, although sometimes they do. But they must share something by way of tradition, history, language, social practice, or cultural forms sufficient for members to constitute themselves as an "us" or "we" to which they belong.

Structural groups are social groups within which the determinate relations group members stand in, with respect to themselves and those at the margins or outside the group, are a function of how they are positioned by the basic social structure of their society when it comes to access to fundamental goods and resources. Structural groups are produced through the institutional mechanisms through which authority, power, labor and production, desire and sexuality, prestige, and the like are socially constituted and organized. *Oppressed groups* are structural groups the members of which are systematically disadvantaged in the distribution of or their access to the basic goods and resources needed to develop and exercise capacities for self-expression, self-development, and self-determination. The members of oppressed groups, for example, African Americans in the United States, are thus disproportionately vulnerable to a wide and serious range of socially produced and avoidable harms; among the most serious of these are poverty, illiteracy, economic marginalization, violence, incarceration, avoidable illness, early mortality, and the like. Describing accurately these disproportionate vulnerabilities and marking out the many and interrelated ways in which they arise out of a basic social structure that systematically disadvantages some but not others is a key task of oppression theory.

The members of structural groups need share no common aim, purpose, or end. And they need neither find nor construct their identity or self-understanding at basic levels through appeal to their membership in the group. Indeed, they may, and unhappily sometimes do, belong to the group without even knowing it. The existence of and membership within structural groups is a function of how persons are objectively positioned socially, relative to one another within and through their basic social structure. The differentiation of structural groups is distinct, then, from the differentiation of associationist groups and cultural or identity groups, for in the latter cases group members must affirm their membership to be group members.

In the United States, blacks, gays, Jews, and various ethnic groups, as well as women, have been and remain to various degrees oppressed structural groups. This social fact does not depend at all on whether blacks, gays, Jews, and so on, *think* of themselves as a group. Of course, it also does not preclude them constituting associationist groups or cultural or identity groups more or less identical in terms of their membership.

It bears emphasizing that the existence of and membership in structural groups generally, or oppressed groups more particularly, is a function of reiterated patterns of social relations and interactions over time. Three things follow from this. (1) First, membership in structural groups is something that may come in degrees, depending on the degree to which one is, over time and in general, implicated structurally in a web of systematically advantageous or disadvantageous social relations.[17] So, particular persons may be more or less black with respect to their membership in the structural group called blacks. (2) Second, membership in, indeed the existence of, a structural group may change over time. So, membership in and even the existence of Jews as a structural group in the United States has and continues to undergo significant change. (3) Third, membership in a structural group is logically independent of membership in associationist groups and cultural or identity groups. So, a particular individual may be marginally—perhaps not even—black with respect to blacks as a structural group but be centrally black with respect to blacks as a cultural or identity group, or vice versa.

Individual members of oppressed groups do not all suffer the same particular, individual socially produced and avoidable harms by virtue of their social positioning. But they are all disproportionately vulnerable to them. And for many, this vulnerability will itself constitute an actualized harm, a sort of psychological weight rooted in a deep sense of anxiety, insecurity, or powerlessness.

To be vulnerable is to be in a distinctively or especially precarious position, to be exposed or at risk to an unusual degree to some injury or harm.[18] To be vulnerable is not the same as simply belonging to a class the members of which merely satisfy some precondition for a particular harm. Only women get ovarian cancer. So, only women are at risk of ovarian cancer. It doesn't follow that to be a woman is to be vulnerable to ovarian cancer. Similarly, only the employed can lose their jobs during an economic recession. It doesn't follow that to be employed is to be vulnerable to unemployment during a recession.

Vulnerabilities can arise from many sources. Some women are vulnerable to ovarian cancer by virtue of their genetic endowment. So, nature is one source of vulnerabilities. The disproportionate vulnerabilities that mark oppressed groups as oppressed groups arise from the "normal" functioning of the basic social structure of the society in which they exist. So, given the structure of labor markets and of authority within most employment contexts today, blacks are more vulnerable to unemployment during an economic slowdown than are whites. They are more likely to be laid off and more likely to suffer adversely from being laid off. And given the historical exclusion of blacks from political processes—something that continues informally today—blacks are more vulnerable to the legislative sacrifice of their interests for the "common good." They are more likely to have their interests ignored during ordinary legislative processes and then to be accused of and marginalized for divisiveness for asserting their interests once ordinary legislative processes are complete. The multiplication of these disproportionate vulnerabilities, covering wide ranges of social life, produce what Marilyn Frye has called the "bird cage" effect: blacks and other oppressed groups find themselves caged by an intersecting network of constraints arising out of the "normal" operation of the basic social structure that limit or undermine their self-development, self-expression, and self-determination.[19]

Disproportionate vulnerabilities are commonly understood to impose special obligations on those especially well placed to prevent harm to, to protect, or to aid the vulnerable, and these special obligations are often legally enforced. So, adults have various special obligations to children. Providers of various services have various special obligations to the elderly, as do providers of medical services to the terminally ill. Those not cognitively impaired have special obligations to those who are cognitively impaired. These obligations arise as moral obligations in each case out of the asymmetry of the respective parties' social relationship or relative positionings. They are given legal backing because of the moral gravity of their violation, although not exclusively for this reason; consequentialist considerations also have a role to play here. Similarly, the special obligations violated in paradigmatic hate crimes arise as moral obligations out of the asymmetry of the respective parties' social relationship or positioning, that is, their group-based relationship or positioning within or through the "normal" functioning of the basic social structure. They are given legal backing in part—and again, consequentialist considerations have a role to play—because of the moral gravity of their violation. The moral intuition or sentiment at work here in the case of paradigmatic hate crimes belongs to the same family as that at work when we judge that stealing from a blind man is morally worse, and thus deserving of or at least eligible for greater punishment, than stealing from a sighted man.

A full defense of the argument from oppression would require much more than the foregoing. However, I hope the foregoing sufficient to give a clear enough sense of how the argument goes and how it differs from and improves on the standard arguments to support a concluding discussion of the claim that hate crimes laws arise out of and express a balkanizing, identity-group politics of resentment.

Hate Crimes Laws: Progressive Politics or Balkanization

Objections to hate crimes laws and the politics from which they arise cannot be assessed apart from assumptions about the justification, aim, and shape of hate crimes laws. Suppose, then, that the argument from oppression is taken as the sound justification for suitably revised hate crimes laws. What then are we to make of the objection that hate crimes laws arise out of and affirm a balkanizing, identity-group politics of resentment?

This objection has been raised in various forms by numerous critics.[20] In their book critical of existing hate crimes laws and the politics from which they seem to have emerged, Jacobs and Potter argue that rewriting particular criminal laws to take into account the racial, religious, ethnic, and such, identities of offenders and victims undermines the criminal law's potential for bolstering social solidarity by redefining crime as a problem of intergroup conflict and encouraging citizens to think of themselves, first, not as citizens but as members of identity groups, ideally victimized and besieged, and ready to exact revenge on their oppressors.[21] This is, of course, not one but many objections. Those who make the sort of objection just sketched typically make one or more of the three following claims:

1. Hate crimes laws arise out of and encourage a politics of resentment that is psychologically harmful to those who engage in it.
2. Hate crimes laws arise out of and encourage a balkanizing, interest-group politics hostile to the common good and at odds with republican and liberal democratic values.
3. Hate crimes laws presuppose a false degree of internal unity within the relevant social groups—blacks, gays, Jews, and the like—and thus encourage these groups to police their own membership in oppressive ways.

As directed at existing hate crimes laws and the standard justifications given for them—the arguments from greater harm, more culpable mental states, and liberal democratic values—these claims are, at least prima facie, not without some bite. But the case against existing hate crimes laws, and the standard justifications given for them, does not depend on the strength of these objections, for the standard justifications are themselves either unsound or weak, as demonstrated earlier. So, rather than assess the force of these objections against existing hate crimes laws and their standard justifications, I want to assess their force against hate crimes laws justified by and suitably revised in light of the argument from oppression.

A Politics of Resentment?

Several critics from the left have argued that hate crimes initiatives, like perhaps slavery reparations or affirmative action initiatives, bear an unhappy relationship to the politics of resentment. The politics of resentment is the politics of those who suffer from and seek to anesthetize the deep hurt of finding themselves in a social world publicly regarded as legitimate or just but within which they are systematically and significantly unable to satisfy their desires. It arises first out of a righteousness or righteous indignation, produced affectively, that overwhelms and thus blocks the subjective experience of weakness, hurt, and suffering. That righteous indignation is then given direction through the identification of some agent or agents as the cause of that weakness, hurt, or suffering. The weakness, hurt, or suffering is then displaced by the inflicting on the causally responsible agent or agents a harm. The aim of this displacement is not to alter the balance of power in the social world, however. It is merely to ease the pain of one's own condition.

Thus, for it to work, the harm inflicted on the external source of one's suffering must carry itself some public mark of legitimacy. The paradigm harm inflicted, then, is punishment, for punishment is what revenge is called by those who hypocritically seek to cloak their acts in the garb of legitimacy or justice. Of course, the imposition of such a harm—revenge or punishment—does not and was not intended to eliminate the source of the hurt and suffering; it does not alter the balance of power in the social world. Those who find themselves systematically and significantly unable to satisfy their desires will continue to so find themselves; and by passing their act of revenge off as legitimate punishment, they will have reaffirmed the very norms that legitimate their suffering. But they will have dulled their pain.

Hate crimes laws, reparations for slavery, and other group-based initiatives are often said to arise out of and reflect such a politics of resentment.

They are the fruits of a politics of revenge cloaking itself in the language of legitimacy and justice. But they are poisoned fruits. They do nothing to change the balance of power in the social world, and they invest those who suffer the most under existing social conditions in their own suffering.

This objection misses the mark, however. Hate crimes laws, reparations initiatives, affirmative action proposals, and the like arise not out of a politics of resentment rooted in the experience of suffering, but from a politics of anger rooted in the knowledge of and struggle against injustice. The aim is not to inflict a harm on some agent or agents held causally responsible for the suffering of those who suffer, but rather to reorder the basic social structure to eliminate the structural and institutional bases of oppression. Of course, this is, according to the critics, just what proponents of hate crimes laws may be expected to say in their defense.

To be sure, the politics of victimhood and resentment has sometimes accompanied hate crimes and similar initiatives. But for the most part, those actually pushing politically for these initiatives are neither deeply invested in their own suffering, nor acting from a self-defeating resentment. They are angry, mobilized, and increasingly politically empowered. Their aim: the chance to participate and advance their own interests in a basic social structure free of group-based oppression. Ultimately, whether theirs is a disabling and disfiguring politics of resentment cannot be determined a priori. Time and social experience will settle the matter. To date, however, there is little empirical evidence to support this objection.

A Balkanizing, Interest-Group Politics?

Critics from both the right and left have complained that hate crimes laws and similar initiatives arise out of and give priority not to a politics of the common good but rather a divisive interest-group politics. In the inevitable clash over which groups are to enjoy which gains, the argument goes, the res publica is lost.

But, if proponents of hate crimes laws and similar initiatives are correct about the realities of oppression, the res publica was never in hand in the first place. What divides proponents from these critics of hate crimes laws, then, is not a commitment to a republican and liberal democratic politics of the common good and treating like cases alike; both share that commitment. What divides them is their evaluation of existing social conditions.

Proponents of hate crimes laws and similar initiatives argue that group-based oppression is a significant feature of these conditions, and that there is, accordingly, no neutral, universal point of view from which all citizens may engage in democratic deliberation over the common good or what in fact constitutes a like case. To insist that some murders or assaults deserve greater punishment than others as a result of the social positioning of the victims and offenders is not to subordinate the common good or the demands of formal justice to the particular interests of one's own group. It is, rather, to insist that social position and point of view matters and, thus, ought not be set aside in public deliberations over what the common good requires or what counts as a like case for the purposes of formal justice. To deny this is either to deny the reality of oppression or to falsely and covertly universalize the social position and particular point of view of the nonoppressed.

Critics sometimes argue that social position and point of view did not, and rightly did not, matter for other marginalized groups at earlier points in U.S. history. In relatively short order, numerous immigrant groups, for example, assimilated into mainstream politics, rarely challenging the unstated point of view from which public democratic deliberation over the common good and the demands of justice proceeded. Why should matters be any different for blacks, gays, Jews, and the like?

The answer is that marginalized *cultural* groups may be assimilated into mainstream democratic deliberation without any fundamental challenge to the unstated point of view from which that deliberation proceeds because, or so long as, they are not also oppressed *structural* groups. Oppressed structural groups cannot participate, or cannot participate effectively, in democratic deliberation over what the common good or justice requires without calling that point of view into question, without refusing to adopt a point of view from which their oppression is invisible or obscured. And so their politics appears to be, indeed is, divisive at some level. But there is no other path to justice and the common good consistent with democratic commitments. The choice between an unacceptably balkanizing interest-group politics and a more or less harmonious republican and liberal democratic politics of the common good is one confronted only in a society free of structural group-based oppression. Only there will a commitment to basic institutional arrangements and norms function as a common point of departure for all social groups in democratic deliberation. In a society not free of oppression, the choice is a false dilemma.

Do We Really Have or Want Social Groups Such as Blacks, Gays, Jews, and so Forth?

It is sometimes said that the sort of politics behind hate crimes laws and similar initiatives presupposes and creates incentives to coerce a degree of internal group unity neither possible nor desirable. So, critics will object to hate crimes laws on the grounds that blacks—or gays, or Jews, and the like—are too varied a group for such laws to be justified and that such laws create objectionable incentives for them to police their own membership for internal conformity to certain criteria of group membership.

This objection arises out of two mistakes. The first is to forget that, within the context of hate crimes laws and their justification, references to blacks, gays, Jews, and other groups are references to structural groups, not cultural or identity groups or associationist groups. Thus, it is entirely beside the point that group members neither share important ends nor self-identify through group membership. The second mistake is to suppose that structural groups are properly defined through some set of essential membership criteria, a set of necessary and sufficient conditions the proper application of which determines whether any particular individual is in or out of the group. But structural groups cannot be so defined. They are constituted and must be understood in terms of how they are related to other structural groups within and through the basic social structure that determines the ability of individuals, and thus groups of individuals, to access basic social resources. Individuals may and often will differ in the degrees to which they belong to various structural groups, depending on how they are positioned within the network of institutional social arrangements that facilitate or frustrate access to basic social resources. This does not preclude speaking intelligently of groups, however, so long as there are—as there in fact are—concentrated nodal points of numerous individuals situated similarly to a very high degree within and by basic institutional norms and arrangements.

To the extent that the argument from oppression presupposes blacks, gays, Jews, and the like as structural social groups, it neither presupposes nor encourages a false or high degree of internal group unity. Indeed, at least with respect to the politics behind hate crimes laws, the term *identity politics* is misleading. It is simply not in the nature of structural groups to make claims as such about their identity or the identity of their members. It is in their nature, instead, to make claims about the justice of how they, and thus their members, are positioned within and through the basic social structure.

To be fair, it must be noted that political initiatives aimed at improving the social positioning of oppressed structural groups are unlikely to succeed in a democracy without substantial support and activism from group members and that, as a strategic and rhetorical matter, cultivating a group-based identity—above and beyond ordinary "consciousness raising"—among group members may prove desirable. But this is a contingent and avoidable feature of such political initiatives. The less the resistance within the democratic polity, the less there is to be gained by such rhetoric and political strategy.

Conclusion

Critics of hate crimes laws are correct about two things. First, the standard arguments given as justification for these laws are either unsound or weak. Second, these laws and the standard justifications given for them at least appear to arise out of and affirm a balkanizing, identity/interest-group politics of resentment. But, the critics of hate crimes laws are incorrect in concluding that there is no compelling moral case for such laws. The argument from oppression is sufficiently compelling to constitute a prima facie justification for such laws. And hate crimes laws justified by appeal to and suitably revised in light of it cannot be saddled with the charge that they arise out of and affirm a balkanizing, identity/interest-group politics of resentment.

Nevertheless, hate crimes laws and the politics from which they arise are undeniably divisive. But that is to be expected and by itself is unobjectionable; democratic initiatives aimed at responding to and remedying structural group–based oppression are almost always divisive. The question with all such initiatives is whether they are so divisive that their cost in terms of social unity outweighs whatever moral and political gains they promise. That is a complex question I have neither asked nor answered in this paper. But two points bear emphasizing, as a final thought, here.

First, among the moral and political gains promised by hate crimes laws and the politics that surround them is a broader, deeper, and more accurate understanding of social and political life. And that is a gain perhaps worth pursuing, even at the—one must hope temporary—cost of an increase in social tension and division between groups. Second, no proponent of hate crimes laws imagines them as a silver bullet capable of working significant social change by themselves. They are just one part of a broader set of social, political, and legal initiatives aimed at responding to and remedying structural group–based oppression. Ultimately, their merits and demerits ought to be assessed in the context of that larger set of initiatives of which they are a part.

Notes

1. On the distinction between victim-selection and group-based animus hate crimes laws, see Frederick Lawrence, *Punishing Hate: Bias Crimes under American Law* (Cambridge, Mass.: Harvard University Press, 1999), 29–30; and Lawrence Crocker, "Hate Crimes Statutes: Just? Constitutional? Wise?" *Annual Survey of American Law* (1992–1993): 486–89.

2. As of 2002, most every state has adopted some sort of hate or bias crimes law. In 1993, the U.S. Supreme Court upheld Wisconsin's hate crimes law against constitutional challenge. See, *Wisconsin v. Mitchell*, 508 U.S. 476 (1993). In 1994, Congress passed the Hate Crimes Sentencing Enhancement Act, covering crimes committed on federal lands. In 1999, the Hate Crimes Prevention Act was introduced into Congress but was not enacted. It would have extended federal penalty enhancements to hate crimes committed (a) with the aim of preventing a person from exercising a federal right, or (b) through the use of firearms or explosives. And it would have extended the classes of persons covered to include sexual orientation, gender, and disability. A virtually identical bill was introduced in 2002 as the Local Law Enforcement Enhancement Act.

3. For views either critical or skeptical of hate crimes laws, see James B. Jacobs and Kimberly Potter, *Hate Crimes: Criminal Law and Identity Politics* (New York: Oxford University Press, 1998); Susan Gelman, "Sticks and Stones Can Put You in Jail, But Can Words Increase Your Sentence?" *UCLA Law Review* 39 (1991): 333; and the following symposium journal issues: *Annual Survey of American Law* (1992–1993): n. 4, 1993; *Criminal Justice Ethics* 11 (1992): n. 1; *Law and Philosophy* 20 (2001): n. 2. For a view sympathetic to such laws, see Lawrence, *Punishing Hate*.

4. For an initial articulation of this argument, see my "Hate Crimes, Oppression, and Legal Theory," *Public Affairs Quarterly* 16, no. 3 (2002).

5. For similar criticisms of the greater harms argument, see Jacobs and Potter, *Hate Crimes*, 80–90, and Alon Harel and Gideon Parchomovsky, "On Hate and Equality," *Yale Law Journal* 109 (1999): 507, and sources cited therein.

6. See Paul Slovic, Baruch Fischhoff, and Sarah Lichtenstein, "Facts and Fears: Understanding Perceived Risk," in *Judgment under Uncertainty: Heuristics and Biases*, ed. Daniel Kahneman, Paul Slovic, and Amos Tversky (Cambridge: Cambridge University Press, 1982).

7. The more culpable mental states argument is sometimes couched as an argument from more vicious character traits. See, for example, Andrew Taslitz, "Condemning the

Racist Personality: Why the Critics of Hate Crimes Legislation Are Wrong," *Boston College Law Review* 40 (1999): 739.

8. For versions of this argument, see Lawrence, *Punishing Hate*; and Michael Blake, "Geeks and Monsters: Bias Crimes and Social Identity," *Law and Philosophy* (Symposium Issue on Hate Crimes Laws) 20 (2001): n. 2.

9. For a helpful discussion of these values, see Andrew Altman, *Arguing about Law* (Belmont, Calif.: Wadsworth, 2000), 262–64.

10. For an alternative account (appealing to equal protection and distributive justice values rather than nondiscrimination and tolerance values) of the moral difference between a racially targeted crime against a black victim from a racially targeted crime against a white victim, see Harel and Parchomovsky, "On Hate and Equality."

11. My argument does not preclude appeal to a weaker and broader notion of nondiscrimination and tolerance that I might violate if I refuse to date Baptists or to frequent bars tended by tall bartenders. I take it as more or less obvious, however, that whatever the moral force of this weaker and broader account of nondiscrimination and tolerance, it is insufficient to merit legal enforcement or affirmation through hate crimes laws.

12. For a general account of structural group-based oppression, see Iris Young, *Justice and the Politics of Difference* (Princeton, N.J.: Princeton University Press, 1990); and Jim Sidanius and Felicia Pratto, *Social Dominance* (New York: Cambridge University Press, 1999).

13. On this disproportionate vulnerability, see Sidanius and Pratto, *Social Dominance*; David Cole, *No Equal Justice* (New York: New Press, 1999); Susan Okin, *Justice, Gender, and the Family* (New York: Basic Books, 1989), esp. chap. 7; Michael Omi and Howard Winant, *Racial Formation in the U.S.*, 2d ed. (London: Routledge, 1994); David Kairys, *With Liberty and Justice for Some* (New York: New Press, 1993), esp. chap. 5; and the discussion by David Wilkins in his "Introduction: The Context of Race" in Amy Gutmann and K. Anthony Appiah, *Color Conscious* (Princeton, N.J.: Princeton University Press, 1996).

14. For an analysis and defense of special obligation to the vulnerable, see Robert Goodin, *Protecting the Vulnerable: A Reanalysis of Our Social Responsibilities* (Chicago: University of Chicago Press, 1985).

15. The argument from oppression, then, justifies treating male rapes of females as hate crimes.

16. My account of oppressed groups draws heavily on the work of Iris Young. See her *Justice and the Politics of Difference*, and her more recent *Inclusion and Democracy* (New York: Oxford University Press, 2000), esp. chap. 3.

17. And this will in turn depend in part on one's ability and efforts at resisting being implicated in such a structural web of disadvantage.

18. My account of vulnerability draws substantially from Ken Kipnis's "Vulnerability in Research Subjects: An Analytical Approach," (unpublished manuscript).

19. See Marilyn Frye, "Oppression," in *The Politics of Reality: Essays in Feminist Theory* (Trumansburg, N.Y.: Crossing Press), 1983.

20. For articulations and discussions of this objection or family of objections, see Jacobs and Potter, *Hate Crimes*, chap. 9; Iris Young, *Inclusion and Democracy*, chap. 3; Susan Bickford, "Anti-Anti-Identity Politics," *Hypatia* 12 (1997): 111–31; and Wendy Brown, "Wounded Attachments," *Political Theory* 21 (1993): 390–410. My discussion draws sympathetically from the views of Young and Bickford.

21. See Jacobs and Potter, *Hate Crimes*, chap. 9.

Chapter 15

Contemporary Germany Faces Multicultural Society

Lester Mazor

Incivility and its discontents are among the causes for philosophic reflection. Various traditions of social, ethical, and political thought point toward different ways to avoid painful conflict and to increase the chances of peaceful interaction, coordination, and cooperation. Some viewpoints preach quietude, some tolerance, others call for assimilation, yet others for exclusion. Some may even address the conditions that encourage cultural pluralism. These do not exhaust the possibilities, but the prevalent discourse, situated as it is within liberalism—in the sense of the social contract among individuals, the rule of law, and the development of civil society—tends to mark out a certain range of approaches that are considered acceptable. Theoretical discourse often arms itself against empirical testing, yet perhaps it may be called to account by reviewing certain historical examples. In this spirit the thoughts about contemporary Germany that follow are offered in evidence.

The issue, of course, concerns modern society generally, confronted as it is by multiculturalism. Yet the ideal of the industrialized and urbanized market society, ruled by law under representative government and grounded in modern ways of thinking, long has been tied to the notion of the cultural nation.[1] Hence, the development of the United States as a self-consciously multicultural society in the last half century has been fraught with struggle and pain. Its outcome still is uncertain. Europe, by contrast, for a while seemed to be moving in the opposite direction, witnessing the breakup of the old pluralistic empires in favor of more singularly national political entities followed by the destruction or expulsion of national minorities. Places like Belgium or Czechoslovakia, combining more than one "people," were understood to be exceptional and, in the eyes of many, unfortunate.

The formula with which all these societies have sought to solve what they conceive as the problems created by the presence of minority cultures within their boundaries is rooted in that Reason born in the Enlightenment and nourished by the virtues of civil society founded on classical liberal premises. It is argued that a society based on a social contract can offer membership and participation to all who are willing to accept its terms, including above all the obligations of citizenship—especially abiding by the rule of law and accepting the society's established values. For achieving domestic peace and maintaining effective social interaction, societies rely on such institutional features as universal education, the separation of the private and public spheres, the anonymity of the market, and the formality of civil rights and liberties. The individual is expected to develop attitudes and practices of respect for human dignity, tolerance of others, and civility in general. The question addressed here is the adequacy of such a framework for the building of a multicultural society, using contemporary Germany as a test case.

Some Events in Germany's Encounter with Cultural Diversity

Example 1: Having completed the education required to become a teacher, F.L. applied for an internship, required for a credential. Her application was rejected on the basis of her insistence on wearing a head covering while teaching. The state education minister overruled this decision, but on completion of the internship she was denied a license to teach, on the ground that a public school teacher is a role model for students and a representative of the values and norms of the state. Her insistence on wearing a head covering, said the education authorities, demonstrated disregard for the welfare of her students, who might interpret her dress as a political symbol. The case drew considerable attention in the media and was the subject of lengthy debate on television.[2]

Example 2: A fourteen-year-old, called "Mehmet" in the press, was jailed, accused of a holdup. He had a long record of juvenile offenses. When the local authorities sought to deport him, they faced the legal obstacle that he had not yet been tried, much less convicted. They chose to deport his *parents*, resident in Germany more than thirty years, and "Mehmet" with them, on the ground that they had failed to raise him properly. The event came to a head in the midst of a mayoral election campaign and was the subject of considerable media attention.[3]

Example 3: The Berlin city-state senator for internal affairs called for quotas to be established for the number of foreigners who may reside in any one of the city's then twenty-three districts. The stated goal of the proposal was to counteract the formation of strong ethnic communities. In the energetic public debate that followed, he rejected suggestions that Berlin should be a "multicultural" city, although he did not object to the representation in the city of a variety of cultures. He emphasized that already there were some parts of the city in which native Germans did not feel at home.[4]

Example 4: During elections for the state legislature in one of the new states carved out of the former German Democratic Republic (GDR), neither of the main national parties could claim a majority because a hitherto unknown party, the German People's Party (DVU) received almost 20 percent of the vote. Postelection polling revealed that those who had voted for it were unfamiliar with its platform and candidates but welcomed its posters and literature, featuring slogans like "Foreigners Are Taking Our Jobs" and "Deport Criminal Foreigners." Less than 1 percent of the population of this state are non-Germans.[5]

Example 5: Teachers from several Berlin schools took their mixed-ethnicity classes on outings to places in the surrounding region, the state of Brandenburg. After repeated incidents in which these students were harassed by groups of young people dressed in what is known as the conventional uniform of right-wing extremists, and after some situations escalated into violence that left several students hospitalized, many Berlin teachers decided to end the trips. In an effort at reconciliation, some of the Berlin teachers invited teachers and students from Brandenburg to Berlin to tour the areas where their schools are located. The results were disappointing. The students remained hostile. In a lengthy discussion of the matter on television, the head of one of the Brandenburg schools defended her students, saying that it was well known that foreigners are responsible for a great deal of crime.[6]

Incidents like these provide material for private comment and public debate in Germany. No doubt they do not draw the kind of attention from the global media that has been given to the cases in which, in recent years, hundreds of foreigners in Germany have been beaten, pushed from moving trains, or had their homes set on fire. To this picture we must add the frequent incidents of desecration of graves and houses of worship, and the daily insults and harassment that foreigners undergo—especially those whose distinctive dress or personal appearance makes them easy targets.[7]

No part of modern history, needless to say, is better known than Germany's miserable treatment of its minorities as well as other non-Germans during the first half of the twentieth century. One might stop right there, concluding that Germany is one of the least likely test cases for the claims of liberal institutions and attitudes. To do that, however, would neither do justice to the fullness of German history nor recognize the intense efforts of the Germans since World War II to come to terms with their past, join the ranks of countries showing high respect for liberal values, and design and give force and life to the kind of political, social, legal, economic, and cultural institutions that foster civility. The broad terms of German history since 1945 and the society that has evolved within its territory are familiar to many. On the supposition that specific knowledge about Germany may not be so widely held, I will set out the liberal credentials of contemporary Germany, before turning to the philosophical challenges posed by the prospect of multiculturalism.

The Legal Setting[8]

The Basic Law of the Federal Republic of Germany (FRG), its constitution, was adopted in 1949 as part of the process by which the Western allies began to give up some of their powers of occupation. A constitutional assembly and an advisory council were involved in drafting it for submission to the German states under the control of France, the United Kingdom, and the United States. By its own terms this constitution was provisional, to be replaced by a full-fledged constitution for all of Germany when circumstances would permit. Nevertheless, no new constitution was adopted following the collapse of the GDR, the incorporation of its territory into the Federal Republic, or the signing of the treaty formally ending World War II. Although the FRG has a federal system, most legislation takes place at the national level. Civil law, civil procedure, commercial law, administrative law, family law, labor law, criminal law and procedure, and most other fields are governed by codes, often very detailed, establishing national norms. The judicial hierarchy, likewise, has its apex in a national high court and a separate constitutional court.

Adopted in the wake of the Nazi experience, the Basic Law has many features designed to prevent a repetition of that blot on human history. Prominent among these is the list of *fundamental rights* with which it opens, starting with the general obligation of the state to respect and defend human dignity and the broad right to the free development of one's personality. Freedom of religious belief, freedom of opinion, freedom of the press, and the protection of property are stated as basic rights. There also are specific guarantees of artistic freedom, freedom of scientific inquiry, freedom of association, the privacy of the home, and the right to conscientious objection to military service.

The Basic Law also announces a fundamental commitment to *equality*. It guarantees the rule of law and proclaims that everyone is equal before the law. It also forbids that anyone be disadvantaged or advantaged on the basis of sex, family background, race, language, religion, religious or political beliefs, ethnicity, or country of origin. Germany is declared to be a "social" state, that is, a welfare state. The constitution promises protection and support for marriage, the family, churches, and schools. The state is obligated to provide support to certain classes of persons—mothers and children, for example.

When the Basic Law was adopted, both the Western allies and the Germans were keenly aware of the issue of *political refugees*. The right to asylum for those fleeing political persecution was anchored firmly in the text and over the years has been given broad interpretation and application. By the 1980s, voices were heard questioning the breadth of this provision, but it was not until after reunification of West and East that the major parties agreed on changes narrowing the freedom of asylum seekers to enter the newly unified Germany. The new provision restricts entry for those who are already in a country having a legal commitment to grant asylum.[9] Now that Germany has such countries on its eastern borders, much of the pressure on it to accept refugees is reduced.

Germany long has had no immigration law as such. Apart from citizens of other members of the European Union (EU), who by virtue of that fact are entitled to live in any member country, most of the non-Germans living in the country have had the status of *guest workers*. Their children, and even their children's children were not entitled, until the most recent legal changes, to permanent residence or German citizenship, even if they were born and raised in Germany and lived there all their lives. The guiding principle of German citizenship law has been *jus sanguinis*—a matter of bloodlines—rather than *jus soli*—based on birth or long presence on the soil of the country—which governs in countries such as France or the United States. The citizenship law also has entailed that ethnic Germans whose families have been living in countries like Russia or Rumania for many generations are entitled to come to Germany and claim their rights as citizens. Dual citizenship is not permitted.[10]

Civil Society in Germany

Germany is a modern, industrialized, highly urbanized, technologically advanced country with a high standard of living in world terms. It is a nation-state on a federal model, consisting of sixteen states—three of them city-states and five of which formerly were in the GDR. The government is parliamentary at both national and state levels, with the chief executive chosen by the parliament. The president has only a formal role; the chancellor is the chief national figure. The judiciary is composed of career professionals, organized hierarchically. People trained in the law hold many posts in the extensive bureaucracy at national, state, and local levels. The tradition of the civil service is strong. Its status and privileges are given explicit constitutional protection.

A market economy national in scope and dependent for success on a high export volume functions with strong involvement of major financial institutions. What has been a very large public sector—once including the rail system, national airline, the telephone system, radio and television broadcasting, as well as the post office—has gradually been privatized. With very few exceptions, schools and places of higher education are state funded. Strong unions negotiate agreements covering large numbers of workers in many occupations. The social welfare system includes a system of broad health insurance, generous unemployment benefits, retirement pensions, social welfare payments, as well as rent subsidies and family allowances.

The public sphere is highly developed, including renowned institutions of research and teaching, innumerable museums, as well as subventions for theater, music, and even individual artists. The press is private, independent, and active. Kiosks often offer a dozen daily newspapers or more. Private television and radio are well developed now. One index of the state of the public sphere is that the most widely watched television program is the national evening news. In almost all the media, serious commentary, heated controversy, and intense discussion—often lengthy—demonstrate the earnestness and depth of thought that is a hallmark of German culture.

Most people hold that the old class structure has been dissolved in the turbulence of the twentieth century. The financial, industrial, and commercial class seems to have replaced the old aristocracy in setting the tone of society, but the new class of civil servants and professionals also has great influence. White-collar workers of all types are well organized in professional associations and unions.

Two churches, the Roman Catholic and the Lutheran, are institutionally strong, publicly outspoken, and socially active. They participate in the social welfare system, distributing and deploying state funds. Church attendance, however, is not very high, nor is religious belief especially strong. The society is mainly secular in character.

The political scene in the FRG has been dominated by two large popular parties, the Union (CDU/CSU) and the Social Democrats (SPD), but at the national level and in most of the states, the participation of smaller parties almost always has been necessary to form coalition governments. The successor to the GDR's ruling party (PDS) draws votes only in the states of former East Germany. From time to time extreme right-wing parties have shown some strength, but rarely have they partaken in coalition governments, and some have been banned under the constitutional provision allowing the exclusion of anticonstitutional parties. Opinion studies, however, suggest that as many as one-third of Germans reject the parliamentary system, a trend manifested also in sinking electoral participation.

German society is tightly linked to the rest of Europe, most noticeably through the EU. The national currency reluctantly surrendered to the euro. The role of EU institutions is visible and increasing, including its courts and, most recently, the central bank. With a population of almost ninety million, Germany is the largest single EU country, about one-fourth of the total EU population. Its strong economy has given it more than one-fourth of the say in EU decisions. German high culture, of course, long has been recognized and even revered throughout the world.[11]

Historical Development of German Civil Society

German social and political history has been marked by dramatic ruptures. In just a little more than a century, Germany repeatedly experienced major shifts, known by salient dates: 1871, 1918, 1933, 1945, 1961, and 1989 being prominent among them. The unification of Germany by Prussia, the abdication of the Kaiser and collapse of the Empire, the Nazi rise to power, the Zero Hour at the end of World War II, the erection of the Wall, and the demise of the GDR, leading to reunification—these mark the ups and downs that frame the themes and issues of contemporary German society.

These dates also are a reminder that Germany is one of the more recent of the major political constructs on the European continent. While England was consolidating its power over the British Isles, and Spain, France, the Dutch, and the Portuguese extending their power globally, Germany was still a loose collection of separate states. Although the Rhine roughly marks the western border, Alsace and Lorraine sometimes were part of Germany, sometimes of France. The Saarland voted to be part of Germany in 1955, as it had in 1935. Germany took territory from Denmark in the 1860s. Hitler's annexation of Austria and of the Sudetenland is better known. At the close of World War II, Germany lost not only Austria and northern Bohemia, but also its territory in East Prussia and Silesia, including such cities as Posen, Breslau, Danzig, and Konigsberg. If there are few former colonials in the population today, it is mainly because Germany was such a latecomer to the game of colonialism.

Germany also trailed the other major European powers both politically and economically. Efforts by the middle class to establish parliamentary power failed in the middle of the nineteenth century, and the body that met in the Reichstag in Berlin at the end of that century had little say. Even the brief-lived Weimar Republic had to endure the scorn of much of the educated class, the disdain of professors of law and politics, and rejection by most young people, who accepted the Nazi view that liberal institutions were inappropriate to German traditions. The GDR followed the Soviet model. It is really the fifty-year existence of the Federal Republic that testifies to the institutionalization of a liberal, parliamentary system in Germany. Economic historians often claim Germany gained advantages through relatively late industrialization and also by the necessity to rebuild its industrial plant after World War II. Rapid industrialization clearly was a shock to the class structure in the nineteenth century and led to the establishment of Bismarck's "social state" as far as Konigsberg.

The most infamous chapter of modern history comprises the German experience with non-Germans—if one can put it that way without disrespect to the memory of the victims—now known as the Holocaust. Yet, there was a time when Huguenots found asylum in Berlin in numbers large enough that one in four Berliners spoke French. Through the efforts of Moses Mendelsohn and others, Jews were granted rights to participation in the economy and society that were unusual for European countries. And, by the end of the nineteenth century there was a high degree of assimilation, despite persistent anti-Semitism. In the eastern territories, especially after the partition of Poland, many Poles lived on German territory.[12] The Holocaust and the shift in borders after World War II sharply reduced the diversity of the population. Except for the occupying military forces, there were few non-Germans in the FRG until, in the 1950s, the economy began to prosper and the labor shortage led to the invitation of "guest workers," at first mostly from Italy and then from Yugoslavia and Turkey in increasingly large numbers. The liberal asylum policy permitted people fleeing Soviet domination to enter the country. Some moved on, but many stayed. Many of the people who came as guest workers to West Germany from southern Europe and Turkey have remained and raised families in Germany, and now their children are founding families. The GDR, by contrast, did not respond to its labor shortage with such an aggressive policy, preferring instead to contract with particular countries, mostly from Southeast Asia, for contingents of workers for a definite term of service. They usually were not allowed to bring family members with them and often were kept in barracks removed from the main East German population.

Germany after reunification became a country of more than eighty million people. More than seven million of these are counted as foreigners. Of these, two million are labeled Turkish and about one million come from what was formerly Yugoslavia. There also are some 600,000 Italians, more than 350,000 Greeks, close to 300,000 Poles, and more than 100,000 people each from Spain, Portugal, the United Kingdom, the Netherlands, France, Austria, the United States, Rumania, Iran, and Vietnam. Although it is possible for some of these people to become German citizens, it has not been easy and few have done so. Some are reluctant to give up their ties to their homeland. Some may fear that even citizenship will not provide acceptance or security. There is much evidence that in popular consciousness they would not be seen as Germans.[13]

The "Problem of Foreigners"

Events like those described at the outset of this paper are treated in contemporary German public discourse under the heading of "the problem of foreigners in Germany." The distinctions made in this discourse are not those between citizens and resident aliens, or between the native born and immigrants, or even between legal and illegal resident aliens. Because it has been so widely accepted that Germany is not a country open to immigration, the term *immigrant* really has had no place in the discussion. Germans are people who are German by birth, that is, by blood. Some are Germans returning from other lands, descendants of Germans who left for a life elsewhere at one time or another, often well more than a century ago. Most of the people counted as Germans have resided in Germany all their lives, including the substantial numbers of the older generation who came from the areas lost in the east at the end of World War II.

To many Germans, the presence of anyone else—that is, of foreigners—is seen as a problem. Clearly, they were wanted when they were needed to fill jobs in a scarce labor market. With high unemployment in recent years, that justification is gone. Only very recently have economists and business people suggested that the natural increase of the population will not suffice to sustain the economy, and especially, to support the large number of people who will retire in coming decades. The government has moved to create limited possibilities for highly trained technical workers to come to the country in well defined numbers, but not without a great deal of opposition.[14] Many Germans are of the opinion that most of the foreigners should just go home. For those in this category who have been born and raised in Germany, often it is not so clear where that home is. For those who have been granted political asylum because of the torture and terror they face in their homelands, the suggestion seems even more absurd. There also are large numbers of people waiting to have their asylum applications examined. Most of these eventually will be rejected, but they may still be allowed to stay, under government policies recognizing their hardships and postponing deportation. In the meantime, they are given housing and subsistence—state subsidies that irritate many Germans—but are not allowed to seek employment.[15]

Of course, many of the issues concerning foreigners are not unique to Germany. Bilingual instruction in the schools, which has been tried to some extent with the Turkish population and remains controversial, is one example. Religion is a significant issue. Those who have come in large numbers from Turkey and the Kurdish areas, as well as many others from the Mediterranean and the Middle East, are Muslims. The considerable resistance to the presence of Islam in Germany manifests itself in incidents such as refusals of permits to build mosques. In discourse one can hear an elision from "Islamic" to "Fundamentalist," that threatens to slide into "terrorist." One indicator of the kind of reactions many Germans have to these people is that a newspaper's series of small articles explaining various items of Turkish language and culture evoked a stream of letters from outraged readers, protesting what they saw as the implication that they had a duty to learn about such things. Cultural anthropologists and sociologists comparing German attitudes toward and treatment of these groups with the way similar problems are dealt with in other modern societies often comment that Germany is one of the most xenophobic of such societies. In the view of these interpreters, it is especially difficult for Germans to accept difference because Germans do not believe that one can become German through the passage of time, learning the language, adopting the mores, honoring the laws, or adhering to German values. In fact, people who are not German by blood and who do these things may be suspect. They may be seen as dissemblers.[16]

In the national election of 1998, parties on the right sought to make the number of foreigners in the land one of the main issues of the political campaign. The more moderate large parties in the middle of the political spectrum responded to the public's concerns, first through the amendment of the asylum provision of the constitution to make it more restrictive, then through incentives and pressure on foreigners to return to their homelands, including reductions of social benefits and even deportation of malefactors. The smaller Liberal Party called for dual citizenship. The Greens were alone in calling for a real immigration law, explicitly establishing an immigration policy with quotas and including antidiscrimination legislation; their plan called for implementing the long-unenforced clauses of the Basic Law and other measures in the spirit of accepting an increasingly multicultural Germany.

The buildup to the national election of 2002 also suggests that the topic of foreigners in the society could be a salient feature of the campaign. The ruling majority of SPD and Greens hoped to head that off by adopting the new immigration law, full of compromises as it is. Yet at this writing, the issue is clouded by a procedural wrangle over the validity of the crucial vote in the Upper House, and beyond that lies the uncharted territory of promised constitutional challenges. In the background, the lead candidate for the Conservative Union (CDU/CSU) rumbles that he may choose to make an issue of immigration and asylum seekers. The topic also surfaces, in a more subtle way, in the controversy over reform in education, where newly revealed rankings on internationally normed tests indicate, not surprisingly, that those parts of Germany with the highest concentrations of foreigners scored at the low end of the national results. That the nation as a whole did not score well already is attributed in many quarters to the various effects of the presence of "the others."[17]

History and Future Uses of German Philosophy

There are those who would argue that if the Germans have difficulty in accepting cultural diversity, it is because the Enlightenment did not triumph as thoroughly in Germany as it did in France and many other European countries. Yet, it is difficult to maintain this position, given Reason's reign in so many spheres, both in high culture and in everyday life. The large number and high quality of newspapers and magazines, the character of discourse in the electronic media, the style of German political debate, the nature and content of the educational system, and the great respect for science, learning, and the arts, and many other features of contemporary German culture testify to the breadth and depth of the acceptance of a modern scientific worldview. Critical reason clearly is expected to be the guide to both personal conduct and the shaping of public policy. One commentator on modern societies characterizes Germany and other places under German influence as especially prone to give priority to philosophical questions. Whereas the Anglo-American world asks "How does that work out in practice?" for Germans the most important question is "What are the premises of your argument?"[18] The rather substantial part of the German population that has completed secondary school has more than a minimal familiarity with basic philosophical viewpoints. The names of Kant, Feuerbach, Hegel, and Marx not only adorn street signs; they stand for positions that are well known, intensely debated, and in many ways absorbed into the broader culture.

Kant, especially, continues to have great influence. After the initial period of reception of his work, a major revival took place in the neo-Kantianism of the end of the nineteenth century. That revival especially sought to adapt Kantianism to the encounter with the social issues that came to the forefront with the transformation of economy and society. Kant's imperative of human dignity also often has been the dominant note in the effort to respond to the crimes of the Nazis and, more recently, in dealing with wrongs committed by the East German regime. Kantian ethics offers an approach to the challenges posed by the presence of foreigners in the land by supporting the rule of law, the evenhanded administration of justice, and openness and tolerance as fundamental attitudes. Yet, the Kantian emphasis on the individual has never provided much sustenance for a theory of social institutions. Civil society is important in Kant's social philosophy, but it does not acquire much shape or detail. One consequence is that the range of positions on what to do with the challenge of multiculturalism that can be derived from Kantian principles is extremely wide and contradictory.[19]

Hegel was alert to this problem in Kant's philosophy. In the lengthy treatment of civil society in his *Philosophy of Right*, Hegel seeks to fill the gap between the formation of the moral individual and a fully ethical society with stages of institutional formation that foster a shift from a strictly individualistic to a social perspective and that anchor the individual in a web of social relations. The market, public forums of discussion, and cultural institutions are to serve in this transition. But, Hegel conceded that civil society alone cannot provide sufficient means to harmonize and constrain the egoism and conflicting interests that modernity has set loose through the dissolution of traditional bonds. To accomplish real social peace, he thought that a new kind of ethically based state must be created, founded on principles and organized in a manner the world had not yet seen in his time. It was the German people whom he expected to lead the world into this new stage of human development.

Marx was just as optimistic about the Germans in his own way, thinking that if Hegel could be brought down to earth, grounded in material reality, and made to stand on his own two feet, the progress of material development would offer the conditions for the birth of a new society of equality and freedom. The Kantian impulse to universalism persists in Marx's view that only a universal class, the proletariat, could liberate humankind from centuries of class struggle, and therefore from exploitation, oppression, and war. From his perspective, cultural differences were a residue of the age of superstition at best, and at worst an instrument of the ruling class's strategy to divide and conquer. Ethnic difference needed to be overcome through the solidarity of the working class that was being hastened by the global character of the modern economy.

Weber carried these themes into the twentieth century, urging a Kantian sense of duty in the face of the inevitable crises of modern institutions. In his version of systems theory, the various sectors of society pursue their own interests, finding different forms of legitimation, one of which is rational decision making, especially in the legal sphere. But the old optimism is gone. One form of society is destined to give way to another, but without the promise of progress. No actualization of the ethical is to be realized in an ideal state, nor is it to be expected that there will be an eventual over-coming of class struggle or of material need. For Weber, liberalism is prefer-able to its enemies, but it no longer can inspire enthusiasm. Only a stoical civic duty remains.

Much of postwar German social thought has repeated these themes. Habermas pursues Kant's project in a theory of communication whose ideal is "transparence" in social relations, and he proposes the liberal vision of the citizen as the alternative to the nation as a source of identity. Luhmann deploys biological models in extending Weber's systems theory, to a point where the humanism of the Enlightenment begins to disappear. That mod-ern society is a society of strangers made up of individuals who must accept that they live in a sea of indifferent individuals becomes a commonplace of popular culture. The insecurity it breeds leads away from that attitude of hospitality and curiosity about strangers found in many—though certainly not all—traditional societies. Instead, it points us toward the framing of principles of exclusion that seek to calm the anxieties produced by the alienating conditions of life in a civil society that many experience as bru-tally lacking in civility.

But, now, the conditions that have framed modern German society are changing. Many would argue that the whole modern framework is no longer really beneficial or beneficent. National cultures become less significant as boundaries in the new Europe become more permeable.[20] A new generation learns to identify as itself European, while, simultaneously, the breakdown of the power of the national capitals breathes new life into old regionalisms and localisms. This process, already well developed in places like Scotland and the Tirol, and most painfully so in the Balkans, may one day manifest itself in Germany. It also calls into question the way being German long has been defined. Citizens of EU countries resident in other EU countries are entitled to vote in local elections where they live. Broader political rights likely will follow and cosmopolitanism will be difficult to avoid.

In this process, Germans may be able to take advantage of resources in their philosophic tradition outside a liberal consensus that seems only to offer arid, abstract, and largely empty formal concepts of freedom and equal-ity mixed with a tepid tolerance to cope with the challenges of multicul-turalism. Strangely, it may be German thinkers like Schopenhauer and Nietzsche—whom the Nazis once tried to claim as their own—who pro-vide promise. This promise lies in their explorations of empathy and the transcending of the forms of identity prescribed for us by modernity. Here, there are openings toward a meeting of cultures on a ground that does not have to presuppose homogeneity, universality, a founding consensus, or sameness.[21] It might just be worth the price of a ticket for Germany to draw on some of these other resources in order to embark on a new phase of its historical journey. This phase could become a quest for the chance to experience the rich potential of a multicultural world and the means to face its challenges. After all, so far as we know, that is all that there is.

Notes

1. For a broad range of positions, see Edward Mortimer and Robert Fine (eds.), *Nation and State—The Meaning of Ethnicity and Nationalism* (London: I. B. Tauris, 1999). See also Dieter Haselbach (ed.), *Multiculturalism in a World of Leaking Boundaries* (Muenster: Lit-Verlag, 1999).

2. Derek Scally, "Muslim Teacher Loses Case over Headscarf Ban," *Irish Times*, 27 June 2001; U.S. Department of State, *Annual Report on International Religious Freedom for 1999: Germany.*

3. Alexander Fisher, "Mehmet Nach Istanbul Ausgeflogen," *Sueddeutsche Zeitung*, 16 November 1998.

4. *Frankfurter Allgemeine Zeitung*, 3 June 1998; *Sueddeutsche Zeitung*, 3 June 1998.

5. Lucian Kim, "Ballots for Far Right Reveal East Germans' 'Meager Hopes'," *Christian Science Monitor*, 28 April 1998; "State Elections in Saxony-Anhalt," *American Institute for Contemporary German Studies*, 26 April 1998.

6. Discussion on Berlin television station observed by the author, July 1998.

7. For example, John C. Leslie, "Reemerging Ethnic Politics in Germany: Far Right Parties and Violence," in *The Myth of "Ethnic Conflict": Politics, Economics, and "Cultural Violence,"* ed. Beverly Crawford and Ronnie D. Lipschutz (International and Area Studies Research Series, No. 98., University of California Berkeley, 1998); Bahman Nirumand (ed.), *Angst vor den Deutschen: Terror gegen Auslaender und der Zerfall des Rechtstaates* (Reinbek bei Hamburg: Rowohlt, 1992); Burkhard Schroeder, *Im Griff der Rechten Szene: Ostdeutsche Staedte in Angst* (Reinbek bei Hamburg: Rowohlt, 1997).

8. Reinhard Zimmermann, "An Introduction to German Legal Culture," and Kay Hailbronner and Hans-Peter Hummel, "Constitutional Law," both in *Introduction to German Law*, ed. Werner F. Ebke and Matthew W. Finkin (The Hague: Kluwer Law International, 1996); Donald P. Kommers and Paul Kirchhoff, *Germany and Its Basic Law: Past, Present, and Future* (Baden-Baden: Nomos, 1993).

9. Sam Blay and Andreas Zimmermann, "Recent Changes in German Refugee Law: A Critical Assessment," *American Journal of International Law* 88 (1994): 361. See also Kay Hailbronner, David Martin, and Hiroshi Motomura, *Immigration Controls: The*

Search for Workable Policies in Germany and the United States (Providence, R.I.: Berghahn Books, 1998).

10. The historical process that produced this situation is discussed in works cited at n. 12, infra.

11. The best survey of life in contemporary Germany is John Ardagh, *Germany and the Germans: The United Germany in the Mid-1990s* (Harmondsworth, U.K.: Penguin, 1995).

12. Klaus J. Bade, *Migration Past, Migration Future: Germany and the United States* (Providence, R.I.: Berghahn Books, 1997); Klaus J. Bade (ed.), *Deutsche im Ausland—Fremde in Deutschland: Migration in Geschichte und Gegenwart* (Muenchen: C. H. Beck, 1992); Wolfgang Zank, *The German Melting Pot: Multiculturality in Historical Perspective* (New York: Palgrave Macmillan, 1998).

13. Daniel Cohn-Bendit and Thomas Schmid, *Heimat Babylon: Das Wagnis der Multikulturellen Demokratie* (Hamburg: Campe, 1993); Wolfgang Zank, "Cultural Diversity and the Political System: The German Experience," in *National Cultures and European Integration*, ed. Staffan Zetterholm (Providence, R.I.: Berghahn Books, 1994). See also Ardagh, op. cit.

14. Werner Shiffauer, *Fremde in der Stadt: Zehn Essays ueber Kultur und Differenz* (Frankfurt am Main: Suhrkamp, 1997); Peter Wagner, "Fest-Stellungen—Beobachtungen zur Sozialwissenschaftlichen Diskussion ueber Identitaet," in *Identitaeten*, ed. Alaeda Assman and Heidrun Friese (Frankfurt am Main: Suhrkamp, 1998).

15. The issues were defined anew after unification. See Klaus Bade (ed.), *Das Manifest der 60: Deutschland und die Einwanderung* (Muenchen: C. H. Beck, 1993); Roland Tichy, *Auslaender Rein! Deutsche und Auslaender—Verschiedene Herkunft, Gemeinsame Zukunft* (Muenchen: Piper, 1990).

16. See works cited at n. 14, supra.

17. President Rau finally rendered his decision to sign the law on 20 June 2002, unleashing renewed political controversy, including the threat of a constitutional challenge. At almost the same moment, the European Ministerial Conference took up the issue of tightening Europe's borders. Title story: "Ansturm der Migranten: Europa macht dicht," *Der Spiegel*, no. 25, 17 June 2002, in the wake of Le Pen's electoral gains in France and similar election results in Denmark, the Netherlands, and elsewhere in Europe.

18. Johan Galtung, "Struktur, Kultur und Intellektueller Stil," in *Das Fremde und das Eigene*, ed. Alois Wierlacher (Muenchen: Iudicum Verlag, 1985).

19. Nikolaus Wenturis, "Reflexionen zu Kants Politische Philosophie," in *John Locke und Immanuel Kant: Historische Rezeption und Gegenwaertige Relevanz/Historical Reception and Contemporary Relevance*, ed. Martyn P. Thompson (Berlin: Duncker & Humbolt, 1991).

20. Haselbach, op. cit.; Larry E. Jones (ed.). *Crossing Boundaries: The Exclusion and Inclusion of Minorities in Germany and the United States* (New York: Berghahn Books, 2002); Christian Joppke, *Immigration and the Nation-State: The United States, Germany,*

and Great Britain (Oxford: Oxford University Press, 1999); Riva Kastoryano, *Negotiating Identities: States and Immigrants in France and Germany*, trans. Barbara Harcher (Princeton, N.J.: Princeton University Press, 2001); Barbara Marshall, *The New Germany and Migration in Europe* (Manchester: Manchester University Press, 2001).

21. Daniel W. Conway, *Nietzsche and the Political* (London: Routledge, 1997); Lawrence J. Hatab, *A Nietzschean Defense of Democracy* (Chicago: Open Court, 1995); Bryan Magee, *The Philosophy of Schopenhauer* (Oxford: Oxford University Press, 1997); Rudiger Safranski, *Schopenhauer and the Wild Years of Philosophy*, trans. Ewald Osers (Cambridge, Mass.: Harvard University Press, 1989); Tracy Strong, "Nietzsche's Political Misappropriation," in *The Cambridge Companion to Nietzsche*, ed. Bernd Magnus and Kathleen Higgins (Cambridge: Cambridge University Press, 1996).

CONTRIBUTORS

Erik Anderson is Assistant Professor of Philosophy at Furman College. He has been a Lilly Program Fellow and currently has a postdoctoral fellowship with the Center on Religion and Democracy. Many of his publications focus on the possibilities of religious expression in liberal society; he is working on a manuscript entitled *Religious Freedom after Secularism*.

Joseph Ellin is Professor of Philosophy at Western Michigan University. He is the author of *Morality and the Meaning of Life* as well as of numerous articles in bioethics, political philosophy, the history of philosophy, and professional ethics.

Norman Fischer is Associate Professor of Philosophy at Kent State University. His areas of interest include environmental philosophy, social and political theory, and a broad range of problems in the philosophy of law. His publications include articles on aesthetics and Marxism.

Emily R. Gill is Professor of Political Science at Bradley University and is a past-president of AMINTAPHIL. Her book, *Becoming Free: Autonomy and Diversity in the Liberal Polity*, was published by the University Press of Kansas.

Christopher Berry Gray is Professor of Philosophy at Concordia University in Montreal, and editor of *The Philosophy of Law: An Encyclopedia*. He is co-convenor of the Marriage Law and Culture Workshop in Montreal.

Heidi Malm is Associate Professor of Philosophy at Loyola University Chicago. She has published and presented extensively in the areas of biomedical ethics and legal philosophy. Much of her work has centered on issues of wrongful omissions in law and ethics. She serves on the editorial board of *Philosophy and Public Affairs* and is a member of the Executive Committee of AMINTAPHIL.

Lester Mazor is Professor of Law at Hampshire College, where he also serves as the director of the Hampshire in Berlin Program. He holds the J.D. degree from Stanford University and clerked for the Honorable Warren Burger. His publications include books and articles on utopianism, legal philosophy, and the sociology and history of law.

Joan McGregor is Associate Professor of Philosophy and Lincoln Associate Professor in Applied Ethics at Arizona State University. She is director of a new bioethics program in the life sciences, an adjunct professor in the college of law, and an affiliated faculty member in Women's Studies. Her extensive publications include work in feminist jurisprudence and biomedical ethics. For many years, she has conducted an ethics workshop for sitting judges, and she has served as editor for *Law and Philosophy*.

Thomas Peard is Associate Professor in the department of Philosophy and Religion at Baker University. He holds the J.D. degree from Colorado University School of Law and is a member of the federal bar and the Colorado bar. Much of his writing has focused on problems of hate speech and speech control.

David Reidy is Assistant Professor of Philosophy at the University of Tennessee, where he also teaches in the interdisciplinary program for global studies. He holds the J.D. degree from the Indiana University School of Law. His extensive record of publications and presentations includes work in legal and political philosophy, with focus on the philosophy of John Rawls.

Wade Robison is Ezra A. Hale Professor of Applied Ethics at the Rochester Institute of Technology. He is president of the Society for Ethics Across the Curriculum and past- president of the Hume Society. In addition to numerous articles on Hume and in the area of legal philosophy, he recently published an edited compilation entitled *The Legal Philosophy of Michael Bayles*.

Jonathan Schonsheck is Professor of Philosophy at Le Moyne College, where he also team-teaches business ethics in Le Moyne's M.B.A. Program. He has written on a diverse selection of moral and political issues. He is author of *On Criminalization: An Essay in the Philosophy of Criminal Law* and coeditor of a previous AMINTAPHIL volume, *Law, Liberty, Equality*.

Mortimer Sellers is University System of Maryland Regents Professor and director of the Center for International and Comparative Law at the University of Baltimore School of Law. His publications include *Republican Legal Theory, The Sacred Fire of Liberty, New World Order, American Republicanism*, and *Ethical Education*.

Christine Sistare is Professor of Philosophy and codirector of the Philosophy/Political Thought Program at Muhlenberg College. She is author of *Responsibility and Criminal Liability* and coedited two previous AMINTAPHIL volumes, *Law, Liberty, Equality* and *Groups and Group Rights*. She is codirector of the Society for Philosophy and Public Affairs and a member of the Executive Committee of AMINTAPHIL.

Patricia Smith is Professor and Chair of the Department of Philosophy at Baruch College and a permanent member of the graduate faculty of the City University of New York. Her publications include *Liberalism and Affirmative Obligation, The Nature and Process of Law,* and *Feminist Jurisprudence*. She is a past-president of AMINTAPHIL and currently serves as president of the American Philosophical Association's Committee on Law and Philosophy.

INDEX